DEMURJIAN

OFFICE SYSTEMS:
Methods and Tools

IFIP TC 8/WG 8.4 Working Conference on
Methods and Tools for Office Systems
Pisa, Italy, 22–24 October, 1986

organized by
IFIP Technical Committee 8, Information Systems
International Federation for Information Processing (IFIP)

co-sponsored by
Consiglio Nazionale delle Ricerche
Associazione Italiana per l'Informatica e il Calcolo Automatico

NORTH-HOLLAND
AMSTERDAM · NEW YORK · OXFORD · TOKYO

OFFICE SYSTEMS:

Methods and Tools

Proceedings of the IFIP TC 8/WG 8.4 Working Conference on
Methods and Tools for Office Systems
Pisa, Italy, 22–24 October, 1986

edited by

G. BRACCHI
Politecnico di Milano
Italy

D. TSICHRITZIS
Université de Genève
Switzerland

N·H
P∿C

1987

NORTH-HOLLAND
AMSTERDAM · NEW YORK · OXFORD · TOKYO

© IFIP, 1987

ISBN: 0 444 70241 5

Published by:
ELSEVIER SCIENCE PUBLISHERS B.V.
P.O. Box 1991
1000 BZ Amsterdam
The Netherlands

Sole distributors for the U.S.A. and Canada:
ELSEVIER SCIENCE PUBLISHING COMPANY, INC.
52 Vanderbilt Avenue
New York, N.Y. 10017
U.S.A.

Library of Congress Cataloging-in-Publication Data

IFIP WG 8.4 Working Conference on Methods and Tools
    for Office Systems (1986 : Pisa, Italy)
    Office systems.

    Papers presented at the conference organized by IFIP
Technical Committee 8, Information Systems, International
Federation for Information Processing, and co-sponsored by
Consiglio nazionale delle ricerche and Associazione
italiana per l'informatica e il calcolo automatico.
    Includes index.
    1. Information storage and retrieval systems--
Business--Congresses. 2. Office practice--Automation--
Congresses. I. Bracchi, G. (Giampio), 1944-
II. Tsichritzis, Dionysios C. III. International
Federation for Information Processing. Technical
Committee for Information Systems. IV. Consiglio
nazionale delle richerche (Italy) V. Associazione
italiana per l'informatica e il calcolo automatico.
VI. Title.
HF5548.2.I285 1986   651.8   87-8916
ISBN 0-444-70241-5 (U.S.)

PRINTED IN THE NETHERLANDS

PREFACE

This volume contains the papers presented at the IFIP Working Conference on "Methods and Tools for Office Systems". The conference took place in Pisa in October 1986. It explored both the methodological and the development aspects of Office Information Systems.

Office Information Systems are playing an ever increasing role in business, government and scientific applications. They take advantage of many R&D activities in data base management, information systems, communication techniques, artificial intelligence, organizational theory and behavioral psychology.

Advances are being made through the innovative application of theories, methods and techniques from these various fields. In addition, the office is being explored under different aspects: procedural, information-flow, behavioral, decision-making, and so forth.

The IFIP Office Systems Working Conference Series provides an international forum of specialists to promote research, to exchange experiences gained in advanced design, implementation and use, and to encourage the discussion of new ideas in this growing and interdisciplinary area. The Pisa Conference is a logical successor of the previous IFIP Working Conference on Office Systems that was held in Helsinki, Finland in 1985.

It was a pleasure to observe during this second Conference the continued progress in application and system methods and technologies, the trend towards knowledge engineering, distributed services and system integration, and the consolidated maturity in understanding the basic issues in Office Systems.

We would like to thank the Program Committee members, who fulfilled their role with admirable dedication. In selecting, over a wide range of submitted contributions, the papers to be presented at the Conference, the Program Committee had the help of many well known specialists, and we wish to thank all of them for their contribution. We also want to thank the Organizing Committee, the co-sponsors and the supporters who made this conference possible.

This book deals mainly with issues relevant to Office Information Systems. We hope, however, that it will also be useful to the computer community at large.

The Editors

OFFICERS AND PROGRAM COMMITTEE MEMBERS

OFFICERS

General Chairman	G. Bracchi	Italy
Program Chairman	D. Tsichritzis	Switzerland
Organizing Chairman	C. Thanos	Italy
Local Arrangements and Treasurer	E. Ricciardi	Italy

PROGRAM COMMITTEE MEMBERS

K. Bauknecht	Switzerland
E. Bertino	Italy
C. Ellis	USA
R. Hirschheim	England
F.H. Lochovsky	Canada
P. Lockemann	W. Germany
V. Lum	USA
N. Naffah	France
O.M. Nierstrasz	Greece
C. Rolland	France
J. Roukens	Belgium
E. Sandewall	Sweden
A.A. Verrijn-Stuart	Holland

SUPPORTERS

Istituto Elaborazione Informazione
Societ\` Generale di Informatica
Data Base Informatica
IBM Italia
Gruppo Editoriale Jackson
Booz Allen & Hamilton Italia
Syntax
Systems & Management

CONTENTS

MESSAGE SYSTEMS

SYSTEMS PERFORMANCE

DATABASE ISSUES

OFFICE PROCEDURES

TEMPORAL ISSUES

OFFICE SYSTEMS: Methods and Tools
G. Bracchi, D. Tsichritzis (Editors)
Elsevier Science Publishers B.V. (North-Holland)
© IFIP, 1987

LINCKS: Linköping's Intelligent
Knowledge Communication System

Lin Padgham
Department of Computer and
Information Science
LINKÖPING UNIVERSITY

Abstract

LINCKS is a system which is under development at Linköping University,
Sweden, and is currently in the beginning stages of implementation. It is
an object oriented imperative system, designed for use as an office system,
incorporating automated and intelligent services. The system is designed
around the theme of communication, which is seen as central to an office
environment, as well as to many other environments. The data base is
object oriented, but passive, with events occuring as a result of actions
taken, either by users, or by software *actors*. Objects are represented by
structures of *molecules*, which can be thought of as information chunks.
The system is aware of its history, and is thus able to evolve gracefully
over time. Information is always available concerning objects as they were
at a previous point in time. Team work is facilitated by specific support for
parallel development.

1. Introduction

Office systems is an important and growing area for both computer research and
computer products. There is much eagerness to automate office procedures. However
offices are not alike, and a system developed to suit one office will often not be really
suitable for another [1][2]. We aim to provide an environment with an organisation and
structure suitable for a wide range of situations, plus the ability to easily modify and add
to the environment to create a system customized for a particular situation. This
flexibility and ability to evolve, will also enable the system to develop and change along
with a particular office.

Many of the tasks which one would like to automate in an office are loosely defined and
unstructured. There are many different ways to perform an action and still get the
desired result [2]. The office automation that we aim for is then a collection of intelligent
services, which are able to reason and plan and to operate as expert systems, using the
information within the system to determine a course of action.

Some of the intelligent services, such as those that are able to plan complex action
structures from lower level operations, in order to achieve some goal, are generic and
required in all situations. Others need to be tailored to the specific office and it's specific
tasks. LINCKS provides facilities to make it easy to integrate customized intelligent
services into the base system.

Any particular office, as well as differing from other offices, changes within itself
considerably over time. The objects within the office also are often in a process of change
[1][2]. It is important to maintain and be able to use information about how things in the
environment have changed and developed. In order to do this we keep comprehensive
information about the history of objects, of text, and a command history. This provides
information which can be used both by human users and by the intelligent services within
the system.

Bracchi and Pernici group models for designing office systems into three main classes: data based models, process based models and agent based models. They also discuss mixed models which are some combination of these categories. [2]. LINCKS uses a mixed model, with an integrating theme of communication. Communication happens between agents, using processes, and concerns data base objects. The mixed model approach seems most promising, in that there is a greater possibility of capturing all the fundamental aspects of the office and the relationships between them.

The data base model used by LINCKS is of a networked molecular data base, where objects are represented explicitly as a structure of molecules. Molecules are a uniform data structure, with enough flexibility to capture the rich diversity of objects in the office world.

Processes or actions are equally important in the LINCKS system as objects. They are not strongly linked to particular types of objects as in most object oriented systems. This gives greater flexibility, as well as making operations independent from objects. The representation for actions contains information about the context in which they are able to operate and about the results of their execution. This facilitates the using of rules in planning software to determine consistent combinations of actions. It also enables simple actions to be combined together to form more complex actions.

The agents who are the office personnel, and around whom a model such as the *Structured Office Model* [3] revolves, are represented as objects in the data base, with relationships between them being various types of links. In this way supervisory structures, communication structures, etc are represented. There is in the LINCKS system the notion that agents or actors can be either human users, or intelligent services. Agents act on data objects, using operations. The data base does not distinguish between human and software agents.

The LINCKS system can be described as an object oriented imperative system. This distinguishes it from object oriented systems which are message based and whose data base is active. LINCKS contains a structured but passive data base and actions occur only as a result of commands given, either by human users or by intelligent services.

This paper gives an overview of LINCKS with a recurring example of a common office task - filling in a monthly status report. There is an attempt to strike a balance between an abstract theoretical discussion of the system, and an explanation of how it could actually be used for doing a particular concrete and familiar task. The description of the system is constantly related back to different aspects of the chosen example.

Although the main focus of LINCKS is Office Information Systems, many of the issues and design criteria are wider than this. Consequently the resulting system should be useful in a wide variety of contexts.

2. An Object Oriented System

The core of the LINCKS system is an *object oriented data base*. This means that information within the computer system is an explicit representation of objects in the outside world. Such a data base seems very appropriate for an office system because the office environment contains so many different categories of objects, with relatively few entities in each category (in contrast to an administrative data base which often has few categories but many entities in each).

Objects are understood as things out-side the system, so that internally, they are only *denoted* and *described*. Denotations of objects are distinct entities used in reference to the objects in question. However, the denotations do not give any information about the objects denoted, except that two different objects are assumed to have two different denotations.

Information about objects are contained in *feature descriptors*, each of which describes some features without attachment to any particular object. That is, a feature descriptor contains information that describes some collection of features that are 'things that can be known about some object' (e.g. *length:* 178cm, *weight:* >68 and <73 kg, *eye color:* unknown). The set of all possible feature descriptors can be organised into a lattice according to the notion of *more information.* Each actual feature descriptor can thus be associated to some point in this lattice and thereby compared with other feature descriptors regarding which has more information.

The current knowledge about the objects is represented by associating object denotions to feature descriptors. The *database state* is therefore a mapping from the set of object denotions into the set of feature descriptors.

The basic data structure used to denote and describe objects is called a *molecule.* Molecules have three distinct parts:

*   An *image* of the object. This is uninterpreted information, usually textual or graphic (e.g. a paragraph in a report, or a diagram). It is expected that the textual part of a single molecule will be relatively small - the size of a single paragraph or thought.

*   A number of *attributes* with values (e.g. name or colour). These attributes are things about the object which are not related to other objects.

*   A number of *links* which describe the relationship of the object to other objects (e.g. footnote or reference). These links are pointers from one object denotion to another, and are thus not part of the feature descriptor. However the feature descriptor includes a description of the *link pattern;* which links are incoming and outgoing.

A structure of molecules is the usual way to represent a large or complex object. Such a structure has a single molecule which denotes the object and is the handle by which the structure can be accessed. It is possible to access object structures in varied and flexible ways (e.g. brief description, keywords, reference to position on a printout, etc).

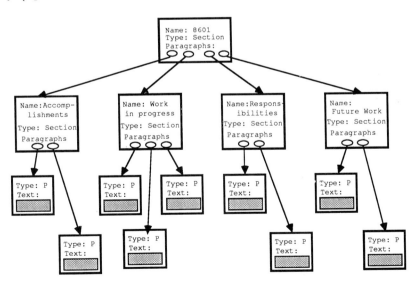

Structure of Molecules Representing a Report

2.1 An Example Object

As an example of a possible object, the monthly report for the month of January 1986 is
chosen. This object is the pieces of paper usually thought of as constituting such a report.
Within the system, extra information is contained in the attributes of the molecules
representing the object. This corresponds to the notes one makes on a paper copy of the
report, or to the notes one simply keeps in mind (e.g. the date the report was turned in,
who was responsible for preparing it this particular month, some extra person that it was
sent to, etc.)

Our report, represented by a structure of molecules, is a composite object made up of
smaller pieces. These pieces are also objects in their own right. When the user wishes to
view the larger object, he sees it as a whole and need not be aware of the molecules which
constitute the report. However it is also possible to focus on a piece (e.g. a section) as an
object and obtain or insert information specific only to that piece (e.g. the report may
have one main author listed, but a particular section may have a different author).

Name: 8601
Type: Monthly report
Author: John Smith

Monthly report for Jan 1986
Accomplishments
Report for upper management finished.

Structure charts for new project started
and preliminary report handed in.

Work in progress
Noise is being eliminated on the main
CPU bus.

Work should now progress   faster on the
Lambda system with less difficulty.

Gandalf has returned from Lothlorien and

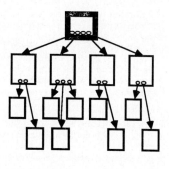

User   **System**

Comparison of User and System View of Report

2.2 Types of Objects

In an object oriented system it is rather common to classify objects as being of certain
types. Thus, the monthly report for January 1986 discussed above, may be seen as of
type *monthly report*. Alternatively it may be seen as of type *report*, and also of type
monthly objects, where the first group includes many different kinds of reports, and the
second includes different sorts of objects that recur every month. The question of which is
the preferred organisation of types is often a matter of personal preference or viewpoint.

Within LINCKS there is for every type a type norm, which is the feature descriptor
required for all objects that are considered to be of the type. The system recognises an
object to be of a certain type, if and only if the feature descriptor associated to the object
is above the type norm, in terms of the *more information* relation. We call this view of
typing *descriptive typing*, since the actual type(s) for an object are derived from what is
known about the object and what is required for the type(s). The type(s) of an object is
not a property of the object, but a property of the (systems) view of and knowledge
about objects. This enables several typing schemas to be used, for instance by different
users within the system. It is in contrast to the usual notion of typing where the type
hierarchy is rather fixed.

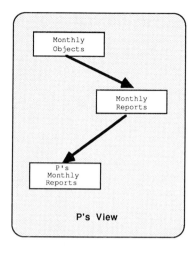
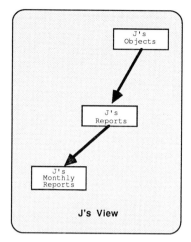

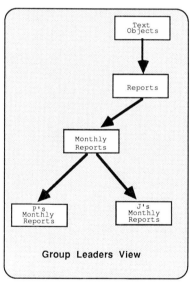
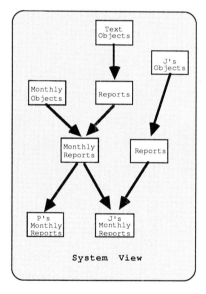

Some Different Views on The Type Hierarchy

Prescriptive typing, as opposed to descriptive, is obtained by stating explicitly in the description of an object that it is of a certain type. The complete feature descriptor for a particular object is then built from the explicit information combined with the implicit information of its prescribed type(s). The additions to this combination may continue recursively if the type norms are also prescriptively typed.

An effect of prescriptive typing is that any change to the information that describes a type will result in changes to the information describing the objects prescribed to be of that type. The prescriptive typing model also conserves storage, since the information required for all objects of a type need to be stored explicitly only as the type norm.

The information that describes a type includes both the type *norm*, which is what information is *required* in the descriptions of objects of that type, and a type *seed*, which is what information is *expected* in the descriptions of objects of that type. The type seed can also be understood as a normal case description that is used as default when a new object is encountered and stated to be of the particular type.

In prescriptive typing, the complete feature descriptor is built using the type seed rather than the type norm, but when the seed information is in conflict with the instance level information the latter will override.

```
Type name:                        Type name:
   Monthly reports                   Monthly reports

Section names:                    Section names:
   Accomplishments                   Accomplishments
   Work in progress                  Work in progress
   Decisions                         Decisions
   Future plans                      Problems
                                     Future plans
Author:
                                  Author:   John Smith
Recipients:
                                  Recipients:
                                     Admin. B
                                     Group leaders
```

      Type Norm   **Type Seed**

2.3 Organisation of Objects

In an office (and therefore in an Office System), objects are not merely classified and typed, but they are also organised in relation to each other. For instance, there are inboxes and outboxes containing mail and other items to be dealt with, files containing various papers, drawers or filing cabinets containing files, reminder boards with notes on them and many other ways in which relationships between objects are expressed. The LINCKS system enables the user to set up these structures and relationships.

All molecules (and hence all objects) in the system, can be linked to each other with any type of link. This means for instance that you can have a drawer and some files and set up links between them to indicate that the drawer contains the files. These links are dynamic and changeable as things are moved around in a workspace.

For example, approaching the time for writing our January 1986 monthly report, an empty report is put into an intray of things to be done this week. As work begins on the report, it is moved to a pile of work in progress, and later to some other persons inbox for contributions. Finally, when it is written and signed by the necessary parties, a copy is sent by electronic mail to the relevant place, and another copy is filed away amongst old monthly reports. As all this happens the links between the monthly report and the other objects in the system are changing.

3. An Imperative System

Although LINCKS is an object oriented system, it is different from many other object oriented systems in that it is imperative rather than message based. This means particularly that actions are seen as important entities in their own right, and not as messages between objects. The actions are not initiated by objects, but are initiated by some actor, to operate on the world of the objects.

Often the actor is the human user of the system who issues commands in the usual manner, but it may as well be an *intelligent service*, which initiates some actions in the system. An intelligent service is not different from a human user, from the viewpoint of the data base. In both cases data is always operated on in a workspace separate from the data base, and is then integrated back into the data base.

3.1 Actions and Operations

In discussing operations on objects, it is important to be clear about the distinction between an operation *in terms of actual code* (the technical point of view), and an operation *in terms of effect* (the usage point of view), more or less the code versus the interpretation of its effect. It is clear, that the interpretation of the effect of performing an operation on one type of objects may be different from the interpretation of the effect of performing (technically) the same operation on another type of objects. Likewise, one operation performed on one type of objects may be understood as the same as or similar to another operation performed on another type of objects. In the following, we refer to the actual code as an operation, and to the interpretation of the effect of an operation as an *action*.

3.1.1 Operations

Operations on objects are defined along with constraints on the descriptors for the objects upon which it applies. Typically, these constraints are lower bounds on the information contained, which is the same kind of constraint as is ensured by prescriptive typing. The statement of constraints in terms of explicit feature descriptors, rather than as prescriptive type names, has two advantages. First, it allows the use of the same operations by users with different typing schemas. Secondly, it ensures that operations are not over constrained because they must be linked to a point where a type is defined.

Operation definitions also contain information about the effects on the feature descriptors of the objects to which they are applied. Whereas the operation constraints are pre-conditions (to be satisfied before the operation can be applied), the effect is regarded as post conditions. This information can then be used in planning what operations can be used to pave the way for other operations.

3.1.2 Actions

An *action* implements a (conceptual) function within a context. It can be understood as a conceptual grouping of operations so that those that are understood as similar (in a given context) can be referred to under the same name. The grouping that constitutes an action may contain structures of operations and actions as well as single operations. This gives a nested model of actions.

The action body is a dispatch table of various implementations of the desired function. Each entry in the dispatch table contains an operation (or operation/action structure), pre-conditions and post conditions. The pre conditions at this level may contain information about what the state must be in order for the action to 'make sense' within this context. Similarly the post condition may contain information regarding the interpreted effect of the action.

For example take the hypothetical action *do monthly report* in some office context. The body of this action may contain a number of implementations of this function. One possibility is to send the appropriate form to person A, with a request to fill it in and return it when completed. An alternative implementation may be to send the form and request to person B. A pre-condition associated with the latter may be that person A is out of town. Obviously this pre-condition is not strictly necessary in order to do the operation, but it is the necessary pre-condition for it to be meaningful in this context.

The pre and post conditions associated with actions enable planning services to build meaningful structures of actions within a given context.

A collection of action definitions existing within a context is called the action schema for that context. It is analogous to the typing schema for objects that exists within each context, and allows the same sort of flexibility.

4. A System with History

An office environment is an environment which is usually changing rather fast. New memos get written, new mail arrives, and new ways are found to organise things. In order to get a full picture of some aspect, it is important not only to see what exists now, but also to see some evolutionary context - how things became as they are.

The concept of evolution is also important for the office system as a whole. One always finds new and better ways of doing and organising things, personnel come and go along with their particular orientations, etc. Consequently, it is important that the computer system is capable of smooth and easy evolution.

4.1 Evolution of Objects

Papers get written and are in process for a while, folders develop and get added to, in and out boxes constantly have their contents rearranged, etc. Working in an office environment, we often use information concerning a previous arrangement of objects (e.g. "Get me the red folder which used to sit on the top shelf", "take out the paragraph that was at the bottom of page three on the first printout", etc). Within LINCKS there is a *version structure* mechanism to keep track of the development of objects over time and to allow retrieval of objects as they were at some past time. This both allows the user to explicitly reference older versions of an object, and provides information for intelligent services to reason with.

For example, writing the monthly report for January 1986, there comes perhaps, a point where the person writing it is satisfied with the result, except for some particular section, which has been rewritten several times and was better in an earlier version. In LINCKS it is quite simple to access the older version of that section and put it back into the current report. Alternatively a copy is given to a colleague to get some feedback while the report continues to be developed. Then a message comes from the colleague saying that it looks good except for the second paragraph in section three. To make sense of this message, it is necessary to have a picture of the report as it looked when it was given to the colleague. LINCKS has such a picture readily available.

4.2 Evolution of Text

The evolution of text rather than of conceptual objects is another important history concept. This is kept track of by a structure called *parent structure*. During word processing, it is quite common to take a piece of text from one place and use it in some new document. The text in the beginning of an edit session is then parent to the text in the end. Rather often the parent structure coincides with the version structure. However, at a point where a piece of text is taken from another object, or when editing occurs on other than the most recent version of an object, the parent and version structures do not coincide.

Again considering our monthly report, we see several occasions where this text history is useful. Suppose for instance that the report contains a section called 'future plans'. In January we are running out of time and therefore we reuse a section from a grant application for the future plans section, as it is very similar to what we want. When we do the February report, the January future plans section is copied, maybe with some minor additions. In March we look at February's report, to use it as a basis for the new report, and see that some things in future plans do not quite seem to fit. We can then look at the edit history of this section of text and see that it originated from a document with a different purpose. This provides a fuller understanding which very often is useful.

The difference between the version structures and the parent structures is that the version structures always trace the development of conceptual objects which exist over time, whereas the parent structures trace the origins (if any) of a piece of text.

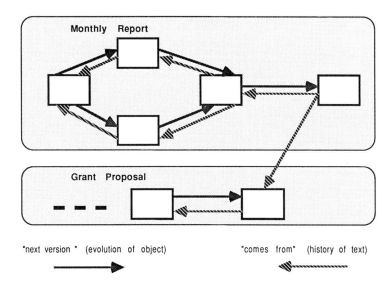

"next version " (evolution of object)   "comes from" (history of text)

Diagram Showing History of Object and Text

4.3 Command History

Commands are instantiated actions and the parameters used in the particular action instantiation. A history is kept of all commands, both those initiated directly by the user, and those initiated by intelligent services. This instantiated action (or command) history is kept in the form of an action structure partially ordered over time. This can then be used by the system in order to reason and to learn. For instance, there might be a group of section leaders, to whom we always send copies of the monthly reports, using some command like *mail to leaders(monthly report X)*, and two other people that we always mail copies to explicitly. After this pattern has occured some number of times the system recognises the pattern, and reminds the user when he forgets to mail copies to the other two people.

The command history is also used by intelligent services to reason and plan about future actions, on the basis of past actions.

4.4 Evolution of System over Time

Since both objects and operations can be reconstructed as they were at a particular point in time, the functionality of the system can be changed and improved, even though some old data is not compatible with new functionality. A conceptual operation, once it exists will never cease to work with data it once worked with, though its functionality may differ depending on the age of the data.

For instance, suppose that there is an operation called *print report* which prints a monthly report with date and headers. As we change this operation so that it also prints a list of all group members, it requires additional information to be noted in the molecule which describes the report. The reports created before the layout change do not contain the information, and we do not want to go through and update them all. Still we may want to print a copy of an old monthly report. Since the system keeps track of how the conceptual operation *print report* has developed over time, the old reports are still printable by accessing the old version of the 'print report' operation.

The view that the system develops gradually over time, and the ability to do it gracefully, makes changes simpler and less costly, thus enabling fine tuning and easy adaptation in a world (such as an office system) that changes relatively often.

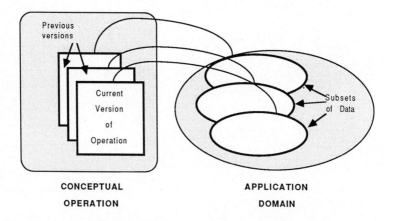

CONCEPTUAL   **APPLICATION**

OPERATION   **DOMAIN**

A Conceptual Operation Never Ceases to Work with Old Data

Even Though the Operation Develops and Changes

5. Multi User Orientation

Most often there is more than one person working in an office, and frequently an office task involves several people. For this reason it is important to use a multi user view in designing a computerised office system. For instance the data base is used and added to by many different users simultaneously. A simple case of this is when the January 1986 monthly report needs to have some sections completed by different team members, requiring a number of people to have access to the report. This can be done sequentially, with each persom completing his work in turn, but it is often more natural to work in parallel on the different sections, ending in a final integration.

5.1 Parallel Work

Parallel work means that more than one person is working on a given task at the same time. This is especially likely and desirable, if the portions of the task being worked on are relatively disjoint. A major advantage of such parallel work is that the given task can be done in a shorter time period. In the monthly report, all contributors should be able to work on their pieces independently, with the results being merged as they become available.

LINCKS has strong support for the concept of parallel work. As one starts work on an object which is already being worked on (i.e. taken to a workspace, some editing done, but it has not yet been checked and put back into the data base) by someone else, the system makes note of the fact that parallel work occurs. The people are also notified of the situation so that they can make a judgement as to whether parallel work is appropriate or not, for instance, if later integration will be too complicated.

In the case of the monthly report, where work is done in parallel on different sections, it would be possible to achieve the same effect of parallel work by having each person work only on a smaller object (the section), and then putting these smaller objects together to make a larger object at the end. However it is often desirable to have, and be conceptually working on, the larger object, although the additions and modifications are limited to smaller pieces.

With our concept of parallel work each user has, and works on, the entire object, with necessary conflict resolution happening later. A user is not constrained to specify exactly what piece he will work on, thus avoiding the unnecessary locks which can result from having to make such specifications in advance. This facility is especially useful when portable computers are considered, as there will be significant periods of time during which work is progressing, without communication between the co-workers.

Merging of work can vary in complexity from a relatively simple task, to be done by an intelligent service (e.g. the monthly report where each person worked on separate sections), to a task where the users must be consulted in order to effect the merge.

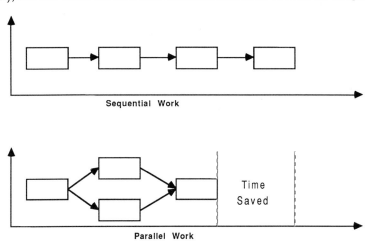

Sequential Work

Time Saved

Parallel Work

Working in Parallel Often Saves Time

5.2 Portables

As well as being a multi user system, LINCKS incorporates a number of different kinds of workstations, including portable laptop computers. This incorporation of portables into a sophisticated system affords a high degree of flexibility. Suppose, for example, that the monthly report should be prepared by a member of the team, who is away at a conference, the week preceding when the report is due. Having LINCKS, he takes all information necessary for doing this task with him, uses the portable to prepare the report, and when he comes back, connects the portable to the main system, so that the report can be processed in the appropriate way. This integration is highly advantageous over the situation where one must change systems (e.g. to pen and paper, or to a non-integrated computer system), in order to work remotely.

Portables cannot of course supply the complete functionality available on the main system but they do *know about* a main system, so those tasks which cannot be done, are queued to be executed later when the main system is connected. Thus, the user can have a sense of having done those tasks on the portable (in that he has given the commands and need no longer think about them), even though the execution is actually done at a later point in time.

5.3 Consistency of the Data Base

The existence of separate workstations and especially the existence of portable unconnected workstations, emphasizes the issue of data base consistency. A user who checks out a portion of the data base and then does some work on it, may well come back to find that the state of the data base has changed in the meantime. This means that checks must be made for conflicts when the material from the portable is integrated.

For example, suppose that we have two separate people (A and B), working together on the monthly report. Person B takes a copy of the report home to work on, after person A has written most of it (except B's sections). While B is working on his sections, A makes some further refinements to what he had written. When B comes back and wants to return the report containing his section to the data base, the changes that A has made in the meantime should not be overwritten and lost. Rather the system must recognise that parallel work has taken place and integrate the documents, or maintain both the versions and ask the users to integrate them.

6. Intelligent Services

In LINCKS *intelligent services* are conceived as software which is able to initiate and do intermediate or high level communication tasks, without direct user control. Intelligent services are in contrast to tools which are interactive, and under the direct command of the user. Many activities done by human users, are done to achieve certain goals, and there are a wide number of possible ways that these may be accomplished. Intelligent services exhibit this same flexibility, in that if they cannot accomplish a task using one means, they will seek other ways of doing it.

The LINCKS system is designed so that intelligent services specific to a particular situation can easily be integrated into the system. Some intelligent services are generic, and useful in all situations, so are included within the core system. Others need to be built specially for the situation. LINCKS provides the structure and environment where this can be easily done.

Tool

**Intelligent
Service**

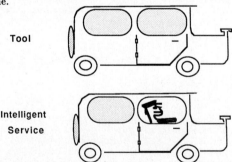

LINCKS Provides Both Tools and Intelligent Services

6.1 Postponed Tasks and Scheduling

One area where intelligent services are always needed is in the area of scheduling of
conflicting tasks, both for the computer and for its users. In scheduling a given group of
tasks, there are many factors to be taken into consideration in order to come up with the
most viable plan. One must consider timing constraints (what things have deadlines, plus
how long things take to accomplish), importance constraints (which tasks and/or which
people's tasks have highest priority), resource constraints (whether more than one task is
competing for a limited resource), etc. These things are inter-related in complex ways.
LINCKS includes such services, although information must be given in order to fit the
service to a new situation.

6.2 Reminders

Another rather general intelligent service is to remind users about tasks that need to be
performed. In order to do this, the system must have knowledge about things that need
to be done at certain times. The system should also know and be able to learn about its
different users. For instance, one user may need to be reminded of a task a week before,
in order to find time to do it, while another user prefers to get reminders closer to
deadlines, such as the day before. In order to offer an intelligent reminder service, the
system must be able to observe actvions and reason about them, and must know about
things that need to be done. E.g. if a person already works on the monthly report several
times one day, it is clearly inappropriate for the system to remind him that it needs to be
started the day after.

6.3 Automatic Routing

Automatic routing of objects to the various people involved in different phases of a task,
is another area where intelligent services can be useful. This includes automatic routing
to folders, or other storage places.

An intelligent service could automatically give partially completed copies of the monthly
report to the people who needed to work on it, but have not yet begun to do so, and
could route the report to various people who need to approve it, before it is sent to the
administration. It could then be sent automatically, and a copy put into a file or drawer.

6.4 Fully Automated Complex Tasks

As the LINCKS system develops we hope to add specific, fully automated office tasks
customized to particular situations. A model for building the intelligent services will make
it easy to design and add new particular services. An example is a service to
automatically generate the monthly report by extracting various data in the data base
and putting it together in a particular way. Because of the lack of a human participant in
fully automated services, it is important that they be extremely robust, and able to
recover from unexpected and unusual situations.

7. Summary

LINCKS can be described as an *object oriented imperative system*, which is designed to
support office automation. The focus of the system is communication, including all of the
tasks that make up effective communication. Because this focus is so broad, the system
should be applicable and useful in several contexts other than office automation.

Many of the issues dealt with in designing LINCKS arise also in designing programming
environments, and it seems that with the addition of a few specialised tools and services,
LINCKS will provide a useful programming environment. Support in LINCKS for parallel
work, solves many of the problems of team work using existing systems. It's emphasis on

evolution rather than simply development, also makes it well suited to system development, where often specification of what the system should be is an ongoing process.

LINCKS also provides a useful environment for a research group. The emphasis on communication is important for research, especially when one includes the concept of communication with oneself. The ability to easily link small pieces of information in many different ways, facilitates creative thinking and writing.

Medical systems also have many of the characteristics which LINCKS aims to deal with. They contain large amounts of data, of many different sorts. Communication is often very important as there are many different specialists who need to communicate concerning any given patient (e.g. radiographers, doctors, laboratory analysts, etc.). Medical expert systems, which have been proved to be very useful, could presumably be integrated into the LINCKS system as intelligent services.

Office automation combines a number of different areas: data base research, expert systems and planning, user interfaces, etc.. Consequently the issues dealt with in designing a system such as LINCKS are applicable to many different fields. The ability to customize the LINCKS system to widely differing office environments, makes it possible to also customize it to other environments.

8. *Acknowledgments*

A number of people contributed time and effort to reading and critiquing this paper. I am especially indebted to Ralph Rönnquist for extensive proof reading and helpful criticism, and to Peter Åberg for help with layout and final details. All members of the LINCKS project group (Johan Andersson, Dimiter Driankov, Ralph Rönnquist, Peter Åberg) contributed to the ideas presented.

9. *References and Bibliography*

1. Zdonik, Stanley B. *Object Management System Concepts.* SIGOA Newsletter, Second ACM-SIGOA Conference on Office Information Systems, vol. 5, no. 1-2, p.13-19.

2. Bracchi, Giampio Pernici, Barbara *The Design Requirements of Office Systems.* ACM Transactions on Office Information Systems, Vol 2, No 2, April 1984, p. 151-170.

3. Aiello, L., Nardi, D. and Panti, M. Structural Office Modelling: *A first step towards the office expert system.* Proceedings of 2nd ACM Conference on Office Information Systems, June 25-27 1984, Toronto, Canada, p. 161-169

4. Barbi, E., Calvo, F., Perale, C., Sirovich, F., Turini, F. *A Conceptual approach to Document Retrieval.* 1984 ACM

5. Biggerstaff, Ted J., Endres, D. Mack, Forman, Ira R. *Table: Object Oriented Editing of Complex Structures.* 1984 IEEE 334-345

6. Croft, Bruce W. Lefkowitz, Lawrence S. *Task Support in an Office System.* ACM Transactions on Office Information Systems, 1984 Vol. 2, Issue 3, p. 197-212.

7. Kimura, Gary D. Shaw, Alan C. *The Structure of Abstract Document Types.* Second ACM Conference on Office Information Systems, June 25-27 1984, Toronto, Canada, p. 161-169

8. Lin, Wente K., Ries, Daniel R., Blaustein, Barbara T. Chilenskas, R. Mark *Office Procedures as a Distributed Database Application.* Data Base, Winter 1984, p. 5-10

9. Lochovsky, F.H. *A Knowledge Based Approach to Supporting Office Work.* Database Engineering, IEEE Computer Society, Vol. 16, No. 3, Sept. 1983, p. 43-51

10. Zisman, M. *Use of Production Systems for Modelling Asynchronous, Concurrent Processes.* In Pattern Directed Inference Systems, Waterman and Hayes-Roth, Eds., Academic Press, New York, 1978, 53-68

OFFICE SYSTEMS: Methods and Tools
G. Bracchi, D. Tsichritzls (Editors)
Elsevier Science Publishers B.V. (North-Holland)
© IFIP, 1987

Integrating Procedure-Automation and Problem-Solving Approaches to Supporting Office Work[†]

Carson C. Woo and *Frederick H. Lochovsky*

Computer Systems Research Institute, University of Toronto
10 King's College Road, Toronto, Ontario, Canada M5S 1A4

Individual office systems are being built to support different types of office work. We classify them into two major approaches: (1) the procedure-automation approach, and (2) the problem-solving approach. In this paper, we argue that there is a need to integrate these two approaches into a common framework, and propose a model for such an integration. A journal editing example is used to illustrate the features of our integrated model.

1. INTRODUCTION

Several models have been proposed to handle office work. As described in [1], they fall into two main categories:

1. the procedure-automation approach
2. the problem-solving approach.

Brief descriptions of these two approaches are given in the remainder of this section. In section two, we will argue the need for integrating the two approaches into a common framework by giving more details about the problems involved in supporting office work. A proposed model to solve these problems will be presented in section three. In section four, we use an example which exhibits more than one kind of office activity to show how our model can be used to support office work. Finally, section five concludes the paper by giving the current status of this research.

1.1. The Procedure-Automation Approach

Automating office procedures is one approach to supporting office work. This approach views office work as primarily an information flow and processing activity and represents it procedurally. This is done by modelling office procedures as a structured sequence of office activities. Furthermore, this approach attempts to partition the office into logical workstations and structure the office work in terms of inputs, outputs, and transactions. The representation of actions performed by office workers and the conditions under which these actions are performed is the main focus of this activity. It is assumed that the office tasks are well understood and all possible circumstances are forseeable. Office tasks that are non-routine or that cannot be rigidly structured are not supported. [2, 3, 4, 5, 6, 7, 8] are examples of proposed and/or implemented office systems under this category.

1.2. The Problem-Solving Approach

The problem-solving approach views office work as primarily a strategy definition and selection activity (in a centralized, single user environment) and represents it descriptively. It attempts to structure the office work in terms of goals and rules. The representation, organization, and use of the rules has been the main focus of this activity. Office tasks that have no explicit representation for their goals and

[†]   This research was supported in part by the Natural Sciences and Engineering Research Council of Canada under grants A3356 and G1360.

rules are not supported. As well, office tasks that are divided into specialized domains handled by different office workers (where cooperation is needed in order to accomplish the work) are not supported [9]. [10, 11] are examples of proposed and/or implemented office systems under this category.

Due to the descriptive nature of the rules, the user cannot easily forsee the outcome of using them together. As well, for most applications, the user cannot at once state all the rules that are required to solve a problem. As a result, the solution computed by a problem-solving system might not always be what the user wants. To overcome this problem, the user is expected to participate in the problem solving by modifying rules and goals until the solution is acceptable (see figure 1). Therefore, problem-solving systems support, rather than replace, office workers' judgment. The overall aim is to improve the effectiveness of their decision making.

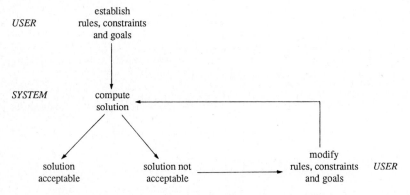

Figure 1: Characteristics of office problem solving[††].

2. MOTIVATION

It is clear from the previous section that there are at least two different ways to view office work. Each view by itself seems to be applicable within a restricted domain of the office environment. Unfortunately, most office work does not fall nicely into exactly one of the two views. As a result, neither approach is entirely adequate to support it.

2.1. A Wide Range of Types of Office Work

Consider the office task of editing a journal. The subtasks of sending an acknowledgement letter to the author (upon receiving his submitted paper) and routing the review form to the appropriate referees are considered to be information flow and processing activities. On the other hand, the subtask of finding appropriate referees to review the paper is a problem-solving activity; it is not possible for the editor to forsee all the possible circumstances of matching the paper with a set of referees, and the computer system (in this case) can only be used to assist the editor, not replace him, in finding the referees. In this simple example, we have demonstrated that some office work exhibits more than one kind of activity. In this section, we will discuss the observations made by several researchers on the different types of office work.

Due to the difficulty of building Management Information Systems (MIS), as early as 1971 people started to notice the wide range of types of office work. In [13], Gorry and Scott Morton show that MIS work falls on a continuous spectrum, with one end of the spectrum representing structured MIS work and

---

[††]   A similar figure is also shown in [12] and [11].

the other end of the spectrum representing unstructured MIS work. Structured MIS work is that of a routine nature for which a prescribed step by step solution is known. Unstructured MIS work is novel and nonrepetitive, and must be solved with creativity, initiative, and originality. Although the work done by Gorry and Scott Morton is intented to help in the design of MISs, the framework is also applicable to general office work.

Almost ten years later, with the same idea in mind, but using different terminology, Panko and Sprague classified office work into Type I and Type II [14] which corresponds to structured and unstructured MIS work (as defined by Gorry and Scott Morton) respectively. The intention here is no different from Gorry and Scott Morton; Panko and Sprague believe that in order to supply more computer technology to offices, we have to first understand the nature of office work, and they provide a framework for this purpose. Using this framework, Panko studied 38 offices and reported his findings in [15]. Although in his study the dichotomy proved to be useful, he emphasized the need to revise the Type I/Type II taxonomy and provide a more detailed taxonomy. The reason is that for some office work, it is hard to fit it in either mould. There is structured work intermixed with some problem-solving work. This agrees with the Gorry and Scott Morton framework in that office work falls on a continuous spectrum of structured and unstructured work.

2.2. The Need for Integration

There are three approaches to building office systems for supporting structured office work intermixed with some problem-solving work:

1. Extend the procedure-automation approach to handle some *limited* problem-solving activity.
2. View all office work as a problem-solving activity.
3. Integrate the procedure-automation and the problem-solving approaches.

2.2.1. Extend the Procedure-Automation Approach

The first approach, besides handling Type I office work well, can detect exceptional cases and provide alternatives to performing a task. This is the approach taken by the POISE system [16] at the University of Massachusetts. Due to the lack of deductive capabilities (i.e., automatically try out various ways of performing a task), all exceptional cases and alternatives have to be programmed explicitly using a procedural specification. For problem-solving activities that require large amounts of knowledge, the programming effort becomes very tedious.

2.2.2. View all Office Work as a Problem-Solving Activity

Theoretically speaking, a procedural specification creates difficulties when used to describe nonprocedural problem-solving work because there is no reasoning mechanism. However, a problem-solving specification can be used to describe procedural work because we can always put the procedural requirements into the rules and goals. Therefore, to describe both Type I and Type II office work, the second approach is more powerful than the first approach. This is the approach taken by the OMEGA system [11] at the M.I.T.

Practically speaking, the second approach does not work out nicely. Description languages (e.g., OMEGA) used by the problem-solving approach are heavily influenced by knowledge-based systems research, and mainly based on logical formalisms (e.g., first order logic[†††]). As a result, they inherit all the major limitations and inconvenience from logical formalisms when used to support certain types of office applications.

[†††] NOTE: the expressive power of OMEGA is more than first order logic [17, 18].

One problem is that to describe an action, we have to describe the states before and after perform-ing the action. For example, let route(d,x,y) describe the action of routing document d from workstation x to workstation y, CONNECT(x,y) describe the fact that a mail path exists from workstation x to works-tation y, and AT-LOCATION(d,z,s) describe the fact that document d is at workstation z in state s. The following formula describes the routing action:

DOCUMENT(d1) ∧ AT-LOCATION(d1,x,s) ∧ CONNECT(x,y)
    ⇒ DOCUMENT(d1) ∧ AT-LOCATION(d1,y,result-state(route(d1,x,y),s))
        ∧ CONNECT(x,y)

Unfortunately, the above description is not complete, we also need to describe what remains unchanged (this is the famous *frame problem* [19] in A.I. planning systems):

(∀d2) (DOCUMENT(d2) ∧ (d2 ≠ d1) ∧ AT-LOCATION(d2,z,s)
    ⇒ DOCUMENT(d2) ∧ AT-LOCATION(d2,z,result-state(route(d1,x,y),s)))

This is required for the following reason. An office task is composed of a sequence of actions. The appropriate actions are selected during the process of proving "the final state can be achieved from the given initial state". During the process of a proof, we cannot delete information that is true at the begin-ning of the proof (e.g., document d1 is at workstation x). Otherwise, we cannot (in general) guarantee the proof is correct. As a result, we are required to include all information in the knowledge base during the proofs; even for a simple action such as routing a document from one workstation to another. One can easily imagine the inconvenience and poor performance caused by this property.

A second problem with using the problem-solving approach exclusively is that users cannot define data structures or specify heuristics for performing a task. In some office applications, this will create unnecessary search and again result in poor performance.

A third problem is that the expressive power of most logical formalisms surpasses what a normal programming language (e.g., PL/I) can handle. For example, in first order logic we can describe state-ments such as "not (assign 19 to X)" and "(assign 5 to X) or (assign 7 to X)", but the corresponding actions cannot be physically performed using a normal programming language.

The language PROLOG is a first attempt to provide a practically usable language based on a logi-cal formalism. However, PROLOG necessarily had to embellish Horn Clausal logic with procedural mechanisms. It finesses the *frame problem* by allowing clauses to be explicitly added or removed by the user. It allows the user to guide search of proofs by means of the cut (i.e., !) operator. The limitation to one positive literal per clause in PROLOG is an expressive handicap (e.g., it cannot return results such as *Mary is either married to John or Joe*). While this is certainly a promising approach, it has other prob-lems. For example, PROLOG cannot describe the following task taken from [20]:

If the editor does not respond within two weeks, generate a reminder letter to him and continue to do so every two weeks. When he does respond, generate letters to each of the referees requesting their services.

Note that the task requires two processes running concurrently (one to remind the editor, the other to gen-erate letters), and if the editor does respond, the reminder process will have to be terminated immediately.

Another problem is that logical formalisms assume a global knowledge base. In this case, incon-sistent office procedures, specified by different office workers, are not allowed. This is not very nice because these different office procedures represent different opinions on common tasks [21]. As well, currently known logical formalisms cannot be used to model office tasks that are parallel, distributed, and require cooperation [19].

Finally, it is clear from Panko's study [15] that the users in the two different types of offices think differently. Consequently, it is not clear whether Type I office workers will accept a system that requires them to think in terms of goals and strategies.

2.2.3. Integrate the Two Approaches

Now, it is clear that although the procedure-automation approach and the problem-solving approach view office work very differently, each one by itself is convenient and *NECESSARY* to describe the type of office work for which the model is intended. Furthermore, we have the following additional comments on the two approaches:

1. For office work that cannot be viewed as either one of these activities (e.g., Type I office work intermixed with Type II office work), neither approach can effectively support it.

2. Some limitations and problems encountered in one approach are handled in the other approach. For example, systems developed using the problem-solving approach are not capable of performing actions. The procedure-automation approach, on the other hand, emphasizes the automation of office procedures (i.e., taking actions automatically).

3. Some Computer Science researchers, e.g., Lochovsky [1], Barber [22], Hewitt and de Jong [23], argue that modern office work is learned mainly by apprenticeship and therefore a task can move in both directions along the spectrum of Type I and Type II office work depending on how much we know about it (i.e., the more properties we know about a task, the closer it is to the Type I office work and vice versa). (Note that due to the open-ended nature of the office environment, it is possible to move an office task in the direction from Type I to Type II.)

Therefore, the need to integrate technologies from both approaches is clear.

Integrating these two different approaches appears to be non-trivial. For example, in the procedure-automation approach, data is rigidly structured using forms and manipulated by a procedural programming language (e.g., C, PL/1), while a LISP-like environment (e.g., descriptions in OMEGA [11]) is used in the problem-solving approach to represent both data and rules. Currently, a common representation for both types of office work does not exist. However, such a representation is necessary if all types of office work are to be effectively supported.

Finally, the procedure-automation and problem-solving approaches should be integrated in such a way that when we use the model, we do not have to identify the type of office work we are supporting. It is the responsibility of the model to decide whether there is sufficient information in the knowledge base to perform a task procedurally or whether it has to invoke the reasoning mechanism to handle the task as a problem-solving activity.

3. AN APPROACH FOR INTEGRATION

3.1. Integration Issues

We make the assumption that all office tasks that display more than one kind of activity can be decomposed into a hierarchy of subtasks where the leaf node subtasks are either Type I or Type II office work. In this case, we can maximize the usage of the technologies in the procedure-automation and problem-solving approaches to support different types of subtasks.

Tasks are required to interact with each other. It would be nice if all the useful facilities provided in the different approaches can, in a consistent manner, cooperate together without resulting in any unwanted side effects. Unfortunately, this is not the case. For some facilities, we don't know how to integrate them. For some others, modifications are needed.

First, we don't know how to integrate disjunctions and negations (from the problem-solving approach) with actions such as routing a document from one workstation to another (from the procedure-automation approach). Furthermore, we are not convinced that disjunctions and negations are useful for performing office work; *What can you do with a task if the knowledge of performing it is incomplete?*

Unless we can find a good use/need for disjunctions and negations (e.g., in logic and data bases, disjunctions and negations are used to enforce integrity constraints[†] [24]), we are not going to include them in our model.

Second, in order to operate the facilities provided in the two approaches in a common environment, in a consistent manner, we need to partition office knowledge into logical units. Note that systems such as OFS and TLA [25, 2], which support Type I office work, have already taken this view to building office systems. However, this concept has not yet been used in building systems for supporting Type II office work [9]. This is necessary for the following reasons:

- different units can be supported by different (i.e., procedure-automation or problem-solving) approaches,

- different, and maybe inconsistent, ways of performing the same office task can be allowed, (Particularly, this is a must for office problem solving. Note that a successful manager is one who can correctly predict what is going to happen in the future. It is very hard to make a good prediction, and normally a good prediction is very different from those made by most other people; otherwise, all businessmen would be rich.)

- office tasks can be executed independently and concurrently.

Third, we need to provide tools for these logical units to cooperate. The mailing tools provided in the procedure-automation approach will serve the purpose. Since we are integrating the two approaches, problem solving tools can be used together with the mailing facility so that communication can also be treated as a problem solving activity [9]. This tool is particularly useful for searching and collecting information located in different logical workstations.

Finally, we need to select a representation for data. We believe that the amount of office information is vast and we would rather trade expressiveness with efficiency. Hence, we will structure office information using forms, as in the procedure-automation approach. Due to the success of VISICALC and LOTUS 1-2-3, we feel that the form representation is promising if we can provide the right set of operations for performing office problem solving.

3.2. Using Objects

It seems natural to view office tasks as objects. However, different people interpret and use the term differently. Therefore, there is a need for us to clarify our interpretation and use of it:

- Object is a natural way to view office tasks that encapsulates some data and the allowable operations on it.

- Objects (i.e., tasks) can be executed independently and concurrently.

- Information in an object can only be accessed, with its permission, via message passing.

- Objects can communicate with each other easily.

Thus, the number "3" is not an object in our model. We will define an object type [26] to consist of:

[†]   Note that disjunctions and negations are operators in a rule (or procedure). It makes sense to use a rule to restrict the additions and deletions of data because rules are used to manipulate data. Unless meta-rules (rules used to reason about rules) are included in an office system, disjunctions and negations cannot be used in a similar way.

```
<object type> : <super class> {
    acquaintances
    variable declarations
    ALPHA rule
    rule_1
        .
        .
        .
    rule_n
    OMEGA rule
}
```

The format for a rule is as follow:

```
<rule name> (parameters) {
    acquaintances
    variable declarations
    preconditions
    actions
} (a value returned to the caller)
```

"Acquaintances" is a list of other object types that can communicate with this object type. Variables are used to provide storage and data structures for the object type. The instances of an object type have the same set of acquaintances and rules, but different values for variables. There are two special rules, called ALPHA and OMEGA, which are used to create and destroy an instance of the object type respectively.

3.3. The PAPS System

The integrated office system we have designed to support a wide range of office work is called PAPS (*Procedure Automation and Problem Solving system*). There are four different classes of object types in PAPS: data objects, task objects, agent objects, and task monitor objects. The relationships among them are shown in figure 2.

Each class of object type plays a distinct role in PAPS. Data objects store inactive information. They serve the same purpose as data bases. Task objects perform actions other than mailing (e.g., create a new entry in a data object). They support Type I office work, and thus include most major facilities available in the procedure-automation approach. Consultation rules in the task monitor objects describe strategies. They support Type II office work, and thus include most integratable facilities available in the problem-solving approach. Note that consultation rules only have to be consistent if they are in the same task monitor object. The architecture of the task monitor object (TMO) is similar to the HEARSAY-II [27] expert system, which is argued by Fox to display characteristics of organizational problem solving [28]. Agent objects are intelligent (i.e., have some problem solving abilities) mailing tools. Unlike all other object classes, agent objects can move around different workstations. To cooperate, the workspace serves as the communication medium for task objects, agent objects, and consultation rules.

As mentioned in section 3.1, office tasks that display more than one kind of activity can be decomposed into a hierarchy of subtasks where the leaf node subtasks are either Type I or Type II office work. In PAPS, a task monitor object (TMO) corresponds to a nonterminal subtask or a leaf node subtask that is Type II office work. The dotted arrow in figure 2 shows how TMOs form this hierarchy. Note that this hierarchy of TMOs cannot be formed without the help of task objects for two reasons. First, TMOs can be (but are not necessarily) geographically separated. It would be too expensive to have them constantly monitoring the activities in their ancestor TMO's workspace. A task object, in this case, resembles the ambassador of a TMO (call it η) on mission to its ancestor TMO (call it ζ). It can, therefore, represent η to make simple decisions and perform simple actions in ζ, while leaving the critical jobs to be done in η. Second, giving the control of a task to its subtasks requires information passing. Since information passing is considered to be an action, only task objects are allowed to perform it.

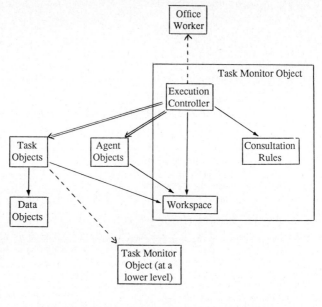

⟹   means supervises the execution of the objects pointed to.

⟶   means allowed to access the information in the objects pointed to.

- - - →   means allowed to pass control to the object pointed to.

Figure 2: Objects used in our model.

3.4. Supporting Structured and Semi-Structured Office Work Using PAPS

In some applications, the sequence of executing the task objects is known or partially known. This is handled in our model by ALPHA and OMEGA rules. As an example, let us consider the task in figure 3 which requires five task objects. The arrows in the figure are used to indicate the execution sequence for the task objects. In this example, an instance of obj_1 is created by one of the following: (1) a user, (2) a task object instance in another logical workstation, or (3) an instance of a data object type which has rules to trigger events. When obj_1 finishes its job, its OMEGA rule will wake up task objects obj_2 and obj_3 at the same time and pass them relevant data. obj_4 can be awakened by both obj_2 and obj_3. However, obj_4 will go back to sleep if one of obj_2 or obj_3 has not finished its job yet. This is handled by the ALPHA rules in obj_4. obj_5 is the last task object to be awakened in this example before the task is done.

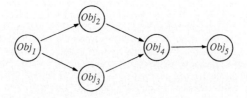

Figure 3: A task that requires 5 task objects.

This representation is very similar to the augmented Petri Net approach as described in [20]. The conditions in the ALPHA rule can serve the same purpose as the conditions in the Production Rules and the OMEGA rule can serve the same purpose as a Petri Net. In more complicated situations, the OMEGA rule can provide alternatives if the task objects it wakes up fail to accomplish their jobs. However, situations might arise for which all of the given alternatives fail to accomplish their jobs. Furthermore, it is also possible that the OMEGA rule contains no information about what task objects to awaken. Under these situations, the TMO will take over and control the execution of the task objects. The TMO handles the execution with the help of the user and the consultation rules.

In the current technology for building information systems, the system analyst is responsible for documenting the flow of information in the manual system using techniques such as data flow diagrams [29]. Due to the complexity of large information systems, drawing a correct data flow diagram takes a long time. In our model, the flow of information from one process to another is represented using the message passing between two task objects. Since the task monitor object is responsible for controlling the execution of task objects, a planner is provided for this purpose [30]. This planning process can therefore replace the work done by the system analyst in connecting all the pieces of a task together. Furthermore, it can also be used to detect conflicting rules among task objects.

In most applications, due to the size of the application and the evolution of the application, office workers cannot relate easily their subtask(s) with respect to the entire application. This does not mean that the task is not procedural. Classifying a task into procedural or problem-solving work sometimes depends on how much one understands about the details of the work [23]. Similarly, if PAPS is used to support an office task, then initially we need to use the planner to schedule the execution of the task objects in that task. As the application begins to run smoothly, we can say that the model begins to understand more about the task. If the task turns out to be procedural, then we would like to execute the task objects in any subsequent instances of that task procedurally. Hence, if planning results are stored appropriately for future use, we can automate this type of evolution in our model.

3.5. Supporting Office Problem Solving Using PAPS

In PAPS, if a leaf node subtask in a hierarchy cannot be supported by task objects, then it is classified as office problem solving and will be supported by a TMO. However, not all office problem solving can be supported by computers either because we don't know how to represent the required knowledge, or because it is cheaper to do it manually. The degree of support (i.e., how many gaps the user has to fill in) provided by a TMO thus depends on how many useful consultation rules it has.

Consultation rules are a special set of rules in the task monitor object. They are only used to assist the task monitor object. They do not perform any office work such as computation or communicating with other objects. Most of these rules are one of the following types:

1. Control rules (e.g., selection criteria when more than one task object is awakened and they cannot be executed concurrently).

2. Default rules which include equivalent information, common sense knowledge, simple implicit knowledge, and so on. Some examples are:
   - (miscellaneous expenses) = (other expenses)
   - December 25th is a holiday.
   - if $X_1, \cdots, X_n$ are true, then can conclude that Y is also true.

3. Reduction rules (e.g., to compute Y, we must first compute $X_1, \cdots, X_n$).

The user can express rules descriptively, and the system will automatically try out all the possible ways of using them until one is successful. However, during the reasoning process, information that cannot be deduced by the consultation rules might in fact be computable by task objects or collectable by agent objects in other workstations.

At this stage, an example would be useful to continue our discussion on PAPS. This will be done in the following section.

4. AN EXAMPLE

We use a journal editing example to demonstrate how PAPS can be used to support office work. When a paper is submitted to the editor-in-chief for publication, he will hand it over to an associate editor for refereeing. Upon receiving the paper, the associate editor is required to select three referees, who are knowledgable in the area of the submitted paper, to review the paper. For the purpose of our discussion, we are only going to concentrate on the process of how the referees can be selected with the help of PAPS. Furthermore, we make the following assumptions:

1. The paper is submitted via electronic mail and the author(s) is required to provide some keywords for the paper.

2. The associate editor has a list of referees and their area(s) of research is represented by keywords.

3. Referees are selected if one or more keywords are matched.

4. In order not to over work a particular referee, the associate editor will not request a referee to review more than one paper in a year.

5. The referees are also using PAPS to support their office work.

To help the selection of referees, we need the following tables in the workspace of the "select_referees_TMO" task monitor object (see figure 4):

1. **referee (name, addr, idleDays, tried)** is used to keep information about the referee name, electronic mailing address, the number of days since he last reviewed a paper, and a boolean variable to be used in the reasoning process.

2. **paperKeywords (keyword)** contains all the keywords of the paper submitted for publication.

3. **haveKnowledge (name, keyword)** provides information on who can review what types of papers.

As shown in figure 4, these tables must be declared and put into the workspace using the "add" statement. Some entries in the tables can be found in data objects. The statement "referee.name := name@refereeData" assigns the "name" field of all the instances in the data object "refereeData" to the "name" column of the "referee" table. The statement "refereeData→getAddr(name)" calls the "getAddr" rule in the "refereeData" object and returns the electronic mailing address for "name" (see figure 5).

For the purpose of demonstration, we assume that there are three stages to go through before we can conclude "a referee is found". These three stages are (1) find a referee by matching keywords, (2) make sure that he did not review a paper within the last year, (3) get an agreement from him to review this paper. In PROLOG like syntax, we can express this information as:

refFound(x) ← **canRef**(x), **notClose**(x), **willingRef**(x)
canRef(x) ← **referee**$(x, \_, \_, \_)$, **haveKnowledge**(x, y), **paperKeywords**(y)
notClose(x) ← **referee**$(x, \_, z, \_)$, $(z > 356)$

where x, y, and z are variables, and _ means any value. A statement of the form:

$$P(x_1, \cdots, x_m) \leftarrow Q_1(y_1, \cdots, y_p), \cdots, Q_n(z_1, \cdots, z_q).$$

is interpreted as a two way traffic: (1) in order to show $P(x_1, \cdots, x_m)$ is true, we need to establish subgoals $Q_1(y_1, \cdots, y_p), \cdots, Q_n(z_1, \cdots, z_q)$ and show that they are true; (2) however, if the subgoals $Q_1(y_1, \cdots, y_p), \cdots, Q_n(z_1, \cdots, z_q)$, with a value for each variable y_i, are facts in the knowledge base or have already proven to be true, then we can conclude $P(x_1, \cdots, x_m)$ is true. Figure 6 shows how consultation rules in PAPS describe the above knowledge. The "?" sign in the figure is used to indicate *null* values.

```
select_referees_TMO: taskMonitorObject {
    alpha(goal.variableName, goal.comparator, goal.value, goal.variableType) {
        goal.variableName, goal.comparator, goal.value, goal.variableType : string;
            ...     /* some more declarations here */
        /* add variables into the workspace */
        add("referee.name": "string");
        add("referee.addr": "string");
        add("referee.idleDays": "integer");
        add("referee.tried": "boolean");
            ...     /* some more variables here */
        /* specify the goal of this problem solving session */
        for each goal
            add(variableName, variableType);
            addGoal (variableName, comparator, value);
        end for

        total_referees := 0;
        /* assign values for the referee table */
        referee.name := name@refereeData;
        for each referee
            addr := refereeData→getaddr(name);
            tried := false;
        end for
            ...     /* some more actions here */
    }
    consultationRules:
        rule001;
        rule002;
            ...     /* some more consultation rules here */
    taskObjects:
        compute_idle_days;
            ...     /* some more task objects here */
    dataObjects:
        refereeData;
            ...     /* some more data objects here */
    agentObjects:
            ...     /* some agent objects here */
}
```

Figure 4: The task monitor object for selecting referees.

As mentioned before, consultation rules cannot perform any computations. In order to ensure no more than one paper is assigned to a referee for reviewing in a year, a task object (see figure 7) is needed to compute the number of days since the referee last reviewed a paper.

The three rules given above seem to be quite simple and can also be expressed using a task object. However, as the number of descriptive rules increases, the need of using consultation rules becomes clear. The following rules, which are used to deduce more knowledge about a referee, in the select_referees_TMO task monitor object are a good example (we use a short hand notation of "A ⇒ B" to mean if the referee has knowledge in A, then he is also knowledgable in B).

```
refereeData: dataObject {
        name, addr: string;
        lastDayRef: date;

        alpha(Rname, Raddr) {
                Rname, Raddr: string;
                Rname != ?;                  /* pre-condition */
                name := Rname;               /* actions */
                addr := Raddr;
        }

        getAddr(Rname) {
                Rname: string;
                Rname = name;                /* find the right referee */
        } (addr)                             /* return his electronic mailing address */

        getLastRefDay(Rname) {
                Rname: string;
                Rname = name;
        } (lastDayRef)

                .
                .
                .

}
```

Figure 5: Definition of the "refereeData" data object.

Office Automation ⇒ Office Information Systems
Office Information Systems ⇒ Office Automation
Office Information Systems ⇒ Data Processing
Distributed Systems *and* A.I. ⇒ Distributed A.I.
Distributed Systems *and* MIS ⇒ Office Information Systems
A.I. ⇒ MIS
Data Base ⇒ MIS
User Interface ⇒ MIS
Programming Language ⇒ MIS
Knowledge Representation ⇒ Programming Language
Relational Data Base Theory ⇒ Data Base
Logic ⇒ Knowledge Representation
Semantic Network ⇒ Knowledge Representation
Frames ⇒ Knowledge Representation
Knowledge Representation ⇒ A.I.
Expert System ⇒ A.I.
Dynamic Logic ⇒ Logic
First Order Logic ⇒ Logic
Temporal Logic ⇒ Logic
Fuzzy Logic ⇒ Logic

Furthermore, it is not possible for the associate editor to list all the possible keywords and their relationships. PAPS can only be used to speed up his decision of selecting the three referees.

```
rule001: consultationRule {
        /* conditions: in order to compute "refFound" */
        refFound = ?;
        exist(canRef) = false;
        exist(notClose) = false;
        exist(willingRef) = false;
        /* changes: we must first compute "canRef", "notClose", and "willingRef" */
        add(canRef: boolean);
        add(notClose: boolean);
        add(willingRef: boolean);
}

rule002: consultationRule {
        /* conditions */
        canRef = true;
        notClose = true;
        willingRef = true;
        /* conclusion: we achieve one third of the goal */
        total_referees := total_referees + 1;
        /* changes: reset some variables for more referees */
        refFound := ?;
        canRef := ?;
        notClose := ?;
        willingRef := ?;
}

rule003: consultationRule {
        /* conditions: if a keyword matches */
        canRef = ?;
        referee.tried = false;
        referee.name = haveKnowledge.name
        haveKnowledge.keyword = paperKeywords.keyword
        /* conclusion: we found a qualified referee */
        canRef := true;
        currentRef := referee.name
}
```

Figure 6: Some consultation rules.

The most interesting part of this example is to demonstrate the use of an agent object in perform-ing office problem solving. After a referee is selected, we need to get an agreement from him to review the paper. This is done by sending an agent object[†] to the referee's task monitor object. If the referee cannot review the paper, the agent object will ask him to suggest another referee. Information about this referee will be put into the "referee" table in the workspace of the "select_referees_TMO" task monitor object after the agent object returns. The advantage of this additional information is that, when the "select_referees_TMO" runs out of referees to ask for reviewing the paper, it can try the suggested new referee. If the suggested referee agrees to review the paper, the user can save his information (e.g., elec-tronic mailing address, his area(s) of specialization(s)) in the "refereeData" data object. Note that the addition of the new data does not invalidate the deductions that are already done for other referees.

[†]   rules used in an agent object are very similar to rules used in data objects and task objects with the additional ability to communicate with users.

```
compute_idle_days: taskObject {
        referee.idleDays : string;
                ...        /* some more declarations here */

        alpha(_referee.name, _referee.idleDays, _currentRef) {
                /* variables begin with an underscore are the same */
                /* variables (without the underscore) in the workspace */

                /* this rule keeps checking the values of "currentRef" */
                /* and triggers itself when the following conditions */
                /* become true */

                _referee.name, _referee.idleDays, _currentRef : string;

                /* condition: select from referee where name = currentRef and idleDays = ? */
                {
                _referee.name = _currentRef;
                _referee.idleDays = ?;

                /* action: compute his idle days */
                referee.idleDays := findDiff(day(), refereeData→getLastRefDay(referee.name));
                }
                for each _referee
                        referee.idleDays := _referee.idleDays;
                end for
        }

        findDiff(date1, date2) {
                /* task to be done in this procedure is very routine and structured */
                .
                .
                .

        }
        omega() {
                referee.idleDays != ?;
        } (referee.idleDays)                    /* put the value of idle days in the workspace */
}
```

Figure 7: Definition of the "compute_idle_days" task object.

Reasoning systems have the ability to backtrack (i.e., try different values for variables or select different rules). Backtracking can be implemented easily if there are no side effects (e.g., a new data object is created). Unfortunately, undoing an action in an office environment can be non-trivial. For example, after sending out a paper for a referee to review, the associate editor then changes his mind due to the difficulties of finding referees for another paper. He cannot physically undo his original action of notifying the referee to review the paper; he can only notify the referee of his new decision. For this reason, PAPS does not undo an action automatically; this capability will have to be programmed explicitly.

5. CONCLUSION

In this paper, we have argued the need to integrate the technologies provided in the procedure-automation and problem-solving approaches to supporting office work. The incompatibility of the two approaches creates certain problems and difficulties for the integration. Nevertheless, by sacrificing some expressive power used in the problem-solving approach, we have proposed an object-oriented system, called PAPS, for the integration. A journal editing example is used to demonstrate the capabilities of PAPS. In particular, the use of communication tools (e.g., agent objects) is demonstrated to be very useful for some types of office problem solving.

Currently, we are working on the implementation of the PAPS system. As well, we are gathering a real world example to try out the tools provided in our system. At this stage, we believe that the model is useful and promising.

ACKNOWLEDGEMENT

The helpful suggestions and criticisms from Stavros Christodoulakis, Alberto Mendelzon, John Mylopoulos, Ken Sevcik, Dennis Tsichritzis, and John Tsotsos in various stages of this research are highly appreciated. We would also like to thank Eugene Fiume, Gerhard Lakemeyer, Tim Lownie, Steve Weiser, and Grant Weddell for their lengthly discussions on various parts of this project.

REFERENCES

[1]   Lochovsky, F.H., "A Knowledge-Based Approach to Supporting Office Work", Database Engineering, IEEE Computer Society, Vol.16, No.3, pp.43-51, September 1983.

[2]   Hogg, J., Nierstrasz, O.M., and Tsichritzis, D.C., "Office Procedures". In "Office Automation: Concepts and Tools", edited by D.C. Tsichritzis. Springer-Verlag, pp.137-166, 1985.

[3]   Zloof, M.M., "QBE/OBE: A Language for Office and Business Automation". IEEE Computer, Vol.14, No.5, pp.13-22, May 1981.

[4]   Fong, A.C., "A Model for Automatic Form-Processing Procedures". Proc. of the Sixteenth Hawaii International Conference on System Sciences (Honolulu, Hawaii, U.S.A., January 5-7), pp.558-565, 1983.

[5]   Lum, V.Y., Shu, N.C., Tung, F., and Chang, C.L., "Automating Business Procedures with Form Processing". In Office Information Systems (N. Naffah editor), pp.7-38, 1982. North-Holland, Amsterdam.

[6]   Shu, N.C., Lum, V.Y., Tung, F., and Chang, C.L., "Specification of Forms Processing and Business Procedures for Office Automation". IEEE Transactions on Software Engineering, SE-8(5), pp.499-512, 1982.

[7]   Zisman, M.D., "Representation, Specification and Automation of Office Procedures". Ph.D. Dissertation, Department of Decision Science. The Wharton School, University of Pennsylvania, Philadelphia, Pennsylvania, U.S.A., 1976

[8]   Barron, J., "Dialogue and Process Design for Interactive Information Systems Using Taxis". Proc. of the First ACM SIGOA Conference on Office Information Systems (Philadelphia, Pennsylvania, U.S.A., June 21-23), pp.12-20, June 1982.

[9]   Woo, C.C., and Lochovsky, F.H., "Supporting Distributed Office Problem Solving in Organizations". ACM Transactions on Office Information Systems, Vol.4, No.4, October 1986.

[10] Fikes, R.E., "Odyssey: a Knowledge-Based Assistant", Artificial Intelligence **16**, pp.331-361, 1981.

[11] Barber, G.R., "Supporting Organizational Problem Solving with a Workstation", ACM Transactions on Office Information System, Vol.1, No.1, pp.45-67, 1983.

[12] Barber, G.R., "Office Semantics". Ph.D. Thesis, Department of Electrical Engineering and Computer Science, Massachusetts Institute of Technology, Cambridge, Massachusetts, U.S.A., 1982.

[13] Gorry, G.A., and Scott Morton, M.S., "A Framework for Management Information Systems". Sloan Management Review (Massachusetts Institute of Technology, Cambridge, Massachusetts, U.S.A.), Vol.13, No.1, pp.55-70, Fall 1971.

[14] Panko, R.R., and Sprague, R.H., "Toward a New Framework for Office Support". Proc. of the First ACM SIGOA Conference on Office Information Systems (Philadelphia, Pennsylvania, U.S.A., June 21-23), pp.82-92, June 1982.

[15] Panko, R.R., "38 Offices: Analyzing Needs in Individual Offices". ACM Transactions on Office Information Systems, Vol.2, No.3, pp.226-234, July 1984.

[16] Croft, W.B., and Lefkowitz, L.S., "Task Support in an Office System". ACM Transactions on Office Information Systems, Vol.2, No.3, pp.197-212, July 1984.

[17]   Attardi, G., Private Communication. 1985.

[18]   de Jong, P., Private Communication. 1985.

[19]   McCarthy, J., "Epistemological Problems of Artificial Intelligence". Proc. of the Fifth International Joint Conference on Artificial Intelligence (Massachusetts Institute of Technology, Cambridge, Massachusetts, U.S.A., August 22-25), pp.1038-1044, 1977.

[20]   Zisman, M.D., "Use of Production Systems to Model Asynchronous, Concurrent Processes". In Pattern Directed Inference Systems (Edited by D. Waterman and F. Hayes-Roth), New York: Academic Press, pp.53-68, 1978.

[21]   Tsichritzis, D.C., "Objectworld". In "Office Automation: Concepts and Tools", edited by D.C. Tsichritzis, Springer-Verlag, pp.379-398, 1985.

[22]   Barber, G.R., De Jong, P., and Hewitt, C., "Semantic Support for Work in Organizations". Proc. of IFIP conference (Paris, France, September 19-23), pp.561-566, 1983. North-Holland, Amsterdam.

[23]   Hewitt, C., and De Jong, P., "Open Systems". In "On Conceptual Modeling". Edited by M.L. Brodie, J. Mylopoulos and J.W. Schmidt, Springer-Verlag, pp.147-164, 1984.

[24]   Gallaire, H., Minker, J., and Nicolas, J., "Logic and Databases: A Deductive Approach". ACM Computing Surveys. Vol.16, No.2, pp. 153-185, June 1984.

[25]   Tsichritzis, D.C., Rabitti, F.A., Gibbs, S., Nierstrasz, O.M., and Hogg, J., "A System for Managing Structured Messages". IEEE Transactions on Communications, Vol.COM-30, No.1, pp.66-73, January 1982

[26]   Twaites, K.J., "An Object-Based Programming Environment for Office Information Systems". M.Sc. Thesis, Department of Computer Science, University of Toronto, Toronto, Ontario, Canada. 1984.

[27]   Erman, L.D., Hayes-Roth, F., Lesser, V.R., and Reddy, D.R., "The Hearsay-II Speech-Understanding System: Integrating Knowledge to Resolve Uncertainty". ACM Computing Surveys, Vol.12, No.2, pp.213-253, June 1980.

[28]   Fox, M.S., "An Organizational View of Distributed Systems". IEEE Transactions on Systems, Man, and Cybernetics, VOL.SMC-11, No.1, January 1981.

[29]   Gane, C., and Sarson, T., "Structured Systems Analysis: Tools and Techniques". Prentice-Hall, 1979.

[30]   Woo, C.C., and Lochovsky, F.H., "A Logically Distributed Planning Model". In Technical Report CSRI-183, Computer Systems Research Institute, University of Toronto, Toronto, Ontario, Canada. 1986.

OFFICE SYSTEMS: Methods and Tools
G. Bracchi, D. Tsichritzis (Editors)
Elsevier Science Publishers B.V. (North-Holland)
© IFIP, 1987

AN ARCHITECTURE FOR DIALOG MANAGEMENT IN OPAL

Stefan BRITTS
Matts AHLSÉN

SYSLAB †
Department of Information Processing & Computer Science
University of Stockholm
S-106 91 Stockholm
SWEDEN ‡

OPAL is an object oriented, combined application development and run-time system. An architecture for the user interface has been designed in order to meet requirements such as uniformity, customizability, device independence, and robustness. This paper describes the design of the user interface architecture and relates it to stated requirements.

1. INTRODUCTION

Office Information Systems

The OIS field seems to be an ever expanding area. As the field grows, new types of applications and new groups of users will be approached. At the same time the distinction between traditional data processing and OIS is fading away. A short characterization of this fuzzy area would encompass concepts such as: management of complex data structures, communications, integration of various applications, distribution, frequent change of routines, exception from rules, and a high degree of interactiveness.

Todays' commercial OIS-products seem to have hard to live up to all these characteristics. The problem of designing better OISs is therefore tackled by developing both new software architectures and more advanced user interfaces.

Object Orientation

Object oriented systems are good representatives of a promising software architecture. It is promising because it facilitates integration and handling of complex data structures as well as communication and distribution by representing everything as objects and providing a common identification scheme.

In addition, object oriented systems are usually based on the theory of abstract datatypes [1] . This means that objects support modularity, encapsulation, and the separation between specification and implementation. Object orientation therefore in itself supports a good software design practice.

Examples of object orientation can be brought up from many different areas such as:

- Operating Systems: Hydra and S/38 [2] ,
- Data Bases: RM/T [3] and GemStone [4] ,
- Programming Languages: Smalltalk [5] , Simula [6] , and CLU [7] ,
- Conceptual Modeling: CMOL [8] , an office data model [9] , and DAPLEX [10] ,
- and Artificial Intelligence: Semantic Nets [11] and Frames [12] .

In the OIS-field ideas have been brought together from several of these areas. This has resulted in systems like: TAXIS [13] , SBA [14] , ENCORE [15] , Oz [16] , and of course, OPAL [1].

Advanced User Interfaces

As OIS-applications are highly interactive not only the underlying software architecture but also the user interface must be considered carefully. A user interface must be powerful and yet simple to use and learn, also for occasional users. Commonly stated general requirements on the user interface are:

---

† This work is supported by the National Swedish Board for Technical Development (STU).

‡ USENET: decvax!mcvax!enea!suadb!stefan

- uniformity within and across applications,
- customizability for different users, including support for multiple dialog styles,
- robustness (smooth user error handling), and
- device independence.

In addition, experience has shown that direct manipulation, or WYSIWYG-interfaces, have become very popular [17, 18] . It is therefore desirable to support this style of interaction.

Today's object oriented systems do not meet all stated requirements on the user interface. These are usually fixed or standardized in that they presuppose a certain style of interaction, e.g. menus and a desk-top interface [19, 20, 21] . This may have to do with system designers interest for exploring the capabilities of a certain type of interface rather than building customizable user interfaces.

The objectives of OPAL are to provide a powerful, object oriented, combined application development and run-time environment. A central goal is to meet the stated requirements on the user interface.

Overview of the paper

In the following sections our approach will be presented in more detail. First, the overall architecture of OPAL is outlined. Then each level of the architecture is described in more detail.

2. SYSTEM ARCHITECTURE

It has been noticed that generalizing and separating dialog management functions from the rest of an application offers several advantages to traditional approaches [22, 23] , such as:

- Reduced user interface implementation efforts.
- More powerful user interfaces can be built and maintained.
- Designing user interfaces can be separated from designing applications.

This separation of concerns has much in common with generalizing and incorporating data management functions into a DBMS. The corresponding approaches concerning user interfaces are often called User Interface Management System (UIMS) [20, 22] , Dialog Management System (DMS) [24] or Display Management System [25] .

These observations have strongly influenced the design of the OPAL user interface. All user interface facilities have been incorporated into a Dialog Management System (DMS) which is a part of OPAL.

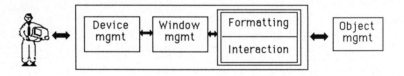

FIGURE 1. DMS Functions

The DMS performs four main functions: formatting, interaction, window management, and device management. Each function is implemented by one or more objects. These objects operate on other objects representing devices, the information to be displayed, etc.

From a user interface perspective OPAL and its DMS is organized in a three-level architecture: the application level, the dialog level, and the I/O-level.

Application level:

Here the semantics of applications is defined. That is, their functional behavior. This is expressed mainly by the concepts of object and view plus operations on, and relationships among, objects.

Dialog level:

Interactions between executing applications and end-users are handled on this level. The problems tackled are how to format and compose data into a suitable layout. Also user input is taken care of here, e.g. menu selection and data entry. The dialog level mediates between the application level and the I/O-level, hence relieving applications from dialog management details.

I/O-level:

On the lowest level interactions are mapped to input and output device management. This is usually referred to as physical I/O. Among the problems tackled are: how to present data on a particular output device, e.g. a bit-map or character display, and how to interpret input from e.g. a keyboard or a mouse. Another I/O-level function is synchronizing I/O between simultaneously executing applications and a common set of I/O-devices.

This architecture is the overall framework for the OPAL user interface. Each level in the architecture forms a level of abstraction which is basically independent of other levels. Naturally, there must be a well defined interface between each level. The architecture is refined by a set of objects implementing the functionality of each architectural level. The result is a clean structure of the user interface where higher level objects need not care about details on lower levels.

Using this approach applications will largely become independent of the actual dialog style and how data are formated and composed on e.g. a page. The former is sometimes referred to as *dialog independence* [26] . Dialogs will in their turn be independent of physical device characteristics, i.e. *device independence*. The whole policy of separation of concerns is called *application independence* [22] . Obviously, this architecture helps in fulfilling listed requirements on the user interface.

The ideas presented here on applying an architectural model to user interface design are not new. Similar models of user-interface architectures can be found in e.g. [27] , [19] , [28] , [20] , and [29] .

In the following three sections a more detailed description of the design of each level in the architecture will be given.

3. APPLICATION LEVEL

3.1. Basic Application Level Functions

The purpose of an OIS is to support various types of activities in an office. The activity support is given by tools or applications. Together, the applications define the semantics of the information system, i.e. what users can do, and the meaning of their actions.

Applications may be both of a specific nature, e.g. accounts receivable, or of a more general nature, e.g. text processing. Regardless of their area of applicability any application program usually encompasses general functions such as creating, processing, distributing, and deleting information. Of course, general functions like these are specialized to the needs of different applications.

Today, designing and implementing applications also incorporates designing and implementing dialogs. In our approach, dialog development is separated from application development. This makes it possible to concentrate on the functional behavior of an application on this architectural level. As we shall see below, however, the application level is still very important in achieving stated requirements on the user interface.

Next section gives an overview of the underlying software system - OPAL - to be interfaced. A more elaborated description of OPAL is found in [30] .

3.2. Application Level Design

As already mentioned OPAL is an object oriented system. It is aimed to be used in a decentralized environment. An *OPAL-system* consists of one or more *nodes*. Each node corresponds to an autonomous unit of an organization, e.g. a department. Every node has an *information base* which provides persistent storage of objects in a single level store.

Everything in OPAL is regarded as objects. We distinguish between object *types* and object *instances* An object type is a description of an object while an object instance is created according to one or more object types. Also object types are regarded as object instances and can be manipulated just like other object instances. Objects can be specialized through a mechanism for multiple inheritance. In accordance with the theory of abstract datatypes an object defines a data structure and a set of operations by which the structure can be manipulated. There is no way to bypass the operational interface and to access the data structure directly.

There are two basic types of objects - datatypes and entities [2]. *Datatypes* are the basic units by which data is defined, e.g. integer, character, and sequence. A difference between the two basic object types is that instances of datatypes (values) cannot have an independent existence while an entity can. Datatypes are always bound to an entity instance. In addition to operations and data structures, *entities* provide e.g. an entity reference container and are subject to synchronization and access control. Some entities are active in the sense that they have the capability of making things happen in the system. These are called process objects.

For any object type - entities as well as datatypes - one or more views may be defined. A *view* restricts and/or transforms the available set of operations on an object. This mechanism is used both for authorization and transformation purposes. The concept of group is used for defining the access rights of different users.

3.3. User Interface Considerations

As mentioned above, the application level is largely independent of, but not unimportant to, the user interface. Several requirements on the user interface - uniformity, robustness, and WYSIWYG capabilities - are strongly dependent on the design of the application level.

In a *uniform* user interface the same command name and syntax should be used for performing similar operations on different types of objects, e.g. DELETE document, DELETE chapter. In OPAL this can easily be achieved by taking advantage of the inheritance mechanism. This way generic operations can be created. That is, operations defined for a certain object type are automatically inherited to all its sub-types, c.f. generic commands [31] . Hence, uniformity is given support in the basic object model.

Robustness is the ability of the user interface to handle user errors smoothly. An example of a user error of the worst kind is performing a DELETE-operation by mistake. The system should provide an undo-capability which permits the user to reset the system state to a point immediately before the mistake was done [32] . To recover from such errors basic support for the undo type of operation must be given at the application level. OPAL provides a version management facility by which previous states of entities can be retained.

Finally, to achieve a *WYSIWYG interface* two more fundamental requirements must be fulfilled. First, it must be possible to perform data entry in any order. That is, a value visible on the screen must be changeable just by e.g. pointing at it and typing a new value. This is sometimes referred to as two-dimensional I/O [33] . Second, it must be possible to specify dependencies among data used in an application. This is necessary in order to have all dependent values automatically recalculated upon the change of a value.

In OPAL this is done by permitting dependencies among data to be specified explicitly by the designer. Dependencies can be specified for all data, both internal and external to an entity. Recalculations are triggered when a data value is assigned a new value.

4. DIALOG LEVEL

4.1. Basic Dialog Management Functions

The dialog level is an intermediary level between the application level and the I/O-level. One could say that this level mediates between OPAL applications and the external world (represented by devices operated by end-users). The dialog level is also the central part of the OPAL-DMS. Here the human-computer dialog is conducted on a level of abstraction where device characteristics and application details are irrelevant.

The main functions performed on this level are:

   - Transforming output data from an internal representation to an external representation suitable for presentation.
   - Formatting output data and composing layout structures.
   - Transforming input data from an external representation to an internal representation that can be handled by OPAL-applications.
   - Prompting questions and receiving user commands, parsing these, and invoking corresponding operations on underlying objects.

In the rest of this chapter the objects implementing these functions will be given a closer examination.

4.2. Dialog Level Design

Application Objects: entities and datatypes

Applications in OPAL are built out of structures of *entity types* having operations defined on *datatypes*. Thus, operations of an entity return or take input parameters in terms of values of these datatypes, e.g., a Document entity type may have an operation which returns a piece of "text" corresponding to some paragraph, and, an Invoice may return a "real" when the "Amount Due" operation is invoked, and so on. These values (or instances of datatypes) are internal to the applications and must be organized in appropriate ways for interactive use. Stated differently, the logical structure of an application must be related to a corresponding layout for presentation without cluttering up the application entities with dialog code.

Layout Objects

The external data representation (or layout) for entity types intended for presentation, is referred to as a *layout object* (actually an instance of a the Layout entity type). An application entity is always viewed and operated upon through this in dialogs. In general, a layout object defines a two-dimensional space for presentation on some display surface. Using graphics terminology, we can call this the World Coordinate Space (WCS) in which the components of a layout object are organized. Lower software layers in the DMS architecture are responsible for the subsequent mapping to devices. The principles for layout objects are basically the same as for the ECMA Office Document Architecture [34] .

The basic structure of a layout object is a pure tree where the nodes are called *frames*. These are simply rectangular display areas used to hold external data representations. All frames have attributes defining their size and position relative to an immediate enclosing frame. The frame at the top effectively defines the available layout space and the value of its position attribute can be thought of as the reference point of the WCS. Those frames being the leaves in the tree are related to the actual content (datatype values) of application objects, and are referred to as *blocks* They have the necessary formatting specifications for the content, such as size, font, alignment, lead texts etc.

The relations between blocks and the application objects, are expressed in terms of the operations of the underlying entity types and the datatypes (i.e., definitions) they use. In addition to the relations implied by the tree structure of layout objects, frames may also be related by "links", e.g. so as to allow the content of one frame to "overflow" into another. A frame can also be use to browse through the contents.

Layout objects may be associated with icons [3]. A number standard icons are supported by the system.

Interactor Objects

The interactor is in essence a "dialog manager" responsible for managing layout objects, reading and interpreting input, providing help on request, and handling user errors etc. There is one interactor for every executing application. This object is independent of the application it serves, although they communicate.

An interactor may have different dialog styles available for use (such as command, menu, question-response, and form). These may be interchangeable or used in combination. An entity operation may e.g. be invoked by means of menu selection (often implying some sort of "mode") or by a direct ("modeless") command corresponding to the operation. For data presentation and data entry purposes command-response and form styles are usually the most appropriate. An obvious task for the interactor in this context is command completion and explanation.

The interactor must at all times "be aware" of the interaction state and act accordingly. Input events generated by a user (at some device) as well actions triggered by the underlying application are caught by the interactor. The mappings between layout objects and application entities are essential for this. Changes in the underlying entities that have significance for the dialog must immediately be propagated to the interface so that the current state of the application is reflected in the interface.

4.3. User Interface Considerations

Objects on the dialog level mediate between applications and I/O-devices. All central dialog management functions are conducted here. Hence, objects on this level will largely be responsible for fulfilling the user interface requirements.

Uniformity is accomplished through the separation between dialog management and applications. Consequently user interface design will be carried out separately from application design. Dialog management policies can then be made uniform both within and across applications.

Both *Customizability* and *dialog independence* are also enhanced through the policy of separation described above. Since the interactor has alternative dialog styles available these may be interchangeable in a dynamic way. For example, in the middle of a session a user can ask the system to use pop-up menus instead of commands. The separation of concerns also provides for flexibility in defining layouts. Different layouts may be created for the same object. Changes and additions to these are easily made.

The *robustness* requirement is taken care of by the interactor. Apart from checking user input the interactor aids the user in correcting errors, completing commands, giving help, etc. In conducting its tasks the interactor may take advantage of the OPAL "data dictionary" facility.

WYSIWYG capabilities are also largely the responsibility of the interactor as it keeps track of what objects are displayed and which are currently being manipulated.

Device independence, finally, is supported by the architecture as such. No device capabilities are known at this level.

5. I/O-LEVEL

5.1. Basic I/O-Level Functions

On the I/O-level the human-computer dialog is mapped to input and output devices. Two main functions handled here are Device Management and Window Management. The goal of Device Management is to control physical I/O-devices. However, in order not to be tied to certain physical devices a level of indirection is introduced through the concept of Logical Device. Window Management is concerned with the mapping of layout objects onto a display surface (e.g. a bit mapped display or printer). This includes managing (multiple) partitions of the display surface, called Viewports, and maintaining mappings between viewports, windows and layout objects.

5.2. I/O-level Design

Window and Viewport

In order to present application objects according to certain layouts (objects), windows and viewports are used to control the actual presentation process. A *window* extracts a rectangular portion of a layout object. The portion extracted may represent the whole layout object or just a part of it. A *viewport* represents a rectangular portion of a display surface. By mapping windows to viewports in a 1:M-fashion the contents of a layout object can be made visible on some physical device. [4]

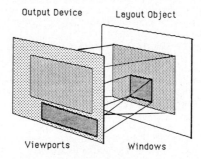

FIGURE 2. Mapping windows to viewports

Windows are defined on some part of the coordinate space (WCS) represented by a layout object. In this sense, a window can be "moved" in all directions across a layout object. Thus, objects such as text documents, images and so on, whose original dimensions are too large for the available display surface space, can be presented in part. Other types of objects, such as forms, can most often be presented in whole by letting a window cover the whole layout object. Several, possibly overlapping, windows can be defined for a single layout object.

Viewports are defined in a device-independent coordinate space (Normalized Device Coord, NDC) for logical devices (see next section). The mapping of windows to viewports is thus a transformation between their respective coordinate spaces. Viewports may optionally be provided with a frame, a name (application name), information about the contents, an icon image etc. Examples of contents information is an overview of a document currently being edited (e.g. table of contents), and current position of the window in the document. In addition, viewports can be partitioned into sub-viewports. This is useful e.g. for structuring the area within a surrounding viewport into a data presentation part, a data entry part and a message display part.

Handling viewports and window mappings is controlled by the *window manager*. Depending on the physical device characteristics, the window manager can handle several, possibly overlapping, viewports simultaneously. Only one viewport at a time is active and the window manager assists in switching between different viewports, recognizing input events and directing output. In essence, the duties of a job control facility.

Windows and viewports can be seen as having the common characteristics of objects in OPAL. Operations defined for viewports on a screen display surface are: 'open', 'close' (to iconic form), 'move' and 'change size'. Windows defined on layout objects can be moved and have their size changed. The mapping between viewport and window can thus be used to realize image transformations such as scaling.

As evident, the facilities described above largely correspond to the functionality provided by a standard window package [5], supplemented with the viewport-window-layout object mapping by means standard graphics concepts.

Logical Device

The next step in transforming dialogs into physical I/O, and vice versa, is to direct I/O-operations to logical devices. A *logical device* introduces a level of indirection between dialog level objects and physical I/O objects. The purpose is of course to achieve device independence by hiding the characteristics of individual physical devices from higher software layers.

Logical devices are specialized through property inheritance into input and output devices which in their turn are specialized further. Examples of specializations following graphics standards for logical input devices are [28] : locator, stroke, valuator, pick, button and keyboard. A Locator returns a location (in NDC) for a display surface, while a Stroke returns a series of locations. A Valuator returns a scalar value, Pick returns an identification of a selected displayed object, Button returns selection from a set of alternatives. Keyboard, finally, returns a text string. Examples of logical output devices are bitmap/raster and character devices.

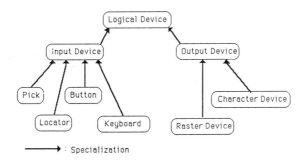

FIGURE 3. Specialization of logical devices

A viewport is mapped to a logical output device. For graphics workstations this is a raster device. The raster is regarded as a normalized device coordinate space (NDC). For character displays, which usually are limited to 24*80 characters display surface, only one viewport at a time is normally mapped to the device.

Device limitations obviously pose problems for the presentation of complex layouts. For example, layout objects containing graphical data cannot be properly presented on a character display. Thus, if character displays are to be supported, a certain loss of information must be accepted. Different approaches can be taken to control this loss, in order to preserve as much as possible of the original meaning and structure of layout objects. The approach taken in e.g. IBM's DCA/DIA architecture [35] permits the document creator to specify which deviations are allowed from the original document upon presentation. For example, losing certain fonts and sizes of characters is a minor problem which might be accepted. However, losing images and graphs expressing aspects not covered by the text in a document can be disastrous, and is therefore forbidden.

Concrete Device

Physical devices interfaced by OPAL are internally represented as instances of concrete devices. A *concrete. device* type simply defines the capabilities of a certain type of physical device (i.e., a device driver in conventional terms). This means that every capability to be used must be expressed in terms of codes understood by the physical device if sent to it or by the system if generated by the device. Examples of concrete devices are VT100 or SUN-2 displays, mouse, keyboard, etc. A property of concrete raster devices, is the Physical Device Coordinate space (PDC) corresponding to the NDC of a logical device.

Higher layers of the software architecture can take advantage of this information in order to decide which operations are possible to perform and which are not. For example, if no mouse is available the system should not present pop-up menus for mouse selection but rather menus for keyboard selection (command or function-key).

A concrete device is actually a leaf in the specialization graph of logical devices. The reason for introducing a new concept is the special status of concrete devices as being the actual interface to the outer world. Concrete devices are mapped 1:M to physical devices.

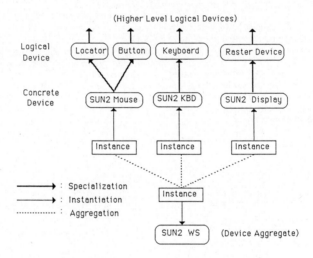

FIGURE 4. Concrete devices and device aggregates

Each physical device in a particular system is represented by an instance of a concrete device. Aggregates of instances of concrete devices can be created to denote the set of devices constituting e.g. a SUN workstation (mouse, keyboard, plus display). This is referred to as a *device aggregate object*. The device aggregate object can be used by application objects to dynamically allocate different component devices e.g., depending on need or availability.

5.3. User Interface Considerations

Both logical devices and the window manager account to *uniformity*. Logical devices provide a common set of I/O-operations, independently of which concrete devices are actually used. The window manager provides a set of standardized viewports on which the dialog is built.

Customizability is also supported on this level. Users are permitted to control which devices should actually be used. For example, instead of using both mouse and keyboard for input a user could request that only the keyboard should be used. The system then adapts the dialog to the desires of the user. Similar requests can also be made from application programs.

Device independence is achieved through the concepts of logical and concrete device [6]. The designer is encouraged to develop all dialog management routines in terms of logical devices, which is a fairly stable set of objects. The problem of incorporating a new physical device into the system is then reduced to defining a new concrete device as a specialization of one or more logical devices.

Another factor improving device independence is the use of standard graphics concepts such as window, viewport, locator, etc. The user interface of OPAL can then largely be implemented using available standard software packages.

A *WYSIWYG interface*, finally, can be built using standard graphics software routines. These have built in functions for keeping track of displayed data and the mapping to underlying data structures. For example, by pointing on the screen using a locator the corresponding image segment is identified. From this, higher layers of the user interface architecture can determine which object is affected by the operation.

6. CONCLUSIONS

In this paper we have described the design of the OPAL user interface architecture. The object oriented nature of OPAL and the layered user interface architecture helps in fulfilling stated user interface requirements.

The idea with the proposed design is to make dialog management independent of application programs as far as possible. This is done by generalizing dialog management routines and grouping them into a separate dialog management system (DMS).

FOOTNOTES

1. The OPAL system described here should not be confused with another very similar system, Gem-Stone, in which the object oriented language unfortunately has been given the name OPAL [36] .

2. In previously published papers the term "packet" has been used to denote "objects". A packet is actually an implementation device, used to represent concepts modeled as objects. In order to enhance the understanding of this paper we use familiar modeling concepts instead of OPAL-terminology.

3. An icon is an alternative visual representation for an object or application, usually in the shape of some "cute" little image to be displayed on a graphics screen.

4. Window and viewport are used in the same sense as in graphics data processing standards such as Core and GKS [37, 38] .

5. The OPAL window system is designed using the SunWindows function libraries and the Core graphics standard, provided by SUN Microsystems Inc. SunWindows provides a standardized interface to both UNIX and OPAL applications. Even though SUN-products are used the design is more generally applicable.

6. The distinction between logical and concrete device can be compared to the distinction between virtual terminal and terminal.

REFERENCES

[1] Liskov, B.H. and Zilles, S., "Programming with abstract data types," *ACM SIGPLAN Notices,* vol. 9, 1974.

[2] Levy, H.M., *Capability - Based Computer Systems,* Digital Press, 1984. ISBN 0-932376-22-3

[3] Date, C.J., *An Introduction to Database Systems,* Addison-Wesley Systems Programming Series, 1983. Volume II

[4] Copeland, G. and Maier, D., "Making Smalltalk a Database System," *ACM SIGMOD Proceedings,* pp. 316-325, Boston, Ma, June 18-21, 1984.

[5] Goldberg, A. and Robson, D., *Smalltalk-80 The Language and its Implementation,* Addison Wesley, 1983.

[6] Birtwistle, G., Dahl, O-J, Myhrhaug, B, and Nygaard, K., *Simula Begin,* Auerbach, Philadelphia, 1973.

[7] Liskov, B., Snyder, A., Atkinson, R., and Schaffert, C., "Abstraction Mechanisms in CLU," *Communications of the ACM,* vol. 20, no. 8, pp. 564-576, August 1977.

[8] Bubenko, J. and Lindencrona, E., *Konceptuell Modellering - Informationsanalys,* Studentlitteratur, Lund, Sweden, 1984. (In Swedish)

[9]   Gibbs, S.J., "An Object-Oriented Office Data Model," CSRG-154, CSRG University of Toronto, Toronto, Jan. 1984.

[10] Shipman, D.W., "The functional data model and the language Daplex," ACM Transactions on Database Systems, vol. 6, no. 1, pp. 140-173, March 1981.

[11] Brachman, R.J., "On the Epistemological Status of Semantic Networks," in Associative Networks: Representation and Use of Knowledge by Computers, ed. N.V. Findler, pp. 3-50, Academic Press, New York, 1979.

[12] Minsky, M., "A framework for representing knowledge," in The psychology of computer vision, ed. P. Winston, pp. 211-277, McGraw-Hill, 1975.

[13] Greenspan, S.J. and Mylopoulos, J., "A Knowledge Representation Approach to Software Engineering: The Taxis Projext," in Taxis'84: Selected Papers, ed. B. Nixon, pp. 1-12, CSRI, University of Toronto, Toronto, Canada, June 1984. (Proceedings of the Conference of the Canadian Information Processing Society, Ottawa, May 16-20, 1983)

[14] DeJong, S.P., "The System for Business Automation (SBA): A Unified Application Developement System," Information Processing Proceedings, 1980.

[15] Zdonik, S., "Object Management Systems for Design Environments," IEEE Database Engineering Bulletin, vol. 8, no. 4, pp. 23-30, Dec. 1985.

[16] Weiser, S.P., "An Object-Oriented Protocol for Managing Data," IEEE Database Engineering Bulletin, vol. 8, no. 4, pp. 41-48, Dec. 1985.

[17] Shneiderman, B., "Direct manipulation: A step beyond programming languages," IEEE Computer, vol. 16, no. 8, pp. 57-69, August 1983.

[18] Kay, A., "Computer Software," Scientific American, vol. 251, no. 3, pp. 41-47, Sept. 1984.

[19] Fähnrich, K.-P. and Ziegler, J., "Workstations using Direct Manipulation as Interaction Mode - Aspects of Design, Application and Evaluation," INTERACT'84, First IFIP Conference on Human-Computer Interaction, pp. 203-208, London, 4-7 Sept. 1984.

[20] Shaw, M., Borison, E., Horowitz, M., Lane, T., Nichols, D., and Pausch, R., "Descartes: A Programming-Language Approach to Interactive Display Interfaces," ACM SIGPLAN Notices, pp. 100-111, June 1983. Proc.Symp.on Programming Language Issues in Software Systems

[21] Smith, D.C., Irby, C., Kimball, R., and Harslem, E., "The Star User Interface: an Overview," Proceedings Natl. Comp. Conf. AFIPS, 1982.

[22] Hayes, P.J., Szekely, P.A., and Lerner, R.A., "Design Alternatives for user Interface Management Systems Based on Experience with COUSIN," ACM CHI'85 Conference Proceedings, pp. 169-175, San Francisco, April 14-18, 1985.

[23] Schulert, A.J., Rogers, G.T., and Hamilton, J.A., "ADM - A Dialog Manager," ACM CHI'85 Conference Proceedings, pp. 177-183, San Francisco, April 14-18, 1985.

[24] Hartson, H.R., Johnson, D.H., and Ehrich, R.W., "A human-computer dialog management system," INTERACT'84, First IFIP Conference on Human-Computer Interaction, pp. 1.57-61, London, 4-7 September 1984.

[25] Carlson, E.D., Rhyne, J.R., and Weller, D.T., "Software Structure for Display Management Systems," IEEE Transactions on Software Engineering, vol. SE-9, no. 4, pp. 385-394, July 1983.

[26] Hägglund, S. and Tibell, R., "Multi-Style Dialogues and Control Independence in Interactive Software," in The Psychology of Computer Use, ed. et al, Academic Press, 1983.

[27] Beech, D., "A reference model for command and response languages," in Proceedings of the IFIP 9th World Computer Congress, ed. R.E.A. Mason, pp. 793-797, North-Holland, Paris, France, Sept. 19-23, 1983.

[28] Coutaz, J., "Abstractions for User Interface Design," IEEE Computer, vol. 18, no. 8, pp. 21-34, Sept 1985.

[29] Bennett, J.L., "The concept of architecture applied to user interfaces in interactive computer systems," INTERACT'84, First IFIP Conference on Human-Computer Interaction, pp. 2.156-161, London, 4-7 September 1984.

[30] Ahlsén, M., Björnerstedt, A., and Hultén, C., "OPAL: An Object-Based System for Application Development," IEEE Database Engineering Bulletin, vol. 8, no. 4, pp. 31-40, Dec. 1985.

[31] Rosenberg, J.K. and Moran, T.P., "Generic commands," INTERACT'84, First IFIP Conference on Human-Computer Interaction, pp. 1.360-364, London, 4-7 September 1984.

[32] Vitter, J.S., "US&R: A New Framework for Redoing," *IEEE Software*, vol. 1, no. 4, pp. 39-52, October 1984.

[33] Shaw, M., "An Input-Output Model of Interactive Systems," *CHI'86 Conference Proceedings*, pp. 261-273, Boston, April 13-17, 1986.

[34] Horak, W., "Office Document Architecture and Office Document Interchange Formats: Current Status of International Standardization," *IEEE Computer*, vol. 18, no. 10, pp. 50-60, Oct 1985.

[35] IBM,, "Office Information Architectures: Concepts," GC23-0765-0, IBM, March 1983.

[36] Maier, D., Otis, A., and Purdy, A., "Object-Oriented Database Development at Servio Logic," *IEEE Database Engineering Bulletin*, vol. 8, no. 4, pp. 58-65, Dec. 1985.

[37] Foley, J.D. and Dam, A. Van, *Fundamentals of Interactive Computer Graphics*, Addison Wesley, 1983.

[38] Hopgood, F.R.A., Duce, D.A., Gallop, J.R., and Sutcliffe, D.C., *Introduction to the Graphical Kernel System (GKS)*, Academic Press, London, 1983.

OFFICE SYSTEMS: Methods and Tools
G. Bracchi, D. Tsichritzis (Editors)
Elsevier Science Publishers B.V. (North-Holland)
IFIP, 1987

PAGES: INTELLIGENT FORMS, INTELLIGENT MAIL AND DISTRIBUTION

Heikki HÄMMÄINEN
Reijo SULONEN

Laboratory of Information Processing Science
Helsinki University of Technology
Otakaari 1 A, SF-02150 Espoo 15, Finland

Christian BÉRARD

GRAI Laboratory
University of Bordeaux 1
351, cours de la Libération, 33405 Talence Cedex, France

End-user oriented understandable system development and maintenance tools are needed for integration of dezentralized systems and activities in office and factory automation. The conceptual model and the user interface considerations of an end-user oriented, Intelligent Form based, and object-oriented application generator called PAGES and the way it is accommodated into a distributed hardware environment through an intelligent mail system is described.

1. INTRODUCTION

The well known organizational and mental gap between the manufacturing and the office organizations in large corporations can be recognized on the technical level, as well. Office automation and production automation are often implemented as completely separate systems. However, along with the increasing automation and distributed data processing power lying on the shop floor, the *semi-automated discrete manufacturing* systems - our main interest - are becoming closer to the office systems. This trend opens interesting possibilities for factory-wide control and data communication based on flexible tools and methods originating from office automation concepts. Obvious benefits are reached if the same tools can be applied on both areas. The basic ideas and the prototype system presented here are an attempt to extend the *object-oriented office automation concepts* into the factory environment. We want to build a system for managing flexibly both the *automatic* and the *interactive* office-oriented procedures in discrete manufacturing.

In a distributed environment the role of data communication is important and in our approach it is emphasized even more. Essentially two kinds of data communication mechanisms are required in a factory environment. The real-time control of robots, NC-machines, etc., uses specialized methods, which are not interesting from our point of view. More relevant is the higher level, non real-time data communication aiming at the overall management of the factory. This has many similarities with the data communication of a distributed office environment, e.g., messages and documents are exchanged both freely and according to strictly controlled procedures.

PAGES is an application generator prototype that is used for experimenting user interfaces suitable for "end-users" to create *loosely coupled distributed applications* on their own. The user interface is considered to be the key into more advanced end-user activities and its significance is stressed throughout the text. PAGES is based on the concept of INtelligent FOrm, i.e., INFO [1], which is a rather independent hierarchic form object containing the *form appearance*, *data*, and processing *rules*. The original INFO concept aimed at development of local applications, but the natural way in which the object-orientation seems to adapt to distributed systems encouraged to modify and extend it for the the purposes of object-oriented communication or intelligent mail. In this area some interesting experimental prototypes have been presented before [2,3,4]. They concentrate mostly on the problems of extending the capabilities of electronic mail neglecting the interfaces to users and to other parts of a distributed information system, whereas the goal of PAGES is the understandable loosely coupled overall coordination and integration of decentralized activities. From our point of view the most essential questions of intelligent mail are the user interface and the synchronization of disributed operations.

2. WHAT INTELLIGENT FORMS GIVE US?

The philosopher's stone of information system building has for some time been a tool that is comprehensible enough for the so called end-users. PAGES is a test bench for comparing different stones in order to find the right one. A good example of a right choice in a specific application area is the concept of spread sheet. Its undeniable success is based on the decomposition of complex interdependencies into small, readily understandable units called cells and, of course, on the proper visual user interface for this decomposition. The same idea is followed in PAGES by decomposing an application into INFOs, which further contain subobjects with their own processing rules. In a certain sense the INFO can be seen as an extended spread sheet. The spread sheet also serves as a measure for user friendliness. A development tool intended for end users may not essentially exceed its level of complexity.

2.1 PAGES World View

Clearly an object is not a solution for all problems, but its role in a distributed system is central as an integrator. It can be utilized in a naturally object-oriented part of local applications, it offers a consistent user interface for a variety of local and remote services, and it hides many of the technical problems of data communication preserving the advantages of loose coupling and avoiding the rigid monolithic structure.

The distributed world seen from the PAGES point of view is heavily centered around the data communication between the work stations, i.e., sending and receiving *Intelligent Forms* through a mail system driven by the *mail processor* (figure 1). There is no essential technical difference when communicating inside a local area network or between networks, which lowers the barrier of the intercompany office procedures. The other communication services like the distributed database, the virtual terminal protocol, etc., are regarded as supplementary tools for special situations.

The *form managers* are the heart of PAGES system. A user interacts with the system through the user interface of a form manager, which has interfaces to the *database processor*, the external *computational processor*, and the *mail processor*. When a form manager is left active without user attendance, it is called an *electronic secretary* (figure 2), which appropriately characterizes its role as the user's assistant.

The INFO applications communicate with other "traditional" applications by using three different methods: the *cut-and-paste*, the *common database*, or the *form interface*. On the user interface level, i.e., in the windowing system, an enhanced cut-and-paste between forms and their subsets is applied, while the traditional applications normally allow only simple transfer of data. An INFO object can also be defined to interact with preexisting database structures. In special cases a more sophisticated form interface for limited sending and receiving of INFOs might be the right way to connect other applications to the form system. This applies particularly to interfacing the automatic real-time control units of discrete manufacturing.

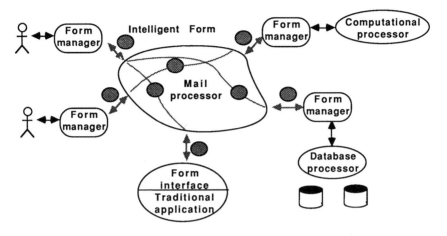

FIGURE 1
The distributed world view of PAGES based on Intelligent Forms.

A simplified formal model of the INFO based distributed object system results from the description of the items belonging to it. We have N *form manager environments* E in a system S, which is considered open in a sense that it is not limited inside a local area network. The environments E reside normally in multitasking workstations equipped with a graphics display and a pointing device, but mainframes are not excluded. Each workstation has one or more E and each E is controlled by one form manager. The external interfaces of an INFO system: the special form interfaced modules, the applications using common databases, and the occasional cut-and-paste linked applications are considered residual Res. Thus the system S is defined as

$$S = \{E_1,....,E_N\} \cup Res$$

Each environment E_i has (figure 2):

a. Form manager O_i (electronic secretary) controlling the other resources.
b. Set of L_i local rule sets R. Only one rule set is active simultaneously defining the characteristics of a personal electronic secretary.
c. Mailbox M_i receiving the incoming mail.
d. Set of J_i INFOs F.
e. Possibly one user S interacting with the form manager and INFOs.

The form manager environment E is summarized as

$$E_i = O_i \cup \{R_1,....,R_{Li}\} \cup \{F_1,....,F_{Ji}\} \cup M_i \cup S$$

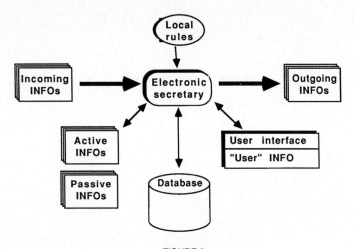

FIGURE 2
Form manager environment of PAGES.

Further each INFO F_i has (figure 3):

        a. Menubar including a set of user defined menu titles and a set of user defined menu
           items under each title, altogether B menu items. Each menu item has a rule set R.

        b. Set R_i of automatic rules, which are automatically processed by the electronic
           secretary without user interaction.

        c. Set P_i of type and state parameters including the definitions for database access.

        d. Hierachy H_i of subobjects. Each subobject belongs to one of the predefined subobject
           types and likewise has its own set R of rules.

Or formally

$$F_i = \{R_1,...,R_{Bi}\} \cup R_i \cup P_i \cup H_i$$

The concept of a rule set R mentioned together with the personalized electronic secretary, the
user defined menus, the automatic rules, and the subobject rules remains syntactically the same
throughout the model. R is always a set of rules, each of which has three parts: a condition (IF),
positive actions (THEN), and negative actions (ELSE). The objective of the rules is not mainly
solving complex problems like for example in the Augmented Petri Netri formalism [5], but
encoding understandably the interactive menu operations and the automatic electronic secretary
operations. In order to satisfy the dual requirements the user can control the order of the rule
firing including a strictly sequential, a pseudoparallel, and a priority based conflict resolution.
The functions in the condition and in the action part mainly operate on the local data structures
of an INFO, but they also include external references to:

        a. Computational processes, which process the parameters passed by the rules.
        b. Database relations by using the database definitions of the INFO parameters.
        c. Other INFOs, i.e., to their menu operations and subobject data.

Intelligent Form

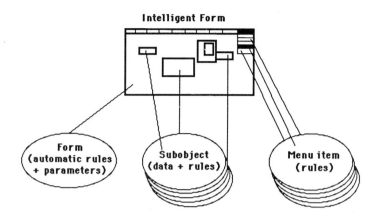

FIGURE 3
The structure of an Intelligent Form.

Formalisms for modelling message systems with automatic processing of messages are proposed before, e.g., by Nierstrasz [7]. Most of them are aiming at the global analysis of the information system and, in this way, detecting and preventing the potential risk of dead locks and infinite loops resulting from automatic processing of messages. The above formalism for PAGES system gives a more exact idea about the model than the visual representation, but it is not fruitful in regard to the global analysis. In PAGES the messages moving between workstations are INFOs, i.e., rather complex objects. This complexity and the fact that the rules may be attached both to the electronic secretary (workstation) and to the INFOs (messages) implies that a global analysis based for example on the Petri net representation is difficult and partly useless. Much of the responsibility of detecting error situations can be transfered to the INFOs, which are able to supervise their own behaviour.

2.2. User Interface

The traditional way of building information systems assumes that the designer designs the system and the user uses it, both having very different mental models and practical tools for interacting with the system (figure 4). The *user's mental model* of the system is based on the application, i.e., on the visual representation of the conceptual model, whereas the *designer's mental model* takes shape in interaction with the *source code*, the *conceptual model*, and the *visual representation*. The conceptual model here means a formal description of the system and its operations written for example in SADT and it is not considered the same as the designer's mental model. If we still take into account that an information system often models or simulates a real physical system, we notice that the designer has four different representations about the same system to balance and combine together in his mental model. This is insuperable for most humans.

It is inevitable to reduce this complexity in order to lower the treshold of end-user activities. In a properly structured distributed environment the applications are split into smaller and more local ones, which increases the need to integrate the roles of the designer and the user. The first step in the integration is to merge all the different models and representations so close to each other as possible.

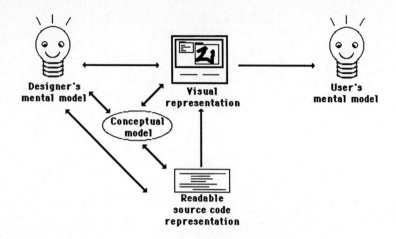

FIGURE 4
The plethora of different representations to be integrated in
an end-user oriented application generator.

An idealistic tool can be envisaged as follows:

a. It allows a "direct" mapping of the real world into the abstract information system reducing the need of a separate formal description tool. Examples exist indicating that the object-oriented approach fulfils this requirement better than the functional one [6].

b. The source code and the visual application are merged together by combining the development and run-time environments through visual programming.

In PAGES this integration problem is solved by a single visual environment, which serves both as a builder interface and a user interface. Building an information system and running it are made as close to each other as possible.

The second general principle in defining the PAGES user interface has been the minimization-maximization approach. This includes two steps:

a. *Minimization*
The diversity is first minimized. The different concepts, functions and features are pruned and integrated together in order to reduce the diversity. Only the essential and necessary remains.

b. *Maximization*
The visibility is maximized. What is left after the MIN step is now shown to the the user to a maximum extent. The user receives continuous feedback from the system, both about its current state and its dynamic changes.

The edit and run-time environment for an INFO (figure 5) is a result of applying these general principles.

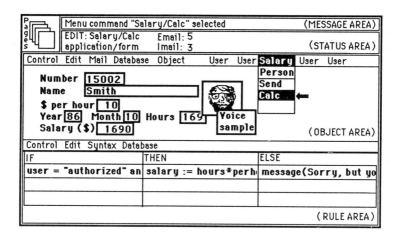

| Pages | Menu command "Salary/Calc" selected | (MESSAGE AREA) |

FIGURE 5
PAGES user interface.

The PAGES user interface lies in a single window which is further divided into non-overlapping subwindows or areas. The meanings of the areas are as follows:

    a. *Message area* shows various system messages (output).
    b. *Status area* shows the environment information and the parameters of the active INFO (output).
    c. *Object area* is the visible part of the INFO showing its subobjects. The subobject is a hierarchical extended version of the traditional field concept (input/output).
    d. *Rule area* is the editing area for the rules of the IF (input/output). Each time a subobject or menu item is activated by clicking with mouse its rules are shown here.

Both the object area and the rule area have above themselves a menu bar, i.e., a row of menu titles. The menu bar is considered to be understandable enough for the end user and it fulfils the requirement that the operations of an INFO are readily accessible all the time. There are two reasons for having two menu bars. Firstly, the size of the PAGES window is arbitrarily modifiable and the physical distance between the object area and the rule area can become too large for the editing operations to be covered with only one menu bar. Secondly, the rule area is not necessary during run-time and it is natural that the rules and there editing functions are made invisible when an INFO application is run.

Zooming is one of our most powerfull methods for understanding the real world. We use magnifying glasses, binoculars and maps for exploring physical objects. To some extent the same idea can be applied in the development of an information system. The object-oriented approach facilitates the dynamic visualisation of the different levels of a system, i.e., the "discrete" *application zooming*. In PAGES this means four levels

    a. *Network level* is the overall representation of a system S. The simplest version is a static map showing the main form manager environments. A more sophisticated implementation visualizes dynamically the status information of a system, e.g., the active electronic secretaries and their active INFOs.

    b. *Form manager environment level* shows the essential items of an environment E:

the INFOs, their states and their mutual dependencies, the status of the INFO mail and the standard electronic mail, and the connected databases.

c. *INFO level* (figure 5) is central both when building and running an INFO. It deals with an INFO and its subobject hierarchy. Any subobject or menu command is activated or edited by selecting it, when the associated rule set appears in the rule area.

d. *Rule level* is reached by selecting a rule of the rule set on the INFO level. The rule level is used for creating and modifying one rule. The "programming" is menu driven as for example in Nexpert [7].

2.3. Building Applications

When an INFO application is built all relevant INFOs are created inside a form manager environment, one at a time. PAGES is set into edit mode on the INFO level. The difference between edit and run modes is a slightly different set of enabled menu commands. Otherwise the user interface remains the same. Modes are, in principle, considered poisonous and PAGES is meant to be as modeless as possible. However the pop-up dialog boxes, which allow the user to enter various parameters, break the mode rule for short periods of time.

The basic elements of every INFO are its form appearance, data, and rules. Ali of them are edited using the select-and-act principle, i.e., first something is selected with a mouse and then an operation selected from a menu is applied to it. Designing the form layout, naming the objects and selecting their parameters are simple tasks even to less advanced users. More challenging is the problem of defining the operations needed to be attached to the INFO data structures. Two factors are intended to enhance the understandability:

    a. Decomposition
    b. Visual programming
    c. Consistent interfacing

By *decomposition* we try to divide the rules of an INFO into rule classes (figure 3). The user enters the same kind of rules in exactly the same way into each of the rule classes. The only technical difference between the classes is the way their execution is initiated during run-time. The *automatic rules* which are attached directly to the highest level of an INFO (the root of subobjects) are processed automatically, if the INFO is defined to be active or an electronic secretary receives the INFO through the mail system. This is the basic function of the intelligent or object-oriented mail. Every subobject of an INFO may have its own *object rules*. They resemble the cell formula concept of spread sheets and can be applied the same way. However, a more common use is the implementation of the pre- and postcondition concept of for example Hogg [4], where part of the object rules are processed when the user wants to activate the object (i.e., moves to the field) and the other part when he wants to finish with the object. The local operations of a subobject, for example integrity checks, are located here. The *menu rules* express the user's special interactive menu operations, but they can also be accessed by the automatic and subobject rule sets. The left part of the menu bar is reserved for the system menus and the other half is left for the user. The user written rules hang on the user menus as part of the INFO. The *local rules* of an object manager are not directly part of an INFO application. They are the operational instructions of an electronic secretary for treating the incoming and active INFOs.

The requirement of *visual programming* is to some extent fulfilled through a related idea usually referred as forms programming. The INFO appearance is part of the user interface and it exposes to the user visually the data structures he is mainly interested in during the development cycle. The forms programming approach also facilitates the editing of an INFO, while the rules and their effect on the form can be seen simultaneously.

Clearly the building of interactive INFOs is more visual and concrete than defining automatic background or remote operations of INFOs. One way of reducing complexity is to apply the *consistent interfacing*, i.e., in PAGES the communication between the user and an INFO is made analog to the message communication between INFOs. When running an INFO the user may activate, read and update subobjects or activate menu commands. These functions are the basis of INFO-INFO messages. The user is seen as a "user" INFO (figure 2).

Even if the INFO is not almighty, its range of applicability is wide. When defining a new INFO two questions are essential. Is it interactive? Is it going to travel? According to the answers the INFOs are classified into three application areas:

a. *Interactive menu driven form applications*
The user defines the subobject data types and rules, the corresponding database relations for multiple instances of subobject sets, and the rule sets for menu commands. This type of form applications are often built with the conventional database oriented application generators.

b. *Event driven applications*
If an INFO is left active under the control of an electronic secretary, its main purpose is to react to the environmental changes such as database values, incoming INFOs, or just time. These conditions and actions are defined in the automatic rules of an INFO.

c. *Intelligent messages*
Any INFO can be sent to another electronic secretary (user). The transfer is initiated by another INFO, the electronic secretary, or the user. If an INFO carries a document or a message to another user, only few automatic rules are normally needed as precautions for example against being forgotten or mishandled. If an INFO has an automatic remore task to accomplish it is likewise defined in the automatic rules.

The above pure INFO types can be mixed together in any combination, which results in interesting but complex multipurpose INFOs.

3. WHAT INTELLIGENT MAIL GIVES US?

When extending PAGES into the distributed environment, a natural decision is to allow the users to send INFOs to each other, even between arbitrary network nodes. It is equally natural to provide an electronic secretary, i.e., PAGES form manager processing the incoming INFOs without user attendance. This mail system is referred to as an object-oriented mail, an automatic mail or an intelligent mail. The most straightforward way of implemention is to use an existing electronic mail system as a carrier between PAGES form managers. More difficult is the decision about the control mechanism of the flow of the INFOs.

3.1. Control Mechanism

In a "completely automated" system, central control and a priori exception handling is inevitable, but a semi-automated system with human users as essential communicants is supposed to survive without an obligatory central control. This seems inevitable when dealing with environments where exceptional situations are frequent. Instead of a heavy centralized control model we propose a loosely coupled tool approach for handling flexibly the disturbances of a distributed system. However, if and when centralized control is needed it can be explicitly defined in the INFOs by having them ask permissions from and send reports (by INFOs) concerning their own actions to a predefined central electronic secretary.

When the control mechanism is distributed, there still remains a choice. The control knowledge may reside in the form managers, or it may be concentrated into the INFOs. PAGES is a compromise. The local rules and some control parameters are attached directly to the electronic secretary and they are matched against the data and rules of every incoming INFO. The local rules (the electronic secretary) are prioritized above the rules of the incoming INFOs (the sender). A practical way to utilize this feature is to have a battery of local rule sets from which to select an appropriate one each time the electronic secretary is activated and left alone.

3.2 Applications

The intelligent mail makes possible the transportation and automatic processing of INFOs, which act like messenger boys carrying messages between secretaries. The user plays, of course,the role of the chief. Possible tasks are, for example, retrieving information from a remote database by traveling there and back, circulating a questionnaire via several users, automatic return, if the receiver of an INFO is not found in a predefined time, or initialization and control of remote tasks. It has to be pointed out that these operations are not supposed to happen in real time.

A potential life cycle of an order INFO "X" might be the following. After the creation it lies active under an electronic secretary in a company A. Some time later one of its automatic rules, that has a condition comparing the database value indicating the stock level of a product, fires. In the condition part of the rule some subobject values of another INFO telling about the situation are updated and that INFO is sent to the production planner. X sends itself to the sales person of a company B. Because of an urgent business trip he has left his electronic secretary Y active with a proper set of local rules. Y receives X and screens it with the local rule set. Y recognizes the sender and the predefined operation and product codes in predefined subobjects, assigns the estimated delivery time, the stock level and the current prizes for different amounts of ordered units set by the sales person, and allows X to make an order, i.e., to be processed automatically. The condition part of an automatic rule in X compares the new current prizes to its own allowable prize ranges etc. and the rule is fired. In action part the order is made by accessing a predefined database relation. The number of ordered items is assigned to a subobject, if it is less than planned. Now X sends itself back with the updated order information. The electronic secretary in A receives X and screens it with the local rules. X is left to the incoming mail queue waiting for the user's manual checking.

4. HOW MULTIMEDIA DOCUMENTS FIT INTO PICTURE?

The human mind flexibly handles different data types like pictures, text and voice, even simultaneously. In computers the integration of data types on the user interface level - the problem of multimedia documents - is a non-trivial task. On the one hand each data type needs its own private space to live in, but on the other hand it has to be able to interact with and accommodate to other data types. From the user's point of view three basic needs of integration can be identified:

    a. Joining different data types freely together as documents for storage, retrieval and manipulation.
    b. Sending any combination of data types (document) from one user to another.
    c. Visual what-you-see-is-what-you-get (WYSIWYG) editing and flexible cut-and-paste for any kind of data inside and between documents.

To satisfy these objectives every subobject of an INFO includes two kinds of operations: rules and functions. *Rules* are directly modifiable and visible to the user and they are responsible for the external interaction between subobjects, e.g., assigning a sum of two other numeric subobjects to the current subobject owning the rules. They realize the unique operations of each subobject . *Functions* are the internal operations unique to each object type. There are two groups of internal functions. The edit functions common for all object types (delete, copy, move, create) are in a standard menu. A separate menu is reserved for type specific functions and the corresponding menu commands change according to the type of the subobject currently activated.

```
struct object {
        int                window_filedescriptor;
        struct             pixel_window;
        struct  pixrect    retained_pixel_rectangle;
        struct  rectlist   visible_clipping;
        char               *object_id;
        struct  rect       rect_place_size;
        struct  object_ops internal_functions;
        struct  ruleset    external_rules;
        struct  menu       *special_menu;
        caddr_t            object_data;
        struct  object     *parent;
        struct  object     *older_sibling;
        struct  object     *younger_sibling;
        struct  object     *oldest_child;
        struct  object     *youngest_child;
        };
```

FIGURE 6
PAGES subobject structure in C.

The subobject structure of INFO (figure 6) shows that the internal functions and object data are hidden in the object and can not be accessed directly. This offers a general framework for implementing new subobject data types and extending the multimedia document capabilities of the INFO. The different role of functions and rules is clearly seen with for example digital voice. An internal function knows how to replay the voice message, but a rule knows on what conditions and when it is replayed.

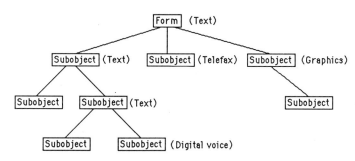

FIGURE 7
An example of the structure of an INFO.

The hierarchic structure of the INFO (figure 7) mainly serves the purposes of subobject grouping and hierarchic visualization. On the rule level the hierarchy is considered too difficult for the end-user, and thus it is not implicitly respected. If the nature of the application presumes a hierarchic processing structure it has to be defined explicitly in the rules.

Evidently, the INFO lacks many characteristics of "pure" object orientation, for example inheritance. The simplifications and selections are made in order to increase the understandability of an end-user oriented application generator. Some of the basic concepts, i.e., template, document, type, and instance, have been flexibly mixed to capture the complexity of multimedia documents. The model of INFO can be classified according to Rabitti [9] as follows:

a. *Datatypes.* All relevant data types are represented, but in practice only those which fit into the relational model can be grouped as subobject instances, i.e., tuples of a relation, and thus accessed efficiently.

b. *Document types.* When an INFO is used as a document, the notion of type is not explicit. An INFO can be seen as a complete transferable document or as a template for relational database access to documents of the same type.

c. *Document internal structure.* This is the INFO structure described above. It is primarily optimized for the user interface and visualization.

d. *Document modification.* The editing operations are based on the cut-and-paste principle, which is powerful when the system is object oriented. The INFO layout and the subobject types are edited using the WYSIWYG principle.

e. *Document presentation.* The internal structure is mainly dictated by the external (visual) structure, which implies that there are no problems of presentation.

f. *Document retrieval.* Essentially two modes of retrieval are needed: by location and by contents. The INFO is accessible by location, but the search based on contents is problematic. It is possible for data types compatible with the relational data model.

g. *Document communication.* For transmission the INFO is encoded into a structured file format suitable for transfer via an electronic mail system.

5. IMPLEMENTATION CONSIDERATIONS

Most features of the INFO concept described above have been tested in a prototype implementation of PAGES. The test environment is a Sun Microsystems workstation [10] running Unix version 4.2 BSD and the following tools are utilized: the C language, the YACC-parser generator and the LEX lexical analyser for implementing the rules, the Sunwindows windowing package and the Ingres relational database system.

The current PAGES prototype makes possible the interactive creation, manipulation, and mailing of INFOs and their automatic reception and processing according to the automatic rules. However there remain difficult decisions and unsolved problems concerning a practical implementation:

a. *Storage and retrieval of INFOs.* Current relational databases do not support all data types needed in documents. Thus only conventional data types are stored in the database and the INFOs together with initial subobject values are stored in the file system. This means that only the database part is accessed rationally.

b. *Complexity of rules.* In spite of the efforts put on the user interface the "programming" is still too complicated. The traditional problem of deciding, which rule functions should be built-in and which should be left to the user is not satisfactorily solved.

c. *Communication between INFOs.* The efficient implementation of this message communication is difficult because of the independent nature of INFOs.

6. EXPERIENCES

We have developped the PAGES prototype in cooperation with two Finnish companies, a diesel engine factory and a cable factory. In the first case the goal was to develop small local applications for handling product information. The speed of building the prototype applications was remarkable, but the run-time efficiency was insufficient due to the non-perfect implementation of the object interpreter and its database interface. The most important experience from our point of view was that the concept of visual programming is essential when trying to increase the understandability of an end-user tool. In the second case the goal was to interface a traditional database application of Honeywell DPS-6 and the PAGES system. The incompatibility problems on the data communication level turned out to be too laborious and we decided to wait for the communication standards.

7. CONCLUSIONS

Data communication is the key word in the automation of factories and offices. However, it is evident that the current tools of data communication do not fully utilize the possibilities of computers in the area where maximal flexibility is needed. To handle automated tasks, exceptions and rapidly changing situations, and to be user friendly, the communication mechanism has to be intelligent. One possible solution is to concentrate the intelligence into the data unit to be transferred and make it a rather independent object. If this object is structured enough, it serves also as a document structure and as a building block for an information system. Being presented to the user in an understandable way, it can be called an INFO, a basic object of an information system.

The PAGES prototype gives a vague idea of the possibilities of object orientation when trying to raise the level of abstraction of the building and use of information systems. In spite of the current efficiency and database problems, the objects seem to be promising, even from the user's point of view.

REFERENCES

[1]   Hämmäinen H., Jahkola J. and Kyhälä A., Intelligent Form - An Approach for an End-User Oriented Application Generator, Proc. of IFIP WG 2.7 (Rome, Italy, October 1985)
[2]   Vittal J., Active Message Processing: Messages as Messengers, Proc. of the International Symposium on Computer Message Systems, IFIP TC-6, Ottawa, 1981, ed. R.P. Uhlig, North Holland Publishing Co (1982)
[3]   Tucker J., Implementing Office Automation: Principles and an Electronic Mail Example, Proc. of the Second SIGOA Conference on Office Information Systems, SIGOA Newsletter, 3(1), 3(2) (June 1982)
[4]   Hogg J., Intelligent Message Systems, Office Automation - Concepts and Tools, ed. Tsichritzis D., Springer-Verlag, 1985
[5]   Zisman M., Representation, Specification and Automation of Office Procedures, Ph.D. Thesis, University of Pennsylvania (1977)
[6]   Booch G., Object-Oriented Development, IEEE Transactions on Software Engineering, vol.SE-12, no.2, pp. 211-221 (February 1986)
[7]   Nierstrasz O., Message Flow Analysis, Office Automation - Concepts and Tools, ed. Tsichritzis D., Springer-Verlag, 1985
[8]   Nexpert User's Manual, Neuron Data Inc., USA (1985)
[9]   Rabitti F., A Model for Multimedia Documents, Office Automation - Concepts and Tools, ed. Tsichritzis D., Springer-Verlag (1985)
[10]   Sun Microsystems, Sun-3 Architecture: A Sun Technical Report, Sun Microsystems, Preliminary Edition (September, 1985)

OFFICE SYSTEMS: Methods and Tools
G. Bracchi, D. Tsichritzis (Editors)
Elsevier Science Publishers B.V. (North-Holland)
© IFIP, 1987

The Construction of User Interfaces

Joëlle Coutaz, Françoise Berthier

Centre de Recherche Bull de Grenoble
c/o Laboratoire de Génie Informatique(IMAG)
BP 68
38402 St-Martin-d'Hères, France

Abstract: The user interface for an interactive application is difficult to design and expensive to construct. This paper is concerned with software tools that improve the quality of user interfaces and reduce the cost of development. Attention is focused on a class of such tools, the User Interface Management Systems (UIMS), whose purpose is to automatically generate the user interface of an application from specifications. The level of abstraction in the specifications is one critical attribute that affects the quality of a UIMS. This paper presents MOUSE (Management Of the User through SpEcifications), a UIMS which allows high level specifications and whose kernel has been implemented in C on a Bull SM90 workstation running Unix. A MOUSE user interface is comprised of two parts: The Application Data Base and the Presentation Data Base. The Application Data Base describes the domain-entities involved in the dialogue. The Presentation Data Base defines the mapping between the domain-entities and entities, called interactive objects, which are expert in man-machine communication. The advantages of interactive objects for expressing the concrete syntax of dialogues are discussed.

Keywords : User Interface Design, User Interface Management System, User Interface Specification, Interactive Object.

1 Introduction

The user interface to interactive systems is difficult to design and expensive to construct. The difficulty results from the very nature of the user interface. The designer is required to be familiar with a wide range of techniques spanning from human factors and cognitive psychology to computer science. The cost of development is not only due to the initial implementation effort[1] but also to the extensive refinement required to produce a satisfying interface. Cost and complexity are increasing as users are more demanding and as powerful personal computers make possible sophisticated interfaces. The opportunity for saving time in designing and implementing interactive systems is obvious.

This paper concentrates on principles and tools that facilitate the construction of user interfaces. One fundamental principle is the separation of the functions of an interactive application system from its user interface. The functions of an application define the tasks that the system is able to accomplish whereas the user interface mediates between the functions and the user. In reality, this division is not easy to achieve due to the lack of enforcing tools. As a result, it is often the case that the code which handles the interaction is intermixed with the code which implements the functionalities of the system. In these conditions, it is difficult or even impossible to put into practice a second important principle in user interface design, the iterative refinement of the user interface [Good 84]. In this paper, we are concerned with tools that encourage this separation.

1-50% of the code in the average database application concerns the user interface [Pilote 83].

Tools for constructing user interfaces can be classified according to the tasks of the user interface implementer [Coutaz 85a]. The implementers' tasks range from physical I/O handling to the management of the dialogue between the user and the system. A tool for I/O handling is described in [Coutaz 85b]. In this paper, attention is focused on dialogue issues, in particular on techniques for the specification and automatic generation of dialogues. The next section presents the "UIMS model", a framework for dialogue specification and dialogue generation. It shows how the model enforces the principles of separation and makes possible the iterative refinement. Then it surveys work related to the area of User Interface Management Systems (UIMS). The remainder of the paper describes our own UIMS, MOUSE (Management Of the User through SpEcifications), which is currently implemented in C on a Bull SPS7 workstation running Unix.

2 The UIMS Model

Dialogue specification was initially introduced to relieve the designer from the complexity of the low level details of the interaction. More recently, it has been used in User Interface Management Systems to factor aspects of the dialogue management that are common to all applications of a workstation. UIMS's can provide higher quality of user interfaces at a lower cost. This section shows how.

2.1 Principles

A User Interface Management System relies on the distinction between the semantics and the lexical-syntactic elements of the dialogue. The lexical elements consist of the input and output tokens built from hardware operations such as mouse-button-clicks for input and color assignment for output. The syntax of inputs refers to the allowed sequences of input tokens (e.g. click an icon) to form input sentences (e.g. delete an object); the output syntax defines composition rules for
output tokens (e.g. the presentation of messages, menus, icons). The semantics is expressed by the functions that the application system performs in response to the user's commands.

A system's implementer initially provides the UIMS with the syntactic specifications of the dialogue between the user and the system. This description defines the abstract syntax that the system is able to recognize at run-time. As shown in the figure 1, the UIMS maintains, for each application system, a database of the compiled specifications and maps the application-visible abstract syntax to the user-visible concrete syntax (and conversely). At run-time, a system communicates with the UIMS according to a protocol which is a simplified version of the actual dialogue: the UIMS strips the low-level syntactic interactive details from the user's commands, and then delivers them in a form directly manageable by a system. Conversely, the UIMS receives reactions from a system and inserts syntactic and lexical adornments before delivery to the user.

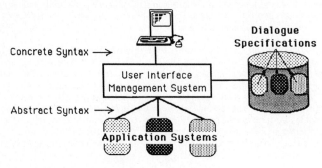

Figure 1: The UIMS Model.

2.2 Benefits from UIMS's

A UIMS not only facilitates the system implementer's task but also opens the way to the construction of "better" user interfaces.

By taking care of user actions that are semantically irrelevant to the system, the UIMS allows the implementer to concentrate on the logical design of the system. For example, a UIMS is able to perform syntactic checkings such as command completeness and parameter type verification. As a result, a file manager system plugged into a UIMS, is not concerned by the way the invocation of "delete a file" is performed (e.g. by keystrokes or selections in menus and icons) nor is it concerned by the user's intermediate actions that lead to the final command (e.g. corrections of typos, requests for local help or for local cancel).

The UIMS model enforces a clean separation between the semantics and the syntax. This property results in three essential benefits for the user: the UIMS allows the concrete syntax to be designed by an expert in the area; it facilitates the iterative refinement of the concrete syntax without modifying the underlying system; it allows several systems to share the same concrete syntax, providing the user with a uniform view of the workstation.

2.3 Related Work and Design Space

The UIMS model has served as the basis for a number of tools for dialogue specification and dialogue generation. These tools can be classified according to three design choices [Hayes 85]: the level of abstraction at which the specification is performed, the localization of the control of the dialogue and the expression of the ordering of events.

The level of abstraction defines the unit of exchange between the application system and the UIMS. The unit of exchange can range from low-level tokens such as keystrokes, to the level of abstraction manipulated by the system such as complete and syntactically correct commands. For example, SYNGRAPH [Olsen 83], a UIMS intended for graphical applications, is based on the low-level notion of logical device (e.g. pick, locator, valuator) which has initially been introduced in graphics packages to hide the functioning of physical devices. Such abstractions concern the surface level of the interaction, that is, the events at the user-visible interface. At the other end of the spectrum, Cousin [Hayes 83] and ADM [Schulert 85] allow user interfaces to be expressed in terms of I/O data or objects manipulated by the applications. These objects concern the application level: they are application-dependent not user-event dependent. The level of abstraction of the user interface specification defines the effectiveness of the separation between the semantics and the syntax of an interactive system. Consequently, it determines the extent to which the implementer is able to concentrate on the logical functioning of the system. As described below, MOUSE emphasizes high level abstractions for dialogue specifications.

The control of the dialogue may be internal, external or mixed [Tanner 83]. The control is internal when it resides in the application system. It is external when it is maintained by the UIMS. It is mixed when the control is alternatively handled by the system and the UIMS. With internal control, the UIMS is implemented as a library of procedures that the application system calls to perform I/O tasks. The Macintosh toolbox [Williams 84] is a library of such procedures. It allows the implementer to build consistent user interfaces for Macintosh systems but it requires him to understand and learn the implicit protocol embedded in the library. In addition to the difficulty of learning for the implementer, internal control may lead to situations where a system procedure traps the user in a kind of local mode by forcing him to reply to a "yes" or "no" question. Finally, by being rooted in the system, internal control does not enforce a clean separation between system functions and dialogue tasks.

Conversely, when the UIMS maintains the control, it is responsible for invoking system procedures in response to specific user actions. The application system is viewed as a collection of procedures which implement the semantic actions of the dialogue. This technique entails a clean separation between semantics and syntax. It opens the way to more modular programs although it may impose a style of programming on the implementer. TIGER [Kasik 82] falls in this category. We believe that the external control of the dialogue should lead to fewer arbitrary constraints on the user, constraints that may be unnecessarily imposed by a system implementer unaware of the basic "do's and don'ts" in user interface design. In particular, one guideline recommends that actions should be initiated at the users' will, not by the system. At the opposite of the internal control, external control operates in accordance with a user-driven style: an external control UIMS listens to the user and calls a system subroutine when it is appropriate to do so.

Between the two extremes, the mixed control allows the implementer to switch freely between internal and external control modes. This flexibility is useful for systems that need to notify the UIMS of asynchronous events (such as the ringing of the alarm clock) or for interactive commands which dynamically require the user to specify some parameter before processing can continue (such as print commands in "more" mode). COUSIN [Hayes 83], ADM [Schulert 85] and MOUSE support mixed control. By doing so, they also facilitate the connection of existing systems to UIMS's. Nevertheless, the flexibility provided by mixed control opens the way to "dirty hacks" inducing the classic software maintance problems (just like the goto statement).

The last criteria for classifying dialogue specification tools concerns the ordering of events. BNF-based specification tools such as SYNGRAPH [Olsen 83], provide an explicit way of specifying the ordering of events. In ATN-based tools, such as USE [Wassermann 85], the ordering of events is determined implicitly. In both cases, the ordering is freezed in a declarative manner. Models used in these tools are well suited to describe contexts. Conversely, the number of allowed actions in a given context may be tedious to specify (for example, the description of the free ordering of command parameters). In addition to the allowed sequence of actions, the designer must exhaustively anticipate exceptional conditions that may arise at run-time. This difficulty is exacerbated when the ordering task is combined to a low-level specification tool. Finally, it is not clear how BNF and ATN based tools account for parallel events. In COUSIN, ADM and MOUSE the combination of external control and high level abstractions provide the means for moving the problem of event ordering outside of the system implementer's view.

3 Management Of the User through SpEcifications: MOUSE

In the 3-D design space defined above and shown in the figure 2, MOUSE is localized at the point: high level abstraction, mixed control and implicit event ordering. This section shows how these design decisions are integrated in the tool MOUSE.

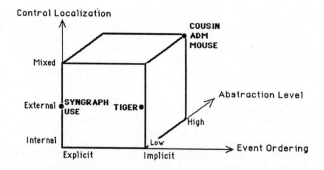

Figure 2: A Taxonomy for User Interface Management Systems

3.1 Principles

The driving design principle in MOUSE is that the system implementer is not necessarily the user interface designer. The problems of the system implementer are distinguished from the task of the user interface designer. For doing so, the specification of a user interface in MOUSE is comprised of two parts as shown in figure 3: the Application Data Base built from the specifications provided by the system implementer, and the Presentation Data Base built from the specifications provided by the user interface designer.

The Application Data Base contains the abstract information that is relevant to the dialogue whereas the Presentation Data Base contains the description for presenting abstract information. The Application Data Base is domain-dependent and user-independent whereas the Presentation Data Base is domain-independent and user-dependent.

At run time, the Application Data Base is used by the MOUSE Controller to build a run-time view of the Application called the Application Interface. The Application Interface is the interface between the Controller and the Application. On the user's side, the Presentation Interface, built from the Presentation Data Base, interfaces the user. The communication between the Application Interface and the Presentation Interface is performed through the Controller.

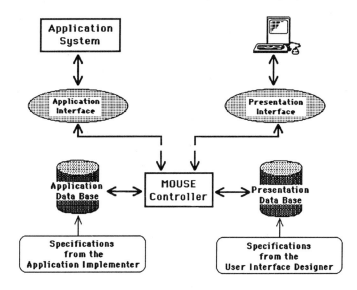

Figure 3: Elements of the MOUSE Architecture

3.2 High-level Abstract Syntax and High-Level Concrete Syntax in MOUSE

The Application Data Base describes the domain entities that are involved in the dialogue. With regard to the application, these entities model the exported semantics objects. With regard to MOUSE, they define the abstract syntax that the application accepts at runtime. They are described by the implementer in a specification part which is external to the code of the application. The formalism used for this specification ressembles the interface part of an Ada package [Le Verrand 85]. By doing so, the application is a true black box with specific entry points. For example, the application "Clock" may export a data structure "Time" which is comprised of three integers (hours, minutes, seconds) and two functions "SetTime" and

"GetTime" to set and read the time respectively. "Time", "SetTime" and "GetTime" are entities that the "Clock" application implements to model the concept of time. Thus, on the implementer's side, the level of abstraction of the dialogue specification rigourously matches the notions manipulated in the application.

The Presentation Data Base defines the mapping between the entities of the abstract syntax and the entities of the concrete syntax. In MOUSE, the entities for the expression of the concrete syntax are interactive objects. Menus, icons, gauges, push-buttons, forms, etc... are examples of interactive objects. The specification of the concrete syntax is therefore performed at a high level of abstraction. It is not expressed in terms of button-clicks nor screen coordinates. For doing so, the user interface designer is provided with a data base of interactive objects (see figure 4). This data base is structured in a manner somewhat similar to knowledge representation networks: objects are organized in a hierarchy of classes with an inheritance mechanism. For example, the abstract object "Time" may be presented as an interactive object composed of three editable, horizontally aligned, integer strings and the functions "SetTime" and "GetTime" may be shown as icons in a menu. Strings, icons and menus are classes of interactive objects predefined in the data base.

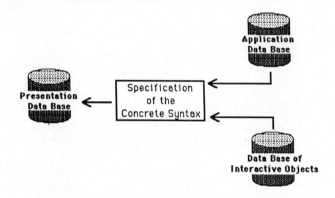

Figure 4: Construction of the Presentation Data Base

In summary, dialogue specification in MOUSE happens at a high level of abstraction for both the abstract syntax and the concrete syntax. By being fully user-independent, the abstract syntax can be mapped to radically different user interfaces (i.e concrete syntaxes). The specification of a concrete syntax is two levels. The higher level defines the mapping between an abstract syntax and the interactive objects. This mapping is mandatory but is not concerned with low-level details of the interaction. The second level is necessary only if the default low-level details need to be tuned through the interactive objects or if the data base does not contain the appropriate interactive objects. (In the latter case, the designer must program a new class and may use an interactive editor for fine tuning) In general, a data base of ready-for-use interactive objects should be sufficient for the rapid prototyping of concrete syntaxes.

3.3 Interactive Objects

An interactive object is a mediating entity between the user and a computer system entity. It has its own expertise in man-machine communication defined by the class of which it is an instance. As a mediator between two partners, it is characterized by two interfaces. One is concerned with the surface behaviour, the other defines the system behaviour. Surface behaviour determines the way the interactive object presents itself to the user as well as what actions it accepts from the user and what reactions it provides. The system behaviour defines the messages that the object sends to or receives from its related computer system entities (which could be another interactive object or an abstract object of the Application Interface or logical devices abstracting mouse and keyboard events). As an example, let's take the interactive object "Time" of type string which represents the time. Its surface behaviour would be defined by the current font, the presence or absence of a frame, the way the user can edit it (by direct manipulation with the mouse and/or with EMACS-like control keys) and the conditions which identify the beginning and the end of the edition (such as a carriage return or the loss of the mouse). The system behaviour allows the string to reply to messages such as the request about its current value.

An interactive object is an active entity . It evolves, communicates and maintains relationships with other objects. Such activity, parallelism and communication are automatically performed by the Object Machine, the generic class of the interactive objects. The Object Machine defines the general functioning that is made common to all of the interactive objects by means of the inheritance mechanism. In particular, each object owns a private finite state automaton for maintaining its current dialogue state. On receipt of a message, an object is thus able to determine which actions to undertake according to its current state. For example, a push-button receiving the message "mouse has left", would switch back to normal video if it is in the "busy" state and would not react otherwise. (In order to be busy, such a button would need to receive a message like "mouse-button-down")

Interactive objects implement the dialogue in a distributed way. The set of automata (one automaton per interactive object) defines the global state of the interaction between the user and the computer system. The control of this interaction is therefore distributed in an evolutive network of interactive objects. At the opposite of usual UIMS's, dialogue control in MOUSE is not handled by a unique monolithic dialogue manager. A monolithic dialogue manager is difficult to implement when one wants a pure user-driven style of interaction. Conversely, interactive objects being able to maintain their own state, it is easy to let the user switch between objects in any order. Thus, the Object Machine provides for free the maintainance of the user's tribulations.

Interactive objects are easily customizable. Our design choice about the concrete syntax has been influenced by the encouraging results of the object-oriented programming languages like Smalltalk [Golberg 83] and Loops [Bobrow 81]. Object-oriented programming languages support data abstraction which makes it possible to change underlying implementations without changing the calling programs. In the present case, this principle allows the internal modification of an interactive object without changing its interfaces. Interestingly, it also allows the modification of one interface without any side-effect on the other interface. For example, one can modify the surface behaviour of an interactive object (such as attaching a different key translation table to an interactive object of type string) without reflecting on its system behaviour. This property allows dynamic adjustments of the user interface without questioning the specification of the concrete syntax.

The data base mechanism provides support for the modification of the interactive objects. The type of dynamic adjustment mentioned above is generally made possible by assigning properties (or attributes) to objects. Because objects are individuals maintained in a special purpose data base, property assignments can be performed through any tool interfacing the data base: outside of the concrete syntax specification as well as in the specification itself. For example, a key translation table is a property of the class string which can be assigned in the specification of the concrete syntax and which can be dynamically overridden by the user's profile at the instantiation time. As another example of external dynamic adjustment, the name, location and size of a field in a form can be edited with an interactive editor similar to the Macintosh Resource Editor. Other modifications go far beyond simple attribute assignments requiring a new implementation of the class or the programming of a new class. This latter task is performed outside of the dialogue facilities currently supported by MOUSE (i.e. programming a new class is to write a C module).

4 Conclusion

MOUSE is currently under development. A number of applications such as those commonly available on personal computers are used as test cases to complete the definition of the specification formalism. The data base of interactive objects has a running kernel written in C on a SM90. Sophisticated objects such as forms and pie charts have been constructed on top of the basic classes. The whole project is now being ported to the Apple Macintosh™ whose basic graphic tools offer an attractive and reliable environment.

At the opposite of other UIMS's, MOUSE does not enforce a particular style for the user interface and it does not make any hypothesis on the nature of the system application. Style independence is achieved through an extensible data base of refinable interactive objects. Application independence results from the driving design decision of a clean separation between abstract syntax and concrete syntax. In addition, this separation allows the system implementer to focus attention on the logical aspects of the system whereas the user interface designer can determine the syntax that best conveys the system's semantics for a given class of end-users.

References

[Bobrow 81] D.G. Bobrow, M. Stefik: The Loops Manual; Tech. report KB-VLSI-81-13, Knowledge Systems Area, Xerox, Palo Alto Research Center, 1981.

[Coutaz 85a] J. Coutaz : Abstractions for User Interface Design; Computer, 18(9), September 1985, 21-34.

[Coutaz 85b] J. Coutaz : A Layout Abstraction for User System Design; SIGCHI, January 1985, 18-24.

[Goldberg 83] A. Goldberg, D. Robson : Smalltalk-80 : The Language and its implementation; Addison-Wesley Publ., 1983.

[Good 84] M.D. Good, J.A. Whiteside, D.R. Wixon, S.J. Jones:Building a User-Derived Interface; Communications of the ACM, October 1984, 1032-1043.

[Hayes 83] P.J. Hayes, P. Szekely: Graceful Interaction through the Cousin Command Interface; International Journal of Man Machine Studies 19(3), September 1983, 285-305.

[Hayes 85] P.J. Hayes, P. Szekely, R. Lerner: Design Alternatives for User Interface Management Systems Based on Experience with Cousin; Proceedings of the CHI'85 Conference, The Association for Computing Machinery Publ., April 1985,169-175.

[Kasik 82] D. J. Kasik:A User Interface Management System; Computer Graphics, July 1982, 99-106.

[Le Verrand 85] D. Le Verrand : Evaluating Ada; North Oxford Academic Press, 1985.

[Olsen 83] D.R Olsen, E.P Dempsey:Syngraph: A Graphical User Interface Generator; Computer Graphics, July 1983, 43-50.

[Pilote 83] M. Pilote. A data modeling approach to simplify the design of user interfaces. Proceedings 9th VLDB, October-November 1983.

[Schulert 85] A.J. Schulert, G.T. Rogers, J.A. Hamilton : ADM - A Dialog Manager; Proceedings of the CHI'85 Conference, The Association for Computing Machinery Publ., April 1985, 177-183.

[Tanner 83] P. Tanner, W. Buxton: Some Issues in Future User Interface Management Systems (UIMS) Development. IFIP Working Group 5.2 Workshop on User Interface Management, Seeheim, West Germany, November 1983.

[Wasserman 85] A. Wasserman: Extending State Transition Diagrams for the Specification of Human-Computer Interaction; IEEE Transactions on Software Engineering, 11(8), August 1985.

[Williams 84] G. Williams: The Apple Macintosh Computer; Byte, February 1984, 30-54.

OFFICE SYSTEMS: Methods and Tools
G. Bracchi, D. Tsichritzis (Editors)
Elsevier Science Publishers B.V. (North-Holland)
IFIP, 1987

OBJECT ORIENTED TOOLS FOR THE DESIGN OF HIGH LEVEL INTERFACES : THE KEY FOR ADAPTABILITY

Solange Karsenty
Laboratoire de Recherche en Informatique - Université de Paris-Sud - Bât. 490
91405 ORSAY Cedex
FRANCE

We present a number of tools and concepts to design high level interfaces. The user interface is often crucial for the acceptance of office systems but the same arguments hold more generally for various kinds of applications. The view that we have of a system is first of all its interface. By high level user interface, we mean interfaces using graphics, menus, icons, windows. Designers have to make many choices implicit in the following kinds of questions :
- How strong is the interface dependent on the application ? Should it be usable for others applications ?
- What is the average users's knowledge ?
- What style of interaction should be used ?
- How should the menu/command hierarchy be built ?

We show, through an object oriented environment, that these choices do not have to be definitive, but can be dynamically modifiable to provide many kinds of interaction to many kinds of users. We show also that an interface can really be a distinct part of an application. The concept is to provide a system with which it is easy to specify and implement interfaces, that include a wide range of parameters and allows for the possibility of dynamically changing specifications. Some tools that have already been implemented are described at the end of this paper.

1 - Human factors

The consideration of human factors in system design is often ignored : namely the user [1]. Systems are made for computers, but an interactive system requires a dialogue between humans and computers ; this interaction gives a new dimension to programs. Most modern workstations have a bitmap screen, window management, a mouse and other special facilities. They provide new environments [2]. But while these new tools facilitate design of highly sophisticated interfaces, they must be used carefully to provide user-friendly interfaces.

To a large extent, the determination of what makes an interface user-friendly is a matter of personal taste of the user. Assuming the number of users is arbitrary large, there cannot be an interface for each user. There is usually one static interface and users are forced to adapt themselves to this one alone. We present some basics concepts of interaction independant of the system to be used, which can lead to adaptable user-friendly interfaces.

1.1 - User knowledge

The concept is to consider the user as a part of the total system being designed. Many problems result from the fact that the system doesn't "know" what the user knows. How do we match the expected actions with the capabilities of the user ? For example, to keep the user from activating a invalid command, the interface can allow the user only a subset of all the commands at a given time. Whatever the user's knowledge is, the system will be protected. But in the case of a command sequence that an knowledgeable user wants to group under one command name, there is

This work was partially supported by the Meteor Esprit project.

usually no solution. In this case, a novice user will appreciate this explicit sequence, while an advanced user will find the interface inconvenient.

Another example is the feedback of an interface. Feedback is the way of showing the user that he is doing what he thinks he is doing. Echoing the characters is a standard feedback. Similarly, it can be in the form of text, pictures, or graphics presentation (e.g., cursors and windows). Each piece of feedback information is associated with the activation of a specific command. The user has the feeling that the system knows what he is doing. Depending on the user's knowledge, this feedback may include either too much or too little information. This points out an important property : it should be possible for the user to adapt the interface to his knowledge.

1.2 - Ease of use and learn

The goal of any interface is to facilitate the use of a system. Therefore it must be both easy to use at a beginner level, and easy to progress at higher levels. Ease of use and learn is essentially a problem of consistency. The same mechanisms must be defined in the same situations. This is similar to the syntax of a language, in our case the interface language, which is never really specified. For instance, some interfaces try to minimize the number of actions to be done, but instead of gaining time, the user is lost : he cannot remember which style of interaction corresponds to a specific function, because there is no relationship between semantics and protocols of interaction. There are certain actions that must be consistent in designing an interface : *selection* of a command or an object, *tracking* of an object, *scrolling* of a menu, and *aborting* a command. The different strategies are clicking, double-clicking, and dragging; they can be combined by associating screen or objects regions to these actions. These associations are proper to the interface and constitute its style of interaction.

More sophisticated styles of interaction are reserved for experimented users. These styles can co-exist with simple ones, assuming the first level of an interface uses the basic actions described previously. Learning is also discovering ; once you know the basics, the set of possible commands is increased by combining the simple actions with use of the keyboard. These new combinations extend the semantic of the functions. For instance, altered clicks (e.g. with control or shift) activate other functions that are semantically close to the original function. Suppose, for example, that in a text editor a simple click selects a word, then a shift-click could select a whole sentence, and a control-click could select a paragraph. The semantic difference between all these clicks is the unit : *paragraph* made of *sentences* made of *words*, but the function is always selection.

These examples point out two essential factors involved in making an interface user-friendly : consistency and homogeneity .

1.3 - Feedback

How is established a dialogue between a human and a system ? There cannot be a real dialogue because the system does not know what the user knows, but it can advise the user of what is happening. Feedback, as we said before, gives informations relative to the current state of the system.

There are several levels of feedback : *lexical, syntactical* and *semantical*. A lexical feedback, as the echo of the characters typed on the keyboard or hilighting a command selected is the most easy to achieve. Syntactical feeback involve checking of user's actions : arguments selected, commands activated. It minimizes the user errors by telling him what is expected from him.The occurence of a syntax error involves an appropriate and meaningful message well integrated in the normal operation of the system. Notice that these two factors depends on the user's viewpoint. Consider the following example : when an invalid command is selected, some users would like to read an explicit message while for others a single beep would suffice. Graphical feedback such as the different representations of a hard-cursor or icons is often better than a long explicit message. Feedback is frequently both syntactical and semantical. It needs to be adapted to the user knowledge. If the interface is really a separate module of the program then the amount of feedback could be parameterized in the interface itself.

2 - General view of the environment

Several works have been done to provide high level tools to manipulate and build interfaces [3][4]. Our goal is to build an environment of tools, general enough to manage all the situations described above. Each interface has two sides : one to the user and the other to the system to be interfaced. Both need to be adaptable. The user wants to adapt the interface dynamically to his taste and knowledge, and the connections between the interface and the program need to be easily and dynamically changed. The object oriented approach with the mechanism of message passing is well-suited to provide such a scheme (figure 1). The consequence is that any interface of this kind could be re-usable for other programs.

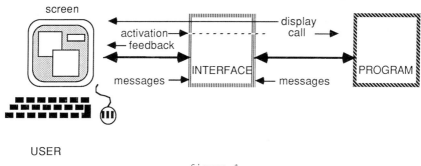

- figure 1 -

The two connections are quite different : the user perceives and activates the program through the interface, and what he sees from the interface is what is displayed on the screen. Displaying comes either from the interface itself, or from the program. But the screen management is controlled by the interface. The interface displays messages relative to the interaction protocol (feedback) and calls procedures activated by the user. The program can also read input from the keyboard or the mouse, but through a protocol defined by the interface. For instance, to enter a string, a special window is created with some basic editing functions. The string is sent to the program only when the user specifies the ending. More generally the user and the program communicate with the interface by message passing.

2.1 - UFO, User-Friendly Objects

To really provide an adaptable environment of this kind, we need abstraction. The tools we present are based on **UFO** [5] [6], an object oriented system specially adapted to interfaces and manipulation of graphical objects . Concepts of classes, messages, subclasses are built into the system, and the portability of **UFO** makes our tools portable as well. The purpose of **UFO** is to separate external and internal representation, and to associate with an object one internal representation , and one or more external representations. **UFO** is written in **C**, as a library. It runs on **ICL Perq** and **SUN** workstations, host/**Unix** ™* + **STEP**§ terminal [7].

Several reasons led us to build tools on top of this system :
- ♦ the object-oriented approach provides real adaptability and flexibility.
- ♦ classes and subclasses lead to a large variety of interfaces. Only a small number of basic

---

* Unix is a trade mark of AT&T Bell laboratories.
§ STEP is a terminal which has a hardwired window management and graphic capabilities.

classes are required to build sophisticated interfaces.

♦ various external representations of the same object are useful for graphics interfaces. Moreover, **UFO** provides mechanisms to specify constraints between objects.

♦ **UFO** is portable : the only part that must be adapted to a given host is the graphic library.

♦ Any program written in **C** or compatible with **C** (e.g. **Lisp** or **Pascal**), can use these classes and be linked with an interface built with these classes.

2.2 - Classes of interaction

The first step consists of defining basic objects to be used when designing a high level interface. Windows, icons and menus are frequently used [8] [9] [10], although rarely are they all combined together. The main reason is the high cost of implementation. Most modern workstation do not provide high level graphic function to build these objects but only basic graphic functions . An other reason is efficiency. Response time has to be considered as a fundamental factor : sometimes the layers added to a system make it unusable because of a bad response time. **UFO** and its classes always care for efficiency toward good response time. Efficiency and adaptability run against one another : usually adaptability means modularity while efficiency means low level programming. The way to combine them is to build classes on an graphic object oriented system such as **UFO**. This will provide an environment of high level functions or messages to build high level graphic interfaces quickly and efficiently .

We have chosen to implement those three classes : windows, icons and menus (figure 2). The structure of each class, along with its messages and attributes, must be carefully chosen since it is both an important factor of efficiency and flexibility of use.

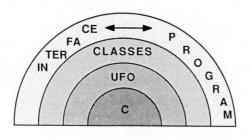

- figure 2 -

3 - Levels of implementation

UFO is a kernel to manipulate objects. Some preliminary steps are needed to provide an environment of tools to facilitate the building of various interfaces. The first step is to define the three basic classes. The second step consists of composing a new class, containing the other three as subclasses. This adds a level of abstraction in the manipulation of objects. For instance, a class *screen* would manage menus, icons and windows (as sub-classes), adding new relationships between them, for example a menu may belong to a window or a window may be abreviated by an icon.

At this level, we are manipulating interactive objects. The two parts of the interface can be built : the part acting only with the user, and the part connecting program functions to some objects. The first one consists of sending messages to create, delete, modify objects and their attributes, and determine the style of interaction. Consider the following example : an icon can be activated to open a window and to display a menu belonging to that window. The activation message is sent to the icon, then to the window, and then to the menu. Attributes concerning the style of interaction can be changed dynamically by sending messages. This means that we have to associate functions of the program with objects. We represent this relationship by storing the name or the address of a function with every object. For instance, selecting a command in a menu activates a program function. This means that the connections between objects and functions can also be changed dynamically.

The interface implementation must include commands relevant to the style of interaction. Their activation send messages modifying objects attributes. Since the class includes all kind of messages to change the specifications of the interface, this allows the user to change dynamically the style of the interface and the function associations.

Since we build the interface with real interactive objects, this is already high level programming. But as we will see in section 3.2, there is another way of building interfaces, which is to build them interactively with an interface editor.

3.1 - The menu class

In this section we describe the menu class. We first show the possibilities offered to the designer and then give some concrete examples.

An **UFO** object is made up of some attributes and a graph. The graph has simple vertices and sub-object vertices. A menu is an object with a set of vertices to be displayed, selected, scrolled, edited : its commands are given in the vertices of the graph. Each vertex contains some attributes. This class is generic : a command can belong to any class and have its own external and internal representation.

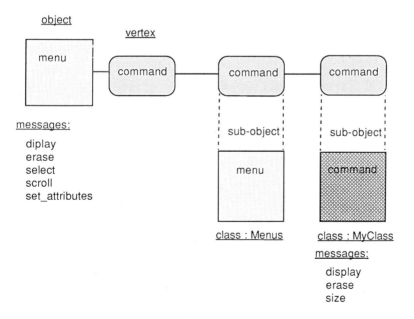

- figure 3 -

This scheme represents a menu with three commands and summarizes the different cases for commands.

An object of the class *Menus* has several attributes :

- ♦ title with font and alignment (left, right, center)
- ♦ commands alignment (left, right, center)
- ♦ number of visible commands (to fix the menu height)
- ♦ space between commands
- ♦ commands highlighting for selection (reverse video, rectangle, none)
- ♦ menu display (horizontal, vertical)
- ♦ space between borders of the menu box and commands.

These attributes can be changed at any time by messages : a general function updates the menus when it is needed.

The messages of the class *Menus* are :

- ♦ display
- ♦ erase
- ♦ select (with or without scrolling)
- ♦ scrolling (smooth or one command at time)
- ♦ set attributes (all described below)
- ♦ add command
- ♦ delete command
- ♦ update (save modifications)

Displaying a menu consists of displaying the menu box, the title, and the commands. Updating a menu consists of computing the size and coordinates of the commands. An instance of the class *Menus* is created by this sequence of messages :

```
/* send the message CreateMenu to the class ClassMenus
to create an instance
*/
instance = Send (ClassMenus ,CreateMenu ,arguments…);

/* for each command send the message Addcommand */
Send ( instance, AddCommand, arguments...);
```

which is followed by messages to set attributes (having default values).

The figure 3 shows different kinds of commands, and describes our notion of generic class. The first one is a simple vertex , and it has the attributes :

- ♦ name
- ♦ keyboard key
- ♦ font
- ♦ number
- ♦ little icon
- ♦ flags of inhibition and visibility

The goal is to give a number of attributes that allow enough possibilities without making them too complicated. The *name* and *keyboard key* are strings displayed with the *font*. These are specified so that a menu can mix different fonts. The number is an identification facility ; it is quicker to compare integers rather than strings. The *icon* is a picture displayed after the name and can be dynamically changed by sending a message. The flags give the possibility of hiding or/and inhibiting commands.

This means that one can interactively edit any command. One can imagine typing some new name of a command, changing the order of the commands, deleting some icon, etc.

The menus are usually organized in a hierarchy. To build this hierarchy, each simple command can be changed to a sub-object, i.e. a sub-menu. This is the second vertex of figure 3. A command of this nature keeps all its attributes, but is also connected to another menu. This connection means that selecting this command will display automatically — if wanted — the sub–menu. The result is often a tree, although any graph is allowed. The graph can be easily changed, again by sending messages, and the advantage is that going through this hierarchy can be completely managed by the interface. Note that a menu can be a sub-menu of several menus. Nothing has to be redefined since it has only to be linked with other menus. For example, this can be useful when a menu (e.g. a top level menu) needs to be accessible from any level in the hierarchy.

Naturally, the structure and the attributes defined for a command will not satisfy every user. So we want this class to be generic. It is possible to completely define your class of commands, *MyClass*, and to transform any command to a sub–object of this class. The definition of this new class is left to the imagination of the designer, but it must be able to answer to three messages : *display, erase* and *size*, in order to diplay/erase and update the menu. *MyClass* has its own attributes, internal and external representation. For instance, in a graph editor, a command can represent a complex object such as a sub-graph. The sub-graph has its own structure and procedures to display and erase it.

There are many possibilities of combination and configuration of menus. For instance, roll-down menus are one horizontal menu — the menu bar — with several vertical submenus for each command of the menu bar. Sub-menus can be built and displayed in several ways. Some examples are shown in the appendix.

This class has been implemented completely. The first application that has been developed with this class is an interactive menu editor (see the appendix), in order to improve the dynamic adaptability to the user. The response time is immediate and the simple commands already provide a large number of different systems of menus.

3.2 - Further developments

The classes *window* and *icon* will not be described here. They are developed in a similar context of adaptability. The next step will be to mix these three classes by adding a new level of abstraction.

Mixing those three classes means that we need to define another class that will use them as subclasses. An instance of this superclass represents the screen of a terminal. Windows, menus and icons are the basic objects and each instance has a position. By position we mean graphic coordinates and also a position in the **UFO** graph. This position defines semantic dependencies with others objects. For instance, a set of menus can be connected to a specific window. Each menu is displayed whenever a particular region of the window is pointed. The icons can symbolise a window or a process belonging to different windows. The relation x "belongs to" y is interpreted as x is a sub-object of y. The relation x "is connected" to y has two interpretations for the **UFO** graph : either it is of the kind "belongs to", or the link is expressed with edges. **UFO** edges are made to express semantic relations between objects. Each edge has a type and one can perform any action on a list of objects connected by a certain type of edge. For instance, when a window is moved with its specific menus, these menus are easily identified to be moved together with the window.

In figures 4 and 5, we show an example of what could be an instance of the superclass combining the basic classes. The screen display is composed of three windows and three icons. The main window has one particular menu. One of the icons symbolizes a process running in a window and creating output in another window, another one symbolizes a file and the last one is a window which is temporary invisible. Figure 5 shows the hierarchy and the relations between objects. This is the **UFO** graph : the vertices represent the windows, menus and icons of the object screen, and the edges represent different constraints. The icon that symbolizes a process has two types of edges : input and output windows. The third type appearing on this example is the representation of a window by an icon. The icon and the window represent the same object but they are really two different vertices in the graph. The edge from one to another is the only way to get this information.

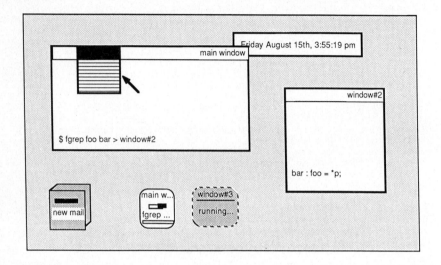

- figure 4 -

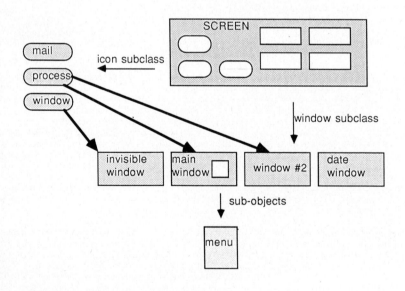

- figure 5 -

We shall see an example of use of these tools, from the point of view of the designer. We quickly described the internal representation of the superclass *screen*. It is now possible to define quite easily a small and sophisticated interface. The following program is the implementation of the main part of an interface. This interface consists of one window, one menu belonging to that window, and an icon. A shell process is created for the window which is represented by the icon.

```
/* initialize the screen */
screen = Send (ScreenClass, Create, …);

/* create a window and a shell process */
win = Send (screen, CreateWindow,…);
Send ( win, CreateProcess, "/bin/sh");
/* create a menu for the previous window */
menu = Send (win, CreateMenu, …);
/* create an icon that represents the window */
icon = Send (screen, CreateIcon, …):
Send (screen, Link, win, icon);

/* top level */
switch (NextEvent(&value)) {
    case ClickMouse :
            /* depending on the object pointed, some
             * action is performed (command selection and
             * activation, moving, opening an icon…)
             */
            Send (screen, MouseClick, value.coordinates);
            break;
    case KeyboardInput :
            /* the string is displayed or/and sent to a
             * process
             */
            Send (CurrentWindow, GetString, value.key);
            break;
    case ProcessOutput :
            /* the window attached to the process scans
             * the output
             */
            w =Send (screen, FindWindow ,value.processid);
            if (w) Send (w, GetProcess);
            break;
}
```

The syntax of the function Send is :
```
Send (Receiver, NameOfMessage, Arguments…)
```
This example does not show the link between the interface and the program. The functions of the program should be linked to the interface when creating the menu and the window. In this example, windows have within their attributes a process identification number to memorize the current process they are linked to.

The most important event is ClickMouse : the message that is sent is sometimes transmitted deeply through several classes before being executed. Consider the following event : the window is deleted. At the *screen* level, a message of deletion is sent to the window together with a signal to the system to kill the process before a redisplay of the screen. Then, at the *window* level, all the connected objects are searched and the message of deletion is also transmitted. Finally, the menu and the icon are deleted as well as the constraint edges that established the link with the window. Through this example, we wanted to show the simplicity of writing such an interface as well as the power of such tools.

Our idea is finally to have an interactive interface to build interfaces. The first application, a menu editor, will be extended to establish the link between objects — commands — and program functions, and will manipulate *screen* objects. The screen topology will be defined dynamically by building windows, icons and menus. The semantic relations will be as well dynamically adaptable. This should prove the great flexibility of this system.

4 - Conclusion

Actually we have programming tools manipulating common interactive objects. The messages are divided in four parts :
- The messages that build the general structure of the interface. These are the basic messages to define objects to be used and their relationships.
- The messages that set the attributes to define the style of interaction. They are not necessary since attributes have default values. They allow dynamic changes and should be accessible from the interface. The user could adapt interactively the interface to his taste.
- The messages that allow the user to adapt the interface to his knowledge. This may involve coordination with the application.
- The messages that make the connection between the interface and the application.

We have shown that designing an interface with the tools described above, provides both adaptability and flexibility for building user-friendly interfaces. However, the basic rules we have described at the beginning of this paper must be carefully applied during the design. The interface is more than a layer between the user and the application; it is also a tool for the user and the designer. The user defines the way he wants to use it, and the designer can adapt it to other applications.

References

[1] Stephen W. Draper and Donald A. Norman. "Software Engineering for User Interfaces". *IEEE Transactions on Software Engineering*, Vol. SE-11, No 3, March 1985

[2] Joseph N. Pato, Steven P. Reiss, Marc H. Brown. "The Browm Workstation Environment" Brown University January 1984

[3] Philip J. Hayes. "Executable Interface Definitions Using Form-Based Interface Abstractions" *Internal report* March 1984

[4] H. Hanusa. "Tools and techniques for the monitoring of interactive graphics dialogues" *Int. J. Man-Machine Studies* 19, pp. 163-180, 1983

[5] M. Beaudouin-Lafon. "UFO : un méta interface graphique pour la manipulation d'objets". *Proc. Congrès AFCET Matériels et Logiciels pour la 5ème Génération* Mars 1985

[6] M. Beaudouin-Lafon. "Vers des interfaces graphiques évolués : UFO, un méta-modèle d'interaction". *Thèse de 3ème cycle* Octobre 1985

[7] M. Beaudouin-Lafon, M. Bidoit, J. Corbin, G.M. Marcoux. " Le logiciel de Step : spécifications de réalisation" Rapport final du contrat CNET Juin 1984

[8] Brad A. Myers. "The User interface for Sapphire" *IEEE Computer Graphics and Applications* Vol.4, No. 12, December 1984 pp.13-23.

[9] Dr David Canfield Smith, Charles Irby, Ralph Kimball, Bill Verplank and Eric Harslem. "Designing the Star User Interface" *Byte* Vol. 7, No. 4, April 1984

[10] Warren Teitelman. "A Tour through Cedar" IEEE Transactions *on Software Engineering* Vol. SE-11 No. 3, pp. 285-302 March 1985

APPENDIX

These are two examples of combination of menus. The menu "title bar" has three submenus. The third submenu is selected. It can be displayed as shown in these examples.

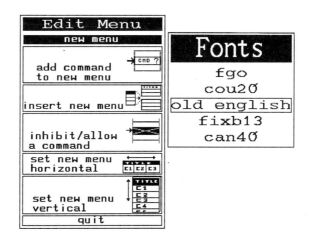

The next examples are hardcopied from the menu editor. The main menu "Edit Menu" gives the possibility to add a new sub-menu. When one selects the command "new menu", several messages and sub-menus are displayed, such as the menu "Fonts", to choose the parameters of the new menu. The last two examples show menus added dynamically – "my menu" and "my sub-menu" – that are selected and displayed.

Select title font

S. Karsenty

OFFICE SYSTEMS: Methods and Tools
G. Bracchi, D. Tsichritzis (Editors)
Elsevier Science Publishers B.V. (North-Holland)
IFIP, 1987

INSEM: AN ELECTRONIC MAIL PROJECT FOR THE EUROPEAN
COMMUNITY AND ITS INSTITUTIONS

R. CENCIONI, S. HOLLAND, R. KROMMES, F. KODECK

Commission of the European Communities,
Jean Monnet Building,
L-2920 Luxembourg

Abstract

The INSEM project (INterinstitutional Service for Electronic Mail)
aims to introduce electronic mail to the daily procedures of the
European Institutions and their contacts with national
administrations of the member states. This will be carried out in two
stages. The first stage uses teletex protocols, and will be
introduced this year. The second stage is based on the message
handling system models and standards produced by ISO (MOTIS) and the
CCITT (X.400). The institutions will pursue a policy of co-operation
and collaboration with the information technology and
telecommunications industry to promote the development of commercial
products which both suit the needs of large administrations, and
conform to the relevant international standards.

1. INTRODUCTION

This paper describes the INSEM project (INterinstitutional Service for
Electronic Mail), which has been established by the European Institutions as
part of the INSIS (INterinstitutional System for Integrated Services)
programme. The background to the project is first considered. The European
Institutions are briefly reviewed, and the aims and approach of the INSEM
project summarised. The architectural guidelines which apply to all information
technology and telecommunications services within the European Institutions are
examined. The standards applicable to the mail service are reviewed, and where
particular selections have been made the choices are explained. The two phases
of the INSEM project are considered in detail, with attention to the
architecture adopted and· the way that the concepts of the models have been
adapted to the actual needs of the users. Finally some considerations for the
future are examined. These include the areas where standardisation work is not
yet complete, and the problems anticipated in moving a large existing
paper-based traffic flow onto an electronic infrastructure.

1.1. Communications Requirements in the European Institutions

To set the background to the INSEM project, let us briefly recall the nature of
the European Community and its Institutions.

The European Community comprises 12 member states with a total of more than 320
million inhabitants. It aims to secure economic and social progress through
coordinated action.

The community tasks are handled by its various institutions: the Commission of
the European Communities, the Council of Ministers, the European Parliament,
the Court of Justice and the Court of Auditors, assisted by the Economic and
Social Committee and the European Investment Bank. They exchange written

information among themselves in forms ranging from short information notes to large texts of formal procedures. Most institutions are also in daily contact with the administrations of the Member States.

The institutions activities have three main seats (Brussels, Luxembourg and Strasbourg) in three different countries, in addition to which there are four scientific research centres and almost one hundred delegations, press and information offices spread around the world. At a local level there is also a wide dispersal: in Brussels the institutions occupy more than thirty buildings.

The scale of the telecommunication and data processing resources currently employed within the Commission of the European Communities (usually referred to as the Commission) gives an idea of the extent of the service INSEM will eventually be called upon to provide:

> the telephone exchange in Brussels has approximately 12000 extensions and nearly 900 outside lines,

> the automated telex exchange handles two to three thousand messages a day,

> the Commission uses four large mainframes, forty medium range computers, around 1400 terminals, eight hundred word processors and a growing number of personal computers,

> over one hundred facsimile machines are currently installed.

It is planned that by 1990 200 departmental mini-computers, 2000 personal computers, and 2000 terminals and word processors will be in place.

The Institutions have been installing word processing systems since 1977. The first few years saw the arrival of numerous incompatible systems. During the same period the first message systems, such as SCRAPBOOK, were introduced on a pilot basis, on sites serving limited user populations.

In 1982 a rationalised strategy for the introduction of document production and communication systems began to emerge. Message systems such as TARANIS, SEMS and KOMEX were introduced. These provided facilities for message preparation, transmission, consultation and processing more suited to the needs of their users.

By 1986 the emphasis has shifted from simply providing support for typing services to integrating office automation functions on standardised computing resources (MS-DOS personal computers and UNIX V multi-user systems). Electronic mail is increasingly important as a means of transmitting documents, in contrast to its previous use for short informal messages.

The problem now facing the Institutions is how to draw together document production and interchange within the framework of the electronic office, while permitting access to public text communication services such as telex and teletex. It is to solve this problem that the INSEM project was launched.

1.2. The Informatics Guidelines

The Commission of the European Communities (CEC) has produced a set of guidelines(1) for the way information technology services should be deployed and used within its own administration. They lay the foundations for a well coordinated plan for procurement and implementation of information technology services across the European Institutions.

The basic aim of this plan is to allow the European Institutions to adopt and integrate new technology independently of the policy of individual manufacturers. A number of subsidiary objectives have been defined as means to achieve this aim. These are:

> To modernise the administration of the European Institutions and organise the information flow between them and the Member State administrations,

> To promote a multi-vendor procurement policy, showing that it is economically justifiable in a standardised environment,

> To promote cooperation between manufacturers in adopting and adhering to standards through the use of European functional standards,

> To strengthen interinstitutional cooperation in information technology allowing the sharing of benefits resulting from the combination of the purchasing power of separate institutions,

> To set an example to public bodies in Europe in procurement policy for information technology products.

Key elements in the strategy through which the guidelines aim to achieve these objectives are:

> A coherent policy in implementing standards,

> A rational deployment of information technology resources, reflecting more closely the way user communities are organised.

The guidelines set out a common architecture for the integration of information technology resources. This architecture is treated in detail later.

To ensure that these guidelines result in concrete achievements, the institutions have launched the INSIS programme and its subsidiary projects, which address areas such as electronic mail, database access and videoconferencing.

1.3. Aims of the INSEM Project

The INSEM project is part of the INSIS programme. This programme is based on user needs and priorities, and aims at improving the quality of communications within and between Institutions of the European Communities and the Member States by making effective use of advanced information technologies and telecommunications techniques. Its direct objective is to improve the efficiency of the administrations of the Community by providing fast and reliable communication systems and services.

INSEM has to provide a mail service which will satisfy the requirements of its potential users in the European Institutions. In this respect, a number of the requirements of the Institutions are basically those of any commercial organisation:

- the service provided must be reliable and cost effective,
- it should not be tied to a single supplier,
- document production, distribution and presentation facilities should be improved,
- the software should be portable, so that investment is preserved as hardware is replaced.

The electronic mail service which INSEM must provide will supplement (and in
the long term largely replace) existing postal services. Consequently INSEM
must provide a service at least functionally equivalent to the service provided
by the current postal, telex and internal mail services.

It must therefore be possible to convey both short simple messages of the
memorandum style, and large documents with complex structure and formatting
requirements. This latter requirement introduces the problem of how the
attributes of documents are to be conveyed in the electronic mail services.

It is envisaged that the solutions adopted by INSEM for the Institutions will
also be suitable for large national administrations, since their requirements
are fundamentally similar.

INSEM therefore aims at building its services out of commercial and competitive
products. It does not aim to be a vehicle for research and development.

In this respect it can be seen that the aims of INSEM (like the other INSIS
projects) differ from those of ESPRIT (European Strategic Project for Research
in Information Technology). The ultimate aim of INSEM is to build an
operational system targeted at the needs of a specific user community. It
should therefore make use of proven technologies and industrial products.

Projects within ESPRIT aim at producing R&D prototypes. Most notable among them
as far as INSEM is concerned is the Information Exchange System (IES), an
electronic mailing system which has been developed as a tool for the
communities of researchers engaged in ESPRIT projects, and the ROSE and THORN
projects it has given rise to. ROSE covers the development of OSI tools in a
UNIX environment, while THORN investigates directory services. Such research
will only achieve its full potential if there is a market opportunity to
justify its commercial exploitation. One of the aims of INSIS projects is to
stimulate that opportunity.

It will be impossible for INSEM to avoid dependence on a single supplier unless
products obtained from different sources are fully capable of interworking.
This can only be foreseen if the products conform to international standards.
Even this is not enough in itself; consistent selection from the profusion of
standards is necessary. To help ensure this, the Community is actively
promoting the use of functional European standards based on international
standards, and their adoption is required throughout the projects launched by
INSIS.

1.4. Review of the Approach taken

INSEM was launched in January 1984. Since at that time the requirement was
ill-defined, an initial study period was necessary, with the objective of
establishing the project planning in the short, medium and long term. The first
studies concentrated on three main areas:

> how to achieve better use and greater integration of the equipment
> already in place or about to be installed,

> definition of the tools necessary, particularly the nature of the
> servers required, the information needed in the delivery envelope, and
> the protocols required for the submission and delivery of documents,

> evaluation of the possibility of introducing a harmonised language for
> the representation of documents during transmission, a problem which
> occurs when documents are exchanged between systems of different types.

In these and subsequent studies, external consultants were used. A number of companies were involved, so that a spread of expertise was available and a single view was not allowed to dominate.

The plan which was formulated at the end of this period called for a staged approach to the installation of services. This plan reflected the market situation of the period, the status of the relevant standards, and the need to ascertain the user requirements.

A process of consultation with representatives of industry and national administrations was launched to ensure that plans and specifications produced would correspond with the direction the market was moving in, and would align to the requirements of the administrations for interconnection.

In early 1985 a second series of studies was launched, based on the results of the first series. These studies aimed at consolidating the work plans, and also addressed the problem of providing directory services, with particular emphasis on the requirements to be met.

Two phases were identified for the implementation. The first of these phases (which are described in detail in section 4) was begun in 1985.

In 1986 attention is focused on the problems of managing the electronic mail service. The tools required in the service and the organisational apparatus necessary are being defined. At the same time preliminary investigations are being carried out into the possibility of integrating facsimile services within the overall mail architecture.

Throughout this period these essentially technical studies have been complemented by a series of studies into the needs of the intended users, the information flows and document distribution patterns, and the impact of the future system on the current methods of document administration.

The phase one service is being installed in selected test sites, while specifications for phase two are being finalised. The architecture of the service which will be installed in phase two has been defined(2). A call for tender for the supply of systems to provide the phase two service is being prepared.

In 1987 it is planned that the phase one service will be widely available and used. At the same time the products which will build the phase two service will be evaluated and selected.

Full phase two service should be installed and in use by about the second half of 1988. At this stage electronic mail services should be fully integrated with office automation packages.

2. The Overall Informatics Architecture

The guidelines referred to above in 1.2 set out the overall architecture within which information technology and telecommunications services will be introduced. In defining the overall architecture for the European Institutions, account has been taken of the organisational structure of the intended user population.

The European Institutions are autonomous organisations, each with responsibility for their own resources. Each organisation therefore forms a separate management domain. These separate domains communicate with each other, with the Member State Administrations, and with public domains using public communication networks.

Within a domain the users are further organised into administrative units
(directorates in the Commission, for example) which may be widely dispersed
geographically. This has led to the adoption of a policy of distributed
processing. Furthermore, the degree of independence between the administrative
units means that they may equip themselves with equipment and software from
different manufacturers, within the guidelines set out by the informatics
directorate.

The administrative units form cohesive bodies in which there is a high degree
of interaction between the users. This leads to the concept of the local
support unit (LSU), the collection of resources dedicated to and administered
by a single user community with a close working relationship.

However, not all information technology resources can sensibly be distributed;
some services can only reasonably be supplied in a centralised manner. This
results in the definition of the common support unit (CSU), which is defined to
be a resource common to a domain as a whole.

Internally to a domain communication among LSUs and CSUs is over the Domain
Corporate Network (DCN), which in principle is a private network, although
currently it is a public data network used with appropriate safeguards to
protect against unauthorised access.

Within a domain each LSU is in principle free to communicate with any other.
However, most institutions have strict rules concerning communications outside
the domain, while the PTTs as providers of public communication services have
stringent service requirements for the connection of equipment to their
services. These two factors combine to justify a particular type of CSU known
as a Telecommunication Centre (TC).

The TC provides the gateway into and out of a domain: all traffic entering or
leaving the domain must pass through it. It provides access to the various
communication technologies which must be used for communicating outside the
domain: ie telex, teletex, and later MHS and possibly facsimile.

Concentrating external communications through one centre means that the extra
investment required to meet service requirements for (for example) attachment
to the public teletex service is not necessary in every LSU which might require
it: pass through facilities can be provided. From the point of view of
administration of communication services, procedures such as registration of
incoming mail, archiving and filing, and approval of outgoing communication can
all be centred in the TC.

An overview of the architecture is presented in figure 1.

Within this architecture, three items can be seen to be of particular
importance to INSEM: the structure and function of the TC, the architecture of
the LSU, and the protocols for communication among LSUs and the TC.

This last item is addressed to some degree in the guidelines, since a number of
services in addition to electronic mail will require communication between
distributed systems. It is a fundamental principle that the OSI model shall be
adhered to, although this does not solve all problems. The refinements which
have been necessary in the development of INSEM specifications are discussed
below.

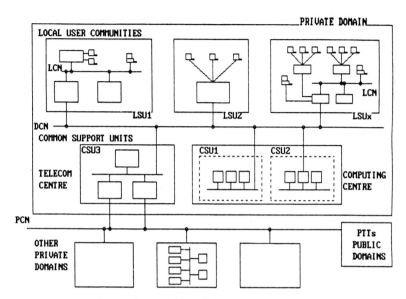

Figure 1: Overall Informatics Architecture

3. Standards adopted by INSEM

As mentioned in the introduction, INSIS users are not prepared to depend upon a single supplier, and have consistently pursued a multi-vendor procurement policy. By implication the suppliers come from different countries, and so their products can only be expected to interwork if they conform to international standards. It is therefore necessary for INSIS projects, in this case INSEM, to select and promote the standards to be applied and to promote their application by the suppliers.

This ties in with a wider objective of promoting the use of European functional norms, which are based on international standards and define sets of conventions and options to be selected in products. Use of these functional standards is important in the establishment of a common European market for information technology and telecommunications products.

INSEM's study of the standards applicable to electronic mail and open systems interconnection (OSI) have resulted in the following conclusions:

3.1. OSI

The principles and protocols of OSI up to layer 5 (session) are now well established and are supported by a wide range of manufacturers. However, OSI has been conceived in such a way that in the lower layers different protocols (and options within the protocols) may be selected, reflecting the variety of communication technologies existing.

It is necessary that coherent sets of options be selected for pairs of communicating entities in order to permit satisfactory interworking. This has specific relevance to layers one to three of the OSI model (physical, link and network) where a wide range of standards are defined, and layer four (transport) where selection of the class employed depends on the characteristics of the underlying layers.

For INSEM this problem is overcome by adoption of sets of standards and options in line with the appropriate CEN/CENELEC functional standards, covering for example connection to X25 networks and LANS.

3.2. Teletex

The label teletex can be applied to two things: the set of protocols and codings defined in the CCITT recommendations T.70, T.62 and T.61, and the service offered by a number of PTTs. The latter comprises the former plus a set of service requirements covering the characteristics of equipment which may be connected to the service.

As a public service, teletex has the advantage of immediate availability in a large proportion of the member states, and will be used in the short to medium term for communication between national administrations and the European Institutions.

The public teletex service is not considered suitable for use within INSEM domains for a number of reasons. The main reason is that it is only possible to attach approved equipment to the service, and the conditions for approval preclude most of the equipment which is envisaged for the service.

The teletex protocols themselves are not entirely suited to the service INSEM plans to introduce, since they only provide point-to-point communication. However, they do support a sufficiently full character set to support the range of languages used in the Community, and are currently available in a number of products. For these reasons teletex protocols have been selected as a basis for the first service to be introduceed by INSEM.

This selection has two immediate consequences: one is that an application protocol has had to be developed to expand the mail facilities offered by teletex, and the second is that a relay or gateway between the internal teletex operation and the public service is required (the Telecommunication Centre).

3.3. Message Handling Systems

The initial studies indicated that the most satisfactory basis for the mail service is the Message Handling System (MHS) model defined initially by the CCITT in their X.400 series of recommendations, and more recently by ISO in the MOTIS (Message Oriented Text Interchange System) drafts.

The model is suited to the size and heterogenity of the target user population. It should provide a stable architectural model for the future development of electronic mail services and their integration into the increasingly automated office procedures.

An added benefit is that many of INSEM's partners in the national administrations are also planning to base their services in similar projects on this model. This will have the desirable effect of allowing a degree of cross-fertilisation to take place as the various projects proceed.

In selecting the MHS model it has been recognised that the standards contain a wide variety of options, selection of which must be made carefully if heterogenous systems are to be fully capable of interworking. INSEM has therefore closely followed the work of CEPT and CEN/CENELEC in the definition of the A/311 and A/3211 functional standards, which define service and protocol support for interworking between domains. However, the scale of operations of

INSEM will be such that it will also require the as yet undefined A/323 functional standard, which is intended to address the problem of interworking within multi-vendor private domains. In order to avoid having to await definition of this standard, INSEM has defined an intercept based on the A/3211 functional standard.

Within the MHS model a number of areas either await standardisation or the applicable standards are insufficiently stable to form a basis for development. Prominent among these are the directory service standards, naming conventions, code conversions, management operations, and the mailbox service model. These are all important elements in the INSEM architecture.

3.4. Office Document Architecture

It is a requirement for INSEM services to support the distribution of documents in a printable and revisable form in a multi-vendor environment. This implies that documents produced on different word processing systems must be converted in format between the coding schemes used by different manufacturers.

This problem has been recognised from the outset, and it was decided very early on in the project that a single coding scheme was desirable for the interchange of documents. Use of a single scheme both reduces the potential number of conversions, and simplifies the management of the service, since any document in transit is encoded in a single known format.

Initially therefore, INSEM proceeded with the development of an interchange format which was aimed to bridge the gap between the service being operational, and completion of ISO work in the same area. Fortunately however, progress on the ISO standards has been such that a stable kernel of the Office Document Architecture - Office Document Interchange Format (ODA/ODIF) has emerged which is suitable for adoption.

This ODA-kernel is based on the Draft International Standards (DIS) 8613/2, 8613/5 and 8613/6, which are concerned with the common representation of revisable and/or printable documents. They are concerned with character-coded information, and are well suited to the interchange of text prepared on currently available word processing equipment.

ODA defines two structures for a document - layout and logical. The layout structure primarily reflects the print image of a document, while the logical is more concerned with the structure of a document in terms of chapters, paragraphs etc. Since for the purposes of INSEM it is considered important to allow a recipient to revise a document, and less so to present the same image on different types of equipment, a logical structure is required.

The ODA-kernel requires conformance to the levels PDA-3 and CP-3 defined in the standards. PDA-3 provides sufficient facilities to represent the logical structure of documents and physical formatting constraints (eg representation of hard page breaks), while CP-3 allows representation of most word processing system attributes.

4. The INSEM Implementation

Implementation of the INSEM service is planned to follow two stages. The first stage can be seen as a pilot service intended to raise user awareness of the possibilities of electronic mail, and show up any major problems which will have to be overcome before the second stage is introduced. It has been conceived to meet urgent user needs in a timely manner, so that the deployment of electronic mail on departmental servers can begin as soon as possible.

The second stage entails installation of message handling systems based on the
MHS standards described in section 3.

In parallel with the two stages, the telecommunication centre will be
developed. Since it plays a central role in both stages, it will be described
first.

4.1. The Telecommunication Centre

The telecommunications centre has a central role in the domain. In addition to
its purely communication related role, it hosts a central management facility,
and is combined with a support and development centre.

The centre provides access to public services, ie:
- telex,
- teletex,
- public MHS (when available).

It will also provide a gateway to other private domains using public
communication networks. This service may be necessary for an interim period
while public services are unavailable.

The centre provides a gateway between internal teletex based services and MHS
based services. This is essential during the period when phase one mail systems
coexist with phase two systems.

The centre offers the quality of service essential for communication outside
the domain. This means that it provides twenty-four hour operation, and secure
document storage, as well as satisfying whatever service regulations may be in
force.

The centre will incorporate mechanisms to control access to and from external
correspondents. This prevents unauthorised transmission of information outside
an organisation, and may serve to protect users from receipt of 'junk' mail.

The telecommunication centre also contains central management facilities. These
control operation of the mail services and the underlying network and
equipment. Statistics are collected by the equipment in the LSUs and passed to
the centre for corollation and analysis. Accounting is carried out in the
centre. A central register of all service users is held at the centre, and
directory services and update distribution will be coordinated from the centre.

A maintenance facility will be part of the centre. In most domains this
performs a diagnostic and monitoring role, and may eventually carry out
configuration control and software update distribution. In at least one domain
this facility will also be used for development and maintenance of the service.

The development of the telecommunication centre will parallel the development
of the mail services. An initial installation will be provided at the time
phase one becomes fully operational, providing a gateway between the internal
mail service and public teletex services. This initial service will be
progressively enhanced to provide the facilities required in the final service.

The staged approach is made possible by the modular design of the
telecommunication centre. Logically separate functions are provided on
physically separate machines. An internal high speed communication facility is
used to connect the services.

4.2. Phase One

The first phase is aimed at introducing an electronic mail service into the institutions within the shortest possible timescale and without substantial capital investment. It will provide users of existing, communicating word processors and office automation packages with facilities to exchange documents over the DCN using teletex protocols, as discussed in section 3.

The electronic mail service serves two functions: it allows internal interchange of documents, and correspondence with parties outside the domain. The first function is achieved by direct interchange between LSUs. The second requires that messages transit the telecommunication centre.

In order to implement phase one, three items are necessary: access to teletex links, a common interchange format, and a common routing mechanism.

Access to teletex links can be provided in different ways according to the equipment involved. Stand-alone personal computers are in many cases capable of running teletex software, and so can directly access links. In the case of the integrated office packages currently in use on UNIX V systems, either dedicated teletex couplers can be front-ended to the systems in order to allow access to public teletex, or else software packages running under UNIX can be used to give access to internal services. Finally personal workstations which do not support teletex packages can communicate with UNIX V systems using private protocols to access teletex services provided under UNIX.

In general it is economically unsound to provide a DCN connection for a single user system, so that the first of these approaches will not be preferred. Access to the DCN will generally be by a departmental server.

In the preferred approach, ie connecting word processors to UNIX machines or using office packages on the UNIX systems themselves, conversion algorithms had to be developed on the UNIX servers. These convert between the common interchange format and the private document coding formats of the word processors in use within the institutions. This common format preserves most of the formatting information embedded in a document held by a word processor, and so allows documents to be revised when they are received and converted to the format of the recipient system.

Message routing in a teletex environment is not standardised (since the nature of teletex is point-to-point, not store and forward). The definition of P5 in CCITT recommendation X.430 includes the format of a submission control document, used when passing a document to the message handling service from a teletex terminal. This document contains the necessary elements for handling a document in the mail service, and was taken as the basis for the definition of a message submission envelope, known within the project as the 'minimal envelope'. The minimal envelope is contained within a normal document, so that problems associated with generating and processing separate control documents are avoided.

A document that contains the minimal envelope, in fact a specially formatted first page, can be automatically routed, so that messages passing through the telecommunication centre can be handled without operator intervention.

Users of the first service will be provided with tools for the preparation of the minimal envelope. These tools include a basic directory service which provides address list expansion and aliasing. Multiple addressing is possible, and an electronic mailbox is available. The mailbox service includes status enquiry facilities, as well as the fetch and dispatch facility.

A user will be able to send a document to other users served by the same LSU, by a different LSU, or connected to the teletex service.

It is the intention that the phase one service is as near as possible to being functionally compatible with the X.400 based service which will be introduced in phase two. This should ease the problems of transition for the users when the second phase is brought into service.

The first release of phase one is now being installed in a number of test sites within the Commission. General installation of the service will begin in January 1987, and by the end of that year about 30 machines serving more than 400 users should be available.

4.3. INSEM Phase Two

Phase two of the service should be provided by the second half of 1988. It entails the installation of services conforming to the MHS standards as discussed in section 3. The range of text preparation and mail access services available to a user will be integrated with a User Agent Entity (UAE), the collection then being referred to as a user agent (since it acts on behalf of the user). Each LSU will be equipped with a Message Transfer Agent (MTA), a software entity which relays messages submitted by UAEs to other peer MTAs, and ultimately delivers messages to their destination UAE.

In phase two it is intended that all office automation and text processing services are integrated with the mail services, so that documents can be simply transferred through the mail between different systems.

The MTA and UA operate the protocols P1 and P2, the basic mail protocols currently defined. P1 is operated by the MTA, it provides the carrier service to convey messages between UAs. P2 gives meaning to the content of the messages, it provides the inter-personal message service (IPMS) which gives a simple memorandum style format to messages.

Because the IPMS is a very basic structure, INSEM has focussed attention on the coding format for message content, resulting in the adoption of the ODA-kernel as discussed in 3.4.

INSEM requires that the MTA and the UA be clearly distinct software entities. This requirement is imposed so that in the future additional services may be built on the basic mail service. For example, work is currently in progress in the international standardisation arena to produce protocols for electronic data interchange (EDI), based on the P1 service. By maintaining a clear separation between MTA and UA, INSEM keeps the door open for future developments.

To these components, which are the basic components of the MHS model, must be added two others: a Management Services Agent (MSA) and a directory services agent (DSA), both of which are considered necessary for the operation of the system.

A MSA comprises the services necessary to control operation of the mail service. Some of these functions are local to the LSU in which the MSA is located, and will be operated by a Local System Administrator (LSA), while others are concerned with the operation with the mail service as a whole, and are under the control of a management centre, which has responsibility for a complete domain.

A DSA provides services to users in the preparation of messages, and to the MTA in routing them. The naming schemes adopted for the MHS are complex, and not readily suited to direct input by human operators. Therefore directory services are necessary to translate mnemonic names to forms that the MHS can understand.

In order to simplify the directory services and the associated problems of routing messages as much as possible, INSEM has adopted a subset of the name forms defined within the standards. Only names conforming to this subset will be assigned to users of the service. The structure of names in this subset directly reflects the organisational structure of the user communities, which is in turn reflected in the distribution of LSUs. It is therefore possible to use user names directly in the incremental routing algorithms within a domain.

However, there will obviously be problems in maintaining the volume of information which must be held in the directories in the various LSUs. Names may be mispelled, and messages received from outside the domain may contain inadequate routing information. To cope with these problems the INSEM service incorporates a referal service which allows operators to correct the address information held in a message and resubmit it to the mail service. The referal service is built on the notion of the alternate recipient contained in the MHS model.

The implementation of this phase will take place against a background of LSUs evolving with increasing complexity. As the amount of equipment utilised by a local community increases, and the volume of internal traffic grows correspondingly, there will be a strong tendency towards the introduction of local area networks (LANs) to interconnect equipment. This becomes more practical as simple dumb terminals are replaced by personal computers.

Use of LANs is attractive from another point of view, since it allows a physical isolation of the equipment of the LSU (remember that the DCN, which is the alternative means of connecting equipment, will usually be a public network), and so allows greater security to be provided.

Indeed, security and access control requirements are such that a LSU connected by a LAN will only access the DCN through a special gateway, which will perform protocol conversions and contain whatever security mechanisms are required.

Within the LSU the MTA is required to offer a high degree of availability, and so will generally be hosted by a dedicated computer offering the required combination of availability and reliability.

Other equipment making up the LSU could be personal computers, and multi-user UNIX V systems serving users with attached terminals.

This then leads to the type of LSU configuration shown in figure 2.

Clearly the MTA resides on the dedicated system shown on the diagram as the EMAIL SERVER, but what of the other elements?

The MSA is closely related to the operation of the MTA. It provides facilities for the registration of users, update of the routing tables, collection of statistics and control of documents leaving the LSU. It is therefore most logical to place the MSA on the same machine as the MTA.

The DSA is less obvious. On the one hand it provides services to users in the preparation of messages - a task carried out in the personal computers and multi user UNIX systems, and so might be distributed around them. On the other hand, many of the users will require to contact the same correspondents, and it is undesirable to duplicate information in several end systems. It is also highly desirable to store directory information in a system which provides a high degree of protection against loss of data. On balance, the preferred approach is to centralise the directory service on the same machine as the MTA.

However, machines may also provide some degree of directory services, so that
users may build up their own personal lists of correspondents.

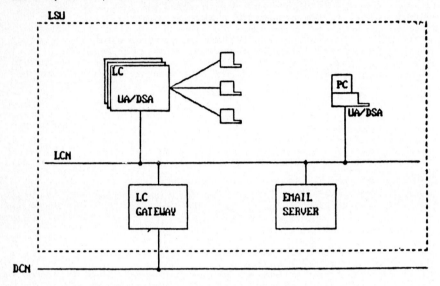

Figure 2: Typical LSU configuration

Finally there is the problem of the UA. Clearly, the majority of the UA
functionality will be located in the system to which a user has access: either
a personal computer, or a multi-user UNIX V system. There is one major problem
however: the storage of messages.

A major principle of electronic mail is that messages shall not get lost. In
this context, this means that a user submitting a message must be sure that
after it has been delivered to the UA of the recipient, it will not be lost or
deleted without the recipient becoming aware of it. If the recipient's UA is
located in a typical personal computer, this simply cannot be guaranteed. The
requirement clearly then is to provide a secure store in which to hold messages
after delivery, and realistically, this cannot be done by upgrading personal
computers.

Therefore, in the INSEM architecture a mailbox model of operation has been
adopted. In this model messages are securely stored in a mailbox which is
located in the same secure environment as the MTA. A user has the ability to
fetch received messages from his mailbox, and deposit messages for transmission
into it. Additional tools for control of the mailbox are also available, such
as status enquiry and logging and recording functions.

A major problem associated with the mailbox model is that no universally agreed
standard for mailbox access and service exists; indeed currently two different
models are being studied, with no clear indication as to which will emerge as
the accepted one. The ISO has taken up the mailbox model proposed by

ECMA in their MIDA service model(3) (often referred to as the P7 protocol), while the CCITT have enhanced the model set out in X.400 with a message store within the message transfer service, and are developing P3+ (an enhanced P3) to provide access to it. The INSEM attitude in the face of this problem is discussed in section 5.

As far as internal communications within a LSU are concerned, the commitment to adoption of international standards still holds. However, since a LSU is under control of a single administrative unit and in terms of the whole domain represents a small portion of the total resources, it may be acceptable to employ some non-standard protocols internally to a LSU.

For communication outside the LSU, adherence to standards is mandatory. Indeed, interworking between LSUs in a multi-vendor environment would be impossible without it. For external communications a LSU must conform to the appropriate standards and to the functional standards, as stated in 3.3 above.

Clearly the mail service proposed for INSEM phase two is technically ambitious, and a large scale development. Since it will not be a special purpose development, but is intended to be built out of stable commercial products, it will require considerable goodwill and effort on the part of the potential suppliers. It is recognised that INSEM cannot expect this to be forthcoming without some effort on its part, and for this reason a policy of cooperation and consultation has been in place for some time now.

It is the intention of INSEM to collaborate with industry in the refinement of specifications for phase two, so that the requirement can be satisfied by commercial products. In order that the products suit the requirement (rather than vice versa), INSEM will provide financial incentive for the development of products which will meet the requirements. This will only be offered for developments which will lead to products which are marketed publicly, so that INSEM services are not supported by unique or prototype packages.

5. Topics for Future Consideration

A number of difficulties must be resolved before the final INSEM service can be launched. These problems lie in both the technical and organisational areas.

Technical problems include the provision of directory services, security aspects, standards for mailbox access, document management services, and operations management services and protocols. In the organisational area the problems of migrating from existing paper based mail, with the attendant problem of gaining user acceptance on a large scale, should not be underestimated.

Directory services have already been touched upon in the discussion of the LSU architecture. Consideration was given to directory services as a user aid. It is clear from the work now being carried out by the CCITT (Study Group VII Question 35) that the role of directory services will be expanded considerably in the future to include such services as authentication. The need for such services, and their eventual integration into the INSEM service, will be questions for consideration in the near future. A set of services which will be provided as user aids has been specified in the procurement policy for phase two. These may be extended in the light of the outcome of the CCITT work.

Security is a major concern in the European Institutions, and in the national administrations with which they interwork. Although the electronic mail services will not be used for the exchange of secret or classified information, the information carried will in many cases be of a sensitive nature, and Member State administrations are unwilling to interwork with a service that provides a lower degree of confidentiality than their own domestic services. Another element to consider is that at a local level users will store information which they may not wish other users to have access to, and hence will require some means of protecting documents in storage. Mechanisms to protect information both in transit and in store will therefore be required before the service will be acceptable to its potential users. This problem is therefore being studied as a matter of urgency within INSEM.

Mailbox service and access protocols are an area of uncertainty at present, as previously mentioned. Two conflicting models are under study by ISO and the CCITT. It is unlikely that this problem will be resolved by the standards bodies in the timescale envisaged for the INSEM project, while clearly there is a need for mailbox service in the INSEM service. In this area it is most likely that work by manufacturers will outstrip the progress made by the standards bodies. The INSEM policy in this area therefore is to await the offerings of potential suppliers, pending the outcome of the standardisation work.

The problem of building document management services into the INSEM service is one that will require considerable study both by INSEM and in the standardisation bodies. The mail service as conceived only moves messages around, whereas the institutions (like most organisations) all have requirements for the treatment of messages after submission by the originator and before reception by the destinee. Actions such as document registration, archiving and filing and the granting of approval for a document to be issued externally are all best integrated with the service which actually transfers the document. However at present this would represent a considerable departure from the models, and so either the mail protocols must be enhanced, or additional protocols above the mail protocols must be developed.

Many of these problems will only be resolved when an operational service is provided and hands-on experience is gained. One major benefit that the project can expect from phase one is the knowledge and experience of operating an actual electronic mail service.

The final technical problem is that of managing a large distributed mail service. Preliminary studies have identified a number of topics which must be addressed, such as distribution of routing tables, collection of statistics, registration of users and control of the components of the service. The next question to be addressed is the definition of the services and protocols necessary to centralise management of the service in a domain control centre.

The organisational questions are closely linked: migration to the new services will only be possible with the cooperation and goodwill of the potential users. This in turn will only be achieved if the service is easy and attractive to use, fulfills the user needs, and offers a noticeably improved service compared to the existing services.

To make the service attractive to the users, two aspects must be considered: presentation and penetration. The presentation of the service to the user, the man machine interface, must be simple to use, and not demand any great level of technical expertise. This can be achieved by well designed menu style interfaces, and is an area that any manufacturer wishing to present a saleable product is likely to consider in detail.

The penetration aspect is a problem for INSEM and the various institutions. Electronic mail is only useful if potential recipients can actually receive messages submitted to the service. This problem can be approached from two directions.

The first and most obvious is to try and provide as many users as possible with direct access to the service. This approach will be followed as far as possible by ensuring that, once service is available, mail software is installed on all LSU equipment.

However, not all mail service users will have access to such equipment in the foreseeable future, and so it must be possible for users to submit messages through the electronic mail to users not equipped to receive them. This can be achieved by providing gateway facilities to existing transmission services such as telex, teletex, facsimile and the hard-copy postal service. This last is clearly an organisational rather than a technical problem to resolve, since at some point in the path of a message human intervention wil be required to complete the delivery of such messages.

Finally, how will the impetus be provided to begin the migration to electronic mail? The most effective lever in the introduction of a new service is the enthusiasm of existing users which infects potential users. To provide the initial spark, INSEM has identified pilot user communities which can be used to demonstrate the benefits of electronic mail. By careful selection of suitable targets, it should be possible to accelerate user acceptance of the service.

6. Conclusions

Clearly the INSEM project represents a major effort by the European Institutions to stimulate progress in the information technology industry. It is an ambitious project, both technically and in terms of scale. The benefits which can be expected from its success are considerable, and encompass a number of aspects.

Firstly the benefits to the institutions themselves will be considerable. Electronic mail should streamline the working and administrative procedures, thus increasing efficiency.

A side effect may be felt by other large administrations and organisations, since the needs of the institutions are shared by any similar organisation. The solutions evolved by the INSEM project should be applicable to other potential consumers of electronic mail.

Finally, the information technology industry is in a position to benefit from the technical and financial stimulus that INSEM can offer. INSEM is prepared to collaborate on a joint venture basis with companies offering potentially suitable products to assist in development. The basis for this collaboration is that funding will be made available for the development of products that are to be marketed on a commercial basis, in addition to the purchases that the institutions may make. The Commission will stimulate favorable market conditions for the acceptance of such products by its pursuit of multi-vendor standardised procurement policies, and by using its influence to encourage other bodies to do likewise.

7. Abbreviations used in this Paper

CCITT	– International Telegraph and Telephone Consultative Committee
CEC	– Commission of the European Communities
CSU	– Central Support Unit
DCN	– Domain Corporate Network
DSA	– Directory Services Agent
ECMA	– European Computer Manufacturers Association
ESPRIT	– European Strategic Project for Research in Information Technology
INSEM	– Interinstitutional Service for Electronic Mail

```
INSIS   - Interinstitutional System for Integrated Services
IPMS    - Inter-Personal Message Service
ISO     - International Organisation for Standardisation
LAN     - Local Area Network
LC      - Local Computer
LCN     - Local Communications Network
LSU     - Local Support Unit
MHS     - Message Handling System
MOTIS   - Message Oriented Text Interchange System
MSA     - Management Service Agent
MTA     - Message Transfer Agent
ODA     - Office Document Architecture
ODIF    - Office Document Interchange Format
OSI     - Open Systems Interconnection
P1      - Message Transfer Protocol
P2      - Inter-Personal Messaging Protocol
P3      - Submission and Delivery Protocol
P5      - Teletex Access Protocol
P7      - Mailbox Access Protocol
TC      - Telecommunications Centre
UA      - User Agent
UAE     - User Agent Entity
X.400   - CCITT Recommendations X.400, 401, 408, 409, 410, 411,
          420
X.430   - CCITT Recommendation X.430
```

ACKNOWLEDGEMENTS

The authors would like to thank the members of the INSEM team for their contributions to the project to date.

REFERENCES

(1) Guidelines for an Informatics Architecture (CEC Document
    IX/E-6(86) S10 1043)

(2) INSEM Project Distributed Electronic Mail Services and
    Operations (CEC Document IX/E/5 D/133)

(3) Distributed Application For Message Interchange (MIDA)
    Mailbox Service and Mailbox Service Access Protocol
    (European Computer Manufacturers Association, November 1985)

OFFICE SYSTEMS: Methods and Tools
G. Bracchi, D. Tsichritzis (Editors)
Elsevier Science Publishers B.V. (North-Holland)
© IFIP, 1987

STORAGE AGENTS IN MESSAGE HANDLING SYSTEMS

Jaime Delgado (1)
Manuel Medina (1)
Berthold Butscher (2)
Michael Tschichholz (2)

(1) E.T.S.I.T. - U.P.C.
Barcelona (Spain)

(2) HMI-Berlin (Bereich D/M)
Berlin (F. R. Germany)

Nowadays, there is an increasingly awareness that a standard about message (or document) storage (or filing & retrieval, or archiving) services should exist in Message Handling Systems (MHS).

In this paper, we try to present some of the more advanced existing proposals that are more or less related to message storage services. Eventually, we show the need for specialized storage agents, and propose some possible solutions.

This paper has been written thanks to the support given by the Spanish government (CAICYT 85-509(2)) and by the Comission of the European Community (COST 11ter, AMIGO).

1. INTRODUCTION

The storage agents that we present here are included in a X.400 - MHS (Message Handling System) |1| / MOTIS (Message Oriented Text Interchange System) |2| framework. The paper begins with a brief review of the X.400 recommendations of the CCITT. These are very similar to the corresponding ISO standard (MOTIS), so we will concentrate on the first one, which is more widely used.

The second section is devoted to the existing partial solutions to the storage problem, and its advantages and drawbacks are discussed.

The first use of storage in standards is related to the personal computers (PC's) access to MHS. Due to the special features of these computers, a temporary storage for incoming messages to the PC users is needed. This kind of storage is usually achieved by a Message Store (MS). The first two parts of section 3 deal with two approaches to these message stores. We conclude that the MS cannot perform the desired task on its own, so that a storage agent endowed with capabilities similar to those of database management systems is needed. At the end of the section, we describe a proposal for a storage agent (SA) that treats the SA like an Interpersonal User Agent (IP-UA) with an extension of the P2 protocol (these two terms, IP-UA and P2, are explained in section 2). Some limitations and possible improvements are then discussed.

In section 4, we list the needed features for the SA that we are looking for, and develop several feasible solutions that could carry out those features and fit in a MHS framework.

Finally, some conclusions are drawn.

To sum up, the paper has four sections, apart from this introduction (section 1), devoted to the framework (section 2), the existing partial solutions (section 3), the proposed solutions (section 4) and the conclusions (section 5).

2. FRAMEWORK: X.400 RECOMMENDATIONS

The X.400 recommendations |1| of the CCITT define a model and several protocols for a Message Handling System (MHS).

In the model, the MHS is composed of User Agents (UA's) and the Message Transfer System (MTS). The later comprises one or more Message Transfer Agents (MTA's). The human users interact with a UA in order to send messages to another UA. The transfer of messages is done through the MTS.

From a layered point of view, two sublayers in the application layer of the Open System Interconexion Reference Model of ISO |3| are defined. The upper sublayer holds the UA entities, so it is known as UA layer (or sublayer). The other sublayer, Message Transfer (MT) layer, contains the MTA entities.

There is another entity in the MT layer, called Submission and Delivery Entity (SDE). The SDE is necessary when a system has only UA functions, and has not MTA functions. In this case, the SDE provides the UA with the access to the remote MTA services.

The peer protocols needed to interconnect the named entities are:

- Message Transfer Protocol (P1): it defines |8|, basically, the transfer of messages between MTA's.
- Interpersonal Messaging Protocol (P2): it is the protocol that defines |11| the structure of one kind of data units, called Interpersonal messages,

transferred between UA's. These UA's are called Interpersonal UA (IP-UA).
- Submission and Delivery Protocol (P3): it defines |8| the access from a UA
entity to MT layer services. Actually, it is a peer protocol between a SDE and
a MTA entity.

Because the MHS defined by the X.400 recommendations is devoted to
Interpersonal messages, sometimes it will be referred as Interpersonal
Messaging System (IPMS).

Figure 1 illustrates the sketched concepts.

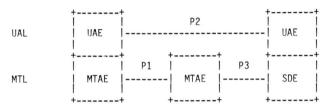

FIGURE 1: Layered description of the Interpersonal Messaging System.
List of acronyms:
- UAE: User Agent Entity.
- UAL: User Agent Layer.
- MTAE: Message Transfer Agent Entity.
- SDE: Submission and Delivery Entity.
- MTL: Message Transfer Layer.
- P2: Interpersonal Messaging Protocol.
- P1: Message Transfer Protocol.
- P3: Submission and Delivery Protocol.

3. EXISTING PARTIAL SOLUTIONS

3.1. Mailbox Service Access Protocol (P7)

3.1.1. Overview

This protocol proposed by ECMA (European Computer Manufacturers Association) is
based on the Client-Server model, and is known as "P7" (|4| or |5|). In this
way, the user agent (UA) function is distributed between a Mailbox Server
Entity (MBSE) and a Mailbox Client Entity (MBCE). The corresponding model can
be represented as in figure 2 (*).

This model allows a PC (having the MBCE) to access to a remote Message Transfer
Agent (MTA) in a host computer (having the MBSE over the MTA Entity).

The definition of this protocol needs a Message Store (MS) in the MBSE to store
the messages delivered by the MTA. All messages going to the distributed UA,
implemented with a P7 protocol, will be stored in that MS. Due to this
circumstance, the MBCE does not need much storage requirements, and does not
have to worry all the time about its messages. These will be received by the

----

* The final version of the P7 protocol is expected by the end of 1986.
Actually, every new version has important modifications with respect to the
previous one. Anyway, although some issues can become obsolete in few months,
we have based our work on the third draft |4|.

user through a Mailbox Client Agent (MBCA), at his/her request. Each message
will stay in the MS until being deleted by the user.

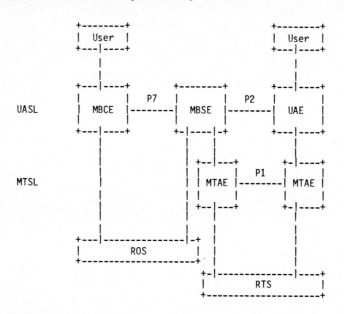

FIGURE 2: Mailbox Service Access Layered Model.
List of acronyms:
- MBCE: Mailbox Client Entity.
- MBSE: Mailbox Server Entity.
- UAE: User Agent Entity.
- UASL: User Agent Sublayer.
- MTAE: Message Transfer Agent Entity.
- MTSL: Message Transfer Sublayer.
- ROS: Remote Operation Service.
- RTS: Reliable Transfer Service.
- P7: Mailbox Service Access Protocol.
- P2: Interpersonal Messaging Protocol.
- P1: Message Transfer Protocol.

Thus, from a Mailbox Client (MBC) point of view, the Mailbox Service Access
Protocol provides the following:

- Message Transfer and User Agent services, as for a usual Interpersonal UA
(IP-UA).
- Storage for delivered messages.
- Retrieval facilities on the MS.

The access protocol (standard way for clients to gain access to a service
agent) is defined in terms of the Remote Operations macro (|6| or |7|).

The third P7 draft allows for the concept of a multi-user mailbox (in the
server system): a unique and singular UA that allows multiple (and
simultaneous) access. However, every mailbox (MBSA) has a unique owner that
permits other subsidiary authorized users (MBCA's) to access to its mailbox.
This implies the need of an access control list for the mailbox.

To manage the MS (mail storage, of incoming messages, notifications and reports, in the Mailbox Server Agent (MBSA)) there are facilities to:

- "Fetch" messages from the MS to the MBCA.
- "List" the messages in the MS.
- "Forward" messages from the MS to other UA's.
- "Delete" messages stored in the MS.

The IP-UA facility to "submit" messages to the Message Transfer (MT) sublayer is transparent to the MBCE: the user may "dispatch" messages to the MBSE.

Other facilities of the MBSA are:

- "Register" capabilities at the MTA and at the MBS (user agent information).
- "Mail Log": it is an optional facility that provides the user with simple information about both the sent and received messages.
- Other "logs": Autocorrelation Log and Action Log.

The P7 uses a special terminology, as we do, in order to avoid confusion when talking about message interchange between MBC, MBS, UA sublayer and MT sublayer (see figure 3):

Terms related to the Mailbox are:

- "Dispatch": from a client entity (MBCE) to a mailbox (MBSE).
- "Fetch": from a mailbox (MBSE) to a client.

Terms related to the MT system are

- "Submit": from a UA sublayer entity to a MTA (going to other UA sublayer entities).
- "Deliver": from a MTA to a UA sublayer entity (UA or MBSE).

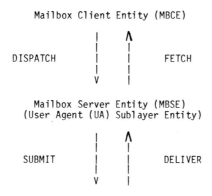

Mailbox Client Entity (MBCE)

DISPATCH   FETCH

Mailbox Server Entity (MBSE)
(User Agent (UA) Sublayer Entity)

SUBMIT   DELIVER

Message Transfer Agent Entity (MTAE)

FIGURE 3: P7 terminology.

3.1.2. Storage related topics

As we mentioned before, the main storage related topic is the message storage function. Moreover, the two mail logs (Inlog and Outlog) are also interesting.

The P7 protocol MS is actually intended to give a temporary storage for incoming messages. It is not properly a message database management system (DBMS) where we are able, for example, to make a search (based on some attribute values) of a message, a part of a message, or a set of messages.

Usually, the objects handled by the Message Store (MS) are P2 messages, reports or notifications. These objects contain a MS-Envelope (general MS and delivery/notification information) and, frequently, the usual IP-Messaging objects |11|.

The Message Storage service elements (closely related to the facilities mentioned in section 3.1.1) are:

- Request message store state: it indicates the number of messages held in the MS, grouped in several classes.
- List MS messages: selection is possible on some MS-Envelope fields.
- Fetch MS message: it presents a complete message or a bodypart.
- Forward user message: a new user message, which in turn can be composed of other messages in the MS, is submitted.
- Delete MS message: the message is specified with its MS number.

The Mail Log objects contain selected information about the messages delivered to the MBSE (stored in the MS), Inlog, and dispatched by the user, Outlog.

The Mail Log service elements, one for each Mail Log, are:

- Request Mail Log state: it indicates the current MS-Sequence Number (see next section).
- List Mail Log entries: the selection is on a range of entry numbers.
- Delete Mail Log entries: a sequence of adjacent entries is deleted.

3.1.2.1 Storage objects

Message Store:

The general structure of the objects handled by the MS has been shown above. Apart from the complete message (or not complete if there is information in the last field explained below), the MS objects contain the MS-Envelope that is composed of:

- MS-Sequence Number.
- Mailbox-message type: all possible (P2 user message, UA report, probe, non-P2 message and notification) except Probe.
- MS-Status: information about the operations performed by the user on that message. The feasible states of a message are "listed", "not listed" and "processed". This last state means, in general, that the message has been either completely fetched or autoforwarded.
- Fetched status: bodyparts which have not yet been fetched.
- Delivery/Notification information: this field, when filled, has information about the message. It contains the parameters from the MT-Deliver or MT-Notify service primitives.

Mail Inlog:

These objects comprise:

- The MS-Envelope of the stored message, except the last field. There is an additional value for the MS-Status field, namely, "deleted".
- Delivery information depending on the message type.

Mail Outlog:

These objects comprise:

- Dispatch sequence number.
- Mailbox-message type: one of five possible.
- Submission information depending on the message type.

3.1.2.2. Limitations of P7 storage operations

As it was explained before, the only storage related operations allowed on the MS are:

- List: very limited.
- Fetch: without search query.
- Delete: only on message numbers.

Therefore, the message store is not a real DBMS, because it has not query facilities, and, in addition, we cannot have data structures and relations between messages (apart from the very limited relations supplied by the Autocorrelation Log).

Furthermore, it is not possible to store the sent messages (or waiting to be sent). We have only a Mail Outlog option.

Moreover, we could note the lack of other convenient features (see 4.2).

3.2. Enhanced "Submission and Delivery" X.400 protocol (P3+)

3.2.1. Overview

With the current X.400 recommendations |1|, the only way for a personal computer (PC) to access to a MHS, apart from working like a remote terminal, is by implementing the P3 protocol |8|. But this has several problems that have been studied by a CCITT special group |9|.

First of all, they studied the shortcomings of P3. Those more related with message storage and PC's are:

- Much storage requirements.
- Poor control of message flow between a MTA and a Submission and Delivery Entity (SDE).
- Problems with mobile users.
- Message redirection not possible within the message system.
- No distinction whether non-delivery is caused by the use of the "Hold For Delivery" service element, or other reasons.

One of the proposed solutions was to add functionality to the Message Transfer Layer while leaving the UA Layer unchanged. This new model is very similar to the CCITT model |10| because there are no new functional entities. The only difference is the addition of a message store for delivered messages in the MTA Entity (MTAE), and the substitution of the P3 protocol by the P3+ protocol.

The P3+ protocol is the P3 protocol enhanced with the following service elements:

- Hold for Delivery: this solution enables the UA to "list" and "select" messages awaiting to be delivered.
- Non-delivery Notification: this solution allows the MTS to indicate to the originator that delivery was prevented by exercise of the "Hold for Delivery" service element.

3.2.2. Message Store

In this model the Message Store (MS) is in the MTAE, but its database capabilities are very similar to those of the P7 model.

It is necessary to add (to the P3 protocol) the following operations on the MS:
- List.
- Select.
- Delete.

One restriction of this MS against the P7 MS is that we have not P2 heading information |11|, only P1 envelope information |8|. Remember that in the P7 model the MS is in the UA layer. Here, it is in the MT layer.

The conclusion is again that a MS is not a real DBMS, as we are looking for. Almost all things commented when talking about the P7 message store are also true for the P3+ message store.

3.3. Storage Agents (SA) using P2+

In this section, we are not talking yet about message stores, but more properly about storage agents (SA's), that are intended to store (for long term and multiuser) messages in a way closer to a real DBMS.

We saw the limited capabilities of MS's in P7 and P3+. The following SA's are one more step towards our goal: a real message (or document) database service, a SA with real DBMS capabilities, and compatible with the current MHS standards.

3.3.1. Document Storage and Retrieval proposal

This proposal (|12| or |13|) is based on the idea of specialized storage agents accessed by an IP-UA with a P2+ protocol (an extension of the current X.400 P2 protocol |11|), or by special storage user agents (SUA's), all within the framework of the X.400/MOTIS recommendations.

In this model, the messages can be stored in these SA's, that are actually IP-Message stores. Moreover, these message stores could mainly act as a tool for message distribution between MHS users (group communication). Messages are sent to the IP-Message store in the same way that they are sent to another IP-UA.

Figure 4 represents this model.

The SA's are able to handle additional data structures such as:

- Relations between messages (message-message).
- Sets: relations between messages and an O/R (Originator/Recipient) name that identifies the set. Each element of a set has a link (type of message-O/R name relation) and a sequence number, apart from the message.

The operations that can be performed on these SA's are (the terminology conforms to the original proposal):

- Store (user --> store): it is similar to the Deliver X.411 operation.
- Search (user --> store): the search query can be composed of O/R name-message relations, message-message relations, calendar date attributes, and textual attributes (even text within the message).
- Retrieve (store --> user): the store gives the user a list of message identifiers, or a reference to a set, in response to a search operation.
- Get (user --> store): the user requests messages (usually those found by a search operation).

- Delivery (store --> user): the store sends to the user the messages requested. It is equivalent to the X.411 Submit.

A combined search & get operation is also proposed.

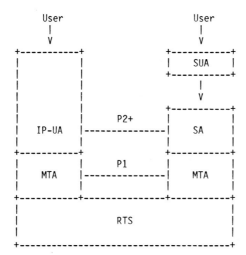

FIGURE 4: Specialized Storage Agent with P2+ protocol.
List of acronyms:
- SUA: Storage User Agent.
- SA: Storage Agent.
- IP-UA: Interpersonal User Agent.
- MTA: Message Transfer Agent.
- RTS: Reliable Transfer Service.
- P2+: Extension of the Interpersonal Messaging Protocol.
- P1: Message Transfer Protocol.

The P2 protocol extensions proposed in order to get the so-called P2+ protocol are:

- Make the IP-Message identifier globally unique.
- Allow relations between messages at the innermost level of a multipart message, as in |14|.
- Add several new message-message and message-O/R name relations as fields for the P2 heading.
- Partial IP-Messages: new field(s) are needed in the IP-Message heading.

With the above suggested modifications, this model does not need the change of the P1 and P3 protocols.

The database access related operations are encoded into the P2+ information.

3.3.2. Limitations and possible extensions

From a message DBMS point of view, this model has some limitations. The following is a list of restrictions and proposed improvements that are not or cannot be achieved with this model. We must remember that one of our goals is to obtain a storage agent with as many general message DBMS capabilities as possible.

Restrictions on sets (the sets handled by this proposal are very useful for group communication (computer conferences, e.g.), but not for general storage & retrieval):

- Only one set (with its O/R name and sequence number series) for all kind of links to an O/R name.
- Links may only be on message-O/R name relations, not on message-message relations.
- Relations between sets are left to the directory system.

Therefore, a possible improvement on sets could be to permit links between messages, and, furthermore, a compound link facility (creation of links with expressions and value relations).

One possible improvement on operations could be a better search query with the enhancement of search based on textual attributes, and the use of fields filled by the storage system, being these new fields (for time store and other storage controls) also an enhancement.

Other improvements could be the addition of new operations like:

- Create sets from queries: facility for the construction of a set with messages found from a query on the message database.
- Modify a document: this implies the creation of a new document with or without the deletion of the old version.

The basic operations "create set" and "delete message" are not mentioned in the proposal, but we assume that they may be implemented.

With the added features, this kind of store could be useful as a group storage as well as a personal storage.

4. PROPOSED STORAGE AGENTS

4.1. Summary of existing proposals

We have studied three kinds of message stores. The first two are related to their corresponding protocols (P7 and P3+), and their functions are mainly devoted to provide temporary storage for delivered messages. Both MS's are very similar. They show some restrictions, already noted.

The last proposal is slightly different. It is also related to a specific protocol (P2+), but in a very different way: the protocol is necessary to implement the storage. In the two former models, it was the other way round. In this later proposal, the message store function is intended for long term storage, and it has some general database capabilities. It also allows the user to store and retrieve messages by means of his/her IP-UA, because the store is a special SA, with the P2+ protocol, that can act as an IP-UA.

4.2. Required features

In the following, we list some of the features that a general SA with DBMS-like capabilities and within the X.400/MOTIS framework needs. The required features for our proposed SA can be grouped into three classes:

Database functions:

- Retrieval with a search based on partial or full attribute values (and text content), and any combination of them. Also search by browsing and tree structured menus (as ISO recommends in |15|) could be convenient.

- Selection of retrieved data: field(s) or part of field(s).
- Document access control.
- Data structures: all kind of data structures based on relations between message (or document) attributes should be available. Also would be convenient to add fields to the message definition in the store.
- User control of the stored data: operations like "add" (or "store"), "modify" (with its consequences), and "delete" are needed.
- Management operations: creation of data structures, creation and modification of the sequence of a list of documents (sorting), facilities for linking or merging files of documents (the last two are ISO recommendations |15| that can be implemented from a logical point of view, not physical), etc.

IP-Messaging functions:

- Knowledge of the X.400/MOTIS semantics.
- Database access through the Message Transfer System (MTS), and/or directly.
- Multiuser access capabilities with access control.
- Archiving of all messages sent and received.

Other functions:

- Possibility of access to the MTS from a PC.

4.3. Proposed models

In the following, we present four possible models for SA's with all or some of the above mentioned features. The general idea is that we do not want a message store as in P7 or P3+, but a general message DBMS within a X.400/MOTIS MHS framework. Nevertheless, since we also try to let a PC access to that storage agent, we will not discard the simple message store as a temporary store for delivered messages (P7 and P3+).

Model 1 is basically the model already mentioned in 3.3.2, where we extended the P2+ solution.

In the second model, the storage system is independent of the Message Handling System (MHS) in a similar way as the directory system is |17|.

The solution of model 3 consists in the improvement of the P7 protocol in order to get a message store with better capabilities, close to those described in section 4.2.

Model 4 would be the result of mixing some of the features of the so-called models 1 and 2.

4.3.1. Model 1

In this proposal, the operations and capabilities of the SA's are those proposed in 3.3.1 (P2+ solution) with the improvements noted in 3.3.2. In this way, and adding the features discussed in 4.2 not yet incorporated to the SA, we can get a real message DBMS.

This can be possible if we structure the message store as a relational message database, using for example the SQL standard, like in |16|. Not all the improvements made on the message store need a corresponding improvement in the P2 protocol, because there is a lot of information managed by the SA that does not need to be transmitted, and the operations on the database can be encoded as P2+ messages.

In order to allow a PC to access to a SA of this kind, this model could be modified as in figure 5. In this new model, a PC with the P7 protocol (enhanced to be compatible with the P2+ protocol) can access to a SA. It could also be possible the use of the P3+ protocol instead of the P7 one. Nevertheless, the reasons explained in 3.2.2 lead us to choose P7 in front of P3+.

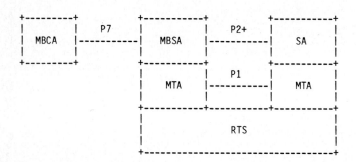

FIGURE 5: Proposed Model 1 (P2+ Model extension).

List of acronyms:
- MBCA: Mailbox Client Agent.
- MBSA: Mailbox Server Agent.
- SA: Storage Agent.
- MTA: Message Transfer Agent.
- RTS: Reliable Transfer Service.
- P2+: Extension of the Interpersonal Messaging Protocol.
- P1: Message Transfer Protocol.

If we want to access to the SA from a Mailbox Client (MBC) Agent, the P7 protocol must be improved to allow the sending and receiving of the added database operations and results. Our goal is to access to the SA as we were in a usual IP-UA.

The Message Store (MS) of the Mailbox Server (MBS) entity is used only to store messages before actual delivery. The real storage of messages is in the SA, that acts as a personal store. After complete "fetching", the messages can be forwarded automatically to the SA and deleted from the MS. Thus, the MS is a small temporary storage, and the actual operations on the message archive are on the SA (message DBMS). The messages sent by the user of the MBC should also be submitted to the personal store (the SA).

Another possibility is to automatically send to the SA all the messages received by the MBS (replication of stored messages).

For any of the above solutions, it is necessary to improve the P7 protocol (as the P2 protocol) in order to be able to submit (automatically or not) all the messages fetched and dispatched by the MBC.

4.3.2. Model 2

In this model, the storage system is independent of the MHS in a similar way as the directory system is |17|. The relation to the MHS can be made, for example, as in |18| (or |19|). We will discuss below this relationship. Figure 6 outlines its general representation.

The idea is that there are two kinds of storage entities (SE's):

- The storage system agent (SSA): it stores physically the documents and is responsible for doing the transfer of documents from one SSA to another.

- The storage user agent (SUA): it is responsible for accessing to the SSA in order to store and retrieve messages. The user (person or another entity) needs a SUA to gain access to the storage system.

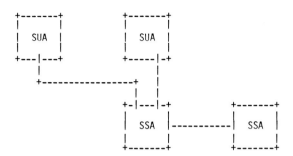

FIGURE 6: Proposed Model 2 (general).
List of acronyms:
- SUA: Storage User Agent.
- SSA: Storage System Agent.

These SE's are, in principle, independent of the Message Handling System (MHS) defined by the CCITT |1|. When a MHS entity has to use a storage service, it needs a SUA to access to it. Thus, an IP-UA will need a SUA embedded in it to store and retrieve messages.

The SSA will have all the required features mentioned in 4.2, that can be achieved by structuring the store as a powerful relational database (to obtain the desired DBMS facilities) and by defining the appropiate protocols. We have not the restrictions imposed by a previous protocol like P2.

Thus, there is a need for a new protocol between storage system agents, and another one between a SUA and a SSA. The direct SUA-SSA protocol could be heavily interactive (without using the Message Transfer System (MTS)), with its advantages.

This model 2 is useful for group and personal stores.

We can extend this model by distributing the UA entity, as we made before, between a Mailbox Client Agent (MBCA) and a Mailbox Server Agent (MBSA). Now, thinking in a personal storage, the problem is the relation between the Message Store (MS) of the MBSA and the message database (real DBMS) of the SSA, because the MTS and the storage system are independent. A solution is to allow the IP-Messaging system to use the storage system through SUA's embedded in its entities.

One feasible solution would be to add a SUA to the MBSA. This is represented in figure 7.

With this model, all incoming messages (to the MBSA) can be sent to the corresponding SSA through the SUA of the MBSA. This operation could be done once the messages have been processed by the MBSA (or once they have arrived at the MBSA). The SSA that stores the messages is a personal store for the client of the MBSA. All outcoming messages (from the MBCA) can also be sent to the SSA through the MBSA/SUA (or even through the MBCA/SUA). To do the above operations, it is necessary to improve the P7 protocol.

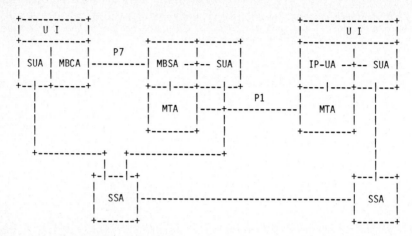

FIGURE 7: Proposed Model 2 (detailed).

List of acronyms:
- U I: User Interface.
- MBCA: Mailbox Client Agent.
- MBSA: Mailbox Server Agent.

- SUA: Storage User Agent.
- SSA: Storage System Agent.
- IP-UA: Interpersonal User Agent.
- MTA: Message Transfer Agent.
- P7: Mailbox Service Access Protocol.
- P1: Message Transfer Protocol.

Furthermore, the MBCA and one SUA are in the same UA entity (they have the same user interface) to provide the user with both IP-Messaging and storage capabilities. For example, the SUA would permit the user to access directly to his/her personal storage.

4.3.3. Model 3

This solution consists in the improvement of the P7 protocol in order to get a message store with better capabilities, close to those described in 4.2.

It is possible to add functions to the Message Store of the Mailbox Server Entity by mixing the delivered message store with a general personal store. These functions should be the DBMS-like features that we mentioned above. The problem is that this store will not be a storage agent, but rather a message database more or less local to the mailbox owner. It will not be, in principle, a real multiuser store. However, if we only want a personal storage, this model could be made correct by adding facilities, for example, to store the messages sent by the Mailbox Client Entity.

If we want to enhance the P7 model so that it becomes a multiuser store, it will be necessary to modify the information stored in the Message Store (by adding some extra fields, for example) in order to mantain different information for every mailbox user.

Nevertheless, there are many problems and restrictions (e.g., P2 access to the database) to try to improve the P7 protocol in this way.

However, all the above considerations are referred to the third draft of the P7 protocol (see 3.1.1). New incoming versions, with significant improvements, could lead us to reconsider this model 3.

4.3.4. Model 4

The last model would be the result of mixing some of the features of the so-called models 1 and 2.

It is possible to think of an independent storage system (with Storage User Agents (SUA's) and Storage System Agents (SSA's), as in 4.3.2), but with SSA's that could be seen as Interpersonal User Agents (IP-UA's). That is to say, some physical stores could act either as SSA's, therefore being accessed by a SUA through an interactive protocol, or as SA's handled as IP-UA's, being accessed through a P2++ protocol (to be explained later). Furthermore, it is necessary an independent communication between SSA's.

This model has the following basic entities:

- User Agent (UA), Submission and Delivery Entity (SDE) and Message Transfer Agent (MTA) as defined by the CCITT in |1|.
- SUA (as explained in 4.3.2).
- SSA (as explained in 4.3.2).
- Double functionality SSA/IP-UA: this entity is a SSA that can be accessed from IP-UA entities, looking like an IP-UA for the accessing entities.

The following protocols are used by this model:

- Message Transfer Protocol (P1), Submission and Delivery Protocol (P3) (when needed), as defined in |8|.
- Interpersonal Messaging Protocol (P2), as defined in |11|.
- Direct and interactive SUA-SSA protocol: Storage Access Protocol (SAP), to be defined.
- SSA-SSA protocol: Storage System Protocol (SSP), to be defined.
- P2++: it is a SUA-SSA protocol (not interactive) embedded in a virtual P2 protocol. We must note that this protocol is in principle different from the P2+ protocol discussed in section 3.3.1. However, both protocols could be very similar, even the same, because this model 4 is partly based on model 1, that makes use of an extension of that P2+ protocol.

We need to define the storage access and storage system protocols. This definition could be based on existing protocols, like P1.

An IP-UA can access to a SSA in two different ways:

- P2++ protocol (through the MTS), if the SSA has this functionality. It is the easiest way.
- Directly from an associated SUA, if the IP-UA has this element and the SSA has the corresponding functionality. It is the fastest way.

Figure 8 shows a possible scheme of the model.

This last model is useful for personal and group storages, and some further extensions (as in former proposed models) are possible.

Making the necessary changes, we will achieve, with this model, almost all the required features described in 4.2.

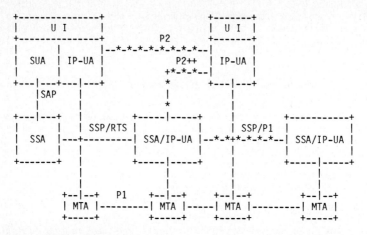

FIGURE 8: Proposed Model 4.

List of acronyms and symbols:
- U I: User Interface (Both U I are not necessarily the same).
- IP-UA: Interpersonal User Agent.
- MTA: Message Transfer Agent.
- RTS: Reliable Transfer Service.
- P1: Message Transfer Protocol.
- P2: Interpersonal Messaging Protocol.
- P2++: Extension of the Interpersonal Messaging Protocol.
- SUA: Storage User Agent.
- SSA: Storage System Agent.
- SAP: Storage Access Protocol.
- SSP: Storage System Protocol (directly over RTS (SSP/RTS), or using the P1 protocol (SSP/P1)).
- "|": Either local service or interactive protocol.
- "--*-*--": Virtual protocol (it uses other application protocols).
- "-------": Direct protocol.

5. CONCLUSIONS

We have analysed the different existing architectures and features of storage agents for MHS. In the last section, four possible alternatives have been proposed.

The goal is to obtain a general storage system architecture with the requirements defined in 4.2. The existing models discussed have helped us to know some feasible message storage structures with its problems and limitations. The four proposed models are based on them and on other standards related to the topic.

If we have to choose one model, we would prefer the so-called model 4, because it has many of the advantages of the previous models, actually being a mixture of them. Nevertheless, the first three models could also be useful.

We hope that these proposals could be introduced into the work on storage agents in message handling systems of the international standardization bodies.

REFERENCES

|1| Recommendations X.400, X.401, X.408, X.409, X.410, X.411, X.420, X.430, "Message Handling Systems", CCITT Study Group VII, Report R 38 and R 39, Torremolinos (Spain), 1984.

|2| ISO/TC97/SC18/WG4 N299, "MOTIS: Functional description and service specification for MOTIS", August 1985.

|3| ISO 7498, "Information Processing Systems. Open Systems Interconnection. Basic Reference Model", 1979.

|4| ECMA/TC32-TG5/85/59: "Distributed Application for Message Interchange (MIDA) Mailbox Service and Mailbox Service Access Protocol" (third Draft), November 1985.

|5| ISO/TC97/SC18/WG4 N319: "ECMA Mailbox Service Standard" (|4| is the same document), January 1986.

|6| ECMA-TR/31: "Remote Operations: Concepts, Notation and Connection-oriented Mappings", 1985.

|7| CCITT Recommendation X.410, "Remote operations and reliable transfer server", CCITT Study Group VII, Report R 38, Torremolinos (Spain) , 1984.

|8| CCITT Recommendation X.411, "Message transfer layer Elements", CCITT Study Group VII, Report R 39, Torremolinos (Spain), 1984.

|9| CCITT, X.400-Series Working Document, "CCITT Special Rapporteur's Group on Message Handling Systems" (Question 33/VII), September 1985.

|10| CCITT Recommendation X.400, "System Model - Service Elements", CCITT Study Group VII, Report R 38, Torremolinos (Spain), 1984.

|11| CCITT Recommendation X.420, "Interpersonal messaging user agent layer", CCITT Study Group VII, Report R 39, Torremolinos (Spain), 1984.

|12| Palme, J., "Amigo: Document storage and retrieval", AMIGO working document, November 1985.

|13| ISO/TC97/SC18/WG4 N316: It is the same document as |12|.

|14| Babatz, R. and Bogen, T., "Referable Documents: Semantic Relations in Message Handling Systems", GMD Draft, May 1985.

|15| ISO/TC97/SC18 N578: "Text and Office Systems Standards Development Relating to Filing and Retrieval: WG 1 Review of Progress and Direction", September 1985.

|16| Delgado, J. et al., "Use of SQL for Message Storage and Retrieval", AMIGO working document, April 1986.

|17| CCITT STUDY GROUP VII, Directory Systems (035/VII), (Version 2) "Draft Recommendation X.ds1 -- X.ds7", January 1986.

|18| Medina M. and Maude T., "An Extended X.400 Architectural Model", AMIGO working document, December 1985.

|19| ISO/TC97/SC18/WG4 N328: It is the same document as |18|.

OFFICE SYSTEMS: Methods and Tools
G. Bracchi, D. Tsichritzis (Editors)
Elsevier Science Publishers B.V. (North-Holland)
© IFIP, 1987

MAIN MEMORY DATABASE SUPPORT

FOR OFFICE SYSTEMS: A PERFORMANCE STUDY

Dina Bitton

Carolyn Turbyfill

ABSTRACT: The availability of larger and inexpensive memories may provide the technology required to answer the needs of modern office systems. In this paper, we present a performance study of a prototype **M**ain **M**emory **D**atabase **S**ystem (**MMDBS**) that is the foundation of the interactive office system **O**ffice-**B**y-Example, OBE. The design of OBE exploits a fast CPU and a large amount of physical memory to simplify the use of the system, while supporting the functions of a comprehensive office system. While the cost of query processing in traditional database systems is measured in terms of disk accesses, we measure the performance of OBE in terms of real and virtual memory requirements, CPU utilization and response time. Based on this case study, we evaluate general design tradeoffs for MMDBS's.

1. INTRODUCTION

The demand for fast response time and the availability of larger and inexpensive memories are motivating office system designers to consider Main Memory Database Systems (**MMDBS**) as a viable alternative to conventional Disk Database Systems (**DDBS**). MMDBS's map the database to main memory, and query processing algorithms are designed under the assumption that all necessary data is in the user's address space. One of the first operational MMDBS prototypes is implemented in the **OBE** (Office-By-Example) system developed at IBM Watson Research Center. OBE is an integrated office system that attempts to mimic manual procedures of business and office systems [Zl82, AHK85, WAB86]. It provides a unified two-dimensional interface for word processing,

Authors' address: Department of Computer Science, Cornell University Ithaca, NY 14853. This research was partially supported by the National Science Foundation under grant DCR-8410889.

data processing, report writing, graphics and electronic mail. A major design goal was to provide a powerful interface that would be easy for nonprogrammers to learn and use. The core of the OBE prototype is a relational MMDBS that exploits the memory residence assumption in its approach to database physical design, query processing algorithms and query optimization.

Database systems that require fast response times and systems on workstations are good candidates for implementation as MMDBS's. The cost of acquiring large memories for a MMDBS can be justified when disk accesses, averaging 30 milliseconds per block I/O, impose unacceptable delays on response time. For instance, meeting user expectations of response time in interactive information systems may require a MMDBS. Office workstations involve a lower range of cost and performance where MMDBS's may become a viable alternative. In workstations, the ratio of main memory to disk capacity is typically 1:10, as opposed to at least 1:100 in mainframes. As the ratio of main memory to disk capacity decreases, the advantage of storing the database on disk diminishes. Furthermore, frequent accesses to slow disk storage incur delays unacceptable to the interactive user, who expects a database system to respond as quickly as an editor [AHK85].

A number of recent studies investigate the implication of memory residency on the design of databases and database management systems [Ki83, KM84, DKO84, AHK85, Sh85, Ya85, LC85, Gr85]. In the performance evaluation of MMDBS's, many of the techniques previously used with DDBS's [BDT83, BT84, BT85, BCH84, BD84] are inadequate because certain performance parameters are specifically related to the main memory residence assumption. In particular, space requirements, in the form of virtual and real memory, and memory management, by the operating system and the database system, are critical parameters in the design of a MMDBS benchmark. MMDBS's must pay careful attention to keeping both the code and the data storage structures compact. Thus, in the design and analysis of a MMDBS benchmark, we contend that performance must be evaluated both in terms of memory requirements and query response time.

The remainder of this paper is organized as follows. In Section 2, we present an overview of OBE, describe the hardware and software configurations of the two IBM systems on which we benchmarked OBE, an IBM 3081 and an IBM 4341. In addition, we describe our benchmarking methodology which is targeted to an interactive office environment. In Sections 3 through 5, we describe and analyze our experiments. In Section 3, we establish that a general CPU metric such as the MIPS rate is a good predictor of the relative performance of a MMDBS on different machines. In

Section 4, we present our measurements of response time and memory requirements for a set of retrieval and update test queries. In Section 5, we present a controlled paging experiment that quantifies the degradation of MMDBS performance when the memory residence assumption is violated. Finally, in Section 6, we conclude by discussing the implications of our results on design and implementation decisions for MMDBS's and office systems.

2. DESCRIPTION OF THE SYSTEM

The OBE prototype was designed for an IBM 370 machine running VM/CMS operating system. In this section, we describe our test environment and give an overview of physical database design and query processing in OBE.

2.1. Hardware and Operating System

We performed our measurements on two machines. The first was an IBM 3081, with 16 megabytes of main memory, running under VM Operating System Release HPO 3.2. The second was an IBM 4341, with 16 megabytes of main memory, running under VM Operating System Release 3.[1] Under VM, each user is given a virtual machine configured with a certain amount of virtual storage and virtual I/O devices. Typically, OBE runs in a virtual machine with 4 to 16 megabytes of virtual storage, depending on the size of the database. Paging is on demand; only referenced pages are kept in real storage.

The VM **INDICATE** command [IBM83, Po85] displays the utilization of and contention for major system resources. A variant, the **INDICATE USER** command, can be used before and after a program's execution to get summary information about resource usage of a single virtual machine. **Vtime**, obtained from the **INDICATE USER** command, is a measure of the CPU time charged to a user's virtual machine. In particular, **vtime** excludes the CPU time incurred when the operating system performs paging and I/O for the virtual machine. In a preliminary experiment [BT86], we found that the **vtime** for a program on a moderately loaded system was always within 4% on the standalone elapsed time for the same program, when the program, run standalone on a machine, required no paging or I/O. In this paper, the measure **CPUtime** is the average **vtime** for a query on a moderately loaded system. Elapsed times, to the accuracy of 13 microseconds, were measured by accessing the TOD clock [IBM83].

---

[1] The 4341 is roughly 6-7 times slower than the 3081. The use of the 4341 led to slower execution of OBE queries, which might be more realistic for an office workstation.

2.2. The Database System in OBE

Detailed descriptions of the design and implementation of OBE can be found in [Zl82, AHK84, Wh85, WAB86]. In this section, we present an overview of the components that are relevant to our performance study: the target environment and the user interface, the physical database design and the access methods.

A pivotal assumption in the design of the OBE prototype was that it would be targeted to an environment where an unsophisticated user would create new database tables and formulate ad-hoc queries with ease. It was assumed that the user would expect response times similar to those of other interactive programs such as editors. The emphasis in the design was on ease of use and simple database design. Performance would be achieved by: 1) Keeping the data in main memory during query processing. 2) Automatically inverting every relation on every attribute.[2]

OBE has kept the QBE [Zl75, Zl82, KMZ83] two-dimensional interface, which is an attractive implementation of the relational domain calculus. The underlying query language is relationally complete and the syntax is very simple. It is based on making entries in skeleton tables instead of writing lengthy declarations and queries. The main steps in writing a select-project query are shown in Figure 1. Using a screen editor and pre-programmed function keys, the user may display skeleton tables (Figure 1.a), relation templates containing a relation name and attribute names (Figure 1.c), and a condition box where complex selection and join conditions are specified (Figure 1.d). By positioning the cursor and using a function key, attributes that are not relevant to the current query can be erased. Table entries may consist of commands, **example elements**, literals or simple qualifiers: "P." for Print, "_X" for **example element** "X", "10" for the literal value 10, and "< 10" for a qualifier.

2.2.1. Database organization and data structures

In OBE, physical database design is automatically done by the system. All relations have the same inverted structure. The user only specifies the logical design including the option of declaring a key. There are three basic data structures that we found to have significant impact on the performance of the system: **relation area**, **TD area**, and **pointer area**. These data structures have two features in common. First, when any one of these areas is created, they are created by a call to

---

[2] Inverting the relations on every attribute is not hard-wired into the implementation. The optimizer does not assume that there is an index on every attribute and can handle other physical organizations [Wh85].

CMS that takes the size of the area as a parameter, and will only succeed if enough contiguous virtual memory is available to fill the request. Second, all pointers to an offset in an area require 4 bytes.

(1) **Relation area:** All relations are stored in the same format, and all attributes are indexed. A relation is stored as an individual area that constitutes a logical, contiguous, relocatable unit of memory. A given value from a domain is stored only once, and a tuple descriptor, TD, is a sequence of pointers to domain values. Tuple descriptors form a double linked list, to facilitate sequential scans. An index is a linear array of pointers to tuple descriptors.

(2) **TD area:** A **TD area** has tuple descriptors and data exactly like a relation area, except that duplicate attribute values for the same domain are duplicated in the data. In addition, a **TD area** does not have any indices. Instead, a hash table used for duplicate elimination is at the bottom of a **TD area**. A hash table slot holds a pointer to the tuple descriptor, TD, of the tuple that hashed to that slot.

(3) **Pointer area:** A **pointer area** contains no tuple descriptors or data. It is always defined as corresponding to a single relation area. At the top of the segment is an array of pointers to TD's in a relation area. The pointer is the offset of a TD from the top of the **relation area** corresponding to the **pointer area**. At the bottom of the **pointer area** is a hash table used for duplicate elimination. A hash table slot contains pointers to the TD of the tuple in the **relation area** that hashed to that slot.

There are three options for the output mode of a query:

(1) **Print:** Result tuples can be displayed by using the "P.", print, command in the desired attribute columns of the relation being queried. When this option is chosen, the result of the query is stored in a **pointer area**.

(2) **User-created output,** abbreviated UCO, is a table that is constructed interactively by entering literals and example elements in a skeleton table. UCO is used to format the result of a query. User-created output is not declared as, and cannot be queried like, a relation. When the result of a query is retrieved into UCO, internally it is stored as a **TD area**.

(3) **Into relation:** To retrieve the result of a query into a relation, that relation must be predeclared by filling in a relation definition table. Internally, the relation being retrieved into will be a **relation area**.

2.2.2. Access methods

Four basic access methods are implemented.[3] The query optimizer [Wh85] uses a branch and bound algorithm to select a query processing plan that utilizes one or more of these access methods.

The optimization phase precedes and is separate from the query processing phase.

(1) **Index-Lookup:** At the bottom of a relation area is an index for each attribute in the relation. Each index is a linear array of 4 byte pointers to tuple descriptors. The index is sorted on attribute value. It is a dense, nonclustered index. Tuples can be accessed according to the value of 1 attribute through a binary search of the index. Updating these indices is made more efficient through a **long move** instruction.

(2) **Simple-Scan:** Selections that involve a single relation can be performed by a very fast scan of the relation. A scan is accomplished by traversing the doubly linked list of TD's in the relation area. Pointers to the TD's that are selected are stored in an array which, if necessary for a join, can be sorted to become an **Temporary-Index**.

---

[3] The designers of OBE use a different terminology and classification for their access methods and data structures [WAB86, Wh85].

Figure 1. The Two-Dimensional Interface

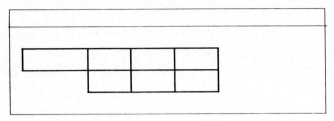

Figure 1.a. Skeleton Table

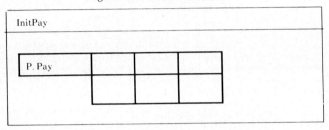

Figure 1.b. Invoking a Relation Template

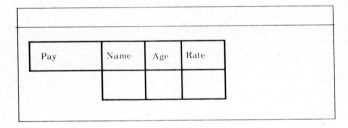

Figure 1.c. A Relation Template

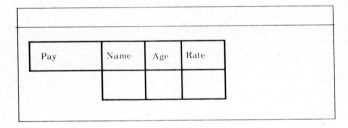

Figure 1.d. A Select-Project Query
Using Condition Box and Example Element "__X"
(Prints the name and age of all hourly employees older than 31)

(3) **Temporary-Index**: A temporary index can be built on one or more attributes on the fly. First, the relation on which the index is being built is scanned using the **Simple-Scan** in order to apply all selection predicates to it. Pointers to all selected TD's (tuple descriptors) are collected in an array. The array is sorted on the join attribute(s) and is used as an index to perform joins.

(4) **Pipeline-Scan**: As part of OBE's pipeline approach to join processing [AHK85], a relation may be scanned a tuple at a time. As each tuple is processed, selections may be applied and the tuple is joined if possible, to qualifying tuples in other relations involved in the join.

There are two implementation decisions in this version of the prototype that should be mentioned.

First, the **Index-Lookup** was never used to perform range selection. Second, single relation

queries were treated as special cases of joins. In addition to the above access methods, sorting and

hashing are employed to process lists of tuples formed during intermediate stages of query process-

ing. A heap sort [Kn73] is used to sort pointers in a **pointer area** for aggregate functions. The

Power's sort [Po80] is an in-place merge sort that has very small storage overhead. In OBE, it is

used to sort TD's in **relation areas** and in **TD areas**, and to sort pointers for the **Temporary-**

Index. Finally, when initially inserting tuples into a **TD area** or a **pointer area**, duplicate elimi-

nation on the tuple being stored is accomplished by hashing the entire tuple and using the hash

table at the bottom of the area.

2.3. Benchmarking Methodology

There can be complex interactions between factors that affect the performance of a MMDBS.

It is important to study these factors in isolation to provide a set of baseline measures. To this end,

we conducted preliminary experiments in single user, standalone mode. By single user, we mean

that there was only one user of the DBMS active when we obtained our measures. This was also

necessary because concurrency control was not implemented in OBE at the time we performed our

experiments. By standalone, we mean that there were no other users on the machine when we per-

formed our experiments. Single user, standalone measures do not provide a realistic estimate of a

DBMS's performance because they reflect its behavior in an underutilized resource environment.

However, measuring query execution time in single user mode is necessary in order to systemati-

cally evaluate schemes for physical database organization, or query optimization and execution

algorithms [BDT83].

2.3.1. Measurement techniques

We wrote a benchmarking program that took the names of OBE query windows from an input

file and obtained measures of interest before and after each query was executed. The query windows were two dimensional images of queries as they would be submitted to OBE from the screen. They were unparsed. The program executed as many queries as were in the input file by invoking the OBE query processor. At least two preparatory queries were always included in the input file to insure that the relations being queried and all OBE code were in virtual memory.

We executed the benchmarking program once per input file to control the effects of fragmentation of virtual memory, which would sometimes cause OBE to abort processing, particularly after a long interactive session. Each input file contained only one query of interest preceded by the necessary initializing queries. Our decision to execute only one query of interest per program is in contrast to our approach with DDBS's [BDT83], where we usually executed 10 queries at a time and then averaged the total to get the time for one query. In a DDBS, this measurement technique was needed to randomize the location of the tuples in the relation that would be accessed, and reduce the probability that the pages they resided on would already be in memory as an after-effect of a previous query. Since, with OBE, the relation was guaranteed to be in memory, the location of tuples accessed was unimportant. The one exception to this case occurs in our paging experiment and it is dealt with in Section 5.

2.3.2. The database

We used a test database consisting of 5 synthetic relations. Each relation has 16 attributes, 13 integer attributes and 3 string attributes. In OBE, all numerical values are stored as variable length floating point numbers. All strings are stored as variable length strings. Out test relations, including statistics on their instantiation in OBE, are summarized in Table 1.

Table 1: A Description of the Synthetic Relations
Used in Benchmarking OBE
Relation is stored as a Relation Area (including indices on every attribute)
Elapsed Time is Standalone Time Required to Read in Relation
From IBM 3380 Disk Using IBM 3880 Channel
(Elapsed Time is in Seconds, Blocks are 4096 Bytes)

RELATION NAME	NUMBER of TUPLES	NUMBER of BYTES	NUMBER of BLOCKS	ELAPSED TIME to READ from DISK
OneK	1,000	360,448	89	0.30
TwoK	2,000	712,704	175	0.58
FiveK	5,000	1,757,184	430	1.29
TenK	10,000	3,465,216	847	2.47

The largest relation, **TenK**, had 10,000 tuples, 16 attributes per tuple. It occupied 3.5 megabytes but could be read in from disk in 2.47 seconds. It was stored on disk as a file with one 3,465,216 byte record. Storing the relation as one record is the optimization that allowed it to be read into virtual memory so quickly. The relation **TenK** is the relation that we used for the majority of our queries. Of the 3.5 megabytes it occupied, the indices alone required 18% of this space: 640,000 bytes. A detailed description of the relations is in Appendix 1.

2.3.3. The test queries

The structure of our test database enables us to generate a comprehensive set of relational queries, with systematic control of the size of the result. In the evaluation of a DBMS, our first goal is to establish baseline measures for a relational instruction set. We achieve this by holding the size of the operand relation and the size of the result constant, and executing each of the 8 query types: Selection, Projection, Deletion, Insertion, Update, Simple Aggregate, Aggregate Function, Join.

In benchmarking DBMS's, one has to consider a range of physical designs options. In the prototype of OBE that we benchmarked, there is only one physical organization. All attributes have a nonclustered, dense index on them. The only choice the designer has is in the design of the relational schema. Thus, the performance of the system on any particular query is both its best and worst case performance.

We initially benchmarked OBE using queries which we had used in benchmarking other relational DDBS's [BDT83]. While these queries were useful in initially making comparisons between systems, we quickly came to the conclusion that they were inappropriate for an interactive office environment for two reasons: 1) We had not included two query types that were important to the environment for which OBE was designed: complex joins and bulk updates. 2) The size of the result of queries in [BDT83] was too large. Most of the results of single relation queries had 100 or 1000 tuples containing 16 attributes. The results of joins had 1000 tuples containing 32 to 48 attributes.

We composed a set of parameters for a **standard interactive query**, (see Figure 2) and varied them systematically to isolate parameters that affected the response time of queries. We consider the following to be reasonable default parameters for a standard interactive query:

    1. 10 tuples and 5 attributes in the result.

D. Bitton and C. Turbyfill

Figure 2. A Standard Interactive Join

JoinAselB					

Tenke	Unique1E	Unique2E		Conditions
	_ A	_Y		_X = _Y _X < 10

Tenkf	Unique2F	TenF	ThousandF	String4F
	_X	_B	_C	_D

UCO	Unique1	Unique2	Ten	Thousand	String4
P.	_A	_Y	_B	_C	_D

Figure 2.a. JoinAselB: A Standard Interactive Join

UCO	Unique1	Unique2	Ten	Thousand	String4
	7095	0	6	267	Oxx...xxOxx...xxO
	4470	1	6	790	Axx...xxAxx...xxA
	4008	2	0	816	Axx...xxAxx...xxA
	9033	3	7	545	Hxx...xxHxx...xxH
	2873	4	9	61	Vxx...xxVxx...xxV
	5674	5	0	338	Oxx...xxOxx...xxO
	9388	6	0	701	Axx...xxAxx...xxA
	422	7	1	667	Vxx...xxVxx...xxV
	425	8	0	684	Oxx...xxOxx...xxO
	4343	9	2	810	Oxx...xxOxx...xxO

Figure 2.b. Result from JoinAselB in User-Created Output Table
(A Standard Interactive Result)

2. "P." result output mode, user-created output for joins (See Section 2.2.1.).
3. Only one relation, the relation TenK, in queries other than joins.
4. 16 megabytes of virtual memory in the virtual machine.

Two factors related to the 2-dimensional interface had a significant effect on query response time: 1) The width of the relation template used in phrasing a query affected parsing time. 2) The use of the condition box sometimes affected the access plan chosen by the optimizer. Both factors could cause substantial variations in query execution time. By phrasing queries in different ways, we isolated the cost of these factors from other query processing costs. Appendix 2 contains a brief description of all our test queries.

3. MIPS RATE

On a 3081 and a 4341, we measured and compared the standalone execution times for a cross section of queries including selections, projections, updates, joins, and aggregates. The same queries were previously benchmarked on a number of disk database systems [BDT83, BT84, BD84, BT85], which included both software systems running on a VAX host and database machines.[4] For this experiment, we made available to OBE the amount of physical main memory required do all processing in core, without paging or I/O. A subset of our measurements is presented in Table 3. The 10,000 tuple relation, **TenK**, was included in every query except **ProjectAll**, which was a projection of the relation **OneK** performed without duplicate elimination.

Table 2: Standalone Query Execution Time in Seconds on IBM 3081 and IBM 4341
Default Result Consists of All Attributes From Operand Relation(s)
Default Output Mode: "P." on Query Table

Query Name	Time on 3081	Time on 4341	Ratio 4341/3081	Query Description
Select1-Eq+	0.5	3.1	6.2	Select 1 tuple
Select100-Rg+	1.3	7.6	5.8	Select 1% of the tuples
Select1000-Rg+	1.6	10.3	6.4	Select 10% of the tuples
Select1000-Rg+	4.7	34.7	7.4	Select 10%, with condition box
Project100	14.3	106.8	7.5	Project 100 tuples, 6 attrs.
ProjectAll	1.0	6.9	6.9	Project all of **OneK**
JoinAB'+	2.6	18.4	7.1	2-way join
JoinAselB+	5.6	37.8	6.8	1 selection, 2-way join
JoinCselAselB+	4.8	30.2	6.3	2 selections, 3-way join
Update1+	4.7	26.2	5.6	Update one tuple
Insert1	2.4	24.1	10.0	Insert one tuple
Delete-Eq+	0.4	2.5	6.3	Delete one tuple
MINIMUM	0.5	3.1	5.8	
MAXIMUM	14.3	106.8	10.0	
AVERAGE	3.6	25.7	6.9	

---

[4] We performed this experiment before we modified our set of test queries to conform with the **standard interactive query** described in Section 2.3.3. Thus the queries in Table 2 are different from those in Table 3.

Our goal was to verify whether the ratio between the elapsed time of the same queries on the 4341 and the 3081 would be different from the known ratio between the MIPS rates of the two machines. For the numbers in Table 3, the average ratio was 6.9. The ratio that is usually quoted between MIPS rates for the 4341 and 3081 is 7. This result indicates that a general CPU performance metric is a strong basis for predicting the effect of CPU speed on the performance of OBE. This distinguishes OBE from conventional, disk database management systems.

4. SPACE AND TIME MEASUREMENTS

Table 3 summarizes the virtual memory and processing requirements of a subset of the interactive queries that we tested. A complete analysis of OBE's approach to query processing can be found in [BT86]. In this section, we present some of the major conclusions of our analysis through a summary of OBE's memory requirements and performance on updates, aggregates and joins.

4.1. Memory Requirements

Except for 3 queries, an update that failed and two aggregates: **Update100, MinKey-U,** and **MinFn-U,** all queries executed in the amount of virtual memory required to hold the operand relations. An important design decision in OBE was to always read operand relations into virtual memory before a query was executed. Thus the time to initialize a query includes the time required to read the operand relations. In Table 3, the first 7 queries are initializing queries used to make sure that all code and data was memory resident. The elapsed times of these initializing queries are strikingly low. It took only 2.47 sec to read the 3.5 megabyte **TenK** relation. This demonstrates that, with proper optimization, the delay of reading in the data before executing a query is acceptable. All queries that executed did so in between 8 and 11 megabytes of virtual memory. 8 megabytes was the lower limit because the OBE program and operating system required approximately 4 megabytes of a user's virtual memory and the relation **TenK** that was included in every query occupied 3.5 megabytes.

4.2. Deletions, Insertions, and Updates

Deletions, insertions and updates take place in two phases. In the first phase, all tuples that are affected are identified. In the case of insertions and updates, extensive validity checking is done. Before the second phase, where changes are actually made to the operand relation, the user

Table 3: Virtual Memory and Processing Requirements For Interactive Queries
Memory in Megabytes, Average (3081) CPU time in Seconds on Loaded System
Default Query Parameters as defined for **Standard Interactive Query**

Query	Memory	CPUtime	Comment
InitParse	7	.07	query to initialize parser
Init1K	7	.30*	read in OneK
Init2Kb	7	.58*	read in TwoKb (OneK already in)
Init2Kc	7	.58*	read in TwoKc (1K,2Kb already in)
Init5K	8	1.29*	read in FiveK (1K,2Kb,2Kc in)
Init10Ke	8	2.47*	read in TenKe
Init10Kf	11	2.47*	read in TenKf, 10Ke already in
Selectkey-Eq	8	.14	equality, select 1 on key, "P."
Select10-Eq	8	.17	equality, thousand = 838, "P."
Select10-Rg	8	.59	range, no condition box, "P."
Select10-Rg-P	8	2.42	range, with condition box, "P."
Select10-Rg-U	8	2.98	range, with c'box, into UCO
Select10-Rg-R	8	3.08	range, with c'box, into Relation
Delete1	8	.23	where key = 838
Delete10	8	1.55	where thousand = 500
Delete100	8	14.97	where hundred = 0
Delete1000	8	139.56	where ten = 0
Insertkey	8	4.19	1 new value inserted in relation
Insertall	8	4.20	16 new values inserted in relation
Update1-key+	8	4.19	all attributes in query window
Update1-key	8	3.68	only key in query window
Update1	8	.29	update 1 tuple on candidate key
Update5	8	.95	update 5 tuples
Update10	8	1.79	update 10 tuples
Update100**	>16	>14.97	update 100 tuples
MinKey-P	8	15.64	minimum on key, "P."
MinKey-U	9	4.53	minimum on key, into UCO
MinFn-P	8	36.98	min on key-10 partitions, "P."
MinFn-U	9	8.01	min on key-10 partitions, into UCO
Join2	8	1.29	10K and 1K - 1000 tuple result
Join4	8	2.19	1K,2K,2K,5K - 1000 tuple result
Join3	9	1.73	1K,2K,10K - 1000 tuple result
JoinAselB	11	2.82	into UCO
JoinAB'	8	.46	into UCO
JoinCselAselB	11	.67	into UCO

* Measure is elapsed time to read relation from disk instead of **CPUtime**.
** **Update100** failed in 16 megabytes of virtual memory.

is informed of any anomalies and asked to confirm or abort the operation. While the details of these operations are beyond the scope of this paper, we did isolate the algorithms that contributed to the cost of each query type. With deletions, the primary cost was in updating the indices which was a linear function of the number of tuples deleted: 0.14 seconds per tuple deleted. For insertions of a single tuple and for updates of a single tuple on the key, the primary cost was sorting the 10,000 tuple relation in the first phase, for validating the update. Using the Power's sort [Po80], sorting the relation **TenK** on its integer key took approximately 3.51 seconds. For insertions, in the second phase, restructuring the 16 indices cost .02 seconds, and inserting 16 new values into the relation cost .02 seconds.

Updates consist of deletions followed by insertions. With deletions, space in the relation is not reclaimed during interactive sessions, so a bulk update may require enlarging the **relation area** of the operand relation. In OBE, enlarging a relation consists of allocating a new, larger **relation area**, and then copying the operand relation into the larger area. If enough contiguous virtual memory is not available for the allocation of the larger **relation area** the update fails. In the case of query **Update100**, due to fragmentation, a sufficiently large block of contiguous virtual memory was not available, so the update failed. Query **Update100**, which updated 100 tuples, failed in 16 megabytes of virtual memory, even though query **Update10**, which updated 10 tuples, required only 8 megabytes of virtual memory.

4.3. Aggregates

The aggregate functions provided a concrete example of a space-time tradeoff. We tested two aggregates, a simple minimum on the key, query **MinKey**, and an aggregate function that computed the minimum for the key in 10 partitions of the relation, **MinFn**. When the result output mode was through a "P.", the queries required 15.64 and 36.98 seconds respectively, and required 8 megabytes of virtual memory. When the result was retrieved into user-created output, the same queries required 4.53 and 8.01 seconds respectively, but required 9 megabytes of virtual memory: a 70% to 75% improvement in time at the cost of 12% more space. The poor performance of these aggregates when the result output mode was through a "P." is accounted for by the use of a **pointer area**. For both queries, the pointers in the **pointer area** were sorted on the attributes relevant to the aggregate function using a space efficient heap sort [Kn83]. Sorting the pointers required referencing the operand relation to actually make comparisons between tuples.

4.4. Joins

We tested 6 joins of 2 to 4 relations. All joins were executed in between .46 and 2.82 seconds and required between 8 and 11 megabytes of virtual memory. No join required more memory, measured to the granularity of a megabyte, than was required to hold the operand relations. OBE uses an optimized pipelined join (nested loops) strategy [AHK85], that is time and space efficient. There were two interesting results with these joins. First, the query **JoinAselB**, which was a selection on the relation **TenKf** followed by a join with the relation **TenKe**, executed 5% faster than the identical selection, query **Select10-Rg-U**: 2.82 seconds elapsed time for the former, 2.98 seconds for the latter. Second, for 1 to 1 joins with the size of the result held constant, the time for the joins increased linearly with the number of relations in the joins.

We conclude that certain query execution algorithms in OBE exploited memory residency effectively, while others suffered for performance problems related to physical database design and memory management. The pipeline join algorithm proves to be very efficient, and correctly optimizes complex joins that involve multiple, large relations. On the other hand, performance problems in OBE were related to two areas:

(1) **Completely Inverted Relations**: Even though OBE was not optimized for updates on the assumption that they would be infrequent, the cost of bulk deletions of over 100 tuples cannot be ignored: deleting 100 tuples took 14.97 seconds.

(2) **Memory Management**: The failure of the bulk update of 100 tuples reflects the problem of fragmentation that has not been solved in this system. The space efficient **pointer area** (that was the source of performance problems for 2 aggregates and 1 projection) was implemented in an attempt to avoid failures due to lack of, or fragmentation of, virtual memory.

5. PAGING

When its physical memory requirements are not met, the MMDBS relies on the operating system for virtual memory management. A ubiquitous criticism of the concept of MMDBS's is that no matter how well they perform when their physical memory requirements are met, paging will unacceptably degrade their performance. Thus it is important to measure the effect of paging on the performance of the MMDBS, and establish a ratio of physical to virtual memory size that will provide acceptable performance.

We measured the effect of paging in a single user, standalone experiment on a 4341 that used a 3350 disk for paging. The 4341 did not have a paging cache. It had 16 megabytes of real memory available, consisting of four 4-megabyte memory modules. To force paging, we could bring the machine up in a configuration that used 1, 2, 3, or 4 of the 4-megabyte memory modules. Then, by systematically varying both the size of the query operand relations and the amount of physical memory made available to OBE, we forced paging in a controlled manner. As our access to the

Table 4: Execution Time of Join Queries under Paging

Standalone elapsed time as function of amount of Real Memory available
Memory Required = Virtual memory in megabytes (4 meg granularity)
Time is in Seconds, Operand sizes in thousand tuples

Sizes of Join Relations	Memory Required	Time with 16 Meg	Time with 12 Meg	Time with 8 Meg	Time with 4 Meg
1K,2K	8	9.80	9.76	10.00	10.62
1K,5K	8	10.01	10.02	10.30	17.88
1K,10K	12	10.07	10.19	10.82	30.83
1K,2K,5K	8	12.92	12.92	13.03	29.46
1K,2K,10K	12	13.03	13.00	16.45	41.42
1K,2K,2K,5K	8	15.83	16.04	16.15	30.34
1K,2K,5K,10K	12	15.98	16.42	30.53	91.90
1K,2K,5K,10K,10K	16	19.97	36.43	75.68	241.08

machine in standalone mode was limited, we restricted ourselves to one query type only. We chose to focus on the pipeline join algorithm, which is the basis of all complex queries in OBE and which had performed most impressively in our previous experiments. We tested 8 joins that joined between 2 and 5 relations. The total number of tuples in the relations range from 3,000 to 30,000, and the total size of the relations range from 828,000 bytes to 9.32 megabytes. The minimum amount of virtual memory required to execute the joins ranged between 8 and 16 megabytes. All of the joins were one-to-one joins on the key, that retrieved all 1,000 tuples from the 1,000 tuple relation. Thus, we could limit the size of the result through the size of the smallest relation, without using a selection. To compensate for an unrealistically large result, we chose to use the "P." output mode, which stores the result in a space-efficient pointer area. From previous experiments, we knew that these joins were correctly optimized.

Table 4 shows the single user, standalone elapsed times of our test join queries on the 4341. Looking at these measurements, we make the following observations:

(1) **With 16 megabytes** of real memory, no paging occurred with any of the joins. Execution time was strictly increasing according to the number of relations involved in the join, with the number of tuples in the relations having a secondary effect. This is most clearly seen by contrasting the 1K,10K join with the 1K,2K,5K join. The 2-way 1K, 10K join took 3 seconds less than the 3-way 1K,2K,5K join.

(2) **With only 4 megabytes** of real memory available, the latter effect was reversed. The execution time for the joins was strictly increasing with the total size of the relations joined, and the number of relations involved in the join had a secondary effect. In this case, the 1K,10K

join required 1.37 seconds more than the 1K,2K,5K join.

(3)   Except when the virtual memory requirement of the join exceeds by far the amount of main memory available, our measurements show that the performance of the pipeline joins degrades gracefully as the ratio of real memory to virtual memory decreases.

Interesting problems, beyond the scope of this paper, are raised by this experiment. A general study of locality in database referencing would provide a more general understanding of the effect of paging on a MMDBS. This may justify the need for new paging strategies, tuned to database management in MMDBS's, analogous to the need for buffering strategies in operating systems for DDBS's [St81].

6. CONCLUSIONS AND FUTURE RESEARCH

We have presented the results of a comprehensive benchmark of the relational MMDBS that is the foundation of the interactive office system, **Office-By-Example**. In the course of evaluating OBE, we have identified issues that must be considered in the design and implementation of MMDBS's.

We evaluated OBE with respect to the 2 goals that directed its design:

(1)   The system must be user-friendly and truly interactive [Gr83].

(2)   The system must have an interactive response time on simple and complex retrieval queries comparable to an interactive full screen editor. With relations occupying up to a total of 2 megabytes of memory, an acceptable response time would be preferably under 1 second, but up to 3 seconds, depending on the query.

In comparison to other systems we have benchmarked, we found that OBE supported a very user-friendly DBMS with full relational capabilities. The two dimensional interface was both easy to learn and to use. Update queries were interactive in that the system provided extensive consistency checking with constructive intermediate feedback, and the option to safely abort. The method of displaying the result was also interactive. The first 8 tuples in the result were displayed and the user was given the option of viewing as much of the remainder as desired. In the prototype that we evaluated, the user was relieved of all responsibility for physical design. One drawback we found was that result tables could not be queried as relations unless the result was specifically retrieved into a predeclared relation.

On a cross section of simple and complex interactive retrieval queries, all queries except 3 executed in .15 to 8 seconds. This is a good level of performance, considering that we used a 10,000 tuple relation that occupied 3.5 megabytes of memory, the same very large relation we previously used to benchmark commercial disk database systems [BDT83, BT84, BT85]. Furthermore, no alternative data structures, such as clustered relations or hashed indices, were explicitly built to achieve acceptable performance for any query. Since there was only one physical design option, automatically implemented by the system, these numbers represent both the best and worst case performance of the test queries.

We identified three performance problems. The first occurred when comparisons were made between tuples referenced in a space efficient data structure, a **pointer area**. This is an implementation problem rather than a problem inherent in the data structure. The second problem was fragmentation of virtual memory that resulted in the failure of a bulk update of 100 tuples. Finally, the complete inversion of relations resulted in a high cost for bulk insertions, deletions and updates, due to the cost of updating the indices.

We also identified the tradeoffs involved in the design alternatives chosen for OBE. Every desirable feature of the system had a related cost. The user-friendly two-dimensional interface could result in significant parsing time. It took .51 seconds to parse a relation template with 16 attributes. Validity checking for updates cost time, a minimum of 3.51 seconds for a bulk update involving the key of our 10,000 tuple test relation. Variable length fields increase the space required to store tuples and increase the cost of comparisons, particularly between numbers. OBE reads a relation into memory when its relation template is invoked in the process of writing a query. This results in improved query response time, when the relation is actually queried, at the cost of space in the form of virtual and real memory. Essentially, the designers of OBE used a fast CPU, a 3081, and a large amount of physical memory to greatly simplify the user interface while maintaining acceptable performance.

This case study reveals two important issues in the design and implementation of MMDBS's. First, the speed of the CPU on the host machine directly affects the relative weight of space and time in design tradeoffs. Second, memory management strategies are critical: Allocation, paging, and fragmentation are aspects of memory management that may require new approaches in the context of MMDBS's.

Acknowledgements

We are grateful to all members of the OBE group for making this research possible, and to Pat Goldberg and Art Ammann for authorizing publication of this paper. Moshe Zloof and Ravi Krishnamurthy initiated this cooperative venture. Kyu Young Whang and Maria Hanrahan described the query optimizer to us, and made many helpful suggestions. We also wish to thank Jim Gray for his insightful comments.

REFERENCES

[AHK85] Ammann, A., Hanrahan, M., and Krishnamurthy, R., "Design of a Memory Resident DBMS", *Proceedings of IEEE COMPCON*, 1985.

[BDT83] Bitton, D., DeWitt, D. and Turbyfill, C., "Benchmarking Database Systems - A Systematic Approach", *Proceedings of VLDB*, 1983.

[BT84] Bitton, D. and Turbyfill, C., "Design and Analysis of Multiuser Benchmarks for Database Systems", *Technical Report 84-589*, Cornell University.

[BT85] Bitton, D. and Turbyfill, C., "Evaluation of a Backend Database Machine", *Proceedings of HICSS*, January 1985.

[BT86] Bitton, D. and Turbyfill, C., "Performance Evaluation of Main Memory Database Systems", *Technical Report 86-731*, Cornell University.

[BCH84] Bogdanowicz R., Crocker M., Hsiao D., Ryder C., Stone V., Strawser P., "Experiments in Benchmarking Relational Database Machines," *Database Machines*, Springer Verlag 1983.

[BD84] Boral, H. and DeWitt, D., "A Methodology for Database System Performance Evaluation", *Proceedings of Sigmod*, 1984.

[DKO84] DeWitt, D., Katz, R., Olken, F., Shapiro, L., Stonebraker, M., and Wood, D., "Implementation Techniques for Main Memory Database Systems", *Proceedings of the 1984 SIGMOD Conference on Management of Data*, June 1984.

[Gr85] Gray, J., "The 5 Minute Rule", *Technical Note*, Tandem Computers, May 1985.

[IBM83] IBM, "VM/SP System Programmer's Guide", Release 3, 1983. *JCIT*, 1984.

[Ki83] Kitsuregawa, M. et al, "Application of Hash to Data Base Machine and its Architecture", *New Generation Computing*, No. 1, 1983.

[KM84] Krishnamurthy, R. and Morgan, S.P., "A Pragmatic Approach to Query Processing", *VLDB*, 1984.

[Kn73] Knuth, D.E., "The Art of Computer Programming", Volume 3, pp. 145-147, 1973.

[KMZ84] Krishnamurthy, R., Morgan, S.P. and Zloof, M.M., "Query-By-Example: Operations On Piecewise Continuous Data", *IBM Research Report*, 1983.

[LC85] Lehman, T.J., and Carey, M.J., "A Study of Index Structures for Main Memory Database Systems", *Technical Report 605*, University of Wisconsin, July 1985.

[Po80] Power, L.R., "Internal Sorting Using a Minimal Tree Merge Strategy" *ACM Trans. on Math. Soft.*, 6:1, March 1980.

[Po85] Potter, D.H., Verbal communications, IBM T.J. Watson Research Center, 1985.

[Sh85] Shapiro, L.D., "Join Processing in Database Systems with Large Memories", *Technical Report*, North Dakota State University, December 1985.

[St81] Stonebraker M., "Operating System Support for Database Management", *CACM*, 24:7, July 1981.

[Wh85] Whang, K.Y., "Query Optimization in Office-By-Example", *IBM RC 11571*, December 1985.

[WAB86] Whang, K.Y., Ammann, A., Bolmarcich, T., et al, "Office-By-Example, An Integrated Office System and Database Manager", *IBM Research Report*, 1986.

[Ya85] Yamane, Yasuo, "A Hash Join Technique for Relational Database Systems", Proceedings of the International Conference on Foundations of Data Organization, May, 1985.

[Zl75] Zloof, M.M., "Query-By-Example", *AFIPS Conference Proceedings*, National Computer Conference 44, 1975.

[Zl82] Zloof, M.M., "Office-By-Example: A Business Language that Unifies Data and Word Processing and Electronic Mail", *IBM Systems Journal*, vol. 21, No. 3, 1982.

APPENDIX 1

A Description of the Test Database

We used a test database consisting of 5 synthetic relations. Each relation has 16 attributes, 13 integer attributes and 3 string attributes. In OBE, all numerical values are stored as variable length floating point numbers. All strings are stored as variable length strings. The relations, including statistics on their instantiation in OBE, are summarized in Table 1 (Section 2.3.2).

The integer attributes in the synthetic relations were all uniformly distributed within specified ranges so that controlling the size of the result of a query would be possible. The range of the integer attribute is implied by its name. For instance, the attribute two has two distinct values, 0 and 1. The attribute thousand has one thousand distinct values between 0 and 999 inclusive. The attributes in relation **TenK** are described in the table below. The smaller relations had the same attributes with identical ranges and cardinalities except where the number of tuples in a relation precluded an attribute from having all of the integer values within the specified range.

Each of the 3 string attributes is 52 characters long with 3 significant characters. The significant characters occur in positions 1, 26, and 52 in the string. The remainder of the positions contain the same padding character. With our unique string attributes, the leftmost significant character was varied most frequently, followed by the middle significant character.

In creating a test database, we sometimes create more that one copy of the same relation. For instance, in the OBE test database, we had two copies of the relation **TenK** which we called **TenKe** and **TenKf**. The attribute names in each relation can also be appended with a letter to make all of the attribute names in the database unique.

Description of the Attributes in Relation TenK
10,000 Tuples in Relation

NAME	TYPE	CARDINALITY	RANGE	ORDER	COMMENT
unique1	INT	10,000	0 - 99,999	random	candidate key
unique2	INT	10,000	0 - 99,999	random	declared key
two	INT	2	0-1	alternating	0,1,0,1,...
four	INT	4	0-3	alternating	0,1,2,3,0,1...
ten	INT	10	0-9	alternating	0,1,...,9,0,...
twenty	INT	20	0-19	alternating	0,1,...,19,0,...
hundred	INT	100	0-99	alternating	0,1,...,999,0,...
thousand	INT	1000	0-999	random	
twothous	INT	2000	0-1999	random	
fivethous	INT	5000	0-4999	random	
tenthous	INT	10,000	0-9999	random	candidate key
odd100	INT	50	1-99	alternating	1,3,5,...,99,1,...
even100	INT	50	2-100	alternating	2,4,6,...,100,2,...
stringu1	CHAR	10,000	A...A...A-V...V...T	random	candidate key
stringu2	CHAR	10,000	A...A...A-V...V...T	alternating	candidate key
string4	CHAR	4	A...A...A-V...V...V	alternating	

APPENDIX 2

Description of Benchmark Queries
Default Query Parameters are as defined for **Standard Interactive Query**
All Joins are Equijoins on Key

Query	Comment
InitParse	query to initialize parser, caused **3 start I/O's**
Init1K	read in OneK
Init2Kb	read in TwoKb: OneK already in
Init2Kc	read in TwoKc: OneK, TwoKb already in
Init5K	read in FiveK: OneK, TwoKb, TwoKc already in
Init10Ke	read in TenKe
Init10Kf	read in TenKf, TenKe already in
Selectkey-Eq	equality, select 1 tuple on key, "P."
Select10-Eq	equality, select 10 tuples on thousand = 838, "P."
Select10-Rg	range, no condition box, select 10 tuples on key, "P."
Select10-Rg-P	range, with condition box, select 10 tuples on key, "P."
Select10-Rg-U	range, with cond.box, select 10 tuples on key, into UCO
Select10-Rg-R	range, with cond.box, select 10 tuples on key, into Relation
Select10-Rg2	range, two inequalities, with cond.box, "P."
Project20-U	20/10,000 tuples, 3 integers and 1 string, into UCO
Project20-R	20/10,000 tuples, 3 integers and 1 string, into Relation
Project20-P	20/10,000 tuples, 3 integers and 1 string, "P."
Project8K-P	7993/10,000 tuples, 3 integers and 1 string, "P."
Delete1	delete (1) tuple where key=838
Delete10	delete (10) tuples where thousand=500
Delete100	delete (100) tuples where hundred=0
Delete1000	delete (1000) tuples where ten=0
Insertkey	insert 1 tuple, 1 new value inserted in relation
Insertall	insert 1 tuple, 16 new values inserted in relation
Update1-key+	update 1 tuple on key, 15 other attributes in query window
Update1-key	update 1 tuple on key, only key in query window
Update1	update 1 tuple on candidate key
Update5	update 5 tuples,where twothous=500
Update10	update 10 tuples,where thousand=500
Update100	update 100 tuples,where hundred=500
MinKey-P	minimum on key, "P."
MinKey-U	minimum on key, into UCO
MinFn-P	minimum on key with 10 partitions, "P."
MinFn-U	minimum on key with 10 partitions, into UCO
Join2	join: TenK and OneK, result = all of OneK, "P."
Join4	join: OneK, TwoK, TwoK, FiveK, result: OneK, "P."
Join3	join: OneK, TwoK, TenK, result: OneK, "P."
JoinAselB	select 10 tuples from TenKf, join with TenKe, into UCO
JoinAB'	join: TenKe with 10 tuple relation, into UCO
JoinCselAselB	join: 10 tuple relation with TenKe and TenKf, into UCO

OFFICE SYSTEMS: Methods and Tools
G. Bracchi, D. Tsichritzis (Editors)
Elsevier Science Publishers B.V. (North-Holland)
© IFIP, 1987

Integrated Access Methods for Messages Using Signature Files.

Christos Faloutsos

Department of Computer Science,
University of Maryland,
College Park, MD 20742

ABSTRACT.

Signature files have attracted a lot of interest [34], [21], [13] as an access method for text and specifically for messages in the office environment. Messages consist of attributes and text. The key idea in the method is to store the messages sequentially in the "text file"; for every message an abstraction ("signature") is created, containing some of the information in the original message; the signatures are stored sequentially in the "signature file". To resolve a query, the signature file is scanned sequentially and many non-qualifying messages are immediately rejected. The method guarantees that all the qualifying messages will be identified; in addition, some non-qualifying ones ("false drops") may pass the signature test. In this paper we design and analyze integrated ways of applying this idea for text and attributes simultaneously. We extend methods that have been proposed for text only, namely superimposed coding and compression-based methods, develop a mathematical model and derive formulas for the optimal choice of parameters.

1. INTRODUCTION.

Traditional data base management systems (DBMSs) are designed for formatted records. Recently there have been many attempts to extend these systems so that they can handle unformatted, free text [5], [8], [16], [23], [34]. Electronic message filing in an office is the application of these systems we shall focus on. Many types of messages circulate in an office: correspondence, memos, reports e.t.c.. These messages consist not only of attributes (e.g., sender, date, e.t.c.) but also of text. In an automated office, there should exist a system that allows electronic storage and retrieval of these messages.

Integrated access methods for text and attributes are useful in many relevant applications:

- Automated law [17] and patent offices [18],
- Computerized libraries [32],   [36],
- Electronic storage and retrieval of articles from newspapers and magazines,
- Consumers' data bases, with descriptions of products in natural language

In this paper we concentrate on the signature file approach, which seems to be suitable for the office environment [34],   [5]. Signature files have been applied for textual data bases (e.g., [24],   [15]), as well as for formatted-record ones [27],   [26]. Here we suggest methods of using signature files for both formatted data and text simultaneously.

The structure of the paper is as follows: In chapter 2 we discuss briefly access methods for attributes and text, we describe the most promising among the known signature extraction methods for text and we illustrate with an example how we can extend these methods to handle attributes, as well. In chapter 3 we describe the problem of optimal selection of the parameters and its mathematical formulation. In chapter 4 we give the analysis and results for the extended superimposed coding. In chapter 5 we discuss the extension of the compression-based methods. In chapter 6 we discuss some practical issues. In chapter 7 we summarize the main results and indicate future research directions.

2. WHY SIGNATURE FILES - HOW THEY WORK.

Our goal is to choose one method for text and one for attributes, such that they are suitable for the office environment and they integrate well. Access methods for formatted data ("secondary keys") have been studied extensively in the past. Some of the most prominent methods are: inverted files [4], multidimensional tree-structures (k-d trees [2], k-d B-trees [28]), extensions of hashing (multiattribute hashing [29], grid file [25]) and signature files [27],   [26]. Access methods for text form the following large classes: Full text scanning [1],   [3],   [20], inversion (STAIRS [19], MEDLARS, ORBIT, LEXIS [32] e.t.c.), signature files [34],   [5] and clustering [31],   [36],   [32].

The office environment, which we are primarily interested in, has the following features:

- Large insertion rates, but few deletions and updates [18].
- Most of the messages in an office are seldom required after they have been filed. Gravina [14] reports that the access frequency of an item decreases very fast with its age.

Under the above considerations, the signature file method seems to be a reasonable choice. Compared to inversion, it requires much smaller space overhead ($\approx 10\%$ of the size of the original data base, compared to 50%-300% that inversion requires). Moreover, insertions can be handled easily with signature files. As a consequence, signature files can be applied on optical disks, which are ideal for archiving [12]. Optical disks can be written only a limited number of times. This is a problem for the inverted file method, because the index has to be re-written upon every insertion or batch of insertions. Signature files create no problems, because the signatures of the new messages can be appended easily at the end of the signature file.

The other popular alternative for text, full text scanning, does not seem to integrate well with access methods for formatted data. Moreover, it may be too slow. Signature files can provide an almost 10-fold speed-up over full text scanning with only $\approx 10\%$ space overhead. The speed-up is due to the reduced I/O requirements (the signature file is smaller than the text file by an order of magnitude) and to the simpler operations required on searching the signatures.

Next we shall discuss in more detail some known signature extraction methods for text only. Analysis in [9] showed that the best candidates for text are Superimposed Coding (SC) and methods based on compression. To illustrate these methods, we shall use messages consisting only of text, with $d = 4$ words on the average.

Superimposed Coding ("SC", for the rest of this paper) works as follows: Each word (string) yields a bit pattern of size F. These bit patterns are OR-ed together to form the message signature. The word signature creation is rather sophisticated and needs more details: Each word yields m bit positions (not necessarily distinct) in the range 1-F. The corresponding bits are set to "1", while all the other bits are set to "0". For example, in Figure 2.1 the word "data" sets to "1" the 3-rd, 9-th, 10-th, and 14-th bits ($m = 4$ bits per word).

In order to allow searching for parts of words, the following method is suggested: Each word is padded with an initial and final blank and is divided into successive, overlapping triplets (e.g., " da", "dat", "ata", "ta " for the word "data"). Each such triplet is hashed to a bit position by applying a hashing function on a numerical encoding of the triplet. In case that a word has l triplets, with $l > m$, the word is allowed to set l (non-distinct) bits. If $l < m$, the additional bits are set using a random number generator, initialized with a numerical encoding of the word.

Word	Signature
data	0010 0000 1100 0100
base	0000 0100 1010 0010
management	0101 0000 1100 0000
system	0001 0001 0110 0000
message	
signature	0111 0101 1110 0110

Figure 2.1
Illustration of the superimposed coding method for text.
$d = 4$ words per message, signature size
$F = 16$ bits, $m = 4$ bits per word.

To search for a word, the signature of the word is created, setting to "1", e.g., positions 2, 3, 6, and 9. Each message signature is examined. If

the above bit positions (i.e., 2, 3, 6, and 9) of the message signature contain
"1", then the message is retrieved. Otherwise, it is discarded. The signature size F affects directly the number of false drops, while m has to be
selected so that approximately half of the bits are "1" in a message signature.

Notice that SC is sensitive to variances in the number of words per
message d. E.g., a message with $d = 10$ words will result to a signature
almost full of "1"'s. A solution to this problem is to divide the body of the
message in "logical blocks" [5], that is, pieces of text containing a fixed
number of distinct words (d in our case). We shall not address this problem further here; for the mathematical analysis in this paper we assume
that d has negligible variance.

The next methods are based on compression. The idea is that we use a
(large) bit vector of B bits and we hash each word into one (or perhaps
more, say m) bit position(s), which are set to "1" (see Figure 2.2). The
resulting bit vector will be sparse and therefore it can be compressed.

data	0000 0000 0000 0010 0000
base	0000 0001 0000 0000 0000
management	0000 1000 0000 0000 0000
system	0000 0000 0000 0000 1000
message	
signature	0000 1001 0000 0010 1000
(uncompressed)	

Figure 2.2.
Illustration of the compression-based methods.
With $B = 20$ and $m = 1$ bit per word,
the resulting bit vector is sparse and can be compressed.

Methods for compressing sparse vectors are:

a) Run length encoding (RL) [22] where the number of zeros between two
   successive "1"s in the sparse vector is encoded.

b) Bit-block compression (BC) and its extension, variable bit-block
   compression (VBC) [9]. The idea is that the the sparse vector is
   divided into groups of b consecutive non-overlapping bits (bit-blocks),
   each bit-block being compressed individually. This method requires
   more space than RL, but it is faster on searching. The size b of the
   bit-blocks is fixed for all messages in the BC method, while it varies in
   the VBC method, to optimize the space requirements.

In the rest of this paper, we shall not commit the analysis to any of
these methods for compression. Instead, we shall study the optimistic
bound in compression, calculating the entropy of the sparse vector. We
shall denote this method as EN (for "entropy").

Notice the similarity between the compression methods and SC. The
only difference is whether we compress the bit vector or not. As a

consequence, the design processes differ slightly: for SC we have to choose the optimal m, while for EN we have to choose the size of the sparse vector B, too. Analysis for text only [9] showed that for EN the optimal m is 1, that EN needs less space than SC for the same false drop probability and that the curves $\ln F_d$ -vs- F are straight lines, with better (steeper) slope for EN. A message whose signature seems to qualify in a query, although the message does not actually qualify, is called a *false drop*. The probability of this event to happen is called *false drop probability* F_d. Mathematically,

$$F_d = \text{Prob}\{\text{the message signature seems to qualify} / \qquad (2.1)$$

the message does not }

All the methods and ideas discussed up to now deal with text only and have appeared in the past. The contribution of this paper is that it shows how to extend both EN and SC to handle attributes and how to choose the design parameters optimally. The main idea is to allow different m_i for each field i, according to the occurrence and query frequencies. For the rest of this paper, the term **field** will indicate part of a message, either attribute or text. For example consider a data base of messages, each one consisting of

- Field 1: sender, with $d_1 = 2$ strings on the average (e.g., "John Smith").
- Field 2: subject, with of $d_2 = 3$ strings on the average (e.g., "data base machines").
- Field 3: body (i.e., text), with of $d_3 = 4$ strings on the average. (e.g., "data base management systems")

Normally, 'body' should have much larger occurrence frequency d_3. We use $d_3 = 4$ just for illustration. If we have many queries on 'sender' and very few on 'body', the words in 'sender' should be allowed to set many bits to "1", at least, more than the words of 'body' do. Suppose that somehow we have chosen the values for the m_i's to be $\vec{m} = (m_1, m_2, m_3) = (3, 2, 1)$. Figure 2.3 shows how the message signature will be created.

Next we examine the problem of optimal selection of the m_i's, to minimize the false drop probability for a given space overhead.

3. PROBLEM DESCRIPTION.

The problem is stated informally as follows:

Given   the signature size (= space overhead)
Find   the optimal m_i's (and the size B of the sparse vector, in EN)
to   minimize the false drop probability F_d.

A rigorous mathematical model is developed next. The following assumptions are made:

1) The occurrence frequencies d_i have zero variance (they are the same in every message).
2) Only partial match queries are allowed, that is, conjunctive queries where parts of the fields of the message are specified. For example,

Sender ($m_1 = 3$)
John	0000 0010 1010 0000 0000
Smith	0010 0001 0000 0001 0000

Subject ($m_2 = 2$)
data	0000 0000 0010 0000 0010
base	0010 0100 0000 0000 0000
machine	0000 0000 0001 0010 0000

Body ($m_3 = 1$)
data	0000 0000 0000 0010 0000
base	0000 0001 0000 0000 0000
management	0000 1000 0000 0000 0000
system	0000 0000 0000 0000 1000

message signature	0010 1111 1011 0010 1010

Figure 2.3
Illustration of using different m_i's, to extend
signature methods to handle both text and attributes. $B = 20$.

"find the messages with 'sender' matching 'John'
AND 'sender' matching 'Smith'
AND 'subject' matching 'machines' ".
Methods to handle range queries on numeric attributes are described in
section 6, but they are not considered in the forthcoming analyses.

3) Queries specify fields independently. For example

$$\Pr(q_1=1, q_2=5) = \Pr(q_1=1)\,\Pr(q_2=5)$$

where q_1, q_2 are the number of strings specified for field 1 and 2
respectively: For example, assuming that the messages are of the form
depicted in Figure 2.3, for the sample query of assumption 2, we have
$q_1=2$ (2 strings specified for the "sender" field) and $q_2=1$ (1 string
specified for "subject").

4) The null query ($=$"give me the whole data base") is not allowed. The
false drop probability is calculated on the rest of the queries.

It is shown [10] that F_d is given by:

$$F_d = \frac{1}{1-P_{null}} \left[\left(\sum_{s=0}^{d_1} P_1(s)w^{m_1 s} \right) * \cdots * \left(\sum_{s=0}^{d_k} P_k(s)w^{m_k s} \right) - P_{null} \right] \quad (3.1)$$

where

$$P_{null} = \Pr(q_1=0, q_2=0, \cdots, q_k=0) = P_1(0)P_2(0) \cdots P_k(0) \quad (3.2)$$

$$w = 1 - \left[1 - \frac{1}{B} \right]^{(\vec{m} \circ \vec{d})} \approx 1 - e^{-\frac{(\vec{m} \circ \vec{d})}{B}} \quad (3.3)$$

Table of symbols	
k	number of fields (including text parts) in the message
F_d	false drop probability
F	signature size after compression (if any)
d_i	number of strings in field i
$\vec{d}$	$=(d_1, d_2, \cdots d_k)$
D	$= d_1 + d_2 + \cdots d_k$ total number of strings in a message
B	size of the uncompressed signature (= "sparse" bit vector)
w	proportion of "1"'s in the uncompressed signature
P_{null}	probability of null query
q_i	random variable - number of strings specified for field i in a query.
$P_i(s)$	Prob. that $q_i = s$ in a query
$\vec{P_i}$	$= (P_i(0), P_i(1), \cdots)$: query frequencies for field i
m_i	number of bits that strings of field i set to "1" in the message signature
$\vec{m}$	$=(m_1, m_2, \cdots m_k)$
ln	natural logarithm (base e)
log	common logarithm (base 10)

$$(\vec{m} \circ \vec{d}) = \sum_{i=1}^{k} m_i \, d_i \quad \text{(dot product)} \tag{3.4}$$

For superimposed coding, we have in addition:

$$F = B \tag{3.5-SC}$$

since the sparse vector is not compressed. For EN, the signature size F is the entropy of the vector B:

$$F = BH(w) \tag{3.5-EN}$$

where $H()$ is the entropy function

$$H(w) = -\frac{1}{\ln 2} \left[w \ln w + (1-w) \ln(1-w) \right]$$

The problems are now well formulated for both methods.

Given   the occurrence frequencies d_i
the query frequency distributions $P_i()$
the desired signature size F

Find   the optimal m_i parameters
(and the size of the sparse vector B, for EN)

To   minimize the false drop probability F_d (eq. (3.1)).

4. ANALYSIS FOR SUPERIMPOSED CODING.

Requiring the partial derivatives of F_d are zero for the optimal set of m_i's, we found [10] that $\vec{m}$ should satisfy the following set of equations:

$$(\vec{m} \circ \vec{d}) = F \ln 2 \tag{4.1}$$

$$\frac{1}{d_i} \frac{\sum\limits_{s=0}^{d_i} s P_i(s) w^{m_i s}}{\sum\limits_{s=0}^{d_i} P_i(s) w^{m_i s}} = \text{constant } \forall i \tag{4.2}$$

Important notes:

1) Eq (4.1), combined with (3.3) and (3.5-SC), implies that under optimal design, $w = 0.5$, i.e. half of the bits in the message signature should be set to "1". This is the case with every SC scheme examined up to now [24], [27], [11]. It is interesting to notice that $w = 0.5$ maximizes the information (= entropy) the message signature conveys.

2) The set of eq. (4.1) (4.2) can be solved numerically with an approach similar to Newton-Raphson:

Algorithm 4.1.

    do
        guess a value for m_1,

        use it to calculate the rest of m_i from eq. (4.2),
    until the resulting $\vec{m}$ fulfills eq. (4.1) within accuracy ϵ

The above method converged for all the cases we tried, as long as the solution was positive.

3) Fast, approximate solution to $\vec{m}$ can be found if
- all the m_i's are large, such that $w^{m_i} \ll 1$, for example, $m_i > 4$, and
- $P_i(0) \neq 0$, $P_i(1) \neq 0$ and they are of the same order of magnitude.
In this case, the following closed form solutions hold:

$$m_i = \frac{F \ln 2}{D} + \frac{\vec{d} \circ \vec{L}}{\ln 2 D} - \frac{L_i}{\ln 2} \tag{4.3}$$

where

$$L_i = \ln\left(\frac{P_i(0)}{P_i(1)} d_i \right) \tag{4.4}$$

and

$$\vec{L} = (L_1, L_2, \cdots, L_k)$$

D is a shorthand for $\sum\limits_{i=1}^{k} d_i$. Then, the F_d under optimal design is

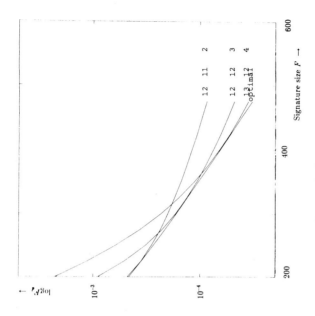

Graph 4.2
Logarithm of false drop probability F_d versus signature size F
for superimposed coding with optimal design.
Case (b): $d = (3, 2, 50)$

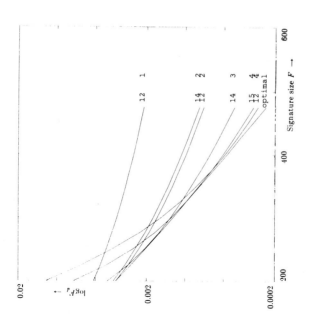

Graph 4.1
Logarithm of false drop probability F_d versus signature size F
for superimposed coding with optimal design.
Case (a): $d = (3, 50)$

given by

$$\ln F_d = \ln \frac{P_{null} \, D}{1 - P_{null}} - \frac{F \, (\ln 2)^2}{D} - \frac{\vec{d} \circ \vec{L}}{D} \tag{4.5}$$

Notice that the logarithm of F_d is again linear on the signature size F. Also, according to Eq. (4.3), large m_i's are assigned to fields with high query frequency (small $P_i(0)$) and low occurrence frequency (small d_i), which is intuitively expected.

4) In the case of messages consisting only of text ($k = 1$), Eq. (4.1) and Eq. (4.3) reduce to the known formula [33]:

$$m_1 d_1 = F \ln 2$$

Graphs G4.1-2 plot $\log F_d$ vs. F under optimal design (curve labeled "optimal"), respectively for the cases:

(a) $k = 2$, $\vec{d} = (3, 50)$,
     $\vec{P}_1 = (0.1, 0.8, 0.1)$
     $\vec{P}_2 = (0.8, 0.1, 0.1)$

(b) $k = 3$, $\vec{d} = (3, 2, 50)$,
     $\vec{P}_1 = (0.1, 0.8, 0.1)$
     $\vec{P}_2 = (0.1, 0.3, 0.6)$
     $\vec{P}_3 = (0.8, 0.1, 0.1)$

The Graphs also contain the curves for some selections of the m_i parameters. Notice that some of these curves "touch", but never cut, the optimal curve. This illustrates the optimality of our solution. The points of "touch" occur whenever the corresponding choice of $\vec{m}$ is the best for the given F.

Tables T4.1 and T4.2 contain the exact and approximate values (upper and lower row, respectively), for the cases (a) and (b) respectively. Eq. (4.3) was used to for the approximate $\vec{m}$, Algorithm 4.1 for the exact $\vec{m}$, and Eq. (4.5) for the approximate value of F_d. Notice the accuracy of the approximate formulas: for F_d, the relative error ranges from ≈ 20 per cent, down to 2 per cent, depending on the approximations used and on the signature size F. The accuracy improves with increasing F.

An alternative approach is based on "disjoint coding", as depicted in Figure 4.1. The message signature is divided into (non-overlapping) sets of bits, of sizes F_1, F_2, $\cdots$, F_k, for each of the k fields. Each of the strings of the first field set m_1 bits to "1", among the F_1 bits; similarly the rest of the fields. The problem is to find the optimal parameters m_i and F_i. It can be shown [10] that the optimal m_i's are the same as in SC, while the F_i's should be such that the ratio of "1"'s in every portion of the message signature is $w = 0.5$. The resulting false drop probability is the same with SC. Thus, the two methods are identical if the occurrence frequencies d_i have zero variance. Otherwise, superimposed coding tolerates variances better than disjoint coding: For example, if a message has 'name'='David Peter Johnson Junior', the F_1 field will be almost full of

signature size		$\vec{m}$		F_d	apprx. F_d (Eq. (4.5))
200	(exact)	11.62	2.08	0.00343853	0.0027895
	(approx.)	12.11	2.05	0.00344999	0.0027895
250	(exact)	12.43	2.72	0.00203942	0.00177288
	(approx.)	12.76	2.70	0.00204253	0.00177288
300	(exact)	13.19	3.37	0.00123672	0.00112676
	(approx.)	13.41	3.35	0.00123753	0.00112676
350	(exact)	13.92	4.02	0.000761838	0.000716119
	(approx.)	14.07	4.01	0.000762043	0.000716119
400	(exact)	14.62	4.67	0.000474386	0.000455132
	(approx.)	14.72	4.66	0.000474436	0.000455132
450	(exact)	15.31	5.32	0.000297527	0.000289261
	(approx.)	15.37	5.32	0.000297538	0.000289261

Table 4.1
Exact and approximate values for $\vec{m}$ (case (a)).

"1"'s; in the original version, the result is not so dramatic, because the additional "1"'s will be scattered over the whole message signature (F bits), instead of just a part of it.

5. COMPRESSION BASED METHODS.

In case of large variance of the occurrence frequencies d_i, even superimposed coding suffers. The compression based methods can tolerate variances better. As a first step, we tried to study the case of zero variance for the EN method. The analysis is similar to the one of superimposed coding, the only difference being that the size of the sparse vector B has to be chosen optimally. Using the method of Lagrange multipliers, the cost function is

$$\ln F_d + \lambda F$$

which yields the following set of non-linear equations to solve:

$$\frac{T_i}{d_i} = \frac{(1-w)\ln(1-w)}{(\vec{m} \circ \vec{d})\ln w} \left[\frac{(\vec{m} \circ \vec{T})}{w} + \lambda B \; H'(w) \right] \quad i = 1, 2, \cdots k \quad (5.1)$$

$$\left[\frac{(\vec{m} \circ \vec{T})}{w} + \lambda B \; H'(w) \right] \frac{(\vec{m} \circ \vec{d})(1-w)}{B(B-1)} = \lambda H(w) \quad (5.2)$$

$$B \; H(w) = F \quad (5.3)$$

signature size		$\overline{m}$			F_d	apprx. F_d (Eq. (4.5))
200	(exact)	11.12	10.30	1.69	0.000461247	0.000356708
	(approx.)	11.70	10.87	1.64	0.000465001	0.000356708
250	(exact)	11.92	11.09	2.31	0.0002749	0.000230475
	(approx.)	12.33	11.50	2.27	0.000276002	0.000230475
300	(exact)	12.67	11.84	2.93	0.000167829	0.000148914
	(approx.)	12.96	12.13	2.90	0.00016814	0.000148914
350	(exact)	13.39	12.56	3.55	0.000104303	9.62156e-05
	(approx.)	13.59	12.76	3.53	0.000104389	9.62156e-05
400	(exact)	14.09	13.26	4.17	6.56516e-05	6.21665e-05
	(approx.)	14.22	13.39	4.16	6.56743e-05	6.21665e-05
450	(exact)	14.76	13.93	4.80	4.16875e-05	4.01668e-05
	(approx.)	14.85	14.02	4.79	4.16933e-05	4.01668e-05

Table 4.2
Exact and approximate values for $\overline{m}$ (case (b)).

Sender $(F_1=8,\ m_1=3)$
   John   0010 0110
   Smith   0011 0100
Subject $(F_2=6,\ m_2=2)$
   data   0010 01
   base   0011 00
   machines   0110 00
Body $(F_3=6,\ m_3=1)$
   data   00 0100
   base   01 0000
   management   00 0010
   systems   00 0100
   message
   signature   0011 0110   0111 01 01 0110

Figure 4.1.
Illustration of "disjoint coding"

where :

$$\vec{T} = (T_1, \cdots, T_k)$$

$$(\vec{m} \circ \vec{T}) = \sum_{i=1}^{k} m_i T_i$$

$$T_i = \frac{\sum_{s=0}^{d_i} sP_i(s)w^{m_i s}}{\sum_{s=0}^{d_i} P_i(s)w^{m_i s}}$$

$$H'(w) = \frac{\partial H(w)}{\partial w} = \frac{\ln(1-w) - \ln w}{\ln 2}$$

and F is the given size for message signature.

Analysis in [10] shows that Eq. (5.2) is satisfied when the m_i's shrink to zero. Since the m_i's are integers, the smallest of them should be at least 1. Thus we try to find the m_i's that satisfy the following equations:

$$\frac{T_i}{d_i} = \text{constant} \quad \forall i \tag{5.4}$$

$$B = \frac{F}{H(w)} \tag{5.5}$$

$$w = 1 - e^{-\frac{(\vec{m} \circ \vec{d})}{B}} \tag{5.6}$$

$$\min_i m_i = 1 \tag{5.7}$$

Essentially, we have replaced Eq. (5.2) from the Lagrange optimization with the practical limitation of Eq. (5.7): $m_i \geq 1 \ \forall i$. Although non-linear, the equations (5.4-7) can be solved as follows:

Algorithm 5.1:
do
    guess w
    calculate B from (5.5)
    do
        guess m_1
        calculate $m_2 \cdots m_k$ from (5.4)
    until the equation (5.6) are satisfied within accuracy ϵ
until eq. (5.7) is satisfied within accuracy ϵ.

The Newton-Raphson method is used to make improved guesses. The initial guesses can use the approximate formulas:

$$m_i \approx \frac{L_i}{\ln w} - \frac{\vec{d} \circ \vec{L}}{\ln w} \frac{F \ln(1-w)}{H(w)D} \tag{5.8}$$

which is derived from (5.4) with similar approximations to the ones of Eq. (4.3). L_i is given by Eq. (4.4). Using (5.8) and requiring that the smallest

$m_i \geq 1$ (eq. 5.7) we can find the following approximate formula that w should satisfy:

$$1 = \frac{L_{\max}}{\ln w} - \frac{\vec{d} \circ \vec{L}}{\ln wD} - \frac{F \ln(1-w)}{H(w)D} \qquad (5.9)$$

where

$$L_{\max} = \max_i L_i \qquad (5.10)$$

Eq. (5.9) can be solved numerically for w, giving good estimates, as we shall see next. We can derive a closed formula for w, using further approximations, that hold for $w \to 0$:

$$\ln(1-w) \approx -w \qquad (5.11)$$

$$H(w) \approx \frac{w}{\ln 2}(1 - \ln w) \approx \frac{-w \ln w}{\ln 2} \qquad (5.12)$$

Then, we have

$$\ln w = L_{\max} - \frac{\vec{d} \circ \vec{L}}{D} - \frac{F \ln 2}{D} \qquad (5.13)$$

In [10] it is shown that an approximate formula for F_d is

$$\ln F_d = \ln \frac{P_{null} D}{1 - P_{null}} - \frac{F \ln w \ln(1-w)}{D} - \frac{\vec{d} \circ \vec{L}}{H(w)D} \qquad (5.14)$$

Notice that (5.14) reduces to Eq. (4.5) for $w = 0.5$. This is expected because, SC requires $w = 0.5$, which means that the compression is unnecessary.

Table T5.1 uses the data of case (a) in section 4 ($\vec{d} = (3, 50)$ e.t.c.). For a range of signature sizes F, it gives the weight w and the parameters $\vec{m}$, chosen according to the above exact and approximate formulas. Specifically, the upper row of each entry used the closed formula (5.13) to estimate w and (5.8) to estimate $\vec{m}$; the middle row used (5.9) and (5.8); and the last row used Algorithm 5.1 to calculate the exact values of w and $\vec{m}$ (and therefore B), using eq. (5.8) and (5.9) for guessing initial values. The last column calculates F_d using the approximate formula (5.14). Notice that the approximate formulas give good estimates, the relative error ranging between 24 to 0.7 per cent. The accuracy improves for larger signature sizes F and, of course, with the use of fewer approximations (eq. (5.9) instead of (5.13) to calculate w).

Table T5.2 gives the same values as T5.1 for case (b) of section 4 ($\vec{d} = (3, 2, 50)$). Again, the relative error of the approximate formulas is tolerable, ranging from 27 to 1.4 per cent, and improving for growing F.

Graph G5.1 plots the logarithm of F_d versus the signature size F for several combinations of the m_i's, as well as the curve under optimal design, for case (a) in Graph 4.1 ($k = 2$ fields, $\vec{d} = (3, 50)$ e.t.c.) The curve labeled "optimal" joins points that correspond to optimal design. As for SC (graphs G4.1-2), the optimal curve is "touched", but never cut, by the other curves. Graph G5.2 plots the same, for case (b) of Graph 4.1 ($k = 3$ fields, $\vec{d} = (3, 2, 50)$ e.t.c.)

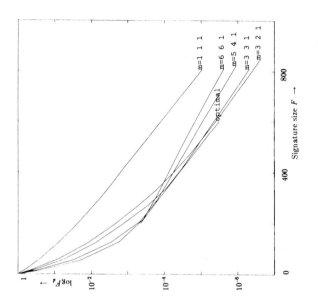

Graph 5.2

Logarithm of false drop probability F_d versus signature size F for the indicated $\bar{m}$'s using the compression method $d = (3, 2, 50)$.

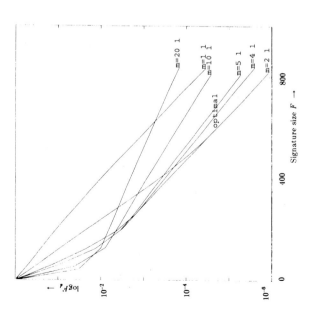

Graph 5.1

Logarithm of false drop probability F_d versus signature size F for the indicated $\bar{m}$'s using the compression method.

Case (a): $d = (3, 50)$.

F		w	$\bar{m}$	F_d	appr. F_d eq. (5.14)
200	(5.13,8)	0.1085	3.84 0.70	0.00294821	0.00244584
	(5.9,8)	0.2303	5.75 1.00	0.0032433	0.00264973
	exact	0.2258	5.45 1.00	0.0032247	0.0026441
250	(5.13,8)	0.0564	3.16 0.74	0.00154022	0.00138027
	(5.9,8)	0.1347	4.48 1.00	0.00175321	0.00154964
	exact	0.1329	4.35 1.00	0.00174711	0.00154664
300	(5.13,8)	0.0293	2.75 0.77	0.000808131	0.000759657
	(5.9,8)	0.0760	3.70 1.00	0.000939017	0.000874046
	exact	0.0753	3.65 1.00	0.000937178	0.000872828
350	(5.13,8)	0.0153	2.46 0.80	0.00042495	0.000410762
	(5.9,8)	0.0416	3.19 1.00	0.000498177	0.000478616
	exact	0.0414	3.17 1.00	0.000497659	0.000478207
400	(5.13,8)	0.0079	2.26 0.82	0.000223498	0.000219443
	(5.9,8)	0.0223	2.83 1.00	0.000262102	0.000256459
	exact	0.0222	2.82 1.00	0.000261957	0.000256332
450	(5.13,8)	0.0041	2.11 0.84	0.000117434	0.000116293
	(5.9,8)	0.0118	2.57 1.00	0.000137028	0.000135446
	exact	0.0117	2.56 1.00	0.000136993	0.000135413

Table 5.1
optimal $\bar{m}$ for case (a)

6. DISCUSSION.

The signature extraction methods described above and their extensions are mainly suitable for attributes that are repeating groups. In the applications of interest, most of the fields will consist of one or more strings: "sender", "receiver", "subject" in the message filing environment, "author", "title", "publisher" in the library environment, e.t.c.. Most of the queries on these fields will be partial match queries, specifying a few strings for some of the fields.

However, numeric fields, such as "date", can be accommodated as well. An elegant idea was suggested by Sacks-Davis and Ramamohanarao [30]. For each numeric attribute they attach a "tag" field to the message signature, of n consecutive bits. For the purpose of the example, let $n = 4$ and assume that the range delimiters are 1960 and 1975. Figure 2.4 shows how the signature of each date is created. For example, the bit #1 is set whenever the date is ≤ 1960. The same Figure illustrates the bits that some range queries set to "1". For the purpose of integration, we suggest that the bits of the tag(s) are interspersed within the message signature, instead of being stored consecutively.

The problem of designing an integrated access method for text and attributes has been encountered before, in two prototype message filing systems: OFP [35], and MINOS [6], [7]. Both systems use a variation of disjoint coding (see Figure 4.1), where the attributes set bits in the first part

F		w	$\bar{m}$	F_d	appr. F_d eq. (5.14)
200	(5.13,8)	0.1484	4.30 4.00 0.64	0.00041397	0.000324745
	(5.9,8)	0.3150	7.04 6.54 1.00	0.000452411	0.000348902
	exact	0.3026	6.47 5.99 1.00	0.000446946	0.000347746
250	(5.13,8)	0.0790	3.44 3.22 0.70	0.000219026	0.000188876
	(5.9,8)	0.1913	5.22 4.87 1.00	0.000250067	0.00021183
	exact	0.1859	4.97 4.63 1.00	0.000248059	0.000211025
300	(5.13,8)	0.0421	2.94 2.76 0.74	0.000116587	0.000106926
	(5.9,8)	0.1118	4.18 3.92 1.00	0.000136898	0.000123804
	exact	0.1097	4.07 3.81 1.00	0.000136233	0.000123419
350	(5.13,8)	0.0224	2.61 2.45 0.77	6.23489e-05	5.9369e-05
	(5.9,8)	0.0632	3.53 3.32 1.00	7.42339e-05	7.00304e-05
	exact	0.0625	3.47 3.27 1.00	7.40311e-05	6.98834e-05
400	(5.13,8)	0.0119	2.37 2.24 0.80	3.34184e-05	3.25232e-05
	(5.9,8)	0.0349	3.08 2.91 1.00	3.99119e-05	3.86278e-05
	exact	0.0346	3.05 2.88 1.00	3.9854e-05	3.85797e-05
450	(5.13,8)	0.0064	2.20 2.08 0.82	1.79203e-05	1.7656e-05
	(5.9,8)	0.0189	2.76 2.61 1.00	2.13156e-05	2.09366e-05
	exact	0.0188	2.75 2.60 1.00	2.12995e-05	2.09221e-05

Table 5.2
optimal $\bar{m}$ for case (b)

	bit #1 ≤ 1960	bit #2 ≤ 1975	bit #3 > 1960	bit #4 > 1975
date	signature			
1955	1	1	0	0
1963	0	1	1	0
1978	0	0	1	1

query	signature			
$1960 \leq \text{DATE}$	1	0	0	0
$1960 < \text{DATE} \leq 1975$	0	1	1	0

Figure 2.4
Signature extraction for numeric fields.

of the message signature, while the strings of "body" set bits in the second part. The choice of parameters is based on intuition. The methods and formulas presented in this work allow optimal solutions to this problem.

Signature files will be used in a prototype retrieval system, which is under implementation as part of the FULCRUM project at the University of Maryland. The system will be written in C, running on an IBM PC-AT under DOS and XENIX. The short-term goal is to store and retrieve abstracts of scientific publications on a PC, to aid researchers at the University of Maryland with the literature search. A Kurzweil scanner will accelerate the document input.

7. DISCUSSION - CONCLUSIONS.

In this paper we have extended signature extraction methods, so that they can handle both attributes and text. The main idea is to allow each string of field i (either formatted or text) to set m_i bits in the message signature, where the m_i's are chosen to minimize the false drop probability. Such integrated access methods for text and attributes have applications mainly in office automation and specifically in electronic message filing [35].

We have examined superimposed coding and compression-based methods in the presense of conjunctive queries and we have suggested a mathematical model for the above cases.

For superimposed coding, we developed exact (numerically solvable) and approximate, but accurate solutions, which allow optimal choice of the m_i's. We discovered that under optimal design, half of the bits in the message signature should be set to "1" (maximum entropy of the signature) and that the logarithm of F_d is asymptotically linear on the signature size F; both observations hold for any SC scheme studied up to now [24], [33] [11].

For the compression methods, we studied the optimistic bound (EN method). Using Lagrange multipliers, we found a set of non-linear equations that the optimal $\bar{m}$ and B should satisfy. This set however led to an infeasible solution. Thus we suggested a heuristic, which allowed numerical solution to the resulting set of equations, as well as closed, approximate but accurate enough formulas.

The contributions of this work are:

1) the design of extended, integrated signature file methods both for text and attributes, using superimposed coding and compression methods,

2) the mathematical formulation of the problem of optimal design for both approaches,

3) the derivation of exact and approximate solutions for the case of the extended superimposed coding (Eq. (4.3)).

4) the proposal of a heuristic for the extended compression methods, and the derivation of numerically solvable formulas for this heuristic (Eq. (5.4-7)), as well as accurate, closed form approximations.

The approximate formulas (4.3), (4.5) and (5.9), (5.13), (5.14) are useful to the practitioner, because they allow fast feasibility studies, to discover whether the corresponding signature method will meet the performance requirements. These formulas give an estimate of the false drop probability for a given signature size. Notice that the response time, mainly dominated by the I/O time, depends linearly on the size of the signature file and on the number of false drops; both need the formulas presented here. If the signature file method seems promising after this rough estimation, the exact formulas can be used (4.1-2), (5.4-7) to find the exact value of the false drop probability and to provide the optimal choice of the design parameters.

Future work can deal with the relaxation of the assumptions of the model, such as: fields independently specified in queries, no variance of occurrence frequencies e.t.c..

References

1. Aho, A.V. and M.J. Corasick, "Fast Pattern Matching: An Aid to Bibliographic Search," *Communications ACM*, vol. 18, no. 6, pp. 333-340, June 1975.
2. Bentley, J.L., "Multidimensional Binary Search Trees Used for Associative Searching," *CACM*, vol. 18, no. 9, pp. 509-517, Sept. 1975.
3. Boyer, R.S. and J.S. Moore, "A Fast String Searching Algorithm," *CACM*, vol. 20, no. 10, pp. 762-772, Oct. 1977.
4. Cardenas, A.F., "Analysis and Performance of Inverted Data Base Structures," *CACM*, vol. 18, no. 5, pp. 253-263, May 1975.
5. Christodoulakis, S. and C. Faloutsos, "Design Considerations for a Message File Server," *IEEE Trans. on Software Engineering* , vol. SE-10, no. 2, pp. 201-210, March 1984.
6. Christodoulakis, S., F. Ho, and M. Theodoridou, "The Multimedia Object Presentation Manager in MINOS: A Symmetric Approach," *Proceedings ACM SIGMOD* , May 1986.
7. Christodoulakis, S., M. Theodoridou, F. Ho, M. Papa, and A. Pathria, "Multimedia Document Presentation, Information Extraction and Document Formation in MINOS: A Model and a System," *ACM Transactions on Office Information Systems (TOOIS)*, 1986. (to appear)
8. Dattola, R., "FIRST: Flexible Information Retrieval System for Text," *JASIS*, vol. 30, pp. 9-14, Jan. 1979.
9. Faloutsos, C., "Signature Files: Design and Performance Comparison of some Signature Extraction Methods," *Proc. ACM SIGMOD*, pp. 63-82, Austin, Texas, May 1985.
10. Faloutsos, C., "Design and analysis of integrated access methods for text and attributes," working paper, Univ. of Maryland, 1986.
11. Faloutsos, C. and S. Christodoulakis, "Design of a Signature File Method that Accounts for Non-Uniform Occurrence and Query Frequencies," *VLDB Conf. Proceedings*, Stockholm, Sweden, Aug. 1985.
12. Fujitani, L., "Laser Optical Disk: The Coming Revolution in On-Line Storage," *CACM*, vol. 27, no. 6, pp. 546-554, June 1984.
13. Gonnet, G.H., "Unstructured Data Bases," Tech. Report CS-82-09, Univ. of Waterloo, 1982.
14. Gravina, C.M., "National Westminster Bank Mass Storage Archiving," *IBM Systems J*, vol. 17, no. 4, pp. 344-358, 1978.
15. Harrison, M.C., "Implementation of the Substring Test by Hashing," *CACM*, vol. 14, no. 12, pp. 777-779, Dec. 1971.
16. Haskin, R.L. and R.A. Lorie, "On Extending the Functions of a Relational Database System," *Proc. ACM SIGMOD*, pp. 207-212, Orlando, Florida, 1982.

17. Hollaar, L.A., "Text Retrieval Computers," *IEEE Computer Magazine*, vol. 12, no. 3, pp. 40-50, March 1979.

18. Hollaar, L.A., K.F. Smith, W.H. Chow, P.A. Emrath, and R.L. Haskin, "Architecture and Operation of a Large, Full-Text Information-Retrieval System," in *Advanced Database Machine Architecture*, ed. D.K. Hsiao, pp. 256-299, Prentice-Hall, Englewood Cliffs, New Jersey, 1983.

19. IBM,, *STAIRS/VS: Reference Manual*, 1979. IBM System Manual

20. Knuth, D.E., J.H. Morris, and V.R. Pratt, "Fast Pattern Matching in Strings," *SIAM J. Comput*, vol. 6, no. 2, pp. 323-350, June 1977.

21. Larson, P.A., "A method for speeding up text retrieval," *Proc. of ACM SIGMOD Conference*, San Jose, CA, May 1983.

22. McIlroy, M.D., "Development of a Spelling List," *IEEE Trans. on Communications*, vol. COM-30, no. 1, pp. 91-99, Jan. 1982.

23. McLeod, I.A., "A Data Base Management System for Document Retrieval Applications," *Information Systems*, vol. 6, no. 2, pp. 131-137, 1981.

24. Mooers, C., "Application of Random Codes to the Gathering of Statistical Information," Bulletin 31, Zator Co, Cambridge, Mass, 1949. based on M.S. thesis, MIT, January 1948

25. Nievergelt, J., H. Hinterberger, and K.C. Sevcik, "The Grid File: An Adaptable, Symmetric Multikey File Structure," *ACM TODS*, vol. 9, no. 1, pp. 38-71, March 1984.

26. Pfaltz, J.L., W.H. Berman, and E.M. Cagley, "Partial Match Retrieval Using Indexed Descriptor Files," *CACM*, vol. 23, no. 9, pp. 522-528, Sept. 1980.

27. Roberts, C.S., "Partial-Match Retrieval via the Method of Superimposed Codes," *Proc. IEEE*, vol. 67, no. 12, pp. 1624-1642, Dec. 1979.

28. Robinson, J.T., "The k-D-B-Tree: A Search Structure for Large Multidimensional Dynamic Indexes," *Proc. ACM SIGMOD*, pp. 10-18, 1981.

29. Rothnie, J.B. and T. Lozano, "Attribute Based File Organization in a Paged Memory Environment," *CACM*, vol. 17, no. 2, pp. 63-69, Feb. 1974.

30. Sacks-Davis, R. and K. Ramamohanarao, "A Two Level Superimposed Coding Scheme for Partial Match Retrieval," *Information Systems*, vol. 8, no. 4, pp. 273-280, 1983.

31. Salton, G., *The SMART Retrieval System - Experiments in Automatic Document Processing*, Prentice-Hall Inc, Englewood Cliffs, New Jersey, 1971.

32. Salton, G. and M.J. McGill, *Introduction to Modern Information Retrieval*, McGraw-Hill, 1983.

33. Stiassny, S., "Mathematical Analysis of Various Superimposed Coding Methods," *American Documentation*, vol. 11, no. 2, pp. 155-169, Feb. 1960.

34. Tsichritzis, D. and S. Christodoulakis, "Message Files," *ACM Trans. on Office Information Systems*, vol. 1, no. 1, pp. 88-98, Jan. 1983.

35. Tsichritzis, D., S. Christodoulakis, P. Economopoulos, C. Faloutsos, A. Lee, D. Lee, J. Vandenbroek, and C. Woo, "A Multimedia Office Filing System," *Proc. 9th International Conference on VLDB*, Florence, Italy, Oct.-Nov. 1983.

36. Van-Rijsbergen, C.J., *Information Retrieval,* Butterworths, London, England, 1979. 2nd edition

OFFICE SYSTEMS: Methods and Tools
G. Bracchi, D. Tsichritzis (Editors)
Elsevier Science Publishers B.V. (North-Holland)
© IFIP, 1987

HETERO

HETEROGENEOUS DBMS FRONTEND

Felipe Carino Jr.
655 South Fair Oaks Avenue #N103
Sunnyvale, California 94086
Tel: (408) 735-1318

ABSTRACT

Hetero is a Heterogeneous Database Management System (DBMS) frontend package that allows heterogeneous DBMSs to *coexist* and *communicate* with each other as if all the DBMSs connected to Hetero were one large uniform relational Distributed DBMS. Hetero integrates one of the most important components in *office automation* systems, namely, the diverse and unconnected databases resident on heterogeneous systems.

This paper *surveys* the technical issues and solutions used in Hetero. Related research done for both heterogeneous and homogeneous distributed databases is mentioned and referenced.

Hetero simplifies the Heterogeneous DBMS problem by requiring that a Hetero frontend layer be added to every DBMS that wishes to be accessed in a heterogeneous database environment. Hetero coexists with the native DBMS and uses native resources to the maximum extent possible.

Hetero creates a relational Distributed DBMS out of existing DBMSs that are based on the relational, network, and hierarchical data models. Hetero can coexist with existing database packages and DBMSs without causing disruptions to existing software, thus making Hetero a valuable frontend package to migrate existing software to distributed and/or relational DBMS.

Hetero introduces the notions of *database pipes* and a priori *knowledge tables* to the database field. The heterogeneous network connection problem is handled by a machine-independent multiplexing strategy that is mapped into the diverse networks supported by the hosts.

Keywords: Heterogeneous Databases, Distributed Databases, and Office Automation.

INTRODUCTION

Hetero is a Heterogeneous DBMS frontend package that can be interfaced to relational, hierarchical, or network DBMSs. A discussion of the three supported data models and semantics can be found in [Ullman 80]. Hetero allows heterogeneous DBMSs to coexist and communicate with each other as if all the DBMSs connected to Hetero were one large uniform relational distributed DBMS.

The relational model's [Codd 70, 72a, 72b] ease of use and distribution make it the logical conceptual model to use in a heterogeneous distributed environment. The Extended Relational Model RM/T [Codd 72b] extends and refines the definition of the relational model. Hetero tries to follow this definition closely when providing relational views to non-relational databases.

Papers that describe what I will term *first generation* heterogeneous database approaches, solutions, and systems are:

[1] GDBMS (Generalized Data Base Management Systems) [Cardenas & Pirahesh 79] at UCLA that uses a global conceptual model based on the entity-relationship model [Chen 77] and an

Acknowledgements: Special thanks go to a former colleague, Mike Bender at Ford Aerospace, with whom I designed the foundations of what evolved into Hetero.

internal model, which uses Codasyl syntax.

[2] A paper by [Gligor & Luckenbaugh 84] explores options in the heterogeneous database field as of 1984 and surveys the following systems: CSIN, GDBMS, XNDM, and Multibase. Distributed transaction management and structured data transfer protocols are also discussed.

[3] Multibase [Smith et al 81] and [Landers & Rosenberg 82] from CCA, uses a functional data model that defines a global schema and a local database interface used in translations.

[4] SIRIUS-DELTA [Esculier 84] [Ferrier & Stangret 82] is a distributed database system which supports cooperation of heterogeneous local database systems.

[5] Mermaid [Templeton 83] and [Templeton et al 86] is a heterogeneous database effort at System Development Corporation.

[6] UDL (Unified Database Language) [Date 80] is a programming language that has been extended to supported relational, network, and hierarchical structures.

Hetero is a *second generation* system that builds on the knowledge and experience of these and other systems. Hetero has many features and capabilities that were added based on a preliminary market survey of various banks that make heterogeneous distributed database use easier and simpler.

Features that are market-driven are:

* *FRIENDLY* - a WYSIWYG(1) visual user interface that integrates querying, report writing, and graphics via a Fourth Generation Language (4GL).

* global views and catalogs.

* database pipes and filters to extend SQL limitations without greatly modifying SQL.

* database *knowledge* protocols to encapsulate common complex actions.

* matrix security protection.

* relational view (and normalization) of hierarchical and network schemas.

Hetero has a *single interface* that resides on top of every DBMS that is supported, and does the necessary work *transparently* to the user. Hetero users can make diverse

DBMSs, possibly remote, behave as if they were a pseudo-distributed DBMS. Hetero is mainly a facilitator and coordinator of tasks between heterogeneous DBMSs. Most of the database work is done by the native DBMS (2) upon which Hetero resides; that is, the existing DBMSs can be thought of as diverse distributed backends which Hetero unifies and interconnects.

Coexistence stems from the fact that users can still use the native DBMS without using Hetero. As far as the native DBMS is concerned, Hetero requests are handled like any other user trying to access data in its database. Concurrency control is coordinated by Hetero, but is actually done by the native DBMS. Major investments in software can be salvaged by using Hetero; at the same time a migration path to new systems is made feasible without major disruptions to existing systems.

Transactions [Gray 80, 81] insure that operations execute to completion or have no effect. A *Two-Phase Commit Protocol* [Eswaran et al 76] using timestamps [Berstein & Goodman 80] is *emulated* when remote database transactions are involved.

A *Universal SQL Language (USQL)* based on the ANSI X3H2 Level 2 SQL [ANSI-SQL 83] is used for querying. The main extensions deal with notation for distributed query processing, environment variables, and database pipes.

The *Hetero-Shell* implements database pipes to overcome limitations in the nested SQL query definition [Date 84] and simplify distributed querying. *Database pipes* connect the output of a query to the input of another query, thus providing a generalized nesting and pipeline facility.

Hetero translates USQL into the appropriate syntax of the target DBMS it wants to communicate with. *DBCAP* is a "*database*" *of transformations* used by a two-pass parser when translating into the native query languages supported. The DBCAP concept is to the Hetero parser what TERMCAP [Unix 4.2BSD] is to the Unix Operating System curses library. Thus, a single copy of Hetero handles all DBMSs on a particular host.

A relational view is provided and the semantics implied by hierarchies and networks are handled in Hetero by inserting them into a *Virtual Relation*. The virtual relation can

---

(1) **WYSIWYG**: What You See Is What You Get.

(2) **Native DBMS**: target DBMS that will really perform the database operations.

be thought of as a directed graph that allows you to construct an *ordering* from a non-ordered relation.

Semantic information in hierarchical and network structures, not present in the relational model, pertains to a *possible ordering* or sequence information between the fields. That is, the *links* between fields may be part of the information in the database. The virtual relation is an internal relation stored in a Catalog.

Catalogs contain traditional data dictionary tables, plus relations that contain information concerning hosts, network, security, views, and audit information about the heterogeneous database network.

Normalization of the virtual relation is attempted when virtualizing - providing a relational view - of hierarchical and network structures and special constructs, such as, *repetition fields* (3). Discussions of normalization, its advantages, disadvantages, and the various normal forms can be found in [Maier 83] (theoretical) and [Date 77] (practical).

Automatic normalization [Meyer & Doughty 84] of the virtual relation into *First Normal Form* (1NF) is attempted. Heuristics are applied to the internal virtual tables generated in an attempt to shrink the tables via non-loss decomposition (not always possible). Papers by [Katz & Wong 82] on Decompiling CODASYL DML into Relational Queries and [Schneiderman & Thomas 82] An Architecture for Automatic Relational Databases, describe earlier work at providing relational views to networks and hierarchies. A more in-depth discussion on Hetero normalization strategies and repetition field handling appears later on in the technical details section of the paper.

A *Global Catalog* is maintained of all the databases and schemas available to the user. *Global Views* [Bertino et al 83] are supported where feasible in a heterogeneous scenario. It is not always possible to provide consistent views of some hierarchical and network schemas. Update semantics associated with views is discussed in [Bancilhon & Spyratos 81]

Security is aided by a matrix authorization and validation scheme described in [Fernandez et al 81]. The security problems associated with distributed databases and introduced by heterogeneous connections are discussed later on.

Hetero provides technical as well as nontechnical benefits in productivity and capital expenditures. Some of these advantages are: coexistence with DBMSs, distributed database access, single uniform interface, database (knowledge) protocols, and normalization of hierarchical and network structures.

Distributed Databases

Distributed Databases such as: SDD-1 [Rothnie et al 80], R* [Williams et al 82], and Distributed Ingres [Stonebraker & Nenhold 77] have homogeneous cooperating backends. They provide a mechanism by which to distribute the data and maintain integrity through a Distributed DBMS (DDBMS).

Organizations have different computing needs which are reflected in their heterogeneous hardware and software. It is unrealistic (and unnecessary) to expect them to run homogeneous software packages. Also, the dynamics of organizations change constantly, as in the case of a merger of two or more distinct organizations. It would be wasteful to throw away and/or rewrite DBMS software because of distributed heterogeneous DBMS needs.

Hetero does not create DDBMS in the pure sense, like SDD-1, R* and Distributed Ingres, a pseudo-DDBMS is created where none existed before. This is because the heterogeneous DBMSs backends cannot support DDBMS features such as split relations or fragments. Hetero provides data consistency and data integrity which are necessary in a distributed transaction processing system.

IPC Multiplexor

An *Interprocess Communication (IPC)* multiplexor is used to route information from a central server on each site that supports Hetero. Only *seven* network-dependent routines have to be changed for every type of network supported. The underlying network is only used to transfer files reliably.

Single Uniform Interface

N^2 mappings would be required to support N support DBMSs in the absence of a single uniform interface to each local DBMS. A single user interface, such as USQL, requires N mappings for N DBMSs, and adding a new DBMS to the Hetero DBMS network requires adding only *one* set of mappings into DBCAP. Otherwise, a new DBMS to the system would require N-1 new mappings.

---

(3) **Repetition Field**: construct used to imply a field is associated with every record.

Database (Knowledge) Protocols

Database (knowledge) protocols encapsulate complex and/or commonly used actions and serve various purposes: (1) Common actions can be pre-optimized into an archive of efficient frequently used routines. Distributing these tables and archives throughout the Hetero network provides a way to limit network traffic by sending small packets and execute queries efficiently. (2) Complex query interaction can be put into pre-compiled executable modules, archived and tuned at every site to use local database resources efficiently.

Non-Relational Normalization

Normalization of relation schemes as described [Maier 83] and [Date 77] belongs in the realm of relational databases. An interesting and unintended byproduct of virtualizing hierarchical and network schemes into relational views is that of non-relational normalization aid.

For example, take a hierarchical scheme and project it into a relational view in a table. Manually normalize the table and create new hierarchies that correspond to these tables. Generally, a *better* hierarchical scheme is the result. This stepwise refinement of schemas can be used to tune performance and provide better integrity, similar to tradeoffs in relational model normalization, or to migrate non-relational structures quickly to a relational DBMS.

HETERO MAJOR COMPONENTS

Hetero's major components are: Friendly - WYSIWYG User Interface, Hetero-Shell, Query Language and Parser, Distributed Query Processing, Database Administration, Global Catalog Management, Distributed Processing and Security Checker.

Friendly - WYSIWYG User Interface

Friendly is a WYSIWYG visual user interface that integrates querying, report writing, graphics, and Hetero-Shell. Users integrate these separate components using a 4GL. Friendly has been designed with high-resolution display in mind. A multiple-window approach is used for ASCII or dumb terminals.

Hetero-Shell

Hetero-Shell contains constructs similar to those found in other database interfaces and the Unix C-Shell, such as environment variables and aliasing. The Hetero-Shell is where database pipes, described subsequently in this paper are implemented.

Query Language and Parser

A query language based on the *tuple-relational calculus* or *"Quel-like"* would conceptually be easiest to use and implement. Our market study shows *SQL-based systems have great penetration*, therefore, it is a moot point. A query language based on the latest SQL standard definition will be extended for distributed processing needs. We call it Universal SQL (USQL) in this document.

The dynamic interpreter used is two-pass. The *first pass* generates an *Intermediate Query Language (IQL)*. An optional optimizer operates on IQL to improve performance. The *second pass* takes the IQL and generates native queries using DBCAP tables or the database protocol entries.

The parser translates USQL into the native DBMS query language using DBCAP, which is a "database" of database translations. The notions behind DBCAP are similar to those of the Unix operating system TERMCAP for handling different terminals (semantic information concerning non-relational DBMS are handled through information generated in the catalog).

The DBCAP table contents must be able to change dynamically and be used by the dynamic compiler generator that eventually is used to translate USQL -> IQL -> Transform (DBCAP) -> Native Queries. Afterwards, the DBCAP entry for each query language of each DBMS supported must be manually and carefully generated.

Distributed Query Processing

Distributed Query Processing is a key factor in the performance equation. Query analysis is done with the information contained in the global catalog and subqueries are then sent to the appropriate (remote) sites. *Distributed Joins* are a special case due to the existence of non-relational structures. The distributed heterogeneous join issues are discussed in the technical section of this paper.

Database Administration (DBA)

In Hetero, the term DBA is a misnomer, since *most* DBA functions (and many others) are performed by the target/native DBMS. Hetero is mainly a *coordinator* of database and inter-database tasks. Hetero is only a frontend package that allows inter-database communication among heterogeneous DBMSs. A very important DBA function is the emulation of a two-phase commit protocol variant for non-cooperating heterogeneous databases, when multiple sites/databases are updated to ensure data consistency and integrity.

Global Catalog Management

Catalog tables are our version of *data dictionary tables*. Every network node has a catalog that contains all the pertinent information about all the databases on the Hetero network. Catalogs contain all the information necessary for the user to formulate queries and for the Hetero DBA to perform its tasks. We have extended traditional catalog contents to include:

* *Virtual Relation(s)*: series of relations that constitute the virtual fields scheme.

* *Network Relation*: relation that contains the nicknames for all hosts supported and routing information.

* *Views Relation*: stores the information necessary to provide global views across databases.

* *Security Relation*: relation of permissions per user on databases.

* *Audit Relation*: audit trail of accesses to individual databases and operations.

A *global catalog scheme* permits us to formulate, partially evaluate, and determine optimal distributed query processing, provided the integrity of catalogs is maintained. Catalog Manager routines needed to accomplish this are described in the technical section.

A global catalog scheme could potentially be explosive in size, since every database, relation, and attribute with the databases must be present at each site. Like the 1NF issues related to the virtual relation, this is acceptable for now, but could lead to space problems in very large database networks.

Distributed Processing

Network facilities are only used to transfer files reliably; all the distributed database knowledge is handled by Hetero. Interprocess Communication (IPC) is handled by a data multiplexer resident at every site. Seven routines are used internally by the heterogeneous IPC handlers which form the basis for the multiplexing strategies. The seven IPC routines are based on a set of routines that are similar to *Unix 4.2 BSD sockets* and are then mapped into the local network resources available.

Security Checker

Security validation is achieved via a table of permissions which indicates user access permission relative to the various databases on the Hetero network. An option permits encryption of packets in the IPC multiplexor for extra safety during routing.

TECHNICAL DETAILS

The technical issues and solutions described in various sections are: Architecture, WYSIWYG User Interface, Universal SQL, Hetero-Shell, Database Protocols, Virtual Fields, Semantics Handling, Catalog Management and Integrity, Distributed IPC Processing, Network Partition, Error Handling, Distributed Heterogeneous Joins, Transaction Processing and Recovery, and Security Issues.

Architecture

Hetero is a frontend software package that is interfaced with every DBMS on the heterogeneous database network. Hetero provides enough capability so that the local DBMSs connected to it appear to create a pseudo-DDBMS. The *Hetero Architecture and components are shown in Figure 1*. The resulting *Hetero Network is shown in Figure 2*.

WYSIWYG User Interface

Friendly is a visual user interface that displays the output of a 4GL which is used to integrate and display the data and pictorial information generated by querying the databases, the graphics package and the report writer. The Friendly user interface is defined in terms of a machine-independent display system which is interfaced to workstation-provided libraries and archives in order to run Hetero windows.

USQL is the supported query language, and graphics routines handle pie-charts and histogram drawing. User interface, query translation, and network IPC handling are the areas where underlying hardware and software capabilities affect Hetero processing the most.

Supporting multi-menu user interface on ASCII or dumb terminals presents separate challenges. The limitations presented by traditional 24 lines by 80 character screens require a different approach. Our strategy is to preserve the multiple-menus and display each menu as it is being used. This approach uses alot of processes and is space intensive since it implements a mini-window managing system, but preserves the user-friendly interface. Pictorial graphical information drawing is supported based on terminal capabilities.

Universal SQL

Hetero USQL is based on extensions to ANSI SQL. The main extensions to the SQL query language are those that specify location (4) of relations or virtual relations in network or hierarchical cases. The introduction of database pipes, implemented in the Hetero-Shell, generalize the notion of nested queries and database filters.

Range variables in SQL FROM can be thought of as pointers that iterate through a table; the pointer points to tuples within a table. The (physical) location to which the pointer points does not affect the logic or syntax of SQL. Therefore, specifying full logical pathnames provides a capability for specifying where the actual data is located. In the future, this will be made more location-transparent.

USQL queries are parsed, decomposed into an *Intermediate Query Language* (IQL), and translated into native DBMS query statements using DBCAP table entries. DBCAP contains the transformations that are used when translating USQL into native DBMS query syntax.

IQL is a small intermediate database language that specifies a pseudo-relational database sublanguage. IQL was designed to facilitate table driven code generation and global optimizations. Relational primitives such as project, select and join facilitate global query analysis.

The USQL translator is two-pass: (1) translation and decomposition of USQL into IQL; and (2) DBCAP table-driven code generator of IQL into target query languages. The technical details of query translation are those traditionally associated with table-driven compilers for multiple instruction sets. The global optimizer has not been implemented yet.

Hetero-Shell

The concepts of *pipes and filters* are well known and widely used in Unix and are powerful tools for building applications. Although SQL already has nested queries that behave like pipes do in Unix, they are not general purpose. A generalized pipe mechanism has been designed and incorporated into the Hetero-Shell which eliminates the arbitrary nesting rules currently in the SQL definition. The " | " notation is used. The introduction of pipes to the data-

base field, connecting the output of one query to the input of another, provided it makes sense, permits the use of query filters. Query filters enhance the ease of use, power, and flexibility currently found in SQL.

Database Protocols

There are *two* types of Database Protocols: *complex* and *simple*. Complex database protocols are similar to canned pre-compiled queries usually composed of a multi-query complex function. They are stored and recognized by a user-supplied name. Simple database protocols are recognized by the USQL parser. After the first pass USQL -> IQL, the *knowledge table* is scanned to see if the user has specified *efficient code* to execute for this particular class of querying and is used in lieu of the code normally generated.

Virtual Fields

Hetero provides a relational view of all data, regardless of what data model the underlying database was based on. Only Relational, Hierarchical and Network DBMS are supported. The Virtual Fields portion of Hetero is what makes it attractive to users with non-relational DBMS.

Virtual fields hide the details of providing a relational view of data to users. The current solution normalizes a non-relational schema into First Normal Form (1NF) by creating a directed graph that describes the non-relational structure. If the resulting 1NF exceeds the maximum allowed size, a mechanical normalization is attempted using the following strategy.

[1] If it is possible to determine a primary key from the non-relational database data dictionary, use this as a key for the table to be generated via projection. If a key cannot be determined from the data dictionary then based on tuple analysis count, pick the attribute(s) that appear the most and use it as the key. Counting is inefficient, but the normalization process and key generation are mechanisms that deal with semantics and content of data.

[2] Decomposing the virtual tables via normalization introduces the problem of *non-loss decomposition*. The non-loss problem actually means you *gain* tuples. When decomposing a table via projections into two tables and joining the two resulting tables it is possible to *generate* tuples that did not exist before in the original table.

---

(4) In the prototype, the user specifies a logical pathname on each range variable.

The only way to insure this does not happen is to count the number of tuples in the original and the re-joined tables after normalization. If tuples were gained then another key is selected and the process is repeated. If there is not enough space and normalization can be performed the operation is aborted and the user is informed.

[3] Repetition fields are used in various DBMSs as a compression construct to associate field(s) with every record. This compression technique when normalizing can lead to data explosion. Repetition fields are factored into the 1NF table to be normalized if the resulting table is *not too big*. Otherwise, the tables are normalized and the field is assumed to be there, although in reality it is a virtual-virtual (subsumed) field.

The virtualizing algorithms used here are simple and are bias towards time complexity in order to save space. The problems associated with these mechanical algorithms are due to the fact they are performing semantic tasks automatically by examining the data.

The algorithms rely on tuple counting and data dictionary entries to generate what is known in database terminology as a *Functional Dependency (FD)*. These FDs are used as the keys by which non-loss decomposition is attempted. Non-loss table decomposition has similar semantic problems, and automating this process is very difficult.

Semantics Handling

The complexity of some heterogeneous DBMS solutions stem from the fact that semantics associated with network or hierarchical structures are handled directly in the query language, or as lateral structures in the case where the native DBMS is mapped into other environments and back to native DBMS syntax when done.

In the latter case, N^2 lateral mappings are required, where N is the number of DBMS. Adding a new DBMS to the system requires N-1 new lateral mappings.

Hetero simplifies the heterogeneous DBMS inter-database problem by having a single query language interface to all DBMSs. This permits users to view the Hetero database network as a single unified universe. The semantics associated with networks and hierarchies are handled using *virtual relations*. Virtual relations are really a series of tables that contain the graph information. For simplicity they are collectively referred

to as virtual relation.

The best way to describe a virtual relation is through a simple example shown in Figure 3. Assume that you have a hierarchy and each box represents a *segment*. These segments contain *fields* (5). (For simplicity, the fields within segments are not shown, but these also have entries in the virtual relation.)

When Hetero is used to create a new network or hierarchy from scratch, there is no mechanism for specifying ordering and a flat structure is produced; a structure with a root and all other fields are direct descendents of the root.

Hetero was never really designed to be used to create *new* hierarchies or networks from the relational USQL. Although allowed, the intention was to permit querying, updating, and even schema modification based on the original schema. Schema modification tries to preserve the tree-structure as much as possible based on the virtual fields. The flat structure created during new table creation is due to the fact that no information is contained within the virtual fields pertaining to the *ordering* of the records.

Catalog Management and Integrity

Catalogs contain information usually contained in the data dictionary, network information for remote communication, and the virtual relation described above. The five Catalog Manager routines that manage contents and integrity of the catalogs are listed and described below.

DB_CREATE: Creates a new global permanent catalog from scratch at the site specified.

DB_SYNC: Updates the network's catalogs every Kth time interval and only if a change occurred.

DB_UPDATE: Updates the local catalog in between DB_SYNCs, if a user uses a database whose schema was modified before the changes were propagated by DB_SYNC.

DB_FSCK: Checks the integrity of the catalogs for inconsistencies or outdated entries.

DB_TMP: Creates temporary entries in the local catalog. DBAs can restrict which databases and sites are resident permanently in the catalogs; this reduces catalog size and content. DB_TMP with some overhead provides the benefits of global

---

(5) IMS terminology for segments and fields are used.

catalogs to infrequently accessed databases. This is a classical case of space versus time tradeoffs.

Distributed IPC Processing

By distributed IPC processing we mean all those functions associated with interprocess communication, network file transfers, distributed knowledge protocol handling, database pipes that pump data across hosts, and the network partition problem.

The original prototype had a user peer-to-peer socket connection for every database logon. The number of processes required per user grew factorially based on the number of hosts involved in a query. This clearly was unacceptable.

A *multiplexing strategy* was designed that directs messages, processes and data within each host. The multiplexer is a machine-independent server that establishes a peer-to-peer communication link between the Hetero frontends on diverse systems. The communication takes place through a single server on each machine, and security can be enforced easier. This added extra burden in data communication packaging, but it also made the server machine-independent and protocol-independent. This makes Hetero portable to many environments.

There are seven routines that emulate Unix 4.2 BSD sockets. These routines are rewritten and mapped into Hetero's pseudo-socket scheme based on the underlying network resources available. The IPC was designed with the provision that exact copies of Hetero exist everywhere on the network where Hetero runs. The seven pseudo-socket routines mapped into the local environment are: [1] rsocket, [2] raccept, [3] rbind, [4] rconnect, [5] rlisten, [6] rrecv, and [7] rsend. For example, if SNA is the underlying communication mechanism, then the above seven routines are rewritten to *behave* like sockets, but actually use SNA calls.

Network Partition

Network partition [Davidson et al 85] has to do with *losing access* to Local Area Networks (LAN) and gateway connection between networks. Hetero handles the network partition problem based on the fact that all the work performed on a database is eventually done by a native database. The native database data is not replicated anywhere and integrity of inter-database updates is maintained via the two-phase commit algorithm used.

Various scenarios must be dealt with when network partition occurs in Hetero: [1] native DBMS node dies, with active users; [2] native DBMS node dies, without active users; [3] LAN or gateway connection is lost, with active users; [4] LAN or gateway connection is lost, without active users.

Native DBMS With User Dies

If the native DBMS node which contains the *real* DBMS dies, then there is nothing Hetero can do and all transactions will be rolled back to the last checkpoint when the DBMS comes up.

Native DBMS Without User Dies

If a native DBMS node with no active user dies, then all requests to it will be blocked by the Hetero DBA until recovery is complete and the global catalogs are updated.

Connection With Users Is Lost

If an active network connection dies, then Hetero will try to find another path. If this fails, then the session will be aborted.

Connection Without Users Is Lost

If a network connection cannot be established, then the user will be informed and told to try later. Furthermore, if the network connection loss impedes global catalog updates, then these will be updated later. The catalog manager guarantees that a user will always see the latest updated schema before allowing access to it.

Error Handling

Various components can detect errors. Based on the type of error, Hetero will rollback some or all transactions and advise the user that an error was detected.

Distributed Heterogeneous Joins

In Hetero, it is possible to join two or more relations from distinct databases at remote sites. The main concept in the Hetero distributed join is that all work is done by moving all the tables involved to a single DBMS and then performing the join.

The environment variable *joinwork* tells Hetero where to execute the distributed join. If joinwork is not specified, then Hetero will try to determine where to execute the query.

The *criteria* for selecting how and where to join tables are ranked below:

[1] Give preference to a relational DBMS over network or hierarchical DBMSs regardless of location and what the user specified That is, move tables to the relational DBMS. Joining a relational

and hierarchical structure at the hierarchical DBMS is too slow, and in some cases does not make sense.

[2] If more than one DBMS involved is relational, then choose the one that has an index involved in the join where-clause.

[3] If all variables are equal and the location issuing requests is involved, then move tables to the requester's DBMS.

[4] If all variables are equal and all DBMS choices are remote, then estimate the size of transfers and move the shortest tables to the longest one.

[5] If no relational DBMSs are involved, then use the same criteria above giving preference to the network model over the hierarchical.

The *distributed heterogeneous join algorithm* can be summarized as follows:

[1] Examine the join query for attributes actually used. Only the retrieved attributes and where-clause conditions participate in a multi-way join.

[2] Set up connections to all locations involved and determine where to execute the join, if not specified in the location environment variable *joinwork*.

[3] Using this information, issue selects to all the sites involved where the where-clauses reflect the limited range of tuples desired. Then further project these tuples to the actual attributes needed as determined in [1] above.

[4] Move these tuples into a temporary relation on the system executing the join.

[5] Finally, join the temporary tables using the local DBMS and clean up when done. This method is very slow when non-relational databases are used.

Transaction Processing and Recovery

Transaction processing in a heterogeneous database environment presents special difficulties. Interconnecting DBMSs that were not designed to be distributed changes the notions of transaction processing from the point of view of the participating DBMSs, and *cooperation* strategies designed into traditional distributed systems are not present. This implies *commit* and *rollback* schemes that are distributed in nature.

A distributed transaction processing superstructure emulates a variant of the two-phase commit protocol with timestamps imposed on top of the participating DBMSs.

Since the participating heterogeneous DBMSs were not designed to cooperate with each other, timing mechanisms and the two-phase algorithm are used to simulate cooperation between the diverse DBMSs. This results in some unnecessary rollbacks and this algorithm will be changed in the future.

Security Issues

Security presents enormous problems in that this issue is user-dependent; here, counterbalancing issues must be resolved. *Performance* versus *Security* needs have to be balanced. Hetero tries to provide security through various measures such as: [1] encryption; [2] user validation; and [3] matrix permission access. This does not guard against hostile attack, but provides an adequate beginning.

Encryption of packets sent to remote location is an option available to users concerned with security.

HETERO EXAMPLES

[1] Shows a Hetero session that transfers 10% of Rockefeller's checking account to Felipe's checking at another location. Hetero-Shell variables are used instead of pipes to demonstrate this feature.

[2] Shows the same example, except that the DBPIPE construct is used to show how database pipes are used.

For simplicity, the examples assume the user knows the location and schema of the databases.

Network addresses such as loc1@ibm are logical. Real network node names are contained within the network relation. The network relation contains all the nicknames that Hetero understands for host names, and is used for finding pathways between hosts. Hetero, using the network relation, would obtain the real network names and paths and establish a communication link.

Example[1]: Remote funds transfer using Hetero-Shell variables only:

```
# start transaction
begin transaction

# database locations
set loc1 = loc1@ibm;
set loc2 = loc2@vax;

# open databases and which
# establishes communication links
open database ($loc1:oracle:checking);
open database ($loc2:ingres:checking);
```

```
# compute 10% of balance
set transfer =
     select  r1.bal * 0.1
     from    s1 $loc1:r1,
             s2 $loc1:r2
     where   s1.acc = s2.acc and
             s2.name = "rockefeller";

# subtract the 10% from rockefeller

update $loc1:bal
set $loc1:bal = $loc1:bal - $transfer
where $loc1:r2.name = "rockefeller";

# add the 10% to felipe

update $loc2:bal
set $loc2:bal = $loc2:bal + $transfer
where $loc2:r4.name = "felipe";

# commit work
end transaction
```

Example[2]: Same example using database pipes:

```
# start transaction
begin transaction
set loc1 = loc1@ibm;
set loc2 = loc2@vax;

open database ($loc1:oracle:checking);
open database ($loc2:ingres:checking);

# current implementation requires
# DBPIPE (...) syntax around
# information to be pumped and
# $DBPIPE where it is to be used.
# DBPIPE does not have to be atomic.

select  DBPIPE (r1.bal * 0.1)
from    s1 $loc1:r1,
        s2 $loc1:r2
where   s1.acc = s2.acc and
        s2.name = "rockefeller"
        |
update $loc1:bal
set $loc1:bal = $loc1:bal - $DBPIPE
where $loc1:r2.name = "rockefeller";
```

Future Work

Hetero is a system that was designed bottom-up to solve a distributed database application problem that needed to create a unified DDBMS from diverse DBMSs on different hosts. A new Hetero system will be redesigned that builds on the knowledge, experience, and market information obtained since the original skeleton prototype was built.

The principal areas of R&D and recode concern reliability, and efficiency issues. Furthermore, the new algorithms must be *proven correct* for Hetero to be useful outside the laboratory environment. The critical areas are:

[1] Replace the two-phase commit algorithm described with a new algorithm that can be proven correct for non-cooperating DBMS backends.

[2] Make SQL querying less cumbersome to use and more database location transparent.

[3] Design new algorithms that more efficiently normalize virtual relation in a non-loss fashion.

[4] Design new strategies to handle data explosion in global catalogs.

[5] Find a better way to handle non-dynamic data dictionary databases; especially IMS.

[6] Design a less process-intensive scheme for the Friendly WYSIWYG when running on ASCII terminals and add long text field management.

[7] Security issues other than a simple matrix permission table and validation and encryption routines in the multiplexer have to better addressed.

[8] The current implementation of database pipes puts the burden on the user to specify where the pipe information is to be pumped. A new consistent and less cumbersome syntax is required.

[9] An item that is market-driven which should be addressed in the future is a natural language interface.

CONCLUSION

Hetero should aid office automation by providing access to diverse databases stored on multiple machines. This integration of information will yield higher levels of productivity by better utilizing distributed computer resources and data. Hetero solves many of the heterogeneous database problems necessary for office automation in a practical way by using a common frontend to all DBMS. It allows coexistence with many environments, salvages current investments, and provides a migration path to a new database technology.

Hetero is written entirely in C, has only seven machine-dependent routines dealing with network communication, and a WYSIWYG user interface that works both on display and ASCII terminals. This makes it highly portable to many environments. Performance is based on overall underlying network performance. Hetero introduces the notion of pipes to DBMSs, provides database protocols to encapsulate actions, and distributed joins capabilities to heterogeneous database users. Future work will certain on developing algorithms that are more efficient and can be proven correct.

Readers' comments on Hetero will be greatly appreciated.

REFERENCES

[ANSI-SQL 83]

X3H3 ANSI Database Committee. Draft Document X3H3-83-152 August 1983.

[Bancilhon & Spyratos 81]

F. Bancilhon, N. Spyratos, "Update Semantics of Relational Views", ACM TODS, Vol. 6, No. 4, Dec. 1981, pp. 557 - 575.

[Berstein & Goodman 80]

P. A. Berstein and N. Goodman, "Timestamp-Based Algorithms for Concurrency Control in Distributed Database Systems", Proc. 6th VLDB Conference, Oct. 1980.

[Bertino et al 83]

E. Bertino, L.M. Hass, B.G. Lindsay, "View Management in Distributed Data Base Systems", Proc. 9th VLDB Conference, 1983.

[Cardenas & Pirahesh 79]

A.F. Cardenas, and M.H. Pirahesh, "Data Base Communication in a Heterogeneous Data Base Management System Network", Information Systems, Vol. 5, No. 1, pp. 55-79, 1980.

[Chen 77]

P.P Chen, "The Entity-Relationship Model-A Basis for the Enterprise View of Data", AFIPS Conference Proc., Vol 46, pp. 77-84, 1977.

[Codd 70]

E.F. Codd, "A Relational Model for Large Shared Data Banks", CACM Vol. 13, No. 6, June 1970.

[Codd 72a]

E.F. Codd, "Further Normalization of the Data Base Relational Model", Data Base Systems (R. Rustin, ed.) Prentice-Hall, pp. 33-64.

[Codd 72b]

E.F. Codd, "Relational Completeness of the Data Base Sub-languages", *ibid.* pp. 65-98.

[Date 77]

C.J. Date, "An Introduction to Database Systems", 2nd Edition, Addison-Wesley, pp. 153- 178.

[Date 80]

C.J. Date, "An Introduction to the Unified Database Language (UDL)", Proc 6th VLDB Conference, Oct. 1980.

[Date 84]

C.J. Date, "A Critique of the SQL Database Language", ACM Sigmod Record, Volume 14, Number 3, November 1984, pp. 8 - 54.

[Davidson et al 85]

S. B. Davidson, Hector Garcia-Molina, Dale Skeen, "Consistency in Partitioned Networks", ACM Computing Surveys, Vol. 17, No. 3, September 1985.

[Esculier 84]

C. Esculier, "The SIRIUS-DELTA Architecture: A Framework for Co-Operating Database Systems", Computer Networks, Vol. 8, pp. 43-48, 1984.

[Eswaran et al 76]

K.P. Eswaran, J.N. Gray, R.A. Lorie, I.L.Traiger, "The Notions of Consistency and Predicate Locks in a Data Base System". CACM Vol. 19, No. 11, November 1976.

[Fernandez et al 81]

E. B. Fernandez, R. C. Summers, C. Wood, "Database Security and Integrity", Addison-Wesley, 1981.

[Ferrier & Stangret 82]

A. Ferrier and C. Stangret, "Heterogeneity in a Distributed Database Management System SIRIUS-DELTA", Proc 8th VLDB Conference, Sept. 1982.

[Gligor & Luckenbaugh 84]

V.D. Gligor and G.L. Luckenbaugh, "Interconnecting Heterogeneous Database Management Systems", Computer, Vol. 17, No. 1, pp. 33-43, Jan. 1984.

[Gray 80]

J.N. Gray, "A Transaction Model", IBM Research Report RJ2895, August 1980.

[Gray 81]

J.N. Gray, "The Transaction Concept: Virtues and Limitations", Proc. 7th VLDB Conference, 1981.

[Irving et al 82]

I.L. Traiger, J. Gray, C.A. Galtieri, B.G. Lindsay, "Transaction and Consistency in Distributed Database Systems, ACM TODS, Vol. 7, No. 3, Sept. 1982, pp. 323 - 342.

[Katz & Wong 82]

R.H. Katz and E. Wong, "Decompiling CODASYL DML into Relational Queries", ACM TODS, Vol. 7, No. 1, March 1982, pp. 1 - 23.

[Landers & Rosenberg 82]

T. Landers and R.L. Rosenberg, "An Overview of MULTIBASE", Distributed Data Bases, H.J. Scheider, ed., North-Holland Publishing Co., pp. 153-183, 1982.

[Maier 83]

D. Maier, "The Theory of Relational Databases", Computer Science Press, 1983.

[Meyer & Doughty 84]

K. Meyer and J. Doughty, "Automatic Normalisation and Entity-Relationship Generation through Attribute and Roles", ACM Sigmod Record, Volume 14, Number 3, November 1984, pp. 69 - 103.

[Rothnie et al 80]

J.B. Rothnie, P.A. Bernstein, S. Fox, N. Goodman, M. Hammer, T.A. Landers, C. Reeve, D.W. Shipman, E. Wong, "Introduction to a System for Distributed Databases (SDD-1)", ACM TODS, Vol. 5, No. 1, March 1980, pp. 1 - 17.

[Schneiderman & Thomas 82]

B. Schneiderman and G. Thomas, "An Architecture for Automatic Relational Database System Conversion", ACM TODS, Vol. 7, No. 2, June 1982, pp. 235 - 257.

[Smith et al 81]

"Multibase-Integrating Heterogeneous Distributed Database Systems", AFIPS Conf. Proc., Vol. 50, pp.487-499, NCC 1981.

[Stonebraker & Nenhold 77]

M. Stonebraker and E. Nenhold, "A Distributed Data Base Version of Ingres", Proc. 2nd Berkeley Workshop on Distributed Data Management and Computer Networks, pp. 19-36, May 1977.

[Templeton 83]

M. Templeton, D. Drill, A. Hwang, I. Kameny, E. Lund, "An Overview of Mermaid System - A Frontend to Heterogeneous Databases", Proc. IEEE EASCON83, September 1983.

[Templeton et al 86]

M. Templeton, D. Brill, A. Chen, S. Dao, E. Lund, R. MacGregor, P. Ward "An Introduction to AIDA - A Frontend to Heterogeneous Databases", Distributed Systems Vol: II, Artech House, pp. 497-504.

[Unix 4.2BSD]

Unix Programmer's Manual, Section (5), 4.2 Berkeley Software Distribution, August 1983.

[Williams et al 82]

"R* An Overview of the Architecture", Improving Database Usability and Responsiveness, Peter Scheuerman, ed., Academic Press, Inc., New York, pp.1-27, 1982.

[Ullman 80]

J. D. Ullman, "Principles of Database Systems", Computer Science Press, 2nd Edition, pp. 73-103, 1980.

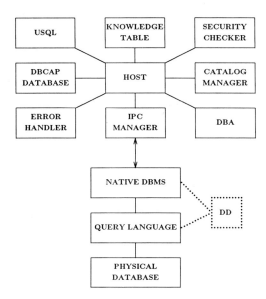

Figure 1. Hetero Architecture

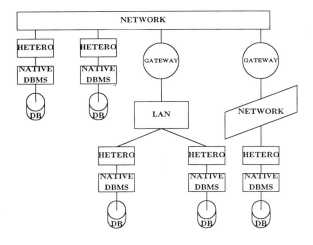

Figure 2. Hetero Network

The virtual relation has many fields. As stated previously, our example is an oversimplification of the real implementation, but it conveys the idea.

MAIN ATTRIBUTES OF **VIRTUAL RELATION** ARE:

vfname: name of a segment.

vfdepth: depth of segment from root.

vforder: order of segment from left to right.

vflink: parent of segment.

virtual relation			
vfname	**vfdepth**	**vforder**	**vflink**
A	0	0	NULL
B	1	0	A
C	1	1	A
D	1	2	A
E	2	0	B
F	2	1	C
G	2	2	D
H	2	3	D
I	2	4	D
J	3	0	E
Q	3	1	E
L	3	2	H

Allows reconstruction of hierarchies, directed graph tables.

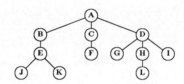

Figure 3. Virtual Relation Example Hierarchy

OFFICE SYSTEMS: Methods and Tools
G. Bracchi, D. Tsichritzis (Editors)
Elsevier Science Publishers B.V. (North-Holland)
IFIP, 1987

THE ARCHITECTURAL REQUIREMENTS AND INTEGRATION ANALYSES OF A DATABASE SERVER FOR OFFICE AUTOMATION *

Steven A. Demurjian, David K. Hsiao and Roger G. Marshall **

Office automation systems are growing both in use and in complexity. The development of a database management system for the office automation environment becomes a high priority, in order to provide an efficient and reliable way to manage the information needs of the office. Therefore, the specification of a database server for the office automation environment becomes a key area of concern. In addition to providing traditional database support, the database server must also provide new database support, so as to meet the unique and many needs of office automation environments. In this paper, we focus on the characterization and specification of a database server for the office automation environment. We also consider how such a database server can be effectively integrated into the office automation environment. We use both heuristics and queueing-theory analyses to evaluate the various integration configurations. In fact, the analysis of the configurations based on the queueing expressions comprises a major portion of the paper. Further, we examine an experimental database system, known as the multi-backend database system (MBDS), as a candidate for the database server in the office automation environment.

1. AN INTRODUCTION

As office automation systems (OAS) become more prevalent in the work place, the need for database support in the office automation environment (OAE) becomes a key issue. In this paper we attempt to provide the characterization of a database server for OAEs. The database server is used to provide traditional as well as new database support in the OAE. In addition, we study various approaches to the integration of the database server into an OAE. In our characterization and study of a server, we focus on the use of an experimental database system, known as the multi-backend database system (MBDS), as the server. Although MBDS may not be an ideal choice, it does serve as a benchmark for measuring the other database servers for OAEs. In the rest of this paper we examine how and why MBDS may be considered as a database server for the OAE.

More specifically, in Section 2 we discuss the architecture and characteristics of a database server for the OAE. In Section 3 we briefly describe the design and implementation of MBDS. We also analyze whether the unique design characteristics of MBDS meet the needs of the OAE. In Section 4 we present how a database server such

* The work reported herein is supported by grants from the Department of Defense STARS Program and from the Office of Naval Research and conducted at the Laboratory for Database Systems Research, Naval Postgraduate School, Monterey, CA 93943.

** S. A. Demurjian and D. K. Hsiao are with the Department of Computer Science, Naval Postgraduate School, Monterey, California 93943, USA. R. G. Marshall is with the Department of Computer Science, Loyola College, Baltimore, Maryland 21210, USA.

as MBDS can be integrated into the OAE by providing a heuristic analysis of the possible design configurations. We focus on the multiple-backend architecture of MBDS and how it satisfies the architectural requirements of the OAE database server. In Section 5, we use single-device and multiple-device queueing models to formally evaluate the design configurations given in Section 4. In Section 6 we present an analysis of the computational results obtained from using the queueing equations of Section 5. The detailed development of the queueing equations for various configurations is included in the Appendix. Finally, we conclude this paper in Section 7 with observations on the results obtained.

2. A CHARACTERIZATION OF AN IDEAL DATABASE SERVER

In characterizing a database server for the OAE, we focus our efforts in two directions. First, we consider the architectural requirements of the database server that will facilitate the smooth integration of the database server into the OAE. Second, we consider the necessary database system features or characteristics of the database server for the OAE. In the following two sections, we examine these two considerations for a database server in the OAE.

2.1. The Architectural Requirements

The basic structure of the OAE consists of a group of workstations connected by a local-area network (LAN). (See Figure 1, where a workstation is denoted with the letter W in a square box.) To successfully meet the needs of this environment, the database server must be integrated into the existing OAE. The integration of the database server into the OAE must be smooth and have no ill-effects on the existing OAS. If the database server runs only on a single workstation, it should be powerful enough to meet the database management needs of the present OAE. However, it may not meet the growing demands of database management of the future OAE. Thus, it seems logical that the database server should consist of, initially, a few workstations and, later, a number of workstations. With multiple workstations, the database server should reduce and distribute the database management load across the variable and multiple workstations.

Whether those workstations which make up the database server act as individual and separate database systems or cooperate to handle the database management needs of the OAE is an issue. It may not be feasible in a given OAE to distribute the database management functionality and load among different database servers on the same network, since the OAS is not a distributed database system. More likely, the OAE requires a central repository of data and programs that is maintained and accessed via a single system, so that the data and programs can be successfully shared throughout the OAE. This calls for a centralized database management system.

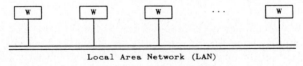

Local Area Network (LAN)

Figure 1.   The Basic OAS

In conclusion. the overall architectural requirements of a database server for OAEs should therefore dictate a centralized database system running on variable and multiple workstations.

2.2. The Six Characteristics

There are six major characteristics of such a database server. They are software portability, software independence, auto-configurability, survivability, versatility, and performance. *Software portability* provides the database server with the ability to be accessible on a wide range of workstations. Specifically, the database server should not be restricted to a particular class of workstations and a specific type of operating systems. Instead, it should be portable across a wide range of workstations and operating systems of the OAE. If the database server is implemented on multiple workstations, the software components of the server running on the separate workstations should be sufficiently independent, so that the database server does not become inoperative when a node (i.e., either one of the software components on a workstation or a workstation itself) becomes disabled. *Software independence* among system components running on separate workstations may eliminate software and hardware interdependencies and the complexity of the database server.

When running on variable and multiple workstations, the database server should be *auto-configurable* and *reconfigurable*. When the OAE grows, (i.e., the number of workstations in the OAS increases) or shrinks (i.e., some workstations becomes disabled or removed) the database server should be able to adjust itself for the addition or loss of workstations. Such adjustment should require no new programming and no modification to the existing software. Further, it should incur no disruption of the OAE or OAS. The database server should also maintain a consistent and up-to-date copy of the database. When a node in the OAE is disabled, it is imperative that the database server still be functional, providing continuous, albeit limited, access to the remaining database. This is also the *survivability* of the database server.

The database server should also be *versatile*, providing the user with more than one way of accessing the database. In an OAE where there is a large group of individuals from diverse backgrounds and with different experiences in using database facilities, the database server should provide different database language interfaces in order to facilitate the database user with various ways of accessing the database. Finally, the database server should be a database system that is oriented towards providing a substantial level of *performance*. As the time goes by. both the use of and repository in the database server increase. To meet the growing needs of the OAE the database server must be able to expand as the OAE expands, and still maintain or increase its performance.

3. THE NEED OF A DATABASE SERVER WITH VARIABLE AND MULTIPLE BACKEND CONFIGURATIONS

3.1. The Proposed Architecture for a Database Server

We advocate that the architecture of a database server be configured with one controller and one or more backends. As shown in Figure 2, the controller and the backends are connected by a broadcast bus. When a transaction is received from a workstation, the controller broadcasts the transaction to all the backends. Each backend has a number of dedicated disk drives. Since the database is distributed across the backends, a transaction can be executed by all the backends in parallel. Each backend maintains a queue of transactions and schedules the transactions for execution independent of the other backends. in order to maximize its access operations and to minimize its idle time. Thus, different transactions can be executed concurrently. On the other hand, the controller does very little work. It is responsible for receiving and broadcasting transactions. routing results, and assisting the backends in the insertion of new data. By minimizing the work of the controller, we are attempting to reduce the chances that the controller may become the bottleneck in the system when the number of backends is increased. The backends do all the database operations. Just how this architecture may have the six characteristics of an ideal database server will be expounded in the following sections by way of an experimental database system which also exhibits an architectural configuration similar to the one depicted in Figure 2.

3.2. The Multi-Backend Database System (MBDS) as a Database Server

To provide a centralized database system, MBDS uses one or more identical workstations and their disk systems as database backends and a workstation as the database controller to interface with multiple, similar or dissimilar workstations or mainframes. We refer to these workstations and mainframes as *hosts*. User access to the centralized database is therefore accomplished through a host which in turn communicates with the controller. Multiple backends are configured in parallel. The database is distributed across all of the backends. The database management functions are replicated at each backend. i.e., all backends have identical software and hardware. They, of course, have accesses to different portions of the database [1, 2, 3, 4].

There are some key issues to be explored in considering MBDS for OAEs. The current implementation of MBDS uses microprocessor-based workstations, Winchester-type disks and an Ethernet-like broadcast bus. There are a number of reasons for preferring microprocessor-based workstations over the traditional minicomputers. First, the 32-bit microprocesser is quickly attaining a reputation as a dependable, versatile and

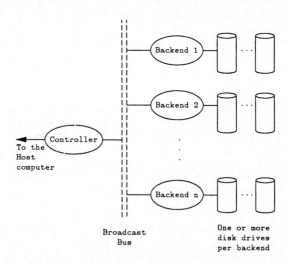

Figure 2. The Multi-Backend Database System.

fast CPU. approaching the speed and performance of the minicomputers of five years ago. Second, the microprocessor-based workstation is cost-effective. This is important when considering that MBDS requires a minimum of two such workstations. It also implies that MBDS can be expanded with relative ease and minimal cost by the addition of backend microprocessor-based workstations [2].

The placement of the user interface is also affected by the use of microprocessor-based workstations. The user interface provides access to MBDS and is run from either a separate host, or as part of the backend controller. When the user interface is on a separate host, the interface interacts with the controller via a bus. In either case, the use of a similar (with respect to the controller and backend hardware) microprocessor-based workstation for the user interface increases the compatibility and the maintainability (with respect to the hardware maintenance and costs) of the database system.

The final major issue involves the ability of MBDS to support multiple data model/language interfaces to the multi-backend database system. These multiple model/language interfaces allow the user to access MBDS using the relational model/SQL language, the hierarchical model/DL/I language, the entity relationship model/Daplex language. or the network model/CODASYL language. These interfaces are also running on either a separate host or the backend controller; and, as such, the issues concerning the user interface also apply here. For a brief introduction to the multi-backend database system MBDS and the multi-lingual database system MLDS, the reader may refer to [5].

3.3. Six Characteristics of MBDS for an Effective Role in the OAE

Regardless of the integration approach that is chosen, MBDS exhibits certain characteristics that are desirable in the OAE. These characteristics include the software portability of the MBDS code, the software independence of the backend code, the auto-configurability and reconfigurability of MBDS on account of its use of identical workstations and replicated software, the survivability of the system resulting from the use of duplicated directory data, the versatility of system due to the ability of MBDS to support multiple language interfaces, and the performance capabilities of the system as a result of its parallel configuration and round-robin data placement. Each of these topics is briefly examined in the following paragraphs.

3.3.1. Software Portability

The MBDS processes, i.e.. the controller processes. the backend processes, and the interface process. are all written in the C programming language. C was chosen as the programming language for MBDS because of its portability and its reputation as a good systems programming language. We estimate that the code of MBDS is about ninety-five percent portable, consisting of 15,000 lines of C code. The five percent of system-dependent code involves the inter-process message-passing code on both the controller and the backends. the inter-computer message passing code for the communications processes, and the disk I/O routines for the record processing process. Thus, the majority of the code is portable. In fact, some of the implementation development for MBDS takes place on a VAX-11/780 running the Unix operating system, where we are able to take advantage of the C-tools provided by Unix. Thus, we feel that we have designed a relatively portable database system that can run on a wide range of the 32-bit microcomputers on the market today, e.g., the DEC MicroVAX and the Sun Workstation.

3.3.2. Software Independence

In examining the software independence issue. we focus on the backend processes. The elegance of MBDS is in that the backend software of one backend is identical to the backend software of another backend. For logical reasons, the directory data, used by each backend when processing transactions. is nevertheless duplicated at every backend. However. the directory data is usually a small percentage of the non-directory data. Furthermore, the only sharing of information by the backends occurs in one phase of the directory search. Otherwise, the directory management, the concurrency control, and the record processing processes are independent of each other. So, when a new backend is configured into the system, the software present on one backend is simply replicated on the new backend. Additionally, the directory data, duplicated at an existing backend, is loaded into the new backend. When bringing a new backend into MBDS, we must also decide on whether to rearrange the non-directory data. On the one hand, we can redistribute all of the non-directory data across the disk systems of every backend. This involves the reloading of data. On the other hand, we can simply leave the data undisturbed, and load only the new data on the new backend. The choice is left to the discretion of the database administrator.

3.3.3. Auto-Configurability

One of the most convenient features of MBDS is the ability to automatically configure and reconfigure the system with ease. When starting the system for the first time, the database administrator simply specifies, using an interface. the number of backends in the system. MBDS then configures itself by notifying the controller and backend processes the number of backends on the system. Using this unique feature, MBDS can be reconfigured when a backend becomes inoperable. In such a situation, MBDS is configured with one less backend. Conversely, when a new backend is added to the system, the system can be configured with one more backend easily.

3.3.4. Survivability

MBDS contains only one copy of the non-directory database. When the database is loaded. it is distributed evenly across all backends' disk systems. However, the directory data. which contains index and cluster information on all data in the database, is duplicated in every backend. The distributed directory data, coupled with the software independence and reconfigurability of MBDS. offers an increased survivability of the database system in the OAE. If a backend or backends become inoperable, the system is still usable. While a backend is inoperable, a log of transactions that modified both the directory and the non-directory data is kept. When the backend is reconfigured into MBDS, the log is run for the purpose of updating the directory and other data. Although portions of the non-directory data become inaccessible with the inoperable backends, MBDS can still access and retrieve the rest of the data. Incomplete data is better than no data, provided that the user is informed of the situation.

3.3.5. Versatility

One of the biggest advantages of having MBDS as part of an OAS is the ability of MBDS to provide support for multiple data models (and therefore data languages) through the use of multiple language-based interfaces. In the OAE, where users are from diverse backgrounds, such a utility is a unique feature in a database management system. In fact, the language interfaces can be tailored by the workstation. One workstation could have a SQL interface, another a DL/I interface, a third a Daplex interface, and yet another a CODASYL interface. By tailoring the language interfaces by workstation, the software required for each interface process could be reduced. Conversely, with a wide range of language interfaces available at every workstation, the workstation becomes more accessible to a wide range of users.

3.3.6. Performance

The performance capabilities of any DBMS are important in an OAE, since the DBMS tends to serve as a repository of all the permanent data and programs of the OAE. As the repository becomes large and the database activities increase, the DBMS as a database server may become the performance bottleneck. However, MBDS is specifically designed to provide for capacity growth and performance enhancement. The performance metric of major concern is the response time of a transaction. The *response time* of a transaction is the time between the initial issuance of the transaction and the receipt of the final results for the transaction. MBDS has two original design goals. First, if the database capacity is fixed and the number of backends is increased, then the response time per transaction reduces proportionately. For example, if a transaction has a response time of 60 seconds when there is one backend, the same transaction should have a response time of nearly 30 seconds when there are two backends, and of nearly 15 seconds when there are four backends, provided that the database size has remained constant.

The second goal is that, for the same transactions, if the response sets are increased due to an increase of the database size and the number of backends is increased in proportion to the increase of the response sets, then the response time per transaction should remain the same. For example, if a transaction had a response time of 60 seconds when there is one backend with 1000 records in the response set, then the same transaction should have a response time of close to 60 seconds when there are two backends and 2000 records in the response set.

The underlying concept in each goal is that MBDS in the OAE would supply a database system that would grow as the OAS grows, and would either maintain a constant response time per transaction by 'growing' its backends or halve a given response time per transaction by 'doubling' its backends. On the basis of our preliminary analysis, the operational MBDS can indeed meet the two goals. The analysis is also published and documented in [6, 7].

4. THE INTEGRATION OF MBDS INTO THE OAE

In this section, we first focus on the ways to integrate MBDS into the OAE. In this focus, we consider five possible configurations as candidates for integrating MBDS into the OAE. Our second focus examines the relative advantages/disadvantages of the integration configurations. In this examination, we are interested in presenting a heuristic analysis of the five configurations.

4.1. Five Approaches to the Integration of a Database Server

Recall that the basic OAS, consists of a group of workstations, connected by a local-area network (LAN) such as an Ethernet [9]. Such a design has been shown in Figure 1. Given this basic characterization, we now consider the integration of MBDS into the OAS. In the first approach, MBDS is added on as a separate group of workstations in the OAS, with its own LAN. We characterize this approach as the *non-integrated dual-LAN design*. In this approach, the additional workstations are dedicated to the database operations. As such, they are inaccessible for non-database activities. We provide the interface process (which may include one or more language interfaces) as a part of the user-accessible workstations. i.e.. hosts. The resulting OAS is shown in Figure 3. In this and the remaining four approaches. the placement of the interface software (i.e.. the number of hosts and which hosts have the interface software) is left to the discretion of the database administrator.

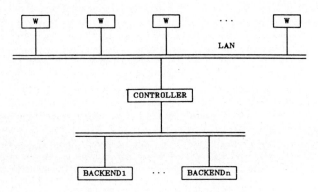

Figure 3.   The Non-Integrated Dual-LAN Design

The second approach is the *non-integrated single-LAN design*. In this approach, as shown in Figure 4, MBDS and the OAS share a common LAN. However, the MBDS controller and backends still remain as separate workstations in the OAE.

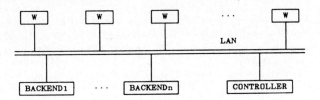

Figure 4. The Non-Integrated Single-LAN Design

The third approach, the *partially-integrated design*, integrates and replicates the backend software as permanent background processes into some of the OAS workstations. The remainder of the MBDS may have the backend software replicated in user-inaccessible workstations. The distribution of the backend software within the user workstations is controlled by the database administrator in the OAE. The controller is the key component in MBDS, and is devoted to overseeing the management of the database system. Therefore, the controller software is placed in a separate workstation, that is not directly utilized in the OAS. The partially-integrated design is shown in Figure 5.

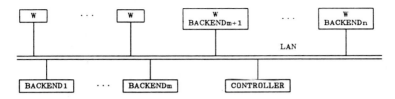

Figure 5. The Partially-Integrated Design

In the fourth approach, the *isolated-controller design*, the MBDS backend software is integrated and replicated into the existing workstations. As in the partially-integrated design, the controller software is implemented in a user-inaccessible workstation. The backend software is installed as permanent background processes in one or more workstations. The isolated-controller design is shown in Figure 6.

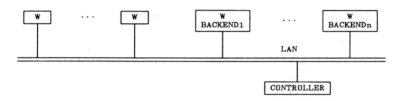

Figure 6. The Isolated-Controller Design

In the fifth approach, the *fully-integrated design*, the MBDS software is completely integrated into the OAS. The controller software is installed as permanent background processes on one workstation. The backend software is installed and replicated as permanent background processes on one or more workstations. The fully-integrated design is given in Figure 7.

Figure 7. The Fully-Integrated Design

In the non-integrated dual-LAN design, we are using the LAN as a logical two-way communications device for MBDS. Messages are passed from the interface process of a particular workstation to the controller and from the controller back to the interface process. In the other four designs, we are using the LAN as a logical five-way communications device. Messages are passed from the interface process to the controller, from the controller to the backends, between the backends, from the backends to the controller, and from the controller back to the interface process.

4.2. An Analysis of the Five Designs: A Heuristic Approach

Informally, let us consider the trade-offs resulting from one approach to another, which depend on various performance and cost considerations. The non-integrated approaches differ only by the cost of a LAN, but the corresponding performance gains of the dual-LAN approach probably outweighs the cost of the extra LAN. In particular, the load on the LAN for the OAS is significantly lower in the dual-LAN design. However, in both these approaches, a high price is paid as the database and transactions of MBDS grow in size and intensity. The integration of more backends into MBDS and therefore the OAS is costly, since the new workstations are only accessible to the database management system.

In such a situation, either the partially-integrated design or the isolated-controller design becomes an attractive alternative. In either case, keeping the controller on a non-accessible workstation is a good choice for performance. In the partially-integrated design, as the database grows, more user workstations can be configured into the database system. Further, if a workstations is entirely devoted to either the backend software or the OAS software but not both, additional workstations can be easily added to either MBDS or OAS. Thus, in the partially-integrated design, these workstations can be added as either dedicated database backends or user workstations. Again, in either case, the addition of more backends into MBDS is more cost-effective, even if the backend software is added as part of the user workstations. We feel that the fully-integrated design is the least desirable. The controller as part of a user-accessible workstation would substantially degrade the performance of MBDS as the non-database use of the workstation at which the controller resides increases.

Overall, the non-integrated dual-LAN design may yield the highest performance and have the greatest cost. (See Figure 3 again.) The performance of the non-integrated single-LAN and partially-integrated designs are about the same. However, the partially-integrated design is more versatile in performance gain and is still cost-effective. The isolated-controller is not versatile in performance, although it excels in cost-effectiveness. Finally, while the fully-integrated design is cost-effective, its performance may leave a lot to be desired.

5. A FORMAL ANALYSIS OF THE FIVE INTEGRATION DESIGNS

In this section we provide a formal examination and analysis of the five configuration designs presented in Section 4.1. Our basic intent is to provide a framework by which the configurations presented earlier can be analyzed and compared. In the process, we can determine just how well our heuristic analysis in Section 4.2 measures up to a queueing-model analysis of the configurations.

In order to compare the five approaches to integrating MBDS into an office automation environment, we use simple queueing models for single and multiple devices. To avoid the possible confusion in the use of the term 'server', we refer to the servers of queues as *devices*. An analysis of the message types in the five approaches indicates that both the single- and the multiple-device models must be applied to each approach, due to the variety of workstations in each configuration, i.e., we have several workstations, several backends and one controller in the configurations. Whether the controller is dedicated or incorporated into a workstation is taken into account in the analysis.

As mentioned in Section 4.1, the local-area networks are used either as 2-way logical communication devices as in the dual-LAN design or as a 5-way logical communication device in the other four single-LAN designs. To reduce the complexity of the queueing analysis, we assume that the backends do not communicate with each other; a similar assumption holds for the workstations. These assumptions are reasonable. In other words, we limit the communication paths in the configurations to: workstation-to-controller. controller-to-backend, backend-to-controller, and controller-to-workstation.

However, this does not necessarily limit the actual message types that are present in each of the five configurations. By examining the operational aspects of the five configurations we note that there are five distinct types of devices; workstation (W), backend (B), controller (C), workstation-backend (WB), and workstation-controller (WC). In the WB device, the workstation functions are combined with the backend functions. (See Figures 5, 6, and 7 again.) In the WC device, the workstation functions are combined with the controller functions. (See Figure 7 again.) Given this characterization, we can summarize the distinct message types for each of the five configurations. These are presented in Table 1.

Let us briefly explain the notation used in Table 1. The entities on the right of the arrows represent the devices which receive and service the message. The entities on the left of the arrows represent the origin of the message. For example, W ====> C, indicates that a message that is serviced by the controller (C) and is received from a workstation (W). Compound letters (e.g., WB, BW, and CW) are used to represent an integrated workstation. The first letter in the abbreviation indicates the part of the integrated unit that is intended as the originator or recipient of a message. In our analysis. we assume that each message type has a distinct message service time associated with it. While it would have been appropriate to model the dual-LAN configuration by representing the LAN itself as a device in its own right, in our modeling and analysis, we have chosen not to do so.

5.1. The Queueing Equations

In order to apply simple queueing theory to the problem at hand, we must continue to add to our list of assumptions. In particular, the following assumptions need be

Configuration	Input to MBDS				Output to Workstation			
Non-Integrated Dual-LAN	W	====>	C		B	====>	C	
	C	====>	B		C	====>	W	
Non-Integrated Single-LAN	W	====>	C		B	====>	C	
	C	====>	B		C	====>	W	
Partially-Integrated	W	====>	C		B	====>	C	
	WB	====>	C		BW	====>	C	
	C	====>	B		C	====>	W	
	C	====>	BW		C	====>	WB	
Isolated-Controller	W	====>	C		BW	====>	C	
	WB	====>	C		C	====>	W	
	C	====>	BW		C	====>	WB	
Fully-Integrated	W	====>	CW		BW	====>	CW	
	WB	====>	CW		CW	====>	W	
	CW	====>	BW		CW	====>	WB	

Table 1. A Summary of Message Types

made: the *inter-arrival times* of messages follows a Poisson process, the *service times* of messages are exponentially distributed, and the items in the queue are serviced on a first-come-first-serve (FCFS) basis. All of these assumptions are used to simplify the queueing equations that are used to evaluate and compare the five configuration designs. In our queueing analysis, we are interested in calculating the waiting time of individual devices and the total waiting time of all devices. The *waiting time* of individual devices, is the time spent by an item in a queue of a particular device type before the item is serviced. The *total waiting time* of all devices is the sum of the waiting times of an item for **all** of the devices. Now let us proceed with the specification of the queueing equations (i. e., the waiting-time equations) for the single- and multiple-device models.

For the single-device model, given the average service time (s) and the average number of messages (l), the average number of items waiting to be served is given by the equation, $w = \frac{p}{1-p}$, where p is the device utilization and is equal to $l \times s$. The waiting time in the queue is given by $t_w = \frac{w}{l}$.

In the multiple-device model, if there are M identical devices, the average number of items waiting to be served is given by $w = B \times \left(\dfrac{p}{1-p} \right)$ where $p = \dfrac{l \times s}{M}$, $B = \dfrac{1-A}{1-pA}$ and $A = \left(\displaystyle\sum_{i=0}^{M-1} \dfrac{(pM)^i}{i!} \right) \Big/ \left(\displaystyle\sum_{i=0}^{M} \dfrac{(pM)^i}{i!} \right)$. The waiting time is, as before, given by $t_w = \dfrac{w}{l}$. Depending on the particular message type, we apply either single-device or multiple-device queueing theory and obtain the corresponding equations for the waiting time. In either the single- or multiple-device model, we use the individual waiting times to calculate the total waiting time, T_w, where $T_w = \displaystyle\sum_{\text{all devices}} t_w$.

In order to specify the queueing-time equations (i.e., the total waiting time) for the five different configurations, we must add once again to our list of assumptions. In particular, we assume the following:

(1). There is a maximum of, k, workstations, irrespective of whether a workstation is integrated or not with a backend or controller. Each workstation generates a total of a messages. In other words, the number of workstations and the number of messages generated by a workstation are fixed.

(2). There is a total of, m, backends. If n of these are dedicated backend workstations, then there are $(m-n)$ integrated workstations and $(k-(m-n))$ dedicated workstations. Each backend generates a total of b messages.

(3). There is exactly one controller. If the controller is integrated into a workstation, then the number of dedicated workstations is reduced by one. The controller does not generate any messages of its own and thus merely acts as a relaying mechanism for message types between the workstations and the backends.

(4). Associated with each distinct device type is a unique message processing time. We call this time the *service time*.

These service times are represented as subscripted quantities, viz.. S_W. S_C, S_{WB}. etc.

(5). Unless otherwise specified, all performance parameters in the equations represent average values.

The total waiting-time equations for the five configurations are given in the Appendix.

5.2. A Queueing Analysis of the Five Designs

To obtain a quantitative determination of which of the configurations is better suited to an office automation environment, we compute the total waiting time for each of the five configurations. We begin by assuming that the workstations generate a fixed number of queries and that the backends generate a fixed number of responses. Next, we determine the values for the variables that have been listed in the previous section. Specifically, we must assign values for k, m, n, a, b and the service times. For our analysis, we pick $k = 4$, $m = 2$, $a = 1$, and $b = 1$. The number, n, of dedicated backends will vary, depending on the configuration. For the service times, we choose $S_W = S_B = S_C = S_{WB} = S_{WC} = S = 0.1$.

Given this scenario, we can now present a synopsis of the device structure in each of the five configurations. This synopsis is presented in Table 2. Briefly, let us examine the distribution and functionalities for the devices in each configuration. In both the non-integrated single-LAN and dual-LAN designs, there are a total of seven devices, with 4 dedicated workstations, 2 dedicated backends, and 1 dedicated controller. The partially-integrated design has six devices, with 3 dedicated workstations, 1

Configuration	Device Distribution and Functionality			
Non-Integrated Dual-LAN	4 W	2 B	1 C	
Non-Integrated Single-LAN	4 W	2 B	1 C	
Partially-Integrated	3 W	1 WB	1 B	1 C
Isolated-Controller	2 W	2 WB	1 C	
Fully-Integrated	1 W	2 WB	1 WC	

Table 2. The Device Structure

device having both the workstation and backend functions, 1 dedicated backend, and 1 dedicated controller. In the isolated-controller design, there are five devices, with 2 dedicated workstations, 2 devices having both the workstation and backend functions, and 1 dedicated controller. Finally, in the fully-integrated design, there are four devices, with 1 dedicated workstation, 2 devices having both the workstation and backend functions, and one device having both the workstation and controller functions.

Using this device structure and working with the variable values defined above, we can calculate the total waiting times for each of the five configurations using the equations in the Appendix. The computed results for the total waiting times are summarized in Table 3, where T_u is the total waiting time and T'_u is the total waiting time that is common to all of the configurations.

Configuration	$T_w - T'_w$
Non-Integrated Dual-LAN	0.04
Non-Integrated Single-LAN	0.042
Partially-Integrated	1.58
Isolated-Controller	0.051
Fully-Integrated	0.282

Table 3. The Total Waiting Times

Based on the numerical results presented in Table 3, it can be seen that the dual-LAN configuration has the best performance. This is to be expected since the dual-LAN structure allows for the concurrent processing of messages between the hosts and the controller on the one hand, and between the backends and the controller on the other. Of the remaining four, the non-integrated single-LAN performs the best, barely outperforming the isolated-controller configuration. Surprisingly, the isolated-controller configuration seems to outperform both the fully-integrated and the partially-integrated configurations. A plausible explanation is that the isolated-controller configuration has fewer distinct message types than either the fully-integrated or the partially-integrated configurations. (See Table 2 again.) For similar reasons, the fully-integrated configuration outperforms the partially-integrated configuration. The partially-integrated configuration has the largest number of distinct message types associated with it, requiring the discrimination of these message types and the routing of messages of different types to various elements in the system. This may be a plausible reason as to why the partially-integrated configuration performs poorly. Overall, we observe that the heuristics presented in Section 4.2 have been in general agreement with the above results, with the exception of the partially-integrated design.

6. A SENSITIVITY ANALYSIS OF THE QUEUEING EXPRESSIONS

In this section we discuss how the total waiting time of the system is affected by changes in the various parameters in the queueing expressions obtained in Section 5. In particular, we are interested in establishing the sensitivity of the total waiting time due to the changes in the following system parameters:

(a). an increase in the number of dedicated workstations,

(b). an increase in the number of dedicated backends,

(c). an increase in the number of integrated backends,

(d). relative changes in the servicing time of a message for each of the different types of devices which comprise the OAS, and lastly,

(e). a variation in the ratio of the number of messages or queries generated by the workstations to the number of messages generated by the backends.

In Figures 8 through 14 we plot the natural logarithm of the total waiting time (defined in Section 5.1) against the one parameter which is being varied while all other parameters in the queueing expressions are kept constant at some specified values. In each of the figures, there are four curves plotted and these are labeled N, P, I, and F representing the non-integrated, partially integrated, isolated controller, and fully-integrated single-LAN configurations, respectively. We have not included any results from the dual-LAN configuration, since we feel that there is no way to normalize the results of the single-LAN and dual-LAN queueing expressions in any meaningful manner for comparisons.

In Figures 8 and 9, the total waiting time is plotted as a function of the number of workstations. For each input message from a workstation, we assume a single response or message is generated by a backend. The service times of all of the different types of devices in the OAS are assumed to be identical. The service-time value is taken to be 0.1 in Figure 8, while it is set to 0.05 in Figure 9. An examination of the figures indicates that T_w is at least an order of magnitude greater for the partially integrated configuration than for any of the other three configurations. In the case of the fully integrated system, we note that the curve for the total waiting time reaches a certain minimum value, shows a gradual increase and eventually merges with the waiting time curve for the isolated controller configuration. The non-integrated configuration given by curve N shows the lowest waiting time of the four configurations under consideration. The curves in Figure 9 are practically identical in behavior to the curves in Figure 8, the only difference being in the magnitudes of the two sets of curves.

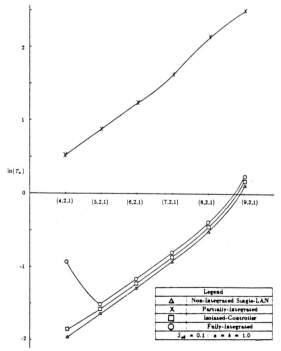

Figure 8. The Total Waiting Time as a Function of the Number of Workstations with Long Service Time.

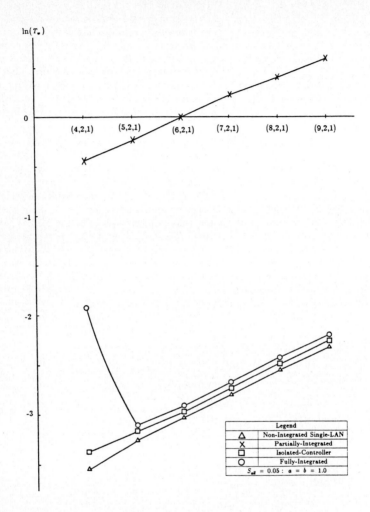

Figure 9. The Total Waiting Time as a Function of the Number of
Workstations with Short Service Time.

In Figure 10, we have plotted the total waiting time against the number of
workstations assuming identical service times of $S = 0.1$ for the different device types.
However, the number of queries generated by the workstations and the number of
responses generated by the backends, while being equal to each other, are now one-tenth
the values used in plotting Figures 8 and 9, i.e., $a = b = 0.1$. The waiting times for the
four configurations are significantly lower when compared to the case where $a = b = 1.0$
(in Figure 8) and this is to be expected, since the total volume of messages being
processed by the entire system. irrespective of the configuration. is much lower. As for
the relative behavior of the four curves. remarks made in the previous paragraph apply
here as well.

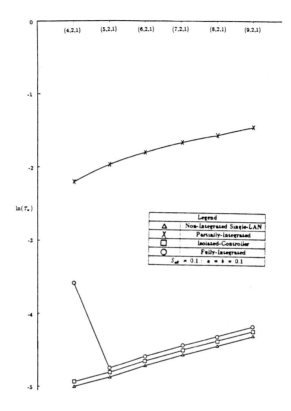

Figure 10. The Total Waiting Time with Identical Service Time
and Different Devices.

In obtaining the curves in Figures 8, 9 and 10, we varied the number of workstations from four to nine while keeping the total number of backends (integrated as well as dedicated) at two. In Figure 11, we increase the total number of integrated and dedicated backends to four while the number of workstations is varied from six to nine. We note that the I and N curves merge when the number of workstations is seven and the the F curve merges with the I and N curves when the number of workstations is increased to eight.

The P curve is still an order of magnitude greater than the N, I and F curves. Note, however, that whereas in Figures 8, 9 and 10, there is a noticeable dip in the F curve, there is no such dip in the F curve in Figure 11. A reason for this seems to be the existence of an optimum number of backends which provides the lowest waiting time for the fully integrated configuration.

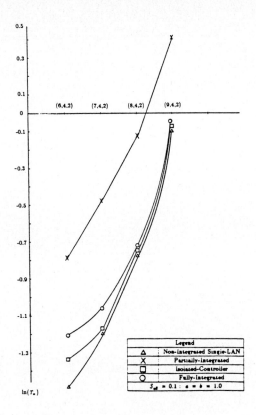

Figure 11. Of a Total of Six to Nine Workstations there are Four
Database Backends.

The effect of varying the number of backends on the system is investigated next.
Figure 12 shows the impact on the total waiting time as the total number of backends is
increased from two to six. Here the total number of workstations is held constant at
eight. Several interesting points are to be noted in regard to Figure 12. First, the total
waiting time for the partially integrated configuration shows a drastic decrease (or
reduction) when the number of backends is increased from two to three. As the number
of backends is increased from three to six, the waiting time becomes more or less
constant; there is a slight upturn when the number of backends is eight. The N, I and F
curves practically coincide when the number of backends is increased beyond four. The
F curve shows the steepest increase in value, while the N curve has the slowest rate of
increase. The N, I, and F curves parallel the behavior of the P curve in that they also
show a dramatic drop in waiting time when the number of backends is increased from
two to three. The result strongly reinforces the suggestion that there is an optimum
number of backends that can be incorporated into a system having a fixed number of
workstations which will result in a certain minimum waiting time. In addition, the
results suggest that either too few or too many backends would adversely impact system
performance.

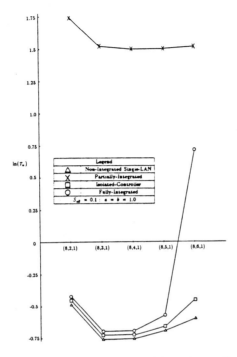

Figure 12. The Backends are Increased from Two to Six while the
Number of Workstations Remains at Eight.

Next, we investigate the effects of proportional changes in the number of messages (queries) input by workstations to the number of responses generated by backends. In Figure 13, the axes are the total waiting time and the ratio of the number of messages produced by the backends to the number of messages produced by the workstations. This ratio is varied from 0.01 to 1000. In plotting the curves in Figure 13, we assume there are four workstations and two backends; the service times of the different devices are assumed constant and equal to 0.1. We note that the I and N curves are more or less identical and they both show a dramatic increase in waiting time as the $\frac{b}{a}$ ratio decreases from 1.0 to 0.01. For large values of $\frac{b}{a}$, the P and F curves are almost identical. However, as the ratio $\frac{b}{a}$ decreases, the waiting time for the partially integrated configuration increases tremendously as indicated by the P curve.

In practical terms, Figure 13 can be explained as follows. The greater the number of queries generated by the workstations and the fewer the number of responses generated by the backends, the waiting time gets to be quite significant. This result is independent of how the system is configured. Also, this result is independent of the size of the database, how the database is organized and what kinds of access mechanisms are provided.

To study the effects of relative changes in the service times of the different types of devices which comprise the OAS, we set the service time of those workstations which are integrated backends to 0.1. The service times for the remaining types of devices are

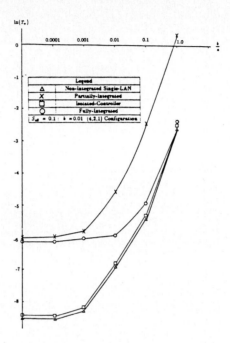

Figure 13. The Total Waiting Time vs. the Ratio of Backend Messages
and Workstation Messages.

assumed to be equal to 0.05. We also assume that equal number of messages are
produced by the workstations and the backends. The results are plotted in Figure 14.
The lowest waiting times are to be found for the N curve, i.e., the non-integrated single-
LAN configuration. This is hardly surprising since this is the only configuration which is
independent of S_{wb}, the service time for an integrated workstation-backend. As expected,
the P curve has the highest waiting time values. The I and F curves merge as the
number of workstations is increased. The waiting time for the fully configured system
attains a minimum value and then starts increasing as the number of workstations is
increased. This minimum value is obtained obtained when the number of workstations
is set to five. Note that Figures 8, 9 and 14 are strikingly similar.

7. CONCLUSIONS

We have shown how MBDS can play an important role in the OAE as an database
server. Specifically, we have shown how MBDS can provide both traditional and new
database support. We have also shown why and how MBDS should be integrated into
an OAS, i.e., what MBDS has to offer to an OAE. In particular, MBDS can be
integrated into an OAS in a number of ways, depending upon the needs of the office
automation environment. Once MBDS is configured in an OAS, the reconfigurability
feature, coupled with the replicated backend software, permits the database server to
grow as the needs of the office information system grow. Additionally, when MBDS
expands, the response time per request for the system decreases proportionately, as long

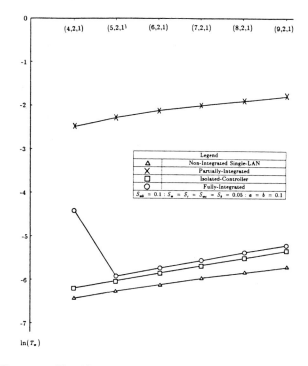

Figure 14. The Effects of Service-Time Changes of Workstations
and Backends.

as the database size remains constant. As the database grows in size and consequently
the responses, MBDS can maintain the response time for the same type of database
services by expanding its backends.

As a multi-lingual database system, MBDS offers the ability to access the database
using a variety of language interfaces. From the native data language of MBDS to
sophisticated data languages such as SQL, Daplex, CODASYL and DL/I, the user can
select a language to query the database. The high degree of software portability
exhibited by MBDS, allows the system to be implemented on a wide range of
microcomputers, offering database support for a wide range of office automation systems.
Overall, we feel that MBDS is close to an ideal database server for the office automation
environment.

At the queueing-analysis level, we have presented the preliminary work in Section 5.
In Section 6 we presented a more complete analysis of the five configurations. We have
investigated how well each configuration performs under different assumptions, i. e., for
different values of the queueing variables. We have been able to determine when the
performance of a particular configuration begins to degrade, given an increase in the
number of devices in the configuration. The existence of an optimal number of backends
for the maximal performance has already been noted in our analysis in Section 6.

Finally, we must also investigate the other relevant considerations when choosing a particular configuration for a specific OAE. Basically, the choice of a configuration depends not only on quantitative data of the configurations' performance, but on external considerations, such as the environment into which the database server is integrated. If an OAS consists of a fixed number of workstations, say two, and there is no growth of the system in terms of additional workstations, then the logical choice is to adopt the fully-integrated approach where the controller is on one workstation, the backend on the other, and the database interfaces on both. If, instead, the OAE is large enough to demand a dedicated database server, then the logical choices are either the non-integrated single-LAN or dual-LAN approach.

ACKNOWLEDGEMENT

A brief version of this paper (without the indepth analysis of the queueing expressions as presented in Section 6) has been published in the *Proceedings of the 1985 ACM Conference*, [8].

REFERENCES

[1] Boyne, R., et al., "A Message-Oriented Implementation of a Multi-Backend Database System (MBDS)," in *Database Machines*, Leilich and Missikoff (eds.), Springer-Verlag, 1983.

[2] Demurjian, S. A., Hsiao. D. K., and Menon, J.. "A Multi-Backend Database System for Performance Gains, Capacity Growth and Hardware Upgrade." *Proceedings of the Second International Conference on Data Engineering*, IEEE Computer Society, February 1986.

[3] Kerr, D.S., Orooji, A., Shi, Z. and Strawser, P. R. (1982). "The Implementation of a Multi-Backend Database System (MBDS): Part I - Software Engineering Strategies and Efforts Towards a Prototype MBDS," *Advanced Database Machine Architecture*, Hsiao (ed.), Prentice-Hall, 1983.

[4] He, X., et al., "The Implementation of a Multi-Backend Database System (MBDS): Part II - The First Prototype MBDS and the Software Engineering Experience," *Advanced Database Machine Architecture*, Hsiao (ed.), Prentice Hall, 1983.

[5] Demurjian, S. A. and Hsiao, D. K., "New Directions in Database-Systems Research and Development," in the *Proceedings of the New Directions in Computing Conference*, IEEE Computer Society, August 1985.

[6] Demurjian, S. A., et al., "Performance Evaluation of a Database System in Multiple Backend Configurations," *Proceedings of the 1985 International Workshop on Database Machines*. March 1985.

[7] Demurjian, S. A. and Hsiao, D. K.. "Benchmarking Database Systems in Multiple Backend Configurations." *IEEE Database Engineering Bulletin*, March 1985.

[8] Demurjian, S. A., Hsiao, D. K., and Marshall, R. G., "The Architectural Requirements and Integration Analyses of a Database Server for Office Automation," *Proceedings of the 1985 ACM Conference*, October, 1985.

[9] Metcalfe, R. M., and Boggs, D. R., "Ethernet:Distributed Packet Switching for Local Computer Networks," *Communications of the ACM*, Vol. 19, No. 7, July 1976.

[10] Kleinrock, L.. *Queueing Systems I*, John Wiley & Sons, 1975.

[11] Kleinrock, L., *Queueing Systems II*, John Wiley & Sons, 1975.

APPENDIX. THE TOTAL WAITING TIME EQUATIONS FOR THE FIVE CONFIGURATIONS

In this appendix we provide a synopsis of the total waiting time equations used for each of the five configurations that have been proposed in Section 4. These equations were used to calculate the data presented in Table 3. In the equations below, k is the number of workstations, dedicated or not, m is the number of backends, dedicated or not, n is the number of dedicated backends, and S is the service time. The total waiting time is $T_w = \sum_{all\ devices} t_w$. The reader is referred to [10, 11] for a comprehensive presentation of queueing analysis techniques.

The total waiting time for the non-integrated dual-LAN configuration is:

$$\max\left(\ kS^2/(1 - kS),\ mS^2/(1 - mS)\ \right)\ +$$

$$\max\left(\ B_1/(m - kS),\ B_2/(k - mS)\ \right)$$

$$\text{where}\quad B_1 = \frac{(kS)^m/m!}{(kS)^m/m! + (1 - \frac{kS}{m})\sum_{i=0}^{m-1}\frac{(kS)^i}{i!}}$$

$$\text{and } B_2 = \frac{(mS)^k/k!}{(mS)^k/k! + (1 - \frac{mS}{k})\sum_{i=0}^{k-1}\frac{(mS)^i}{i!}}$$

The total waiting time for the non-integrated single-LAN configuration is:

$$kS^2/(1 - kS) + mS^2/(1 - mS) + B_1/(m - kS) + B_2/(k - mS)$$

where B_1 and B_2 are as above.

The total waiting time for the partially-integrated configuration is:

$$kS^2/(1 - kS) + mS^2/(1 - mS) + B_1/(n - kS)\ +$$

$$B_2/(m - n - kS) + B_3/(k - m + n - mS) + B_4/(m - n - mS)$$

$$\text{where}\quad B_1 = \frac{(kS)^n/n!}{(kS)^n/n! + (1 - \frac{kS}{n})\sum_{i=0}^{n-1}\frac{(kS)^i}{i!}}$$

$$\text{and}\quad B_2 = \frac{(kS)^{m-n}/(m-n)!}{(kS)^{m-n}/(m-n)! + (1 - \frac{kS}{m-n})\sum_{i=0}^{m-n-1}\frac{(kS)^i}{i!}}$$

$$\text{and } B_3 = \frac{(mS)^{k-m+n}/(k-m+n)!}{(mS)^{k-m+n}/(k-m+n)! + (1 - \frac{mS}{k-m+n})\sum_{i=0}^{k-m+n-1}\frac{(mS)^i}{i!}}$$

$$\text{and } B_4 = \frac{(mS)^{m-n}/(m-n)!}{(mS)^{m-n}/(m-n)! + (1 - \frac{mS}{m-n})\sum_{i=0}^{m-n-1}\frac{(mS)^i}{i!}}$$

The total waiting time for the isolated-controller configuration is:

$$kS^2/(1 - kS) + mS^2/(1 - mS) + B_1/(m - kS) +$$

$$B_2/(k - m - mS) + B_3/(m - mS)$$

where $B_1 = \dfrac{(kS)^m/m!}{(kS)^m/m! + (1 - \dfrac{kS}{m}) \displaystyle\sum_{i=0}^{m-1} \dfrac{(kS)^i}{i!}}$

and $B_2 = \dfrac{(mS)^{k-m}/(k-m)!}{(mS)^{k-m}/(k-m)! + (1 - \dfrac{mS}{k-m}) \displaystyle\sum_{i=0}^{k-m-1} \dfrac{(mS)^i}{i!}}$

and $B_3 = \dfrac{(mS)^m/m!}{(mS)^m/m! + (1 - S) \displaystyle\sum_{i=0}^{m-1} \dfrac{(mS)^i}{i!}}$

The total waiting time for the fully-integrated configuration is:

$$kS^2/(1 - kS) + mS^2/(1 - mS) + B_1/(m - kS) +$$

$$B_2/(m - mS) + B_3/(k - m - 1 - mS)$$

where $B_1 = \dfrac{(kS)^m/m!}{(kS)^m/m! + (1 - \dfrac{kS}{m}) \displaystyle\sum_{i=0}^{m-1} \dfrac{(kS)^i}{i!}}$

and $B_2 = \dfrac{(mS)^m/m!}{(mS)^m/m! + (1 - S) \displaystyle\sum_{i=0}^{m-1} \dfrac{(mS)^i}{i!}}$

and $B_3 = \dfrac{(mS)^{k-n-1}/(k-n-1)!}{(mS)^{k-n-1}/(k-n-1)! + (1 - \dfrac{mS}{k-n-1}) \displaystyle\sum_{i=0}^{k-n-2} \dfrac{(mS)^i}{i!}}$

OFFICE SYSTEMS: Methods and Tools
G. Bracchi, D. Tsichritzis (Editors)
Elsevier Science Publishers B.V. (North-Holland)
© IFIP, 1987

Distribution and Error Handling
in an Office Procedure System†

Th. Kreifelts
G. Woetzel

Gesellschaft für Mathematik und Datenverarbeitung mbH
D-5205 St. Augustin 1

ABSTRACT

The DOMINO-W office procedure system is a reimplementation of the predecessor system DOMINO. The main objectives with the reimplementation were to extend the system access to users of computer networks, and to enlarge the functionality of the system to a more complete set of exception handling methods within the original office procedure model. With DOMINO-W, the communication between user and system is based on a protocol of mutual requests and responses. The protocol elements allow for handling exceptions in office procedures like cancellation of already executed actions or correction of mistakes produced by other actors. By implementing the communication protocol on top of electronic mail, the components of DOMINO-W (procedure control module, user components) may be distributed over the nodes of an electronic mail network, giving all users of such a network access to the system.

1   Introduction

A few years ago, we developed the office procedure system DOMINO[Krei84]. DOMINO is a tool for the specification and automation of well-structured and fairly formalized cooperative office processes, which we represent as coordination procedures in the framework of a formal model. DOMINO can handle different types of coordination procedures which are described in a specification language and are then translated into an executable control program. When a coordination procedure has been started, DOMINO controls its performance by notifying users about actions due to be performed and by routing the results of such actions to the users who need them for subsequent actions. The state of a running procedure may be checked at any time and an activity log

---

†   This work was conducted as part of the joint project WISDOM and was supported by the German Federal Ministry of Research and Technology and Triumph-Adler AG, Nuremberg.

is produced upon termination of a procedure.

DOMINO is not meant to be an integrated office system but rather a tool for office procedure handling which may be used in conjunction with other tools from the office "tool-kit", like editors, data base systems etc. A mathematical foundation of the coordination procedure model can be achieved by describing the permissible types of information flow in a procedure by a certain class of Petri nets. Our coordination procedure model is an information-action model [Barb83] which centers around the information flow within a group of persons necessary to accomplish a common task. Comparable models and according systems have been described in the literature, e.g. [Elli82, Tsic82, Zism77].

The main features of DOMINO are the following: DOMINO is a fairly small system, which concentrates on the essential coordination function of an office procedure system, it integrates the usual electronic mail with the procedure system communication and it is implemented on UNIX, an operating system which is becoming popular also for small to medium office computers. However, there are two serious limitations in our first implementation: DOMINO runs only on a single UNIX system, and it has almost no possibilities of handling user errors in running procedures. To overcome these limitations, we did a reimplementation of our office procedure system which is called DOMINO-W.

In the following, we will report on the main features of DOMINO-W as far as distribution and error handling are concerned, after having very briefly recollected the underlying office procedure model.

2   The DOMINO office procedure model

We model cooperative office processes by coordination procedures. Coordination procedures describe the information flow necessary to accomplish a common task within a group of persons. A coordination procedure is performed step by step in a predefined manner. Each step, which we call an action, is carried out by a certain person called an actor. In general, an action needs information produced by other actions, and in turn produces information required by other actions. With regard to the office, we call these pieces of information procedure forms or forms for short. Procedure forms are transmitted from one action to another via a corresponding procedure channel, which is characterized by the respective form type.

The information flow of a coordination procedure can be represented graphically in a straightforward manner: actions are represented by boxes, and channels by circles. The "need/yield"-relation between actions and forms is represented by arrows connecting the respective boxes and circles. An example of a coordination procedure is given in figure 1. Notches in action boxes indicate that these actions produce alternative sets of forms and thus contain a decision. As is obvious from figure 1, the process structure of coordination procedures allows for concurrent and alternative courses of activity.

The actions of a coordination procedure are described by the input forms they need and the output forms they produce, i.e. by the way

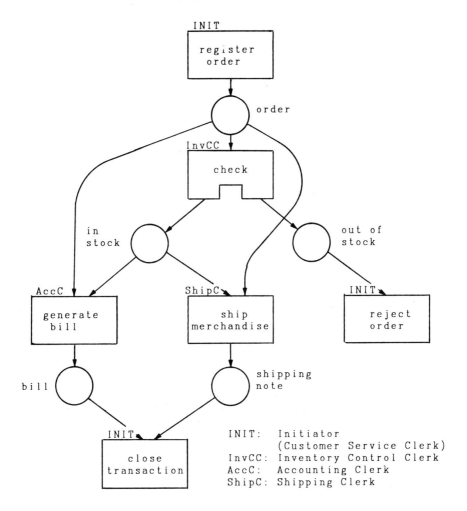

Figure 1. Example of a coordination procedure: Order processing

they communicate with other actions. The procedure does not tell *how* an action should be carried out, but rather *what* its result should be. Every action belongs to a role; the roles of a procedure stand for positions in the organization. Roles are "played" by persons ("actors") who are responsible for the actions of the role. Roles are assigned to certain persons when a procedure is started. One person can play several roles in different procedures; a certain role of a procedure can be played by different persons with different invocations of that procedure.

A coordination procedure is a plan describing how to carry out a certain task, and as such it represents the class of all possible executions of this plan. A respective procedure in progress is an instantiation of this

class. There may be several instances of the same or different
procedures in progress. The execution of a procedure is started with
the role assignment and the execution of the initial action. Subsequent
actions can be carried out when all input forms have been produced.
This process continues until all possible final actions have been
executed, which terminates the procedure.

There are some properties we require of the information flow in
coordination procedures. There must be no cycles or iterative loops in
a procedure; there should be no deadlocks, i.e. regardless of the
decisions made, the execution of a procedure should always lead to a
final action; every action should have the (theoretical) opportunity to
be executed with some invocation of the procedure; no action should
become obsolete due to a concurrently made decision; there should be
no "racing conditions", i.e. actions should not compete for input forms
or the production of output forms.

The above properties are checked by the compiler of the DOMINO system
which accepts coordination procedures written in the specification
language CoPlan-S. An office procedure specification in CoPlan-S has
three parts: the declaration of the roles, the declaration of the forms,
and the description of the information flow which is a list of statements
describing the input-output behavior of the actions. The formal syntax
of CoPlan-S is given in [Woet85]. We give an example by specifying the
coordination procedure of figure 1.

```
ROLE Inventory_Control_Clerk:  woetzel.      # roles
ROLE Accounting_Clerk:         kreifelts.    # declaration
ROLE Shipping_Clerk:           seuffert.

FORM order:                                  # forms
    customer name  : ....                    # declaration
              street: ....
              city  : ....
    article no      quantity
    ....            ....
    ....            ....
ENDFORM
FORM in_stock:
    ordered merchandise is in stock
ENDFORM
FORM out_of_stock:
    ordered merchandise is out of stock
ENDFORM
FORM invoice:
       .
       .
ENDFORM
FORM shipping_note:
       .
       .
ENDFORM
```

```
INITIATOR register_order:                    #  information
   YIELDS order.                             #  flow
Inventory_Control_Clerk check:               #  specification
   NEEDS order
   YIELDS in_stock
   YIELDS out_of_stock.
INITIATOR reject_order:
   NEEDS out_of_stock.
Accounting_Clerk generate_invoice:
   NEEDS order in_stock
   YIELDS invoice.
Shipping_Clerk ship_merchandise:
   NEEDS order in_stock
   YIELDS shipping_note.
INITIATOR close_transaction:
   NEEDS invoice shipping_note.
```

3 The need for error handling

When we talk about errors, we do not mean errors in a procedure specification — which are detected by the compiler — or errors in the underlying computer system, but errors or exceptions caused by users during the execution of an office procedure. There are numerous types of such errors or exceptions:

— The wrong person was assigned to a role.

— The person assigned to a role is on a holiday.

— A procedure form was erroneously filled in which is detected by another actor in a subsequent action.

— A mistake was made in an action which is detected afterwards by the person who made the mistake.

— The initiator of a procedure is no longer interested in its execution due to some "outside" event.

— An actor does not do anything about a pending action and blocks the execution of a procedure.

— An actor detects that the procedure definition is not adequate for the particular circumstances of the case at hand.

A procedure system would not be of much practical value, if one had to pull the emergency break in every case of an error or exception and start the procedure again from scratch. Therefore it is a reasonable requirement that as much errors as possible should be handled whithin a running procedure and without throwing away work already done if not necessary.

Some of the above errors are relatively easy to handle, some require more complicated measures and some can hardly be treated within an office procedure system. The first DOMINO system could only handle the easiest cases which require the manual or automatic delegation of actions to other persons — a process analogous to forwarding in electronic mail systems. The next two items on the above list — errors made in an action which are detected afterwards by the person who made the error or other people involved in the procedure — require freezing, resetting and restarting a running procedure. This sounds easy enough with a procedure consisting of a pure sequence of actions, but is rather complicated with a network of concurrent and alternative actions. Also, the possibility of cancelling and redoing actions or requiring the correction of other people's actions raises the question when an actor can be sure that the execution of a procedure has been successfully completed. The next case, where the initiator is no longer interested in the outcome of the procedure, requires a possibility of cancelling a whole procedure along with a notification of the actors concerned. The last two items are treated best outside the system and usually require talking to people directly. In the case where some actor blocks the progress of a procedure by doing nothing, it might be useful for the initiator to have a possibility of terminating not the whole procedure but only the action in question. When a single actor is assigned to that action, the outcome will be an incomplete procedure, but when more than one actor is assigned to that action (then a so-called simultaneous action), the procedure might carry on with the results produced so far by the other actors. The last case on the above list is the "catch-all exception" with office procedures and requires the abortion of the procedure if no other outside activity helps.

4 The CoPlan-X interface

We have incorporated the error handling measures mentioned above into DOMINO-W. To invoke these (and the other) functions we have designed a new interface through which a user communicates with the system. This CoPlan-X interface consists of user requests and system responses as well as system requests and user responses. All elements of the interface (or: communication protocol) are conceived as messages exchanged between the procedure monitoring part of the DOMINO-W system and a user. There are 15 types of such messages, which are listed below along with a short statement of purpose and content.

System requests:

— Request of the *execution* of an action.
  An actor is requested to carry out an action. The message consists of the input forms needed and templates for the output forms to be produced.

— Request of the *correction* of an action.
  An actor is requested to correct a previously performed action. This message is caused by the cancellation of the action by the actor himself or by the objection of a subsequent actor to one of the forms produced by this action. The contents are the same as with the execution request plus an additional cause for the correction.

User responses:

— *Completion* of an action.
  An actor completes the execution (or correction) of an action as a

response to a respective request. This message contains the alternative chosen (in case of a decision) and the produced output forms.

— *Refusal* of an action.
An actor refuses the requested execution (or correction) of an action. When there is only a single actor assigned to the action, a refusal leads to an abnormal termination of the procedure. This message contains the reason for the refusal given by the actor.

— *Delegation* of an action.
An actor delegates the requested execution of an action to another person. The delegation message contains the name of this person.

— *Objection* to input forms.
An actor objects to one or more of the input forms of an action. This message contains the names of the forms and the reason for the objection and leads to resetting and restarting the procedure with the actions which produced the input forms in question.

User requests:

— *Initialization* of a procedure.
A user wants to initialize a procedure. This message contains the procedure specification in the specification language CoPlan-S.

— *Termination* of an action.
The initiator of a procedure requests the termination of an action the execution of which has been requested but has not yet been carried out. This message contains the name of the action to be terminated. If there is only a single actor assigned to this action, all causally dependent actions of the procedure do not take place.

— *Cancellation* of an action.
An actor requests an action to be cancelled which has been previously executed by this very actor. This message leads to resetting and restarting the procedure with the action in question.

— *Tracing* of a procedure.
An actor requests a record of the activities having occured during the performance of a procedure.

System responses:

— *Confirmation* of an action.
An action is confirmed which means that the respective procedure has been successfully completed as a whole.

— *Rejection* of an action.
An action is rejected which means that the respective procedure has abnormally terminated or has been reset. In the latter case the execution of the action in question might be requested again, e.g. in cases of cancellation of actions.

— *Excess of deadline* of an action.
The initiator of a procedure is notified that some actor has exceeded the deadline for the execution (or correction) of an action.

— Procedure *record*.
This message is produced in answer to a tracing request, and upon
termination of a procedure (for the initiator).

— *Error* in a procedure specification.
The procedure system informs a user that the procedure
specification of an initialization message contained errors. In this
case, the procedure is not started.

Each of the above message types has a formal syntax: it is defined as a
certain regular expression of text lines of different formats. The format
of a line is determined by its first character. There are nine different
formats each designated for a certain type of information: a Z-line
contains message type and procedure identification and is always the
first line of a CoPlan-X message, an A-line contains an action name, a B-
line contains a user name, an S-line contains a procedure form name, a
T-line contains arbitrary text etc. For the complete message syntax we
refer the reader to [Woet85].

A smooth performance of an office procedure would only require the five
message types initialization, execution request, completion,
confirmation, and a closing procedure record. Apart from a possible
procedure specification error message and an intermediate tracing
request all other eight message types are designed to cover exceptional
cases during the performance of an office procedure as mentioned
above. Especially the messages for delegation, objection, cancellation
and correction supply a flexible means to treat a broad class of
exceptions in office procedure processing.

5   The need for distribution

There are strong organizational reasons why it is undesirable for an
office procedure system to be limited to the users of a single time-
sharing system, as it is the case with our first implementation of the
DOMINO system. These reasons are that office workers participating in
an office procedure are distributed over an organization, that an
organization might be distributed over the country, i.e. is not limited to
one site, and that office procedures might even cross organizational
boundaries, i.e. office workers of different organizations might agree on
common procedures which they would like to execute via electronic
media. From a technical viewpoint it would also appear that a single
machine office procedure system is not state-of-the-art: today's office
systems tend to be (local) networks of various types of machines —
personal, server, or time-sharing — rather than one (big) machine; also
there is the wide-spread electronic mail communication facility on
computer networks which one would also like to use for more
structured office communication.

In short, an office procedure system limited to the users of a single
computer does not meet the office requirements and does not fit the
trends in office systems and electronic communication.

6   The DOMINO-W systems architecture

The main objectives with the development of the DOMINO-W office procedure system as compared with the first DOMINO system were to extend the access to the system for users of computer networks and to enlarge the functionality of the system to a more complete set of exception handling measures within the coordination procedure model [Woet85a]. The first DOMINO system [Krei84] was implemented on a single UNIX system. It consisted of the procedure compiler and procedure control software which were installed under a pseudo-user "domino", and a simple user component for carrying out actions. The user component was formed by a slightly modified mail reading program and a forms editor. Whereas the system used the usual electronic mail for the notification of users about actions due, the actual information routing of the procedure forms was done by process coupling via pipes. This latter mechanism is not easily extendable to networks. So it seemed reasonable to use electronic mail also for the transport of the procedure forms in DOMINO-W.

The original design of dividing the whole system into a procedure compiler and control module on the one hand, and user components on the other hand was retained, because this design is a consequence of the coordination procedure model. A coordination procedure specifies a method of accomplishing a goal by describing how elementary steps — the actions — should be combined to do so; the methods to carry out the actions remain in the responsibility of the respective actors. Consequently, the procedure coordinator, i.e. the procedure compiler and control module, executes procedure specifications relevant to a whole group of actors and follows strict rules whereas the user components support specific users with their actions and may be customized as requested. Thus at least potentially, the resulting system is very flexible at the user's end.

For DOMINO-W we have chosen CoPlan-X as the interface between the procedure coordinator and the user components (see figure 2). CoPlan-X is ideally suited for this purpose. The CoPlan-X interface consists of different types of request and response messages. These messages are ordinary text files which are easily transported via electronic mail. In addition, CoPlan-X messages have a formal syntax which can be interpreted and generated by programs, such as the procedure coordinator and the user components. This is the basis for introducing "local" automation in user components.

By implementing the CoPlan-X interface on top of an electronic mail network it is possible to distribute the components of DOMINO-W over the machines of that network: the procedure coordinator, responsible for compiling and monitoring office procedures, will usually reside on a stable and secure server machine, whereas the user components can reside on the particular user's favourite machine, e.g. a personal computer connected to the network. Procedures are initiated and monitored by the procedure coordinator exclusively via electronic mail communication with the partipicipants' user components. It is also possible to have more than one procedure coordinating node in the network if several machines qualify as servers in the above sense. This does not mean that the procedure control itself is distributed: a specific

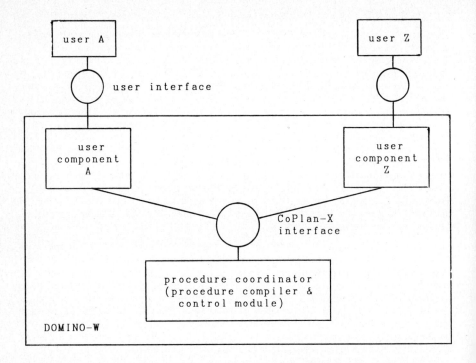

Figure 2. Schematic view of the office procedure system DOMINO-W

procedure is monitored completely by one coordinator (to avoid the additional problems of distributed control like distributed termination etc.), but a user may choose between different coordinators when initiating a procedure for reasons of minimizing network mail traffic.

With this ideas in mind, DOMINO-W was implemented on our local computer network. This network consists mainly of UNIX systems (four VAXes and about 50 smaller systems like Perqs and Cadmus 9000, running different versions of UNIX like V7, System III, System V and BSD 4.2), and connects to some Symbolics Lisp Machines.

A procedure coordinator of DOMINO-W has three main components: the procedure compiler, the control module, and the communication module, the latter being responsible for interpreting and generating the CoPlan-X messages. All components are written in the C programming language. A coordinator is installed as a pseudo-user "domino" on a server machine; in our case we run two coordinators on two VAXes. We have developed two prototype versions of a user component, one very simple version for UNIX systems with a forms editor as local tool and a UNIX-like command dialogue as a user interface, and a more comfortable one for the Lisp Machines which features advanced interaction techniques at the user interface and manages local procedure information in form of procedure and action folders (see

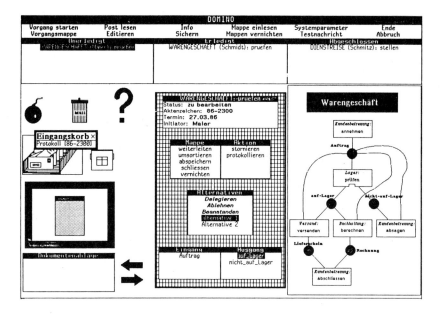

Figure 3. User interface of a DOMINO-W user component

figure 3).

In both cases of procedure coordinator and user component the interfacing to the mail system is done by a mail daemon or spooler which periodically looks for or is triggered by incoming mail, sorts out the procedure mail, i.e. the CoPlan-X messages, and invokes the processing of these messages.

7 Conclusion

We have implemented the office procedure system DOMINO-W which may be accessed by all users of an electronic mail network. The system consists of one or more procedure coordinating nodes and user components. A procedure coordinating node is installed as a pseudo-user "domino" on a server machine. The monitoring of a specific procedure instance is centralized with such a pseudo-user "domino", the user components of the actors involved are distributed over the network. Communication between the procedure coordinator and the user components of the actors is by electronic mail using the CoPlan-X interface of requests and responses by users and system. This interface features important measures for handling exceptional conditions in office procedures like cancellation of actions already executed, and requests of correcting mistakes in documents produced by other actors. The DOMINO-W system is operational on a computer network comprising UNIX systems of different types (VAX 780, VAX 750, Perq, Cadmus 9000) and Symbolics Lisp Machines.

References

Barb83   Barber, G., Jong, P. de, Hewitt, C. "Semantic support for work in organizations", in R. E. A. Mason (ed.) *Proc. IFIP Congress 83*, North-Holland, Amsterdam, 1983, p. 561–566.

Elli82   Ellis, C. A., Bernal, M. "OFFICETALK-D: An experimental office information system", *SIGOA Newsletter* 3, 1&2 (1982), 131–140, also as Proc. SIGOA Conf. Office Inf. Systems, Philadelphia, Pa., 1982.

Krei84   Kreifelts, Th., Licht, U., Seuffert, P., Woetzel, G. "DOMINO: A system for the specification and automation of cooperative office processes", in B. Myhrhaug, D. R. Wilson (ed.) *Proc. EUROMICRO 1984*, North-Holland, Amsterdam, 1984, p. 33–41.

Tsic82   Tsichritzis, D. "Form Management", *Comm. ACM* 25, 7 (1982), 453–478.

Woet85   Woetzel, G., Kreifelts, Th. "Die Vorgangssprache CoPlan", WISDOM-Forschungsbericht   FB-GMD-85-22,   Gesellschaft   für Mathematik und Datenverarbeitung mbH, St. Augustin, 1985.

Woet85a   Woetzel, G., Kreifelts, Th. "Systemarchitektur des Vorgangssystems   DOMINO-W",   WISDOM-Forschungsbericht   FB-GMD-85-23, Gesellschaft für Mathematik und Datenverarbeitung mbH, St. Augustin, 1985.

Zism77   Zisman, M. D. "Representation, specification and automation of office procedures", Ph.D. dissertation, Univ. of Pennsylvania, Philadelphia, Pa., 1977.

OFFICE SYSTEMS: Methods and Tools
G. Bracchi, D. Tsichritzis (Editors)
Elsevier Science Publishers B.V. (North-Holland)
© IFIP, 1987

USAGE: A USER FRIENDLY APPLICATION GENERATOR FOR EVOLUTIVE DOCUMENT
MANAGEMENT SYSTEMS.

Pierre VAN NYPELSEER

AITECH S.A.
87 av Georges Bergmann
B-1050 Bruxelles, Belgium

We describe an integrated office automation tool that takes into
account the full range of document production, modification,
communication and management tasks in an environment where many
people cooperate, possibly in several languages.

It is based on a data dictionary that describes the types of
documents and of actions upon documents. That data dictionary is
accessible to the user, allowing him to define his application and to
make it evolve without the help of a computer specialist. A data
dictionary interpreter gives access to the documents in a distributed
environment, records the actions, and provide all the necessary
facilities for task attribution, follow-up and planning.

The conceptual primitives upon which the system is based are simple
and uniform. They are independent of the data base, word processing
and communication tools they call upon. As a result, the system is
easy to implement and can mix products originating with several
hardware and software suppliers.

1. INTRODUCTION

The work upon documents in administrations is caracterised by change:

- of the document content, as it undergoes creation and modification through
the collaboration of many people

- of the document status, as it progresses through the administrative process

- of the administrative process itself

Organising and keeping track of those various levels of evolution is central to
the administrative work.

We describe here an office system tool that integrates the existing word
processing, data base and communication software operating from plain terminals
to provide a work environment in which evolution is explicitly taken into
account. That environment can support the cooperative work of several thousand
people.

Whereas it is difficult to introduce change management in an existing
conceptual framework, we found that taking change management as our primary
goal trivially solved most of the hard problems associated with cooperation,
such as concurrent update on distributed data bases and modification
notification.

We describe first our evolutive document concept and its implementation. We
then show how to organise cooperative work around a shared follow-up document.
That document controls the access to the data, and is also used as a basis for
change notification, planning and resource allocation.

We then define the data dictionary and the interpreter with the various levels
of service it can offer. Finally we discuss the portability of the system, and
we give our sources of inspiration.

2. DOCUMENT STRUCTURE

From the physical document, as realised on paper, we abstract the notion of
logical document, suitable both for the description of paper based systems and
the realisation of electronic systems.

2.1. Contribution

The paper physical document consists in one or several consecutive sheets of
paper, carrying a main text, signatures, identifications, remarks, archiving
information, ...

The logical document consists in a set of contributions:

- each contribution has a type: "main text", "signature", "identification",
"remark", "index",...

- each contribution can be attached to part or the whole of a single other
contribution, like a "remark" contribution that whould apply to one particular
sentence in the "main text" contribution

- new contributions are added to the logical document as a result of its
progression through the administrative process.

2.2. Occurrence

A new version of a paper physical document can be created from the old, by
producing a modified version of the main text, to which new contributions are
associated. The old contributions (signature, remarks) apply only to the old
main text.

In a logical document, each contribution can have an arbitrary number of
occurrences:

- an occurrence cannot be modified. One can however add a more recent
occurrence to the contribution at any time. A full historical record of the
occurrences of each contribution is kept

- a contribution attached to another is attached to a particular occurrence of
that other, since it has no meaning in relation to another occurrence.

Those two conditions allow the easy management of distributed document data
bases, since the situation at each location is always coherent, old or new, and
the new contributions are always explicitly attached to the occurrences of the
old or of the new situation.

To put it differently, the set of occurrences belonging to a logical document
constitutes a tree on which the only authorised operation is to add a node.
Different parts of the tree can be present at different locations, and
additions can proceed independently at each node.

2.3. View

The main text can exist on paper in many copies, each one a physical document carrying its own associated information. In particular, comments and personal remarks are not all physically present on each copy and are not logically accessible to all the persons having access to the main text.

All the contributions of those physical documents belong to the same logical document. The set of contributions of each physical document constitutes one particular view of that logical document.

A logical view is any set of occurrences of contributions, belonging to one or several logical documents:

- views can be shared, in which case all the participants have access to the new contributions and occurrences added by each to the view. In a paper system, sharing can be organised through duplication and circulation. In an electronic system, there is a single primitive operation by which a participant to a view can grant participation to another. The view content, any later updates and the corresponding change notifications are automatically forwarded by the system to the machine where the new participant resides. The forwarding can be organised through floppy disks or electronic mail; the means are indifferent to the users, except possibly for speed. Views constitute a very high level communication and cooperation mechanism. There is no other communication mechanism in the system.

- a view is accessible only to the participants to that particular view, be there one or several. Views constitute a very high level privacy mechanism.

- finally, a set of new occurences added as a whole to a view can be transmitted to the various locations of a distributed data base as a unit, insuring a higher level of coherence than that guaranteed at the occurrence level by the tree structure.

3. IMPLEMENTATION OF THE LOGICAL DOCUMENT CONCEPT

3.1. Occurrence structure

The basic unit of information in the system is the occurrence. The contribution level information is repeated on each occurrence of the contribution. Each occurrence consists in:

- a profile, that contains the management information. Its format is fixed for all contribution types.

- a body that contains the data content. Its format is fixed for each contribution type.

The profile contains the following information:

- document and contribution type

- document, contribution and occurence number; each of those numbers is independent of the others, contains a creation machine number and is unique within the system

- a short text describing the occurrence

– attachment: occurrence number, field, initial and final position within the field. For some more system oriented contributions, attachement at the contribution level is possible

– language of the occurrence if it contains textual information

– action that created the occurrence, as described below: action type and number, document and personal roles, person electronic visa

– date and time at which the action started creating the occurrence. During creation, an occurrence can be modified, but its access is restricted to the person mentioned in the profile, and it cannot receive attached contributions

– date and time of creation end

The body consists in a pre-defined sequence of fields, each having a name and a format. One of the accepted formats is "word processor text".

3.2. Occurrence implementation

The profile of all the occurrences has the same format, and can be put in a single file of any data base. The system will query the file using the data base access functions. All that is required is inverted files on some fields.

If the data base accepts multiple record types in one file, profile and body can be put together in the same file, the record type is its contribution type. If not, the body of the occurrences of each type of contribution will be in a different file and each profile will contain an index into the appropriate file.

If the data base accepts fields of indefinite length in a record, the "word processor text" can be stored in the record. If not, the record will contain the name of the word processor file used.

The implementation is easier if the data base supports on-line updating, but if not one can program sequential queries on the movement file .

3.3 View structure

A view is a set of contribution occurrences, and is itself represented by contributions. Each view consists in:

– a view header contribution

– one or more view membership contributions, attached to an occurence of the view header

The view header contains a view type and the view number and occurrence number.

Each membership contribution contains essentially a membership type, the number of a contribution or of a contribution occurrence which is made member of the view and the access rights of the view to the contribution or to the occurrence.

3.4. Logical document display

3.4.1. Display of the logical document structure

Example of screen:

```
ABSTRACT            Loan application review guidelines
TEXT       86/3/18  Loan application review guidelines
           SIG           Director
           86/1/13  Loan application review guidelines
           REM           Bad risks
           MOD           Collaterals
```

The screen shows the occurrences of the contributions of the document. It gives
for each its type and description.

The TEXT contribution has two occurrences whose date of creation end are
indicated. Attached contributions are indented to the right below the
occurrence they are attached to. A signature is attached to the most recent
occurrence of the TEXT, and a remark and a modification proposal to the other.

The user can select one of the lines and ask for the display of the profile or
of the body of the corresponding occurrence.

3.4.2. Display of an occurrence profile

The screen shows the list of profile field names followed each by its value.

3.4.3. Display of an occurrence body

The screen shows the list of body field names followed each by its value.
Fields of "word procesor text" format have a "*" value. When the user selects
that line, the text is displayed under word processor control.

If there are contributions attached to a body field or within a word processor
text, the user can request the blinking of each attachment position. The body
of the corresponding attached contribution will appear on a split or alternate
screen. The user can move in both screens trough history from the most recent
to earlier occurrences.

4. ACTIONS UPON DOCUMENTS

4.1. Definitions

An action upon a document utilises and produces contribution occurrences.

- each action has a type: "production of a draft", "translation", "approval"

- each action may involve several persons, which are human resources for the
action. The action consumes part of their time. Each of these resources has a
type and an identity. The type of a human resource might be "secretary",
"statistician",...

- each action may involve several documents which are document resources
accessed or produced by the action. Each document has a type and an identity.
The type of a document might be "certificate of good character", "national
identity card", "form B-327",...

- each resource is associated to the role it performs in the action. A secretary can act as a "meeting organiser" and the "certificate of good character" or the "national identity card" can be used as "proof of nationality".

4.2. Decomposition and chaining of actions

Actions are grouped by case, where the case is a user defined notion. The case is associated with one high level action, case management, which can be decomposed in more elementary actions, which can in turn be decomposed.

The actions are decomposed as follows:

- roles of the more elementary actions can be put in correspondence with roles of the less elementary action, of which they are a refinement

- not all roles of a more elementary action need be the refinement of a role of the less elementary action. This allows the hiding of unnecessary details.

In some situations, the possible sequences of actions at the more elementary level are pre-defined, and constitute an administrative procedure. Each action in the procedure can have several different outcomes, each leading to a different continuation. To represent that fact, each role of an action has an initial state, and one or several final states.

- at the end of the action, the resource associated with each role is in one of the final states for the role

- the actions can be chained through the resources: a resource in a final state of a role of one action can be used as resource in the initial state for one or several roles of other actions, depending of that final state.

One may wish to have the system exhibit a goal-directed behavior, by wich it automatically designs and supervises sequences of actions to reach a given goal. The necessary information consists in a pre-condition, attached to the initial state of each role of the action and that must be verified before the action can take place, and a post-condition, attached to each final state, that is garantied to hold when the state is reached at the conclusion of the action.

4.3. Responsibility for actions

An action manager is associated with each action. He is responsible for the quality of the result and for the schedule of the action. If the action is decomposed in more elementary actions, he is in charge of the decomposition, of the assignment of action managers for more elementary actions, and of the follow-up of progress for those actions.

A resource manager can be associated to each role in an action. He is responsible for providing the resource of appropriate type, quality and quantity on a schedule agreed upon with the action manager.

5. FOLLOW-UP DOCUMENT

5.1. Description

All the actions pertaining to a case are described in a follow-up document. In that document, each action is represented by:

- one action contribution

- one attached role contribution for each role

The contributions representing more elementary actions are attached to the contribution representing the less elementary action. The decomposition of a role is represented by a view attached to the less elementary role and containing the more elementary roles. The sequencing of roles is represented by a view attached to the successor role and containing the predecessor roles.

The action contribution contains the action type, number, planning status and schedule. Each role contribution contains the same, and the type and amount of resources involved.

During the life of an action those contributions are updated many times. To avoid complex duplications, all the attachments are made to the contributions and not to the occurrences.

The document resources involved in the action are made available in views, attached to the corresponding roles.

The human resources, action managers and resource managers are given a view of the actions and roles of the follow-up documents in which they are involved. The views that a person has on all the follow-up documents to which he has access are grouped in his attribution view, a view containing views.

The views on the follow-up document can also be used in the reverse direction, to show all the people involved in an action or a role. This is done on the display of the follow-up document.

5.2. Display of the follow-up document

Example of screen:

```
ACTION    Regulation production    O 14/2/86 2/3/86
          AM          Paul Marin
          REM         Wide consensus required

          ACTION    Drafting    C 15/2/86 19/2/86
                    AM          John Beard
                    ROLE        Regulation      C 15/2/86 19/2/86 12p
                    ROLE        Drafter         C 15/2/86 19/2/86 17h
                    RM          Paul Marin
                    RES         Georges Hopper
                    RES         Albert Griet


          ACTION    Legal advising      P 20/2/86 25/2/86
                    AM          Earnst Habler
                    ROLE        Regulation      P 20/2/86 25/2/86 12p
                    ...
```

The view presented here is that of John Beard, action manager for the drafting action. The display shows the logical document structure for that view of the follow-up document completed with information from the body of the contributions representing the actions and the roles, and the reverse view of the AM, RM and human resources.

One can display the profile and body of each contribution of the follow-up document, for the most recent and for historic occurrences, and add occurrences and view memberships.

5.3. Display of the attribution view

Example of screen:

```
VW   AM        Drafting  C 15/2/86 19/2/86
     INDEX     Loan
     REM       Urgent

VW   RES       Analyst   O 16/2/86 18/2/86 10h
     CONS      C 16/2/86 5h
     CONS      P 21/2/86 5h
```

The display shows the attribution view of John Beard. The first view describes his involvement in the regulation production case whose follow-up document has been given as example above.

The AM view membership contribution is chosen as a representative of the view content for display purposes. Part of the content of the occurrence of the ACTION is shown.

Attached to that view are a remark contribution, and an index contribution that classifies the case. Both contributions have been added by John Beard for his personal use.

The second view describes the involvment of John Beard in another case, for which he plays the role of analyst. The resource consumption contributions represent each a time packet of his time, the first in the consumed status, the second planned.

5.4. Communication through the follow-up document and the attribution views

The communication pattern between the participants in a case is as follows:

- the AM of the less elementary action creates a new more elementary action; the action contribution carries the "requested" status, the earliest date at which the action can start, and the date at which its results are expected. He also creates the role contributions.

- he chooses an AM for the new action, and puts a view of the follow-up document in that AM's attribution view

- the next time the new AM accesses his attribution view, he is notified by the apparition of the view of the new case in reverse video. It remains so until he acknowledges it.

- he accedes the follow-up document; he may decompose the action further, and enter into negociations with RMs and lower level AMs as to dates and resources. When he is able to commit himself on the action beginning and end dates, he creates a new occurrence of the action contribution with those dates, in the "planned" status.

- the new occurrence is within the view of the less elementary action AM. The change in that view puts it in reverse video in that AM's attribution document. He accepts it or continues the negociation.

All AMs, RMs and human resources communicate through the same shared follow-up document, of which they may have different views. They do not explicitly send messages to each other.

The delegation process by itself does not create new actions, but simply gives new people access to existing actions.

This approach is very different from that of most office systems which are driven by document circulation, and not by actions.

6. RESOURCE ALLOCATION

Example of screen:

```
              FEBRUARY                    MARCH
              ..12345..12345..12345..12345..12345..12345.....45..12345..1

Albert Griet    88848  88.68  88888  44888  .....  88888    88  88888

234-1567                      66.   C
567-2914                        ..  44   P
345-2176                     ...888   8  A
214-6789                                      ..  6888   R
```

This screen shows the work assignments of one human resource for a two month period. The first two lines list the official working days; the office happens to be closed on March 17 through 19. The next line is the personal availability, in hours for each day. The following lines give, for each follow-up document the person is involved in as a resource, the status of the resource reservation, the days and the number of hours per day. The periods indicate the extent of the calendar specified in the role.

To schedule a personal resource for an action, the RM selects a person, and the system attempts to reserve the required number of hours while respecting the delays required for the action and the availability of the person.

The resource reservation and consumption are recorded in a CONS contribution, in the person attribution view.

7. ACCESS RIGHT TO THE DOCUMENT ROLES

To each document role is attached a public view, that contains the contribution occurrences that are accessible to all the people that have access to the role.

Each person that has access to the role also has a private view, in which he puts the occurrences that are accessible only to him.

A member of a view can be an occurrence of another view. That other view has a subview relation with the first. The view has access not only to the present content of the subview, but also to the new occurrences that may be added later.

7.1. Display of the document roles

Example of screen:

```
R1      R2
pr  pu  pu

        1   ABSTRACT              Loan application review guidelines
    0   2   TEXT        86/1/13   Loan application review guidelines
    0   2               REM          Bad risks
    0                   REM          Beware of the review board
        1               85/12/6   Loan application review guidelines
        1               MOD          Maximum amount
```

The screen shows the logical document structure for the occurrences of two roles, R1 and R2, selected on a follow-up document.

The user has read the subview 1 from the public view attached to R1. He has produced in his corresponding private view a new occurrence of the text contribution and two remarks. He has created in the public view attached to R2 subview 2 in which he has made public some occurrences of his private view.

The subviews are numbered arbitrarily within the display. "0" means "not in a subview".

All the people that have access to the role R2 are notified of the change by the switching to reverse video of the view of the follow-up document in their attribution view.

7.2. Display of the view participants

It is possible to show all the participants to a given view.

8. COMPLEX EXEMPLES

The examples chosen sofar have been kept simple. A more complex real life example might well be the following: a translation department is asked in an emergency to translate a document in parallel with its creation in the source language. Each delivery of part of the document must be split between translators, within a target language and across languages. A new version of a part that is already partially translated is received... The system that we have described can handle that complexity.

9. USER DEFINITION OF APPLICATIONS

The user can study his own application and describe his contribution types, document types, action types and procedure types.

He then enters his descriptions into a data dictionary. That data dictionary is itself coded as contributions, and all the tools described above are available.

A general interpreter uses the particular content of that data dictionary to drive the particular application.

As the application evolves, the user updates the content of the data dictionary.

10. INTERPRETATION LEVELS

The interpreter can be used to provide several levels of services. All the levels can be mixed, and the user interface remains the same.

10.1. Manual action follow-up

One can enter manually in a follow-up document the actions taken within each case and the role performed by each person and each document.

The system can then display what has been done on a document or within a case, when and by whom, and the progress of administrative procedures can be traced.

10.2. Automatic action follow-up and electronic document access

If the documents are recorded in the system in electronic form, the actions are taken within the system and can be automatically recorded as they occur.

The system will present the user with a choice of cases to process. Each case consists in a higher level action, and a particular document or set of documents to which it applies. Within the case, the system will propose a choice of lower level actions. If the case is governed by a procedure, only the lower level actions that are consistent with the current state of progress of the procedure will be proposed. The action chosen by the user will then be run in manual or assisted mode.

In the manual mode, the user will access himself the documents attached to the roles of the action, through the general facilities offered by the system and described above.

In the assisted mode, a program associated to the action by the data dictionary is run to execute the action. It accesses the documents and possibly enters into a specialised dialog with the user.

As the application evolves, actions that were first run in manual mode can be programmed to run in assisted mode when the action gets better defined or programmer time becomes available.

10.3. Automatic action execution

Within a procedure, the actions that can be executed by a program without dialog with a user can be set-up to execute automatically as soon as the necessary data become available. That availability is indicated by the termination of the preceeding actions, with resources in the appropriate final states.

10.4. Action attribution

Instead of choosing an action to perform, the user can choose an action to attribute to somebody else, by setting up the action in the follow-up document, filling up the roles and assigning an action manager to it. The action manager is notified through his attribution view.

10.5. Manual action and resource planning

The full use of the system as described here entails action attribution, with a specification of requested, planned or effective begin and end date, and management of the resources.

10.6. Automatic action and resource planning

The pre- and post-conditions put on the action's roles descriptions allows an
artificial intelligence planning system to design and monitor the execution of
sequences of actions that fulfills a given goal (post-condition) starting from
a given situation.

Action attribution and manual and automatic planning are possible both for
paper and for electronic documents.

11. SYSTEM PORTABILITY

The data structures that we use are easy to implement in any documentary or
relational data base management system. The integration of a word processor
along the lines that we have described is not difficult. The display exemples
that we have shown demonstrate that any terminal can be used at the user
interface.

The interpreter is quite simple to program, given the uniform data structure it
manages, contributions, and the simplicity of its primitive operations,
contribution creation and display.

All the distributed data base problems are handled by the interpreter, so that
the system can easily be spread across computers. The "forward the changes"
approach gives total freedom in the choice of the inter-computer communication
tools.

As a result, the system can easily be realised in several hardware and software
environments. Those various realisations can be integrated in a single
application, provided that there is a standardised data communication channel
between the implementations. If that channel is equipped for word processor
format conversion, it is even possible to mix realisations based on different
word processing packages.

12. RELATED WORK

The source of our inspiration was the work by Souillart [1], in which a data
dictionary is used to define data modification and data display procedures on a
data base. The users can modify the data dictionary content, and the system
generates screens and screen sequences from it. The data base itself contains a
full history of each field content, and update records are kept indicating who
did what, when and in the context of which procedure.

The system is in use today to manage a 12,000 people personnel data base, on
which 60 people cooperate for data entry, and 120 for interrogation. Started
with 800 fields and 50 screens and screen sequences 4 years ago, it contains
today 1800 fields and 1100 screens and sequences. The same system is also used
to manage a property inventory from acquisition to obsolescence.

In that system, the data is organised according to the object-event formalism.
It suggested for the system described in this paper a representation of the
document as a set of parts, each part being created or modified as a result of
a specific action.

The action formalism that we have chosen gathers most of the data associated
with actions in the methodology literature [2][3], the planning literature, the
office systems literature [4][5][6] and the artificial intelligence literature
[7]. As a result, the corresponding conceptual tools and packages can be

readily used to extend the power of our system.

Access to documents is controlled by "views". A view gives a person access to a set of contributions and people communicate by sharing views. We think that this concept of view is original.

The notion of link between documents, that is realised in our system by a view attached to a contribution and containing a pointer to a position in another contribution is also studied in [8]. Our system gives a solution to a problem mentioned there: how to introduce links that belong to a specific user. Our answer is to consider the linking view as a contribution and to put it within a specific user view.

Many existing OIS tools can in principle be called from our system by an action executed in assisted mode. We provide the sequencing, coordination and follow-up functions that are generally rudimentary in more specialised tools.

REFERENCES

[1] Souillart, C., Koepp, C. and Luisetti, R.: Computerised System for the Management of Staff and Posts at the Commission of the European Communities, in: Proceedings of the 13th Software AG User's Conference (Software AG, Dehmelstrasse 3, D–6100, Darmstadt, Germany, 1984)

[2] Tardieu, H., Rochfeld, A. and Colletti, R.: La méthode Merise (Les éditions d'organisation, Paris 1984)

[3] Teichroew, D. and Hershey, E. A.: PSL/PSA: a Computer Aided Technique for Structured Documentation and Analysis of Information Processing Systems, IEEE Transactions on Software Engineering SE–3 (1977) 41.

[4] King, R. and McLeod, D.: A Database Design Methodology and Tool for Information Systems, ACM Trans. Off. Syst. 3 (1985) 2.

[5] Croft, W. B. and Lefkowitz, L.S.: Task Support in an Office System, ACM Trans. Off. Syst. 2 (1984) 197.

[6] Bracchi, G. and Pernici, B: The Design Requirements of Office Systems, ACM Trans. Off. Syst. 2 (1984) 151.

[7] Barber, G.: Supporting Organisational Problem Solving with a Work Station, ACM Trans. Off. Syst. 1 (1983) 45.

[8] Yankelovitch, N., Meyrowitz, N. and van Dam, A.: Reading the Electronic Book, IEEE Computer (Oct 1985) 15.

OFFICE SYSTEMS: Methods and Tools
G. Bracchi, D. Tsichritzis (Editors)
Elsevier Science Publishers B.V. (North-Holland)
© IFIP, 1987

TIME REASONING IN THE OFFICE ENVIRONMENT

R. Maiocchi [+] and B. Pernici [++]

+ Dipartimento di Elettronica, Politecnico di Milano,
  P.za L. Da Vinci 32, I-20133 Milano, Italy

++ CSISEI-CNR, c/o Politecnico di Milano

In the office environment temporal aspects are important to mark
documents and to coordinate activities. The TSOS time model for
office information systems allows the specification of time aspects.
In this paper a time expert based on TSOS is presented. Temporal
assertions are organized in classes; then, with the time expert, it
is possible to answer questions about temporal assertions. The
answers about time evolution of the office systems are precise to
the maximum possible extent. When it is only possible to give an
approximate answer, this is done with the maximum level of precision
that can be achieved.
The proposed method for dealing with time assertions and the time
expert for reasoning on time are general and can be applied not only
to Office Information Systems, but also to Information Systems and
Database Systems.

1. INTRODUCTION

One of the requirements of Office Information Systems (OIS) is the ability of
dealing with a particular type of data: time data [1].

In the office, temporal information is associated both to static data, such as
documents, and to dynamic data, such as activities.

Besides the possibility of accessing this temporal information, it is also
important to elaborate time assertions to answer queries such as "Is this
activity within schedule?", or "Is this activity performed before that other
activity?".

A particular attention has been given to time related problems in Information
Systems in recent times [2]. A basic classification of existing models of time
consists in the subdivision of models into static and dynamic models. This
classification has been proposed in the literature, even if from slightly
different points of view in [3, 4, 5].

Static time models are those models in which the state of a system is the most
important concept [6, 7]. This view is typical of database systems, where the
current view of data is often the only available one. To consider time related
aspects, either a time attribute (timestamp) is attached to the attributes for
which it is important to keep a temporal record, or several snapshots of the
data are taken and temporal considerations are done on the appropriate subset
of snapshots.

This work was partially supported by European Community under Esprit Project
N. 813, "Automatic Tools for Designing Office Systems" (TODOS) and by the
Italian National Research Council under the APASC program.

In these models, the temporal operations on data consist in querying about
temporal sequences of data, with simple elaborations, and verifying static
(integrity) constraints on data.

In dynamic time models, the time considerations focus on transitions between
states. This view is typical of IS models for modeling relationships between
activities, where dynamic constraints on state changes are specified, for
instance, as preconditions and postconditions on update transactions [8, 9].
The dynamic time modeling approach is also used in artificial intelligence to
plan activities to achieve a given goal or to schedule resource allocation
[10, 11, 12, 13, 14]. In these cases duration of activities and precedence
constraints among activities are specified as constraints in the plan to
achieve. In contrast with static time models, which are based on the concept
of time point, dynamic models are mainly based on the concept of interval of
time. This concept has the advantage of being applicable to different levels
of detail in time specification, with the appropriate semantics. In [15] the
problem of dealing with occurrences of events and activities is handled. If an
event occurs during an interval, this interval is the smallest interval in
which it could have, while an activity may occur in subintervals of a given
interval; however, this does not imply that the activity is occurring during
all the subintervals of the given interval.

The need of specifying imprecise temporal information mentioned in the
previous paragraph is common both to static and to dynamic models. In some
dynamic models, in particular for planning, times are often only indirectly
specified through relationships between activities, and activities are
specified within intervals, and not always as absolute time points such as
dates [10, 11]. Another case in which imprecise times are of interest is that
of distributed systems [16]. In distributed systems, the ordering
relationships on times are not always known, or are only known with a certain
approximation.

In office systems, the problem of time representation has been considered to
insert alerters to signal particular conditions in an office system [17] and
to express triggers for activating system activities [18].

Reasoning on time has been used in the literature mainly for planning
activities to achieve certain goals [15].

Little attention has been devoted to the problems of specifying consistent
time assertions and of answering, precisely or imprecisely, to questions about
the past or future sequences of activities.

In [19] a program knowledgeable about time to deal with temporal aspects of
problem solving is illustrated. In that system reasoning is only used about
temporal references in the past.

Papers about planning can be considered to involve reasoning capabilities
about the future [15]. Another reasoning mechanism is provided by special
operators to manipulate temporal expressions, that allow to compute
relationships among times starting from the given temporal assertions [10,
20].

The TSOS office model proposed in [5] allows the specification of static and
dynamic times, at different levels of detail, with operators and functions for
time manipulation. In TSOS the basic time concepts are that of time point,
time intervals (based intervals and duration intervals), and periodic
intervals.

The purpose of this paper is to illustrate a method for reasoning about time
(time expert), based on time concepts existing in the literature and in

particular on the TSOS model for specifying time aspects in the office environment.

In the present work, we consider only times expressed at the more detailed level, i.e., at the level of minutes, since in our system we do not deal with the problem of times defined imprecisely, that arises from having times at different levels of detail.

In this paper there is no distinction between temporal assertions about past and future and the inference mechanism is able to answer questions about both; both these capabilities are needed in the office environment: temporal assertions about the future are needed for planning, scheduling, and decision making, while those about the past are needed for auditing and analyzing historical information. Moreover, the office is continuously evolving in time; it is therefore difficult to illustrate office states as snapshots.

In Section 2. the TSOS time model for expressing temporal aspects in the office environment is illustrated.

Section 3. presents the organization of different temporal assertions to be used as a basis for the time expert. The methods applied to this organization of times to propagate temporal information are described in Section 4.. The time expert is described in Section 5.

An example of use of the time expert for answering queries about temporally linked activities is presented throughout the paper.

2. THE TSOS TIME MODEL

2.1. Time in the office environment

In office systems the ability of dealing with time specifications is an important and characterizing requirement [1].

Time is present in documents, such as a date on a document, as a date or hour of production of a document, as a period of time in which a document information is considered to be valid, and so on.

Time is also necessary to specify starting and ending times of activities, procedures, tasks in the office; durations of activities, periods of time in which the activities may be performed.

Time relationships between activities, such as the requirement that an activity must be performed before, after or during another activity, need also to be expressed to coordinate the work in the office and to keep deadlines.

In this paper we assume as a reference model for office systems the Semantic Office System (SOS) model proposed in [21].

In SOS it is possible to define the different office elements presented above, in three submodels: the static submodel, the dynamic submodel, and the control submodel. SOS is based on the abstraction concepts characteristic of semantic models: generalization, association, and aggregation. We present here only those aspects of SOS that are relevant to specify temporal aspects; other features will appear from the presented examples.

In the static submodel, document, agent, and event types are described.

Documents are aggregations or association of complex fields, such as:

```
<PAPER> is-a document;
{aggregate-of
  {
    title: text;
    authors: association-of author: AUTHOR;
    publication-date: tp
  }
}.
```

In the above example AUTHOR should have already been defined in the system as an <u>agent</u>, with a syntax similar to that used for documents. Agents are recognized in the systems as elements entitled to start activities.

<u>Events</u> are static elements that describe that a certain fact has happened in the system; they can be used in the dynamic and control submodels to coordinate activities in the system.

A basic event has the following form:

```
<EVENT>;
{aggregate-of
  {event-id: integer;
    time: tp}}.
```

In the rest of the paper references to EVENT times (for instance, EVENT-3.time, where EVENT-3 is an event type) are referred to as EVi (in this case EV3), for sake of brevity.

In the <u>dynamic submodel</u> activity types are defined.

An activity is a manual or automatic activity performed in the system. As for time aspects, the following information is attached to each activity:

```
<ACTIVITY>;
{aggregate-of
  {max-duration: ts;
    min-duration: ts;
    tstart: tp;
    tend: tp;
    events: association-of e: EVENT;
    duration: ti;
    allowed-period: gt;
    ....
}.
```

The meaning of the different time types (tp, ti, gt, and so on) is illustrated in next section.

In the rest of the paper references to ACTIVITY times, i.e., ACTIVITY-1.tstart and ACTIVITY-1.tend, are referred to as S(Ai) and E(Ai) respectively (in this case S(A1) and E(A1)), for sake of brevity.

In the <u>control submodel</u> relationships among elements in the model are expressed. For instance:

```
<RULE-1> is-a RULE;
{aggregate-of
   {declarative-part: aggregate-of
                      {time1: EVENT-1.time;
                       time2: ACTIVITY-2.tstart
                      };
    conditional-expression: time2 = (3 days) after time1;
    body: TRUE
    }
}.
```

RULE-1 specifies that instances of activity type ACTIVITY-2 have to start exactly 3 days after an instance of event type EVENT-1. Rules in which the body is TRUE are rules indicating relationships among times and/or data contained in the declarative part of the rule.

Another example of a rule is the following, indicating that an instance of ACTIVITY-3 has to be started after an instance of EVENT-2 happens:

```
<RULE-2> is-a RULE;
   {declarative-part: aggregate-of
                      {event: EVENT-2
                      };
    conditional-expression: EVENT-2
    body: start ACTIVITY-3
    }
}.
```

The description of the mechanisms for rule invocation is outside the scope of this paper. In the following, we define the time primitives used in SOS and the use of rules to define temporal assertions in the model, as they are needed for reasoning about time in the office.

2.2. Time concepts

In TSOS, the following concepts are defined:

- Time Specification Time Category (TSTC)

  The TSTC is a temporal category formed by relative integers and specifies times such as the distance of a point of time from a fixed reference, the duration of a time interval, and so on. For example: a day, two weeks.

- Time Point Time Category (TPTC)

  The TPTC is the temporal category of time points (tp). This time category is based on the primitive concepts of current time (CT) and starting time (ST). CT takes into account the flowing of time, ST is the origin of the temporal axis. All the other tp $\in$ TPTC are defined as pairs tp=(ts, ref), where ts $\in$ TSTC and ref is CT or ST.
  The functions **is_ts**(tp) and **is_ref**(tp) allow to address the components of a tp.
  It is possible to refer to time points only with their **is_ts**(tp) function when considering the Gregorian Calendar system, thus obtaining dates; for instance, (January 7, 1986) would be expressed as (1986/01/07/00:00, 0000/00/00/00:00) or (1986/01/07/00:00). We use this usual notation in the following.

- Time Interval Time Category (TITC)

  The TITC is a temporal category formed by pairs (starting tp, ending tp),

where starting tp and ending tp are time points. The functions
starting_tp(ti) and **ending_tp**(ti) allow to address the components of a ti.
If the starting (ending) tp is the special tp $-\infty$ ($+\infty$) [22], the time
interval, ti is open to left (open to right).

- Periodic Times Time Category (PTTC)

   The PTTC is the temporal category of periodic times (pt) formed by pairs
   (period, base), where period $\in$ TSTC and base $\in$ TPTC or base $\in$ TITC.
   The functions **period**(pt) and **base**(pt) allow to address the components of a
   pt $\in$ PTTC.
   Formally, pt=(ts, ti0) $\in$ PTTC, with ti0=(tp',tp''), is the collection of
   all ti_j, where $-\infty \leq j \leq +\infty$, such that:
   $ti_j=(tp_j', tp_j'')$ and $tp_j'=tp'+j*ts$ and $tp_j''=tp''+j*ts$.

- General Times Time Category (GTTC)

   The GTTC is the temporal category of general times (gt) formed by a set of
   tp's and a set of ti's.

   Formally, $gt=(tp_1, .., tp_i, .., tp_n, ti_1, .., ti_j, .., ti_m)$.

   A gt is a collection of tp's and ti's without any assumption about their
   ordering and without performing any operations on them (e.g., without
   considering whether intervals are overlapping).
   It is possible to access each element with the following functions:

   i_tp(gt) = tp_i

and

   j-ti(gt) = ti_j.

Operations defined on the time primitives mentioned above are illustrated in
[5]. In this paper we apply time reasoning on time assertions specified using
the subset of operations indicated in Tab. 1..

Tab. **1.** Time relations and operations

Relations

tp1 = tp2	equivalence relationship
tp $\in$ ti	belonging relationship

Operations

from tp	the interval of time starting with tp
until tp	the interval of time ending with tp
ts **after** tp	the time point exactly ts after the tp specified as an operand
ts **before** tp	the time point exactly ts before the tp specified as an operand
ti1 $\wedge$ ti2	the time interval resulting as an intersection of the time intervals ti1 and ti2; null if ending_tp(ti1) < starting_tp(ti2) or starting_tp(ti1) > ending_tp(ti2)
tp $\wedge$ ti	tp if tp $\in$ ti holds; null if tp < starting_tp(ti) or tp > ending_tp(ti)

Temporal assertions may be absolute and relative assertions. Absolutely
defined times (adt) are time elements like, for instance, dates; relatively
defined times (rdt) are defined using as a reference the happening of an
event, or starting, ending of an activity, as a reference for times that are
not yet defined in the system; for instance, EVENT-3.time, where the time

value is not known yet for the considered instance of EVENT-3, is a relatively
defined time.

It is shown in the following section how the temporal assertions in a SOS
model, expressed using the above mentioned primitives, operators, and
relationships, are organized to provide a structure for time reasoning.

3. PROCESSING TEMPORAL ASSERTIONS

This section illustrates how knowledge about relatively defined times is
organized for reasoning purposes: first, temporal assertions are specified;
then they are collected in a relationship graph, an assertion table, and a
reduced assertion table which are presented in the following. In next section
the methods to make time inferences are described. These methods are the basis
of the time expert described in Section 5..

In SOS models occurrences of event types or starting/ending times of activity
types are defined referring to special events or to previously defined time
points. All these times are relatively defined times (rdt) during system
specification. During system operation, relatively defined times may become
absolutely defined times (adt); for example, each relatively defined time that
refers to the same observable event becomes an absolutely defined time when
such an event occurs. The goal of the propagation methods illustrated in next
section is to propagate time knowledge using the temporal assertions specified
in the SOS control submodel.

Temporal assertions are elaborated to be used by a time expert to answer
queries about time. As a first step, temporal assertions expressing
relationships between relatively defined times, contained in conditional
expressions of rules and written using the time relations and operations of
Tab. 1., are organized in the relationship graph illustrated in Section 3.1..

The time reasoning method is illustrated in the paper with an example based on
the temporal assertions of Figure 1..

3.1. The relationship graph

Time relationships expressed in rules are used to build a relationship graph.
The relationship graph is the basis for the following steps of the method,
since it is used to connect all the separate temporal assertions to each
other.

The relationship graph G=(V,E) consists of a finite set of vertices V and a
set of undirected edges E. A vertex V of G represents a relatively defined
time, and two vertices are connected by an edge (V$_i$, V$_j$) if the corresponding
times are related by a temporal relationship, expressed, explicitly or
implicitly, in the SOS specifications; explicit relationships are expressed
through explicit time assertions; implicit relationships are derived from the
semantics of the system (e.g., an activity starting time precedes the ending
time of the activity). Temporal objects modeled by vertices can be time points
of three types: time of occurrence of an event EV, starting time S(A) and
ending time E(A) of an activity A.

In addition to explicit relationships, the following implicit relationship is
defined for each activity, specifying that an activity ends after its starting
time:

   E(A) ε **from** S(A).

For example, the following temporal assertion:

```
EV1 = 1 mo before EV2
EV2 ε until 2w before EV3

S(A1) = EV1
E(A1) ε until EV2

S(A2) = E(A1)
E(A2) ε (from 1 w after S(A2) Λ until E(A5))

S(A3) = E(A1)
E(A3) = 3 d after E(A1)

S(A4) = EV2
E(A4) = 1 mo after EV2

S(A5) ε from E(A3)
E(A5) = 1 d before S(A6)

S(A6) ε from E(A2)
E(A6) = EV3

S(A7) ε from E(A3)
E(A7) ε until EV3

S(A8) = EV3
E(A8) ε until (1 mo after EV3)

S(A9) ε (from E(A8) Λ from E(A4))
E(A9) = 4 mo after EV1

For each activity Ai:
E(Ai) ε from S(Ai)
```

Fig. **1.** Temporal assertions

$E(A9) = 4$ mo **after** EV1

implies the existence of the two vertices E(A9) and EV1, and that of the edge (E(A9),EV1).

The relationship graph for the example is presented in Fig. 2..

3.2. The specification table

Vertices V_i and V_j are <u>adjacent</u> if (V_i,V_j) is an edge of G; a <u>path</u> is a sequence of adjacent vertices $\overline{V_1,V_2,...,V_n}$.

Def. A relationship between two vertices V_i and V_j of the graph G is said to be <u>direct</u>, if the edge $(V_i,V_j) ε G$, <u>undirect</u> if a path connecting V_i and V_j exists in G.

Direct relationships corresponding to edges E are recorded in an <u>assertion table</u>, a square matrix of order g, where g is the cardinality of G.

The assertion table for the example temporal assertions, constructed according to the above mentioned rules, is presented in Fig. 3..

The assertion table information content is antisymmetric, since from (tp1 R tp2) the inverse relation (tp2 inv(R) tp1) can be computed, using the rules illustrated in Tab. 2..

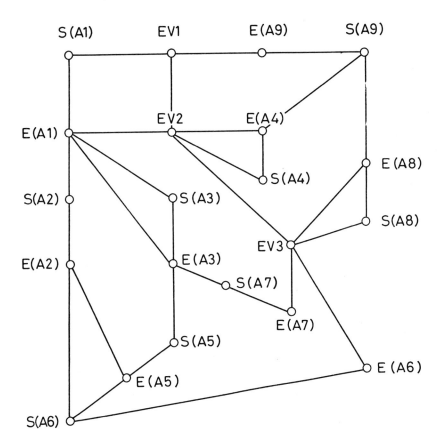

Fig. 2. The relationship graph

Simplifications can be performed according to the time calculus described in
Tab. 3.; for instance, in the example we have:

    E(A2) ε from S(A2)

and

    E(A2) ε from 1 w after S(A2)

let us call:

    tp1 = E(A2)
    tp2 = 1 w after S(A2)
    tp3 = S(A2)

LEFT \ RIGHT	EV1	EV2	EV3	S(A1)	E(A1)	S(A2)	E(A2)	S(A3)	E(A3)	S(A4)	E(A4)	S(A5)	E(A5)	S(A6)	E(A6)	S(A7)	E(A7)	S(A8)	E(A8)	S(A9)	E(A9)
EV1		1 mo before	·																		4 mo before
EV2	1 m. after		until 2W before		from						1 mo before										
EV3		from 2W after												·		from	·	from 1 mo before			
S(A1)	·				until																
E(A1)		until	from			·		3d before													
S(A2)					·		until 1W before														
E(A2)					from 1W after									until	until						
S(A3)					·				until												
E(A3)					3d after		from				until					until					
S(A4)		·									until										
E(A4)		1 mo after							from												until
S(A5)								from					until								
E(A5)						from							from	1d before							
S(A6)						from							1d after		until						
E(A6)		·											from								
S(A7)							from										until				
E(A7)		until														from					
S(A8)		·																	until		
E(A8)		until 1 mo after														from		until			
S(A9)										from								from			until
E(A9)	4 mo after																		from		

Fig. 3. The assertion table

with:

   tp2 ε **from** tp3

Applying the rule from Tab. 3.:

   if   tp1 ε **from** tp2 ∧ **from** tp3
           and tp2 ε **from** tp3
   then   tp1 ε **from** tp2

Tab. 2. Inverse operation

DIRECT	INVERSE
tp1 ε **from** tp2	tp2 ε **until** tp1
tp1 ε **until** tp2	tp2 ε **from** tp1
tp1 = ts **after** tp2	tp2 = ts **before** tp1
tp1 = ts **before** tp2	tp2 = ts **after** tp1
tp1 ε f(tp2) Λ g(tp2)	tp2 ε inv(f(tp1)) Λ inv(g(tp1))

we obtain:

E(A2) ε from 1 w after S(A2).

Its inverse is computed as follows:
1 w after S(A2) ε until E(A2)
S(A2) ε until 1 w before E(A2)

Therefore the entry E(A2)-S(A2) of the assertion table is:

from 1 w after

and its inverse S(A2)-E(A2) is:

until 1 w before

3.3. Reversibility classes

Def. The relationship R: (tp1 R tp2) is called <u>reversible</u> if the assertion of tp1 (tp2) as an absolutely defined time determines tp2 (tp1), <u>irreversible</u> otherwise.

In Tab. 1. relationship "=" is reversible, "ε" irreversible.

An undirect relationship is reversible iff all the relationships in the path are reversible.

Given a precise time knowledge (adt) for a vertex V_i, it can be propagated without introducing any imprecision to vertices either directly or indirectly related to V_i by reversible relationships, while some fuzziness is generated by irreversible relationships. This observation suggests a reorganization of the assertion table, before using it as a basis for time reasoning, partitioning its vertices according to the type of relationship between them.

Def. Two vertices V_i and V_j of a graph G are said to be <u>reversible</u> if and only if there is a reversible relationship (direct or indirect) between V_i and V_j.

Vertices reversibility partitions the vertices of the graph into disjoint subsets defined as <u>reversibility classes</u>, so that two vertices are in the same reversibility class if and only if they are reversible, and are in different classes if there exist only irreversible relationships between them, or if they are not related at all.

Theorem. Reversibility classes partition the vertices of the graph uniquely.

Proof. Suppose there exist two reversibility partitions, P_a and P_b, and that $P_a \neq P_b$. Then there exist two vertices V_i and V_j that are in the same class of one partition and are not in the same class in the other. Since V_i and V_j are in different classes of (say) P_b, there is not a reversible relationship between V_i and V_j, and therefore they cannot be in the same class of P_a.

Tab. 3. Time calculus

IF	THEN
tp1 ε **from**(**from**(tp2))	tp1 ε **from**(tp2)
tp1 ε **until**(**until**(tp2))	tp1 ε **until**(tp2)
tp1 ε **until**(**from**(tp2))	no relation between tp1 and tp2
tp1 ε **from**(**until** tp2)	no relation between tp1 and tp2
tp1 = ts **after** tp2 and	
tp2 ε **from** tp3	tp1 ε **from**(ts **after** tp3)
tp1 = ts **before** tp2 and	
tp2 ε **from** tp3	tp2 ε **from**(ts **before** tp3)
tp1 = ts **after** tp2 and	
tp2 ε **until** tp3	tp2 ε **until**(ts **after** tp3)
tp1 = ts **before** tp2 and	
tp2 ε **until** tp3	tp2 ε **until**(ts **before** tp3)
tp1 ε **from** tp and	
tp ε ti = (tp2',tp2")	tp1 ε **from** tp2'
tp1 ε **until** tp and	
tp ε ti = (tp2',tp2")	tp1 ε **until** tp2"
tp1 ε **from** tp2 Λ **from** tp2	tp1 ε **from** tp2
tp1 ε **from** tp2 Λ **until** tp2	tp1 = tp2
tp1 ε **until** tp2 Λ **until** tp2	tp1 ε **until** tp2
tp1 c ts **after** tp2 Λ **from** tp2	tp1 = ts **after** tp2
tp1 ε ts **before** tp2 Λ **from** tp2	impossible
tp1 ε ts **after** tp2 Λ **until** tp2	impossible
tp1 ε ts **before** tp2 Λ **until** tp2	tp1 = ts **before** tp2
tp1 = tp2 and tp1 ε ti	tp1 = tp2 if tp2 ε ti
	otherwise impossible
tp1 ε **from** tp2 Λ **from** tp3	tp1 ε **from** tp2
and tp2 ε **from** tp3	
tp1 ε **until** tp2 Λ **until** tp3	tp1 ε **until** tp2
and tp2 ε **until** tp3	

Times can be added to both sides of a relationship.
We illustrate here only one case:

tp1 ε **from** tp2   ts **before** tp1 ε **from** ts **before** tp2

To shorten the analysis of the relationship graph in time reasoning, the given graph is transformed into an equivalent graph (reduced relationship graph G_{red}), the vertices of which represent reversibility classes.

In the reduced relationship graph, all vertices belonging to the same reversibility class in the relationship graph are represented by a single node; therefore, card(G) ≥ card (G_{red}).

The reversibility partition has been shown to be unique, thus the classes in the reversibility partition of a graph G define the vertices of G_{red}. The reduced relationship graph G_{red} is constructed in the following way:

1. for each reversibility class a representative is chosen (it may be any of the vertices in the class, as they are all reversible);

2. for each representative, a vertex C_i is added to G_{red};

3. an edge (C_i, C_j) is added between two vertices C_i and C_j if and only if a vertex $V_h ε G$ exists, such that $V_h ε C_i$ and it is directly linked by an irreversible relationship to at least one vertex $V_k ε G$, such that $V_k ε C_j$;

4. the time semantic associated to the generic edge (C_i, C_j) of G_{red} is computed from the time semantic of all possible paths that link the representatives of C_i and C_j in the complete relationship graph. The resulting relationship is always irreversible. The time calculus of Tab. 3. is applied to this computation. It is possible to show that the relationship (if it exists) among any two tp's computed according to the time calculus of Tab. 3. can always be reduced to the following canonical form:

tp1 ε (**from**|**until**) [ts (**before**|**after**)] tp2

or, similarly:

tp1 = [ts (**before**|**after**)] tp2

or intersections of expressions in canonical form.

The relationships between representatives of adjacent classes are specified in the <u>reduced assertion table</u>, a triangular table with cells corresponding to all possible pairs of reversibility classes. The reduced assertion table records such relationships only in one direction since it is always possible to compute inverse relationships according to the rules of Tab. 2..

5. finally, for each reversibility class containing at least two vertices, a <u>class vector</u> is constructed that records the reversible relationships between the vertices of the class and their representative.

For instance, in the example we have:

S(A1) = EV1
EV(2) = S(A4)
EV1 = 1 mo before EV2
E(A9) = 4 mo after EV1
E(A4) = 1 mo after EV2

Therefore, S(A1), EV1, EV2, E(A9), E(A4), S(A4) all belong to the same reversibility class C_1. EV1 is chosen as a representative for class C_1.

The following 10 reversibility classes are identified (selected representative vertices are underlined):

C_1: <u>EV1</u>, EV2, S(A1), S(A4), E(A4), E(A9)
C_2: <u>E(A1)</u>, S(A2), S(A3), E(A3)
C_3: <u>E(A2)</u>
C_4: <u>S(A5)</u>
C_5: <u>S(A6)</u>, E(A5)
C_6: <u>S(A7)</u>
C_7: <u>E(A7)</u>
C_8: <u>E(A8)</u>
C_9: <u>S(A9)</u>
C_{10}: <u>EV3</u>, E(A6), S(A8).

The reduced relationship graph is illustrated in Fig. 4., and the relationships between pairs of adjacent class representatives are summarized in the reduced assertion table of Fig. 5.

Finally, the class vectors are presented in Fig. 6..

Relationships to other classes are computed using relationships to other classes of elements of the class. Simplifications are performed according to

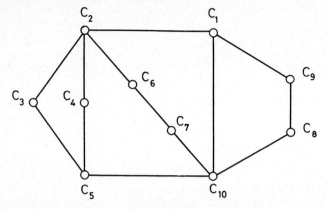

Fig. 4. Reduced relationship graph

time calculus. For C_1, for instance, we have the class vector illustrated in Fig. 6., and the following relationships to class C_2:

    E(A1) ε from S(A1)
    E(A1) ε until EV2

In class C_1 we have the following reversible relationships:

    S(A1) = EV1
    EV2 = 1 mo after EV1

therefore the relationship between representatives of classes C_1 and C_2 is the following:

    E(A1) ε from EV1 Λ until 1 mo after EV1

4. TIME PROPAGATION METHODS

The specification table only expresses relationships between time points. In order to answer queries about when an event has happened or it is going to happen, we must insert precise times (adt's) in the graph. This time knowledge is then appropriately used in the relationship graph.

Time is propagated with two different methods. The first method propagates times directly as soon as they are inserted in the system (forward propagation); the second method (backward propagation of times) is used by the time expert if more information is needed in addition to that obtained from the application of the forward propagation method.

4.1. Forward propagation of times

Using the reduced assertion table described in the previous section, the system is able to make inferences on the related time assertions. A relatively defined time can possibly become absolutely defined time during system operation, thus allowing to infer intervals to which other relatively defined times belong or their absolutely defined time. For example, if a certain limit is defined for the ending time of an activity, it can be propagated to each temporal assertion related to that time. Times obtained in the system mainly at operation time are progressively added to the relationship graph, propagating absolutely defined times (forward) according to the rules illustrated in this section.

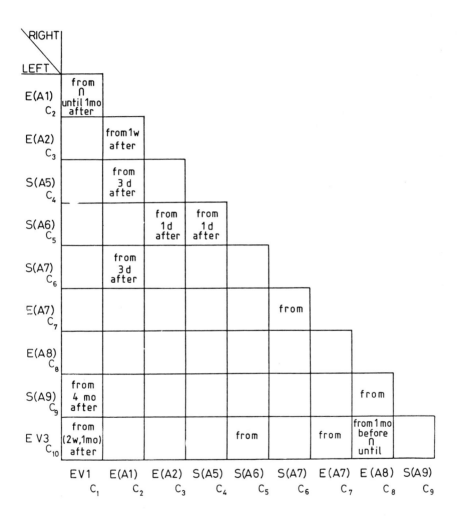

Fig. 5. Reduced assertion table

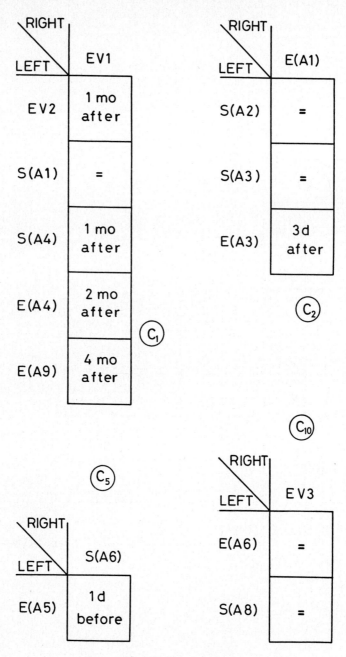

Fig. 6. Class vectors

A difference must be outlined between the propagation of precisely defined tp and of imprecise tp, i.e., tp's for which it is only known the time interval they belong to, since they generate different time knowledge.

Def. A vertex whose associated time is precisely known (as an absolutely defined time) is called TP-vertex; it is called GT-vertex if only a general time is associated to it; the mark I-vertex (imprecise vertex) is attached to a vertex whose associated time is a relatively defined time.

Two algorithms used by the time expert are now presented, one for propagating temporal knowledge from TP-vertices (forward expansion), the other for deducing some temporal knowledge on GT-vertices or I vertices (backward time reasoning).

We propagate absolutely defined times (gt or tp) as soon as they are entered in the system. However, we have chosen to stop this forward propagation as soon as the propagated times become imprecise (gt's), since little information would be added. Further propagation of times is performed successively when needed to answer a query by the backward propagation mechanism.

These algorithms are applied on the reduced form of the relationship graph, while their effects are expanded not only to the class representatives, but also to each time belonging to the involved classes. We recall that there is a reversible relationship between the representatives of a certain class C_i and the other vertices of the class, so the time knowledge associated to the representative of the class can be propagated without introducing any imprecision to other members of the same class C_i; symmetrically, the knowledge of the time associated to a vertex V_i of C_i that is not the representative may be propagated to every vertex in the class using the class vector.

The first algorithm is a forward expansion of absolutely defined times from TP-vertices.

The forward expansion is applied to all known times (absolutely defined times) in the system, one at a time, and consists of two steps:

a. expansion step

b. checking step

Expansion step

1. When a gt time is associated to a vertex V, all the vertices of its class C become GT-vertices. No inference is propagated to vertices of other classes;

2. when the time of a vertex V becomes known as a tp, all the vertices of its class C become TP-vertices. Furthermore, all the I-vertices (and only them) of the classes $C_1...C_n$ directly linked to C in the reduced relationship graph become GT-vertices.

Checking step

After the expansion step a check must be made to detect any inconsistency with the knowledge propagation already recorded; this check can possibly generate further knowledge expansion if the general time associated to a GT-class becomes more precise. For each vertex that has been changed to a TP-vertex or GT-vertex during the previous phase of expansion, all the edges connecting that vertex to either a TP-vertex or a GT-vertex in the reduced graph are examined. Since times are propagated only to I-vertices, those arcs that link two vertices already recording knowledge have not been covered, while the temporal assertions they model may allow to compute more precisely through intersection the gt's determined during the expansion step or, in any case, in checking the consistency of times according to their relationships. The checking step is thus useful not only in testing recorded times, but also in improving those known imprecisely. The following two steps must be covered for TP-vertices first and then for GT-vertices:

1. if the edge leads to a TP-vertex, a consistency check is made based on the time relationship embedded by the edge;

2. if the edge leads to a GT-vertex, possibly its relationship can propagate further knowledge, otherwise a simple consistency check is made; in the first case, the improved time is then expanded forward to other vertices reiterating the checking step.

If any inconsistency is detected, the time expert informs, with diagnostic messages, about the errors discovered (e.g., a starting time of an activity that is later than the corresponding ending time) and asks for non-contradictory information (e.g., a different gt or tp for the expanded vertex). Only if no inconsistency is found, the new information is recorded.

The same rules are applied also when a GT-vertex becomes TP-vertex, i.e., a more precise knowledge has been acquired about a certain time, but only after having checked the compatibility of the new time to the one already recorded.

This process is iterated for each time known in the system other than a relatively defined time. At the end of the application of the forward rules to all known times, some vertices may still not embody any time knowledge: I-vertices retain neither precise (TP) nor imprecise (GT) time. The choice of not propagating temporal knowledge to some vertices depends on the degree of imprecision with which it is possible to define their associated times.

Through the following backward mechanism it is possible to have more information on GT-vertices and I-vertices when needed; the following steps are applied when there is a request that cannot be satisfied only examining the results of the forward expansion of times.

4.2. Backward time reasoning

Time propagation

1. starting from the vertex in the reduced relationship graph to which the required time corresponds, all paths that lead to TP-classes are identified first;

2. moving along these paths, it may be possible to deduce the relationships between the representative of the involved GT-class or I-class and the representatives of the TP-classes from the reduced assertion table; then, the corresponding class vector gives the relationship between the required time and its representative. The possibility of deducing some consistent temporal relationship depends on the semantic of the covered edges, i.e., how time operators and function agree (see Tab. 3. for time calculus);

3. finally, if any relationship has been determined, times resulting as gt's are computed and then intersected for knowledge improving.

By this way, it is not always possible to state the time order between two times even if a precise relationship exists, since gt's computed through backward chaining are much more imprecise as the length of the path grows. In some cases, it is possible to determine the relationships between two nodes not through time propagation, but using only time calculus, as illustrated in the following step.

Time calculus

1. all paths linking the representatives of the classes of the two involved vertices are identified first;

2. moving along these paths, it may be possible to deduce the relationship between the representative of the classes from the reduced assertion table, and then between the required times from the corresponding class vectors. No approximate time computation is made, thus a precise temporal relationship can be specified according to how time operators and function agree (see Tab. 3.).

The following absolutely defined times are propagated in the example graph according to the above mentioned forward propagation algorithm:

EV1 = Nov/29/85/09:00
S(A8) = Jan/20/86/12:00

The resulting complete relationship graph with times associated to vertices is shown in Fig. 7..

5. THE TIME EXPERT

The time expert is able to reason about time to answer queries such as absolutely defined times of events, starting and ending times of activities, relationships between times.

The time assertions organized in the relationship graph with absolutely defined times propagated according to the rules illustrated in Section 4.1. may not be enough to answer these queries. To get more information, the backward reasoning mechanism described in Section 4.2. is used to exploit irreversible relationships.

5.1. Queries to the time expert

After time knowledge forward propagation, the time expert is able to answer questions about time. These questions may be used to handle a variety of situations, e.g., the scheduling of activities in a project management or the control over the evolution of a certain system. The time expert is able to answer about past times since when an event occurs, the corresponding date is recorded and propagated by the system; furthermore, it can make inferences on the future based on the temporal assertions it has recorded.

In the following discussion, the symbols X and Y denote times associated to the vertices of the (non reduced) relationship graph. The corresponding vertices in the graph are denoted with V_x and V_y. C_x and C_y are the corresponding reversibility classes.

The four basic types of questions that can be asked to the time expert are:

Q1. location on the temporal axis
Q2. distance between times
Q3. relationships between times
Q4. possible assignment of time limits

Q1. Location on the temporal axis

This type of questions include questions such as:

"When did (will) X happen?".

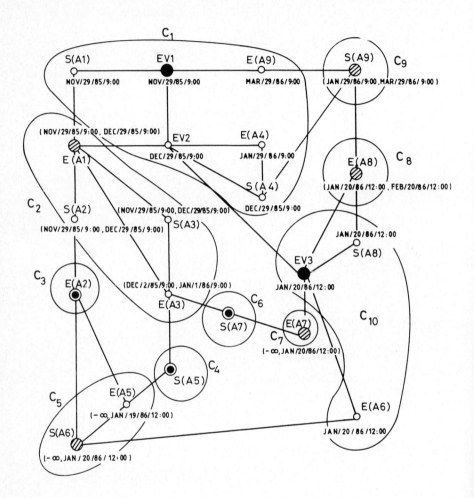

Fig. 7. Time propagation

An <u>absolute time</u> would be the precise answer to this question, but it can be given only if C_x is a TP-class. The time expert can only state the general time of X if C_x is a GT-class; if C_x is an I-class an answer in terms of gt is given only if backward propagation gives a result, otherwise the answer to the query is "unknown time".

The following sample question has been put to the time expert, obtaining answers according to the knowledge previously recorded:

"WHEN WILL S(A7) HAPPEN?"

Since S(A7) is the representative of C_6, and C_6 is an I-class, the backward algorithm for I-vertices must be applied for giving an answer. Vertex C_6 is directly linked to two GT-classes, C_2 and C_7: the edge (C_6, C_2) defines the interval $C_6 \in$ from 3 d **after** C_2;

since $C_2 \in$ (Nov/29/85/09:00, Dec/29/85/09:00) we obtain:

$C_6 \in$ **from** (Dec/2/85/09:00),

The edge (C_6, C_7) defines the interval:

$C_6 \in$ **until** (Jan/20/86/12:00).

Intersecting these results, the time expert gives the following answer:

$C_6 \in$ (Dec/2/85/09:00, Jan/20/86/12:00).

Q2. <u>Distance between times</u>

Queries of this type are queries such as:

"How much time is there between X and Y?".

An <u>interval between two times</u> is the expected answer to this question. An exact response can be given by the system in two cases:

- if $C_x = C_y$, for any type of time class; in fact, as two reversible vertices are related by either a direct or indirect reversible relationship, it is always possible to determine the temporal relationship between them, since they all refer precisely to the same reference event;

- if $C_x \neq C_y$, and both C_x and C_y are TP classes.

Backward propagation is applied in the other cases to get an approximation of the interval; the result of a successful application of the backward propagation must be available, otherwise no answer is possible.

An example of this type of questions is the following:

"HOW MUCH TIME IS THERE BETWEEN S(A3) AND E(A3)?"

S(A3) $\in C_2$ and E(A3) $\in C_2$, thus it is possible to determine the reversible relationship between them using the state vector for C_2:

S(A3) = E(A1) and
E(A3) = 3 d **after** E(A1),

therefore:

E(A3) = 3 d **after** S(A3).

Q3. Relationship between times

Queries about relationships between times are of the following type:

"Did (will) X happen before Y?".

A boolean answer based on the relative time order of X and Y can be given by the system in the following cases:

- if $C_x = C_y$, no matter which kind of knowledge is associated to the class
- if $C_x \neq C_y$, and if their tp or gt times, if necessary computed by the time expert through backward chaining, do not intersect;
- if a precise order can be stated after a successful application of the backward rules using the time calculus, without using computed times. If it is possible to determine the relative precedence between the representatives of two classes, it may be possible to determine the relative precedence between two vertices of these classes through the corresponding class vectors.

Let us consider the following question:

"WILL E(A4) HAPPEN BEFORE E(A8)?"

E(A4) ε C_1, which is a TP-class, and its time is Jan/29/86/09:00, while E(A8) ε C_8, which is a GT-class, and its general time is the interval (Jan/20/88/12:00, Feb/20/86/12:00): since these intervals intersect, the system can give no direct answer, needing a more precise knowledge for a precise response. On the other hand, with the backward algorithm using the time calculus it is possible to determine that E(A8) ε **from** 3 weeks **after** EV1, while E(A4) = 2 months **after** EV1: not even by this way an answer is found, since the intersection is not null.

Q4. Possible assignment of time limits

The last type of queries is about the possibility of a certain limit to a certain relatively defined time such as, for instance:

"Is it possible that X happens before TP?".

In this type of query, the time expert verifies if temporal assertions and propagated times are compatible with the time limit, e.g., if it is possible that an activity become urgent can be performed within a near deadline. The system is able to answer the question if the result of the intersection of TP and X is null (if necessary computed with the backward algorithm), while no answer is given if C_x is an I-class and no inference has been made through backward chaining. A particular computation is required when the intersection is not null, i.e., TP belongs to the interval associated to V_x: since TP can be considered as the upper limit for X, a forward expansion is simulated on that new time. If no inconsistency is detected during the checking step, the time expert realizes that X can happen before that time point and gives a positive answer to the question; otherwise, displays the relationship that is not satisfied.

The time expert handles in a similar way also the question:

"Is it possible that X happens before Y?".

if C_y is a TP-class.

An answer can be given immediately also when $C_x = C_y$. Anyway, after having calculated the intersection of X and Y (of course if it possible to infer something about them), a direct response can be stated if the result is null, otherwise an expansion must be performed to detect any inconsistency before answering.

An example of this type of questions is the following:

"IS IT POSSIBLE THAT S(A5) HAPPENS BEFORE Dec/15/85/17:00?"

The backward algorithm states that, according to the recorded times, $S(A5) \in$ (Dec/2/85/09:00, Jan/19/86/12:00). Since TP belongs to that interval, an expansion is simulated to test if it is possible that $S(A5) \in$ (Dec/2/85/09:00, Dec/15/85/17:00). Since propagating times can be inferred that E(A1) should belong to (Nov/29/85/09:00, Dec/12/85/17:00) and that S(A6) should belong to (Dec/3/85/09:00, Jan/20/86/12:00) and since no inconsistency with the previously defined time assertions is found, the time expert answers "yes" to the question.

6. CONCLUDING REMARKS

This paper presents researches on reasoning about time assertions in the office environment, based on the TSOS model of time for OIS [5]. An improved version of TSOS has been presented, and a method for computing answers to questions about temporal aspects of a systems has been illustrated.

The method consists of two steps. The first step is an elaboration of time assertions expressed within a TSOS model. Temporal assertions are organized in classes and relationships among classes are computed.

The second step deals with updates to temporal information in the model and with answering temporal questions. Each time a new absolute time is available for a relative time in the system, this is propagated (forward propagation) to other nodes until propagations yield imprecise times. When a question is entered into the system, the answer is immediate if a precise time is already available to answer the question. Otherwise, a backward chaining of time assertions is started to get more information (imprecise information).

An example of application of the method with some typical answers to questions has been presented.

ACKNOWLEDGEMENTS

We should like to thank F. Barbic and F.A. Schreiber for their comments and suggestions on this work.

REFERENCES

[1]   Bracchi, G. and Pernici, B., Design Requirements of Office Systems, ACM Trans. on Office Information Systems, 2, 2 (Apr. 1984) 151.
[2]   Panel on Time and Databases, ACM SIGMOD Database Week Proc. (May 1983)
[3]   Kung, C.H., A Temporal Framework for Database Specification and Verification, Conf. on Very Large Data Bases (Aug. 1984)
[4]   Bolour, A., Anderson, T.L., Dekeyser, L.J., and Wong, H.K.T., The Role of Time in Information Processing - A Survey, ACM SIGART Newsletters (April 1982) 28.
[5]   Barbic, F. and Pernici, B., Time Modeling in Office Information Systems, Proc. ACM SIGMOD Conf., Austin, Texas (May 1985)
[6]   Anderson, T.L., Modeling Time at the Conceptual Level, in: Scheuermann, P., (ed.), Improving Usability and Responsiveness, (Academic Press, June 1982)

[7]   Lundberg, B., An Axiomatization of Events, SYSLAB Report N. 12, Univ.
      of Stockholm (Nov. 1982)
[8]   Casanova, M.A. and Furtado, A.L., On the Description of Database
      Transition Constraints using Temporal Languages, in: Gallaire, Minker,
      and Nikolas, (eds.) Advances in Database Theory, (Plenum Press, New
      York and London, 1978) pp. 211-236.
[9]   Castilho, J.M.V., Casanova, M.A., and Furtado, A.L., A Temporal
      Framework for Database Specifications, Tech. Rep. DB 038201 Dep.
      Informatica, Univ. Catolica de Rio de Janeiro (March 1982)
[10] Allen, J.F. and Koomen, J.A., Planning using a Temporal World Model,
      Int. Joint Conf. on Artificial Intelligence, Karlsruhe (1983) pp.
      741-747.
[11] Allen, J.F., Maintaining Knowledge about Temporal Intervals, Comm. of
      the ACM, 26, 11 (Nov. 1983) 832.
[12] Coolahan, J.E. and Roussopoulos N., Timing Requirements for Time-Driven
      Systems using Augmented Petri-Nets, IEEE Trans. on Software
      Engineering, SE-9, 5, (Sept. 1983) 603.
[13] McDermott, D., A Temporal Logic for Reasoning about Processes and
      Plans, Cognitive Science, 6, (1982) 101.
[14] Vere, S.A., Planning in Time: Windows and Durations for Activities and
      Goals, IEEE Trans. on Pattern Analysis and Machine Intelligence, 5, 3
      (May 1983) 246.
[15] Allen, J.F., Towards a General Theory of Action and Time, Artificial
      Intelligence, 23, (1984) 123.
[16] Lamport, L., Time, Clocks, and the Ordering of Events in a Distributed
      System, Comm. of the ACM, 21, 7, (July 1978) 558.
[17] Chang, J.M. and Chang, S.K., Database Alerting Techniques for Office
      Activities Management, IEEE Trans. on Communications, COM-30, 1 (Jan.
      1982) 74.
[18] Zloof, M., Office-By-Example: a Business Language that Unifies Data and
      Word Processing and Electronic Mail, IBM Systems Journal, 21, 3, (1982)
      272.
[19] Kahn, K. and Gorry, G.A., Mechanizing Temporal knowledge, Artificial
      Intelligence, 9 (1977) 87.
[20] De, S., Pan, S-S, and Whinston, A.B., Natural Language Processing in a
      Temporal Database, Data Knowledge & Engineering, 1 (North-Holland,
      1985) 3.
[21] Bracchi, G. and Pernici, B., SOS: A Conceptual Model for Office
      Information Systems, Data Base, 15, 2, (Winter 1984) 11.
[22] Greenspan, S.J., Requirements Modeling: a Knowledge Representation
      Approach to Software Requirements Definition, Tech. Rep. CSRG-155,
      Univ. of Toronto (March 1984)

OFFICE SYSTEMS: Methods and Tools
G. Bracchi, D. Tsichritzis (Editors)
Elsevier Science Publishers B.V. (North-Holland)
© IFIP, 1987

TEMPORAL ASPECTS IN
OFFICE INFORMATION SYSTEMS

Andreas Oberweis and Georg Lausen

Fachbereich Informatik
TH Darmstadt
D-6100 Darmstadt
West-Germany

Abstract

The formal specification of system behaviour including the modelling
of temporal assertions and constraints is essential for appropriately
designing procedures of office information systems. Petri Nets are
a widely accepted means for the specification of time independent
information system behaviour. To model time aspects in Petri Nets
we use a clock based concept first introduced in [Ric85]. This concept
enables us to model temporal assertions that are of relevance in office
information systems, such as the duration of activities, starting times
of activities, time limits, triggering dates and the current date/time.
We take into account the problem of temporal plausibility and outline
an exception handling mechanism based on temporal constraints.

1. Introduction

It has been recognized by many authors that the modelling of dynamic aspects is a very
important issue for the design of information systems (see for example [CRIS82, RoR82,
CRIS83, AnZ84, SoK85]). The modelling of temporal assertions is essential for appropriately modelling the procedures of office information systems (see for example [Ell83,
BP84a, BP84b, BaP85, Gib85]). Such temporal assertions concern the duration of activities, starting times of activities, time limits, triggering dates and the current time/date
([BP84a, BP84b, BaP85]).

Several approaches exist, where Petri Nets are used for the conceptual modelling of office
procedures [Zis77, Ric83, BCL84, HSY84, Nie85, NiV85].

In the Petri Net concept time aspects are excluded. It is assumed that transition occurrences have no duration, that tokens are available for infinite time in places and that the
point of time, where a transition occurs, is not determined. In real systems time aspects

play an important role and therefore a lot of attempts have been made to introduce an additional time formalism into the Petri Net transition rule [BeM83, CoR83, FaM76, Ram74, Raz84, Sif80, Wal82]. The main drawback of these approaches is that the modification of the transition rule causes serious problems when applying most of the results of General Net Theory.

However, in [Ric85] a clock concept for time modelling in Petri Nets is introduced, where clocks are explained in terms of General Net Theory and where the transition rule is not modified: a fundamental change of time is defined by a transition that is called pulse generator. The occurrence of this transition means the beginning of a new basic time interval. This time interval lasts until the next occurrence of the pulse generator transition, i.e. until the next pulse. Everything that happens between two successive basic time pulses is regarded as happening at the same time (cf. also [Dur85]).

Time pulses are managed by a functional unit that is called time-monitor, where the time monitor is connected to the pulse-generator via a so-called time interface. The time monitor can be connected to a transition that needs time information via a so-called clock interface. The time monitor together with its time and clock interface is called clock (see Figure 1).

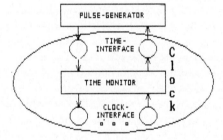

Figure 1: Clock Concept (taken from [Ric85])

Whereas in [Ric85] the general principles for time modelling in Petri Nets are introduced we first shall concentrate on applying these ideas in the specific area of office information system modelling. We describe temporal assertions that are of relevance for office information systems and show what kind of net modules must be added to a given Petri Net to model these time aspects.

Further, we take into account the problem of temporal plausibility. There may exist transitions in a net that can not occur because of contradictory temporal restrictions. Hence there may exist objects that can never be produced. Temporal plausibility means that there are no contradictions in the set of all modelled temporal assertions.

We distinguish between structural and behavioural implausibility. As an example for a structural implausibility consider the following assertion: 'One hour after the production of document X, the production of document Y can start. To produce document X document Y is needed'. This assertion clearly contains a contradiction, consequently neither document X nor document Y can be produced. As an example for a behavioural implausibility consider the following assertion: 'At the first day of every month check the credit facilities for all customers. On Sunday do not check the credit facilities for customers'. This assertion only contains a contradiction for some cases where the first day of a month is actually a sunday.

We claim that structural implausibilities must be elminated from a Petri Net with time modelling while behavioural implausibilities must be solved by an exception handling mechanism. In the before given example a corrective action would be to check the credit facilities on monday if the first day of the respective month is a sunday.

In [BMW84] it is postulated that the description of rare exceptional cases should not disturb the description of the usual system behaviour. We therefore model an exceptional situation by a single transition in a Petri Net: The occurrence of such a transition corresponds to the occurrence of an exceptional situation. However this exceptional transition can be refined by a set of transitions in a separate net specifying the exception handling mechanism.

This paper is organized as follows: The second section deals with temporal aspects of relevance in office environments. The third section describes the types of net modules that are needed to model these temporal aspects. The fourth section introduces temporal plausibility for nets with time modelling. The fifth section deals with the problem of exception handling and the final section gives a short summary and an outlook for future research.

2. Temporal Assertions for Office Procedures

In the context of office procedures different kinds of temporal aspects play an important role. Consider as an office procedure a collection of activities associated with a particular office function where the activities are connected by the involved objects or resources (for similar definitions see [Zis77, Ell79, LCS82]). On the one hand temporal aspects concern activities and on the other hand objects that are involved.

A basic temporal assertion is the duration of an activity. We consider durations as being non-deterministic (rectangular distributed) and denote the minimum duration by T_{MIN} and the maximum duration by T_{MAX}.

An activity can be triggered at a certain date (for example on June 3rd, 1986 production of item XYZ starts). We call this kind of triggering *single fixed date triggering*. Other kinds of triggering are *repeated fixed date triggering* (an activity is repeatedly triggered at certain dates, for example at the first day of every month the salary must be payed to the employees) and *delayed triggering* (an activity is triggered a certain time interval after another activity, for example one day after the arrival day of an order a message must be sent to the customer where the customer is informed whether the order can be fulfilled or not).

Furthermore there exist activities that must happen during a certain *time interval* but it is not determined when exactly (if a request for payment arrives it must be paid at latest four weeks after the arrival date but the exact date of payment is not determined). Sometimes activities cannot start before a certain date (*absolute delay time*) or before a certain time interval has passed after another activity (*relative delay time*). It is possible that two or more activities must start or end at the same time.

In office environments temporal aspects can also be related to information objects that are usually documents. There exist activities in office environments that insert the current date in a document, e.g. the date of an account or of a delivery note. Consequently there must exist mechanisms like clocks and calendars that provide *time/date display* functions.

There exist certain kinds of information that is only available during certain time intervals. Other objects must be consumed by an activity immediately after being produced by another activity, i.e. these objects trigger the respective activity (*immediate triggering*). An example for such a triggering object is an order: As soon as an order arrives it must be checked for correctness, i.e. an activity order-checking is triggered.

Furthermore, the flow of objects like forms in an office environment has a certain *duration* (so it takes a certain time to send a document from one employee to another).

The *temporal units* day, week, month and year are needed for adequately describing dates. To describe durations and points of time in office environments we also need the smaller units hour, minute and second.

In the following we shall first concentrate on Petri Net modules that provide *time / date display* functions. We then describe how to model *repeated fixed date triggering*, *immediate triggering* and *delayed triggering* in Petri Nets and sketch mechanisms to represent *single fixed date triggering* and *absolute/relative delay times*.

3. Modelling Temporal Aspects with Petri Nets

3.1. Problem Statement

Petri Nets or similar techniques are a widely accepted means for the conceptual modelling of office procedures [Zis77, Nie85, BCL84]. High level Petri Nets as predicate/transition nets are especially appropriate for the modelling of the flow of objects taking into account the objects' structure [Ric83,HSY84,NiV85]. In Figure 2 an example is given for the description of a typical office procedure in a predicate/transition net (for a detailed definition of predicate/transition nets see [GeL81]).

The predicates (places) are structured as follows: ADDED-TO-STOCK-ITEM(item, quantity), CHECKED-ORDER(customer,item,quantity), COPIED-ORDER(customer, item, quantity), BILL(customer, item, quantity, price), DELIVERY-SLIP(customer, item, quantity), EXISTING-ORDER(customer, item, quantity), EXTERNAL-ORDER(customer, item, quantity), MESSAGE-TO-CUSTOMER (customer, item), PRODUCED-ITEM(item, quantity), QUANTITY-IN-STOCK(item, quantity), REQUEST-FOR-ITEMS-PRODUCTION(item, quantity), TAKEN-FROM- STOCK-ITEM(item,quantity), WAITING-ORDER(customer,item,quantity).

In Figure 2 the following procedure is modelled: Orders arrive in the system and must

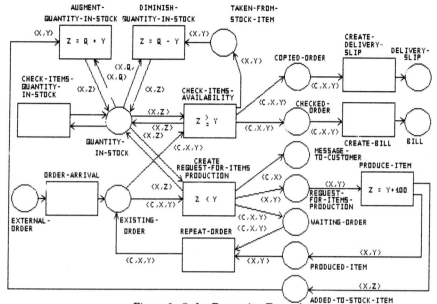

Figure 2: Order Processing Example

be checked for availability of the respective item. If the item is available then the order is copied, the delivery slip and the bill are created and the respective quantity in stock is diminished. If the ordered items are not available then a request is created to produce a certain quantity of the respective item (i.e. the ordered quantity plus a certain additional amount, in this example 100 units of the respective item). A message is sent to the customer where the customer is informed that his order cannot be fulfilled at once. After the production of a sufficient quantity of the item, the order is finally fulfilled.

In the predicate/tranision net description given in Figure 2 certain basic temporal aspects are inherently contained as for example:

(1) An order can only be checked for the items availability after having arrived in the system.

(2) A bill and a delivery slip can only be created after an order was checked and copied.

(3) The activities CREATE–DELIVERY–SLIP and CREATE–BILL can happen at the same time (but it is not modelled that they actually do!).

For adequately modelling the system's behaviour it is necessary to take into account other temporal assertions as for example:

(4) The items quantity in stock is checked at the first day of every month (*repeated fixed date triggering*).

(5) Each order must be checked for availability of the respective item as soon as the order arrives (*immediate triggering*).

(6) The production of items must be started at latest three days after the request for items production is created (*delayed triggering*).

(7) A waiting-order must not wait more than two weeks for being processed (*delayed triggering*).

3.2. Basic Time Mechanism And Repeated Fixed Date Triggering

To model the before mentioned temporal aspects it is necessary to add new active components (transitions) or passive components (places) to the given net structure. We consider them on several levels of abstraction. On the highest level we regard these additional components as agencies and channels in the sense of channel/agency nets (for which, in contrast to place/transition nets and predicate/transition nets, no formal transition rule exists, see [Rei85]). For example we use the notation given in Figure 3 to model assertion (4), the *repeated fixed date triggering*.

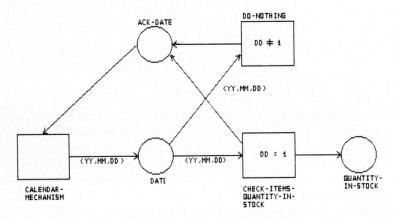

Figure 3: Repeated Fixed Date Triggering

A calendar mechanism provides the current date that can be read by the transitions CHECK–ITEMS–QUANTITY–IN–STOCK and DO–NOTHING. At the first day of every month the transition CHECK–ITEMS–QUANTITY–IN–STOCK can occur, whereas in all other cases the transition DO–NOTHING occurs, i.e. in the corresponding real system nothing happens. For a shorthand notation of Figure 3 the transitions CALENDAR–MECHANISM, DO–NOTHING, the place ACK-DATE and the respective arrows can be omitted.

Refining the transition CALENDAR–MECHANISM leads to the next level of abstraction. The corresponding net is given in Figure 4. It consists of three modules: A basic pulse

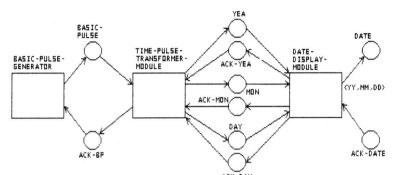

Figure 4: Refinement of the Calendar Mechanism

generator, a pulse transformer module and a date display module.

In this net a formal transition rule is still not modelled. The time pulse transformer module and the date display module therefore have to be further refined for a predicate/transition net interpretation, the lowest level of abstraction.

As done in [Ric85] we use a relativistic notion of time, i.e. we regard events as being logically prior to times (see [BAD82]). Time is defined via events where the occurrence of an event defines a point of time. As events we consider the occurrences of a basic pulse generating transition (see Figure 1). Similar to [Lam78] we assume that there exists a function that assigns a non-negative integer P in ascending order to each occurrence of the basic pulse generating transition.

If we consider the occurrences of the basic pulse generating transition as pulses of unit second then it is possible to transform these basic time pulses into pulses of higher order as minutes, hours, days, months and years. As an example we give the rule to transform pulses of unit second into pulses of unit minute:

Let P be the number of pulses currently being occurred.

Then $PULSE_{SEC}(P) = P$

$PULSE_{MIN}(P) = P \ DIV \ 60$

($x \ DIV \ y$ meaning the integer part of x divided by y)

The transformation rule for minute pulses can be described by using a predicate/transition net as given in Figure 5.

This net contains two counting transitions: One of them (inscribed with '$T_0 < 59$') increases an integer variable T_0 by 1, the other transition (inscribed with '$T_0 = 59$') sets this variable back to zero when it reaches the value 59. Assume an initial marking with one token in SECOND-PULSE and the integer value '0' in place A.

When similarly modelling the other transformation rules the final result is a hierarchy of time pulse transformers that we call time pulse transformer module. This module

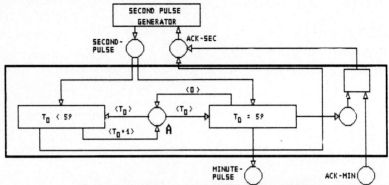

Figure 5: Transformation Rule for Minute Pulses

contains a net interface where different kinds of time pulses are available for transitions as tokens in places. If a transition reads a time pulse then a new pulse can only occur after the transition has acknowledged the pulse. Similarly the minute pulse generator must acknowledge the time pulses of unit second, the hour pulse generator must acknowledge the time pulses provided by the minute pulse generator and so on. Note that for each transition which reads a certain time pulse we have to introduce an extra pair time pulse and acknowledgement. Several pulse transformer modules have to be connected to a single basic pulse generator module (cf. [Ric85]) for synchronization.

In Figure 6(a) a net is given as a gross description of the complete hierarchy of time pulse transformers where the places and transitions are again interpreted as channels and agencies. The transitions of the respective kinds of pulse can be refined similarly to the minute pulse transition in Figure 5.

As a shorthand notation for Figure 6(a) we use the functional unit time pulse transformer module given in Figure 6(b).

The time pulse transformer module provides pulses of unit second, minute, ..., year. To manage these time pulses and to compute the current time/date we use a clock/calendar mechanism called time/date display module. The date display module provides the current date, the time display module makes the current time available.

Let the following sets be given:

$$SEC = \{0, 1, 2, \ldots, 59\}, MIN = \{0, 1, 2, \ldots, 59\}, HOU = \{0, 1, 2, \ldots, 23\},$$
$$DAY = \{1, 2, 3, \ldots, 31\}, MON = \{1, 2, 3, \ldots, 12\}, YEA = \{0, 1, 2, \ldots, 99\}.$$

A date is defined as an element of the set $DATE$, where $DATE$ is a subset of the cartesian product of the sets DAY, MON and YEA:

$$DATE \subseteq YEA \times MON \times DAY$$

A point of time can be defined similarly as an element of the set POT, where POT is the cartesian product of SEC, MIN, HOU:

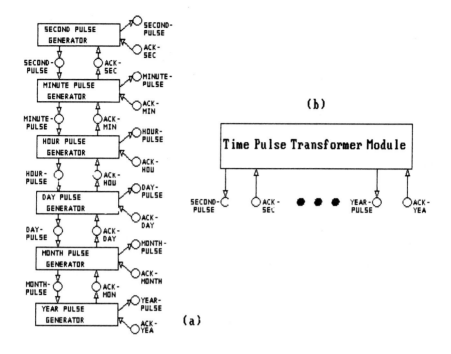

Figure 6: Hierarchy of Time Pulse Transformers

$$POT = HOU \times MIN \times SEC$$

To get the current second-, minute, hour-, day-, month- and year-value of a certain date or point of time, we have to introduce certain functions that transform a number of pulses of the respective time unit into elements of the sets SEC, MIN, HOU, MON, YEA. As an example we give the function POT_{SEC} that transforms the number $PULSE_{SEC}$ of already occurred pulses of unit second into the corresponding value of the set SEC.

$$POT_{SEC}(PULSE_{SEC}(P)) = PULSE_{SEC}(P) \; MOD \; 60$$

($x \; MOD \; y$ meaning the remainder after x is divided by y)

The time/date display module is linked to the basic time pulse generator and a time pulse transformer module. In Figure 7 a time display module is shown that transforms pulses of units second, minute and hour into elements of the sets SEC, MIN and HOU.

A transition that is connected to this time display module can read the current time. After having read the time the respective transition must send an acknowledgement to the time display module. A new basic time pulse can only occur after this acknowledgement. Note that each time point must be read by a transition to get the acknowledgement (see also 3.3.1.).

256   *A. Oberweis and G. Lausen*

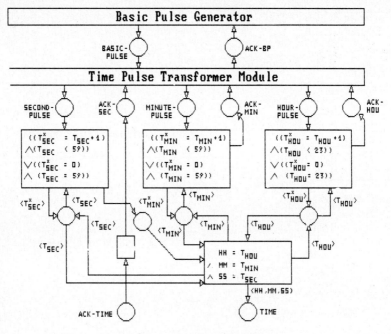

Figure 7: Time Display Module

Similarly a date display module can be constructed that transforms pulses of unit day, month and year into elements of the sets DAY, MON and YEA.

As a shorthand notation for time/date display modules we shall use the simplified nets given in Figure 8 (see also Figure 3). The current date or time is given as an individual token in a predicate $TIME$ (e.g. $TIME(9, 15, 25)$), a date is given in a predicate $DATE$ (e.g. $DATE(86, 09, 11)$). The respective tokens are produced by functional units called time display module or calendar display module. Hence points of time and dates are available in predicate/ transition nets to be used in the logical formulas assigned to transitions and for the labelling of arcs.

3.3. Applications

3.3.1. Single Fixed Date Triggering and Absolute Delay Times

The use of a calendar mechanism enables us to model *single fixed date triggering* of activities. A transition A that should occur on July 6th, 1986 must be inscribed with the expression $'date = (86, 07, 06)'$. Together with a transition $\neg A$ inscribed with $'date \neq (86, 07, 06)'$ A has to be connected to a calendar mechanism as done in Figure 3. Transition A is only enabled if the current date equals July 6th, 1986, $\neg A$ occurs in all other cases. By the acknowledging mechanism it is guaranteed that each day either A or $\neg A$ occurs, because the calendar mechanism can only proceed after having received acknowledgement

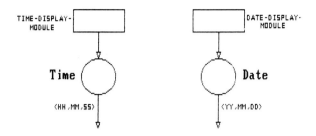

Figure 8: Shorthand Notation for a Time/Date Display Module

of either A or $\neg A$. Consequently A must occur during the specified day (cf. [Dur85]).
The modelling of *absolute delay times* for activities is a bit different to the modelling of
single fixed date triggering: A transition A that must occur after July 6th, 1986 has to be
inscribed with the expression $'date > (86,07,06)'$ whereas the complementary transition
$\bar{A}$ has no inscription.

3.3.2. Immediate Triggering of Activities

Let us now have another look at the example given in Figure 2 and the corresponding
temporal assertions. Assertion (5) meant that each order must be checked for availability
of the respective item as soon (i.e. in the same basic time interval) as the order arrives.
This immediate triggering can be modelled by using the pulses of unit second that are
provided by the pulse transformer module (see Figure 9). For reasons of simplification
we consider the transition CHECK–ORDER as a coarsening of the transitions CHECK–
ITEMS–AVAILABILITY and CREATE–REQUEST–FOR–ITEMS–PRODUCTION.

We add to the given net structure a transition NO–ORDER–ARRIVAL that is connected
by arrows to the places IMP_{SEC} and ACK_{SEC} to ensure that at each basic time interval
'something' happens: Either an order arrives or no order arrives (where we regard NO–
ORDER–ARRIVAL as an activity too). In the former cases, a new pulse of unit second
can only occur after the occurrence of CHECK–ORDER, i.e. CHECK–ORDER is forced
to occur in the same basic time interval as ORDER–ARRIVAL. In the latter cases, where
no order arrives, the transition NO–ORDER–ARRIVAL acknowledges the pulse. By each
occurrence of NO–ORDER–ARRIVAL it is expressed that no order arrived in the respective time interval.

Note that in this net it is assumed that at most one order arrives during one basic time
interval (second). Hence this mechanism is not acceptable for specifications like 'at the
same day' or 'in the same month', i.e. for time intervals where usually more than on order
arrives. For such specifications we have to use a delayed triggering mechanism as described
in the next section.

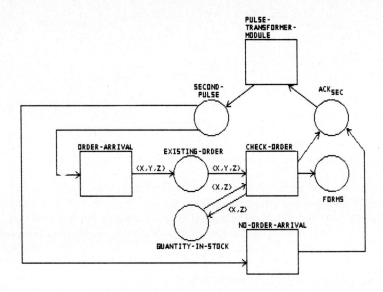

Figure 9: Immediate Triggering of an Activity

3.3.3. Delayed Triggering of Activities

Let us now have a look at the temporal constraint (6) concerning the example given in Figure 2: The production of items must be started at latest three days after the request for items production is created.

To model this delayed tiggering we again have to add new functional units into the given net structure. If we consider these additional components as agencies and channels we can use the notation given in Figure 10, where a so-called min/max delay module is introduced between the two transitions CREATE–REQUEST–FOR–ITEMS–PRODUCTION and PRODUCE–ITEM.

The min/max delay module is a functional unit that provides a signal T_{MIN} time units after having received a start time. If the signal is not acknowledged then it is repeated each time a basic time pulse occurs. After T_{MAX} time units a signal is given that must be acknowledged, i.e. a certain transition is forced to occur at latest T_{MAX} time units after the start of the delay interval. As input this module needs a start time or start date, a miniumum/ maximum delay time value T_{MIN}/T_{MAX} and an additional attribute specifying a certain object that is related to the delay time. This additional attribute is necessary, because in predicate/transition nets there may exist several different objects in a marking which enable a transition (see e.g. [GeL81]). The attribute specifies the objects that should be removed from the input places of the respective transition.

To fulfill temporal constraint (6) in Figure 10 the value '0 days' is assigned to T_{MIN} and '3 days' to T_{MAX}. This means that the earliest firing date of the transition PRODUCE–

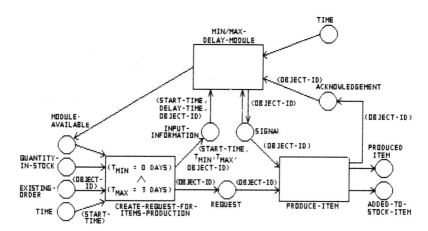

Figure 10: Delayed Triggering of an Activity

ITEM is the firing date of the transition CREATE–REQUEST–FOR–ITEMS– PRODUCTION. At latest 3 days after the request's creation the production of items must start.

Refining the functional unit min/max-delay-module leads to the predicate/transition net given in Figure 11. In this net we use a function

$$time - difference(HH, MM, SS, HH', MM', SS')$$

as inscription of several transitions. This function computes the time difference between the current point of time (HH, MM, SS) and the point of time where the delay time started (HH', MM', SS').

Starting with a marking where the only tokens are in place A and in place TIME the following basic occurrence sequences are possible:

- { *transition*1 – *transition*2 – *transition*5 }:
  No external transition starts the delay module and the current time is acknowledged. This sequence is repeated during each basic time interval until the module is started by an external transition.

- { *transition*1 – *transition*2 – *transition*3 }:
  An external transition starts the delay module. The minimum delay time is not yet reached and the current time is acknowledged. Then the sequence { *transition*1 – *transition*3 } is repeated until the minimum delay time is reached.

- { *transition*1 – *transition*2 – *transition*4 – *transition*7 },

  { *transition*1 – *transition*2 – *transition*4 – *transition*6 }:
  An external transition starts the delay module. The minimum delay time is reached or already exceeded but the maximum delay time is not yet reached. A signal (token)

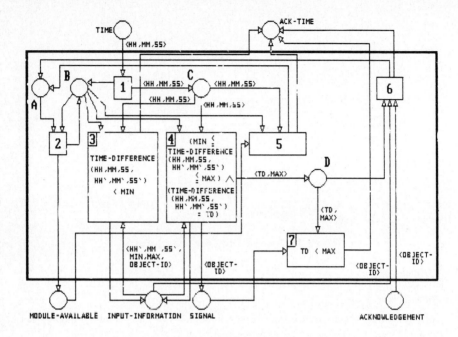

Figure 11: Min/Max-Delay Module

is provided in the place SIGNAL that can be read by an external transition. If no external transition reads the signal then *transition7* acknowledges the current time. If an external transition reads the signal then this transition must acknowledge the signal and *transition6* acknowledges the current time.

If the maximum delay time is reached then *transition7* cannot occur, i.e. the signal must be read by an external transition that also has to acknowledge the signal.

(Note that we denote by external transitions such transitions that do not belong to the min/max delay module.)

By using a min/max delay module and assigning the same value T to T_{MIN} and T_{MAX} it is possible to model a fixed trigger time for a certain transition. After T time units a specified transition must occur.

The use of n min/max-delay-modules where all modules are started by the same transition and where the same delay time with T_{MIN} equal to T_{MAX} is assigned to each module enables us to force n transitions to occur in the same basic time interval.

3.3.4. Durations of Activities

If we want to model durations associated to the occurrences of transitions then we have to proceed in the following way (cf. [GeS80,Ri85]): For a given transtion $TRANS$ we have to introduce two transitions $TRANS_S$ and $TRANS_E$, where the first represents the starting and the second represents the ending of an occurrence of transition $TRANS$. Furthermore we introduce a place $PLACE_T$. A marking of that place represents the duration of $TRANS$. In the following we denote by $\bullet TRANS$ the set of all input-places of a transition TRANS and by $TRANS\bullet$ the set of all output-places of $TRANS$. For the refinement of transition $TRANS$ by the two transitions $TRANS_S$ and $TRANS_E$ it must hold: $\bullet TRANS_S = \bullet TRANS, TRANS_E\bullet = TRANS\bullet$ and $TRANS_S\bullet = \bullet TRANS_E = PLACE_T$. By introducing a min/max delay module between $TRANS_S$ and $TRANS_E$ it is possible to model minimum/maximum durations for transition $TRANS$. The minimum duration of $T\overset{\vee}{R}ANS$ equals the minimum delay time, the maximum duration equals the maximum delay time.

3.3.5. Relative Delay Times

Another application of the min/max delay module is the modelling of *relative delay times*. If a certain time interval T_{DEL} must elapse after the occurrence of an activity A before another activity B can start, we have to introduce a min/max delay module between A and B, where the minimum delay time equals T_{DEL} and the maximum delay time equals '∞' (infinity). If T_{DEL} for example equals 14 days then the min/max delay module sends a signal to B 14 days after the occurrence of A. This signal, which is repeated each following day, must not be acknowledged by transition B, i.e. in contrast to the *delayed triggering* B is not forced to occur.

4. Temporal Plausability

The modelling of temporal assertions produces plausibility problems. Temporal plausibility of a procedure means that the collection of all temporal assertions concerning this procedure is reasonable, i.e. without contradictions. As examples for unreasonable collections of temporal assertions let us consider the following two situations:

(1) An activity is triggered at a certain date where some needed input objects for the respective activity are not yet available because of the duration of the producing activity.

(2) An activity needs two input objects where the one is only available until a certain point of time t and where the other object is not available before $t + 1$.

We distinguish between two kinds of temporal implausibilities: structural and behavioural temporal implausibilities. Structural temporal implausibility of a procedure means that for all possible durations of the activities there exists a transition that can never occur because of the temporal assertions in the net. Behavioural implausibility means that in some cases (depending on the actual durations of the activities) an activity cannot occur. Structural temporal implausibilities must be eliminated from a net, behavioural temporal implausibilities are treated as exceptions.

For the order processing example in Figure 2 we gave a temporal constraint postulating that a waiting order must not wait more than fourteen days for being processed. A behavioural implausibility occurs if the transition PRODUCE–ITEM takes more than fourteen days.

Behavioural implausibilities are considered as exceptional situations which must be clarified by an exception handling mechanism (see section 5). A structural implausibility exists, if we add as a further temporal assertion that the activity PRODUCE–ITEM takes at least three weeks and at most four weeks. This is an obvious contradiction to the constraint that a waiting order must not wait more than fourteen days for being processed.

5. Exception Handling

Petri Nets usually are used in such a manner that no deadlocks can occur, i.e. all exceptional situations that may occur are clarified in the given net. In the context of time modelling we define an exceptional situation as a situation, where a transition is triggered without being enabled. Therefore exceptional transitions must be modelled that are enabled whenever a not enabled transition is triggered. In predicate/transition nets there exist two possiblities why a transition is not enabled (if we assume that the token capacity of all predicates is infinite):

(1) There are not enough individuals in the input predicates of the transition.

(2) The logical formula inscribed to the transition is not fulfilled for any assignment of individuals available in the input predicates to the variables in the formula.

An exception handling mechanism in a predicate/transition net must cope with both situations. In [BMW84] it is postulated that the description of rare exceptional cases should not disturb the description of the usual system behaviour. We therefore model exceptional situations by single transitions where the occurrence of such a transition corresponds to the occurrence of an exceptional situation. For each transition an exceptional transition must be added to a given net structure so that the exceptional transition can only occur if a time signal arrives and the corresponding regular case transition is not enabled. This exceptional transition can be refined by a set of transitions in a separate net specifying the exception handling mechanism.

As an example for an exceptional situation, let us have a look at Figure 2 and the corresponding temporal constraints. A waiting-order must not wait more than two weeks for being processed. An exceptional situation occurs if the production of items takes more time than usual. We now want additionally to specify that an exceptional transition is triggered if the production of items takes more than fourteen days. To model such an exceptional transition we first have to introduce a min/max delay module (here again interpreted as an agency in a channel/agency net; for a predicate/transition net interpretation see Figure 11) between the two transitions CREATE–REQUEST–FOR–ITEMS–PRODUCTION and REPEAT–ORDER (see Figure 12).

The minimum delay time is 1 day, the maximum delay time is 14 days. After 14 days a signal is released that must be acknowledged. If the transition REPEAT–ORDER can not occur because the respective item is still not produced then the exceptional transition occurs that acknowledges the time signal. The exceptional transition can be refined by a separate, new net. In this net it must be specified how the exceptional situation can be clarified. In the given situation such a clarifying mechanism would be for example to

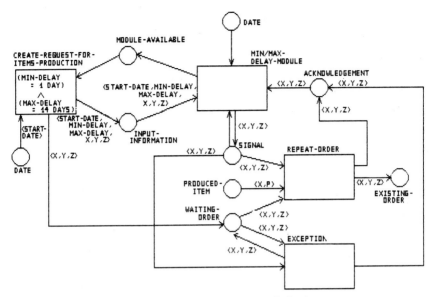

Figure 12: Exception Handling Mechanism

send an excusing message to the customer and to extend the waiting time of the respective order.

6. Summary and Outlook

We have described a method for the modelling of temporal aspects that are of relevance for office information systems such as the duration of activities, the starting times of activities, time limits, triggering dates and the current time/date.

An important issue of this clock-based approach is the ability to model the triggering of activities whereas in Petri Nets without clock mechanism the point of time where an enabled transition fires is not determined. We gave examples where we extended given Petri Nets by a pulse generating module, by a time/date display module and by a min/max-delay module to model repeated and single triggering of activities at fixed dates, immediate triggering by an arriving object, delayed triggering as well as relative and absolute delay times.

The modelling of temporal assertions causes certain problems of temporal plausibility. We distinguish between two kinds of temporal implausibility: Structural temporal implausibilities that must be eliminated from a given net because certain transitions can never occur and behavioural implausibilities that are treated as exceptional situations.

We introduced an exception handling mechanism based on timing constraints. For each exceptional situation we add an exceptional transition into the given Petri Net structure. These transitions can be refined in separate nets to detail the exception handling mechanism.

A special characteristic of office information systems is that the knowledge world is open-ended [Bar83,CrL84,Mae84]. Especially in the field of exception handling the complete set of relevant actions is usually unknown. Therefore an additional knowledge-based mechanism must be incorporated in the model as a specific transition to handle unforeseen situations that have not been specified before.

Further research work still has to be done in the field of temporal plausibility checking. A computer assisted mechanism is needed that automatically finds contradictions in the set of given temporal constraints. Such a mechanism can be implemented similar to the ideas presented in [NVW84, NiV85] where an office simulator is described based on predicate/transition nets with Prolog inscriptions.

References

[AnZ84] Antonellis, De V.; Zonta, B.: A Causal Approach to Dynamics Handling, Database Engineering (quarterly bulletin of the IEEE computer society technical committee), Vol. 7, No. 4, 1984

[BAD82] Bolour,A.; Anderson, T.L.; Dekeyser, L.J.; Wong, H.K.T.: The role of time in Information Processing: A Survey; SIGMOD RECORD, Vol. 12, No. 3, 1982

[BaP85] Barbic, F.; Pernici, B.: Time Modeling in Office Information Systems, Proceedings of ACM-SIGMOD 1985 International Conference on Management of Data, SIGMOD RECORD, Vol. 14, Nr. 4, 1985

[Bar83] Barber, G.: Supporting Organizational Problem Solving with a Work Station, in: ACM Transactions on Office Information Systems, Vol. 1, No. 1, 1983

[BCL84] Blaustein, B.T.; Chilenskas, R.M.; Lin, W.K.; Ries, D.R.: Office Procedures as a Distributed Database Application, in: Data Base, Vol. 15, No. 2, 1984

[BeM83] Berthomieu, B.; Menasche, M.: Timed Petri Nets for Analyzing and Verifying Time Dependent Communication Protocols, in: Specification, Testing and Verification III, Ed.: Rudin, H.; West, C.H., North-Holland Publishing Company 1983

[BMW84] Borgida, A.; Mylopoulos, J.; Wong, H.K.T.: Generalization/ Specialization as a Basis for Software Specification, in: On Conceptual Modeling, Ed.:Brodie, M.L.; Mylopoulos, J.; Schmidt, J.W., Springer-Verlag 1984

[Bor85] Borgida, A.: Language Features for Flexible Handling of Exceptions in Information Systems, ACM Transactions on Database Systems, Vol. 10, No. 4, 1985

[BP84a] Bracchi, G.; Pernici, B.: The Design Requirements for Office Systems, ACM Transactions on Office Information Systems, Vol. 2, No. 2, 1984

[BP84b] Bracchi, G.; Pernici, B.: SOS: A Conceptual Model for Office Information Systems, in: Data Base, Vol. 15, No. 2, 1984

[CoR83] Coolahan, J.E.; Roussopoulos, N.: Timing Requirements for Time-Driven Systems Using Augmented Petri Nets, in: IEEE Transactions on Software Engineering, 1983

[CRIS82] Olle, T.W.; Sol, H.G.; Verrijn-Stuart, A.A. (Eds.): Information Systems Design Methodologies: A Comparative Review, North-Holland 1982

[CRIS83] Olle, T.W.; Sol., H.G.; Tully, C.J. (Eds.): Information Systems Design Methodologies: A Feature Analysis, North-Holland 1983

[CrL84] Croft, W.B.; Lefkowitz, L.S.: Task Support in an Office System, in: ACM Transactions on Office Information Systems, Vol. 2, No. 3, 1984

[Dur85] Durchholz, R.: Causal Dependencies in Deadline Requirements, Information Systems, Vol. 10, No. 3, 1985

[Ell79] Ellis, C.A.: Information Control Nets: A mathematical Model of Office Informations Flow, ACM Proc. Conf. Simulation, Modeling and Measurements of Computer Systems, 1979

[Ell83] Ellis, C.A.: Formal and Informal Models of Office Activity, Proceedings of the IFIP 9th World Computer Congress, North-Holland 1983

[FaM76] Farber, D.J.; Merlin, P.: Recoverability of Communication Protocols, in: IEEE Transactions on Communications, Vol. 24, No. 9, 1976

[GeL81] Genrich, H.; Lautenbach, K.: System modelling with High Level Petri Nets, in: Theoretical Computer Science, 13, 1981

[GeS80] Genrich, H.; Stankiewicz-Wiechno, E.: A dictionary of some Basic Notions of Net Theory, in: Net Theory and Application, Ed. Brauer, W., LNCS 84, Springer-Verlag 1980

[Gib85] Gibbs, S.J.: Conceptual Modelling and Office Information Systems, in: Office Automation, Ed. Tsichritzis, D.C., Springer- Verlag 1985

[HSY84] Horndasch, A.; Studer, R.; Yasdi, R.: An Approach to (Office) Information System Design Based on General Net Theory, Proceedings TFAIS 85, IFIP TC 8.1,1985

[Lam78] Lamport, L.: Time, Clocks and the Ordering of Events in a Distributed System, in: Comm. of the ACM, Vol. 21, No. 7, 1978

[LCS82] Lum, V.Y.; Choy, D.M.; Shu, N.C.: OPAS: An office procedure automation system, in: IBM System Journal, Vol. 21, No. 3, 1982

[Mae84] Maes, P.: Goals in Knowledge-Based Office Systems, in: GWAI-84 Proceedings of 8th German Workshop on Artificial Intelligence, Springer-Verlag 1984

[Nie85] Nierstrasz, O.M.: Message Flow Analysis , in: Office Automation, Ed. Tsichritzis, D.; Springer-Verlag 1985

[NiV85] Niehuis, S.; Victor, F.; Modellierung von Büroprozeduren mit Pr/T-Netzen und Prolog, in: Büroautomation 85, Berichte des German Chapter of the ACM, Bd. 25, Teubner-Verlag 1985 (in german)

[NVW84] Niehuis, S.; Victor, F.; Wisskirchen, P.: Ein rechnergestützter Bürosimulator auf der Basis von Pr/T-Netzen und Prolog, in: Angewandte Informatik, Bd. 5, 1984 (in german)

[Ram74] Ramchandani, C.: Analysis of Asynchronous Concurrent Systems by Petri Nets, Report MAC TR-120, Cambridge, Mass. 1974

[Raz84] Razouk, R.R.; The Derivation of Performance Expressions for Communication Protocols from Timed Petri Net Models, in: Computer Communication Review, Vol. 14, No. 2, 1984

[Rei85] Reisig, W.: Systementwurf mit Netzen, Springer-Verlag 1985 (in german)

[Ric83] Richter, G.: Realitätsgetreues Modellieren und modellgetreues Realisieren von Bürogeschehen, in: Informationstechnik und Bürosysteme, Teubner-Verlag, Stuttgart 1983 (in german)

[Ric85] Richter, G.: Clocks and their use for time modeling, Proceedings TFAIS 85, IFIP TC 8.1, 1985

[RoR82] Rolland, C.; Richard, C.: Transactions Modeling, Proceedings of the International Conference on Managemant of Data, Orlando, Florida, ACM SIGMOD, 1982

[Sif80] Sifakis, J.: Performance Evaluation of Systems Using Nets, in: Net Theory and Applications, LNCS 84, Springer-Verlag 1980

[SoK85] Solvberg, A.; Kung, C.H.: On Structural and Behaviour Modelling of Reality, in: Proc. IFIP TC-2 Working Conference on Database Semantics 1985, North-Holland (to appear)

[Wal82] Walter, B.: Transaktionsorientierte Recovery-Konzepte für verteilte Datenbanksysteme, Dissertation, Stuttgart 1982 (in german)

[Zis77] Zisman, M.D.: Use of Production Systems for Modeling Asynchronous Concurrent Processes, PH.D. Dissertation, The Wharton School, University of Pennsylvania, 1977

OFFICE SYSTEMS: Methods and Tools
G. Bracchi, D. Tsichritzis (Editors)
Elsevier Science Publishers B.V. (North-Holland)
© IFIP, 1987

OFFICE PAPER DOCUMENT ANALYSIS

E. Meynieux*, W. Postl**, S. Seisen*, K. Tombre***

* TITN ZI La Vigne aux Loups F-91380 CHILLY-MAZARIN
** SIEMENS AG 9, Koppstrasse D-8000 MUNCHEN
*** CRIN B.P. 239 F-54506 VANDOEUVRE CEDEX

The electronic handling of Office Documents at a workstation requires an easy input of existing paper documents. The Automated Document Entry system provides a set of sophisticated enhancement and recognition processes resulting in a standardized electronic representation of a paper document captured by a multi-level scanner. The main processings are introduced here, with emphasis on the segmentation of different content types and the recognition of the document structure as well as geometric elements.

1. INTRODUCTION

Facing the increasing use of office systems for processing, storing and transmitting documents of any sort, standardizing the document description seemed to be necessary.

This resulted in the definition of office document standards : the *Office Document Architecture (ODA)* and *Office Document Interchange Format (ODIF)* [1].

According to the ODA, an office document is described by its logical structure dividing it into sections, paragraphs, titles, figures... and its layout structure separating it into pages and nested rectangular areas. Each basic object is associated with a content classified in three main types: characters, raster graphics (described by a pixel array) and geometric graphics (described by geometric primitives). A document is an instance of a document class, and the standard provides ways for defining individual document classes.

The *ESPRIT** Project *HERODE†* aims at implementing and testing the ODA. It will result in an integrated system allowing the archiving, transmitting and editing of electronic documents.

Within the framework of this Project, the *Automated Document Entry (ADE)* objective is to provide an automated way for transforming information in paper form into its electronic representation. From a paper document, the ADE must extract its layout structure that describes the location of the different information types, enhance and recognize the contents.

Such a system may be used for inserting parts of an already printed document in another one being edited, as well as for archiving complete documents with a high compression ratio.

This paper introduces the general ADE architecture and focuses on the segmentation of the different content types as well as the recognition of the layout structure and geometric elements, respectively.

---

* *ESPRIT* stands for European Strategic Programme for Research and Development in Information Technology, and is partially funded by the European Community.

† *HERODE* : Handling the Electronic Representation of Office Documents based on ECMA 101 standard. ESPRIT Project 4.2 / 121, raised by Siemens AG (Munich) and TITN (Paris), with the collaboration of Queen Mary College (London) and CRIN (Centre de Recherche en Informatique de Nancy).

2. INFORMATION IN A DOCUMENT AND ADE ARCHITECTURE

In what follows, processings applied to a scanned document are described sequentially. This has been done mainly for clarity reasons. The implementation consists in an embeddding of such processings, some of them being transparent for the user. Moreover, the ADE design allows the concurrent running of some processings.

The document is captured using a CCD camera, whose spatial and intensity resolutions (200 pixels per inch and 8 bits per pixel, respectively) are sufficient for the segmentation of both typed and printed material including text, drawings and halftone images. A preprocessing module corrects the deficiencies associated with the scanning, such as unequal illumination and skew scanning. In an office document, the main directions are generally the horizontal and vertical ones. Therefore, searching for the main oblique direction in the scanned image results in determining the skew with which the document has been scanned and is followed by a corrective rotation.

The scanned image generally contains the three following texture types:

- Discrete color (The term "tone" is often used instead of "color". We consider the latter to be more adequate.)

The printing technology uses one or an overlay of the four following substractive basic print colors: black, cyan, magenta and yellow on a common background, typically white. As a result, a discrete color pattern of this type may combine 2 to 17 different colors.

- Continuous color

Typically, a "black and white" or "color" photo.

- Halftone

This is an attempted simulation of a continuous color for the human eye using a discrete color pattern. Any printed reproduction of a photograph is produced with this technology. For a scanner whose resolution is poor when compared to the halftone screen density, a halftone pattern behaves like a continuous color texture. This rarely occurs with the scanner we use.

If required, the chromaticity is acquired with three sequential scannings using different color filters. Each pixel is then represented by a byte 3-uple.

Concurrently to the classification by texture, different content portions of a typed document may be classified in terms of information color. "Discrete color" and "multicolor" mean that the area in question will be optimally reproduced either by a few colors (which applies to text and graphics) or by as much as possible different colors (which applies to photographs). In terms of electronic representation, we speak of "discrete level" and "multilevel" information. In this paper, we generally restricted ourselves to a mono-spectral scanning; as a result, "bilevel" replaces "discrete level" for convenience.

So, in the next processing step, the bilevel and multilevel information are separated for the most adequate representation and specific enhancements of the respective content portions. Indeed, the bilevel and multilevel information enhancings have not the same objective: enhancing the multilevel information generally aims at increasing the contrast, whereas enhancing the bilevel information corresponds to smoothing the shapes.

The bilevel information is changed from a multilevel to a bilevel representation, more appropriate for the following processings as well as more compact. It is then segmented into characters and graphical objects.

Now, we must define a third information classification restricted to the bilevel information; it is related to the isolation of connected components in the image. The information is divided into "intra-component" and "inter-components" information. The "intra-component" information allows to transform the iconic representation of an element into a symbolic one, e.g. a character or a graphical primitive. The "inter-components" information consists of a set of topological relationships between components. The layout structure, some semantic information such as underlining and even some content types are recognized from these relationships. For instance, Japanese words are identified as word according to the relationships between their elements, not to the character shapes (at least by most European people).

The segmentation between multilevel and bilevel information does not require an analysis of the relationships between elements, because photographs differ mainly in their texture. On the contrary, the segmentation between graphics and characters and the search for the document structure may not ignore these relationships

A layout structure is built from both these segmentations.

The representation of graphical objects is then changed into standard CGM graphical primitives [2]. The characters are likely to be submitted to an Optical Character Reader. The multilevel information "recognition" mainly consists in classifying the scanned object (mono- or multichrome, screened or not), and recognizing the possible screening pattern. This will allow data compression and optimal rendition on different devices.

Fig: 1. summarizes the ADE architecture.

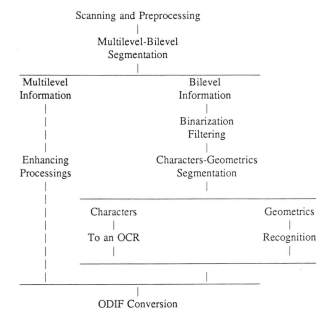

Fig. 1 : ADE ARCHITECTURE

3. BILEVEL - MULTILEVEL SEGMENTATION

This processing step aims at detecting the connected areas with a uniform texture, more exactly, those with multilevel information on the one hand and uniform color information on the other hand. The latter are to become components of bilevel information.

This segmentation is derived from the histogram of the scanned image smoothed to reduce the number of spurious maxima. Detecting hues would require a multispectral scanning and the evaluation of a multispectral histogram accordingly [3]. Each of the significant relative maxima in the histogram is interpreted as corresponding to an area of quasi-uniform absorptance which is, at this stage, the only color descriptor. Level ranges are determined from each maximum and allow us to build a corresponding mask from the original image. The connected black areas satisfiying pre-defined criteria (minimum size, compactness, regularity of shape) are searched for in each of these masks and their contents analysed.

At this step, we are mainly interested in extracting areas with a uniform grey-level density. The latter may be uniformly colored objects such as a logo or big characters or for instance objects filled with a pattern thin enough not to have been detected by the scanner (hatched boxes or halftoned areas). A texture analysis based on two main processings is performed for achieving this classification. The joint value/gradient distribution [4] of selected areas allows to check their uniform density whereas the Fourier analysis emphasizes the screening of haltoned areas.

So, the bilevel information areas are kept in a mask and by inverting the latter another one with the remaining areas is generated. The black areas in this mask correspond to those that have been rejected during the previous analysis or that have grey-level values beyond the grey-level ranges selected from the maxima. All those black areas are considered as potentially multilevel.

Connected components are extracted again but that time on the multilevel mask. Each of them is analysed using the same criteria as above though adapted to multilevel information. Finally, this segmentation yields a mask of the multilevel areas. This mask will be used during the following segmentation on bilevel information which will have to fulfill the following functionalities:

- agglomerate in a single photographic object some areas separated because of texture differences.

- keep the bilevel and mutilevel information separated such as characters overlaying multilevel information.

Recognizing substructures in a multilevel object thus contributes to the derivation of a layout structure.

All these segmentation steps are illustrated by the processing of a clipping (Fig. 2.1) from a typical magazine page with a logo (1), a quasi-signature (2), two lines of large characters (3), text (4), a haltone image (5) as well as two fields (6) and (7). The components (1), (2), (4) and (5) are printed in black and (3), (6), (7) in blue ink; the background is a glossy white.

The processings have been restricted to a monospectral analysis; indeed, the chromaticity information is of little relevancy in this document.

Fig. 2.2 shows the smoothed histogram from which four grey-level ranges and the corresponding masks are derived (Figs. 2.3.1, 2.3.2, 2.3.3, 2.3.4).

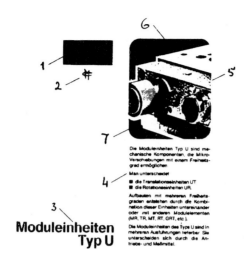

Fig. 2.1 : Binarized version of a scanned magazine page

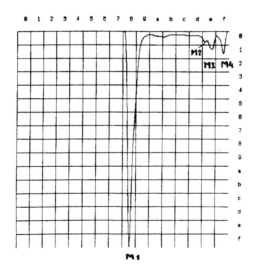

Fig. 2.2 : Smoothed histogram of the scanned image
with localized maxima

Fig 2. : BILEVEL - MULTILEVEL SEGMENTATION RESULTS

The following results are obtained submitting these masks to the detection of the bilevel areas:

- Fig. 2.3.1 : the area (1) is selected as bilevel.
- Fig. 2.3.2 : no area selected.
- Fig. 2.3.3 : the areas (1) and (2) are selected as bilevel.
- Fig. 2.3.4 : the area (1) is selected as bilevel.

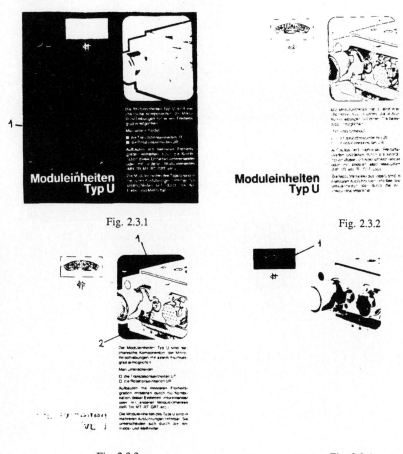

Fig. 2.3.1

Fig. 2.3.2

Fig. 2.3.3

Fig. 2.3.4

Figs. 2.3 : Binarized version of the same image,
thresholded in four ranges around the four maxima
Fig. 2.3.x corresponds to the maximum Mx

Fig. 2 : BILEVEL - MULTILEVEL SEGMENTATION RESULTS

The inverted mask of the bilevel areas is shown in Fig. 2.4 and the multilevel areas detection applied to it provides the multilevel mask illustrated by Fig. 2.5. Note that the elements (6) and (7) in (Fig 2.1) considered as bilevel objects are merged into the neighboring multilevel area during the bilevel segmentation based on the topological relationships study taking the multilevel mask into account.

Fig. 2.4 : Bitmap of the detected non-uniform areas
submitted to the detection of the multilevel areas

Fig. 2.5 : Final result - Areas detected as multilevel

Fig 2 : BILEVEL - MULTILEVEL SEGMENTATION RESULTS

4. BINARIZATION AND FILTERING

To make further processings easier and cheaper, the bilevel information is changed from a multilevel to a bilevel representation; each pixel must be defined as belonging to the background (white pixel) or the information (black pixel). Emphasis should be laid on the fact that the results of the document structure analysis greatly depend on this binarization. The information extracted during the previous segmentation, when analysing the histogram, may be used in this step.

The binarization methods can be divided into two classes. The image may be submitted to an absolute thresholding, considering as black (corresponding to information) those pixels with a grey level above a fixed value and as white (corresponding to background) those left. Much work has been done on the automatic searching for the optimal threshold (see for instance [5]). However, results may be adversely affected by the global nature of this method, when the information grey level varies in the document.

In the second class, more adaptative, a decision is made at a point according to the grey level values of neighbouring pixels. Such a method is introduced in [6]. In the method we implemented, both the internal and external contours are first detected evaluating the black and white potentials on each pixel. An oblique propagation is then used for contours filling.

Choosing the parameters in all these binarization methods is often critical. Optimal parameters of the previously introduced method, independent of the analysed document, have been extracted.

Fig. 3. illustrates the differences between both binarization classes.

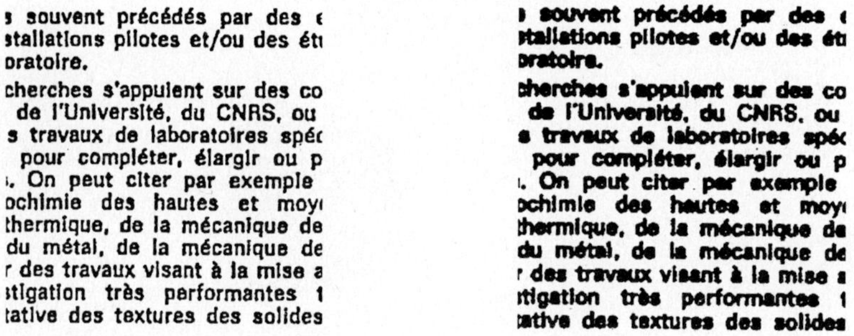

```
s souvent précédés par des (        I souvent précédés par des (
stallations pilotes et/ou des éti    stallations pilotes et/ou des éti
oratoire.                            oratoire.
cherches s'appuient sur des co       cherches s'appuient sur des co
   de l'Université, du CNRS, ou        de l'Université, du CNRS, ou
   s travaux de laboratoires spéc      s travaux de laboratoires spéc
   pour compléter, élargir ou p        pour compléter, élargir ou p
i. On peut citer par exemple         i. On peut citer par exemple
ochimie des hautes et moyi           ochimie des hautes et moyi
thermique, de la mécanique de        thermique, de la mécanique de
du métal, de la mécanique de         du métal, de la mécanique de
r des travaux visant à la mise a     r des travaux visant à la mise a
itigation très performantes t        itigation très performantes t
tative des textures des solides      tative des textures des solides
```

Right : Absolute thresholding
Left : Adaptative binarization

Fig. 3 : BINARIZATION RESULTS

The obtained image is then filtered for contour smoothing. The choice of a filter depends on the type of information considered as noise and on the processings to be applied on the resulting image.

Many filters do not keep thickness 1 information, considering it as insignificant. The scanning obviously results in a one pixel width imprecision on each contour, but the existence of a thickness 1 line is a significant information.

The resulting image has to be submitted to a module that codes the connected conponents by their contours; because of this, the filters have to be evaluated according to the following criteria :

- Thickness 1 information preservation

- Connectivity preservation

- Reduction of the number of detected contours and their coding.

- Result stability when the filter is applied twice (idempotence).

A filter which satisfies all those requirements has been implemented. It removes all the horizontal and vertical, black and white, contour runs considered as insignificant. A run is said to be insignificant if its length is lower than n (where n is a fixed integer depending on the resolution) and if, perpendicularly, it is wedged between two runs whose colors are different and lengths greater than n. The stability is ensured by the order in which runs are suppressed.

5. GRAPHIC - CHARACTER SEGMENTATION AND LAYOUT STRUCTURE RECOGNITION

This processing aims at separating the graphical parts from characters and building the layout structure. A survey on segmentation can be found in [7]. This is performed in the two following steps : first, a structure describing the different connected components and their topological relationships is generated ; this structure is then analysed.

5.1. Connected components extraction

Both the black and white connected components are detected and coded sequentially scanning the image. The coding, derived from the Cederberg coding [8], consists of a chained list of partial contour codes, describing direction changes and length in each of the five directions shown in Fig. 4.

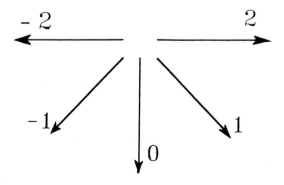

Fig. 4 : CODING DIRECTIONS

Such a coding is illustrated in Fig. 5.

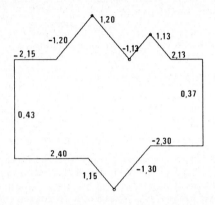

Fig. 5 : CODING EXAMPLE

(a,b) means length b (in pixels) in direction a
O indicates a contour end

For each component, internal information (e.g. position, surrounding rectangle, eccentricity, density of points and runs, center of gravity position, surface...) is evaluated. Each component is thus associated with an internal description, independent of the other document elements. All those internal descriptions consitute the "intra-component" information.

The detected components are simultaneously stored in a hierarchical structure representing the main topological relationships : inclusion and proximity. On the one hand, each component is included in another one with the opposite color, its father; on the other hand, it is related to a set of neighbouring elements with the same color.

The four horizontal and vertical directions (North, South, East and West) and the four angles (North-East, South-East, South-West and North-West) define two aspects of the proximity notion.

Two components are said to be horizontally or vertically related (h-v-related) if a line with the following properties can be drawn :

• Parallel to the given direction

• Joining two points of component contours

• Not intersecting other components

The number of such lines is called the neighborhood degree. The minimal distance is stored in the relationship. Each component associates a sense with such a relationship.

For each component, some of the h-v-relationships are removed, taking account of the distance and the relative neighborhood degree defined comparing the degree with the greatest possible one. For instance, relatively far (compared to the size of the current element) components are removed if the relative neighborhood degree is lower than a threshold. These removings are based on adaptative criteria. Because the relative neighborhood degree depends on the considered sense, there may be a North relation without the South corresponding one.

However, the fact that some relationships have been removed is recorded.

In each oblique direction, the current object is related to the closest component and the minimal distance is stored. This component may be h-v-related to the current one, or not.

A structure is associated with each h-v-related component. It describes all the neighborhood relationships with the current object. Indeed, two objects may be h-v-related in different directions, either horizontally and vertically or obliquely, thus indicating a partial surrounding. Because this set of relationships is updated while scanning the image, contour embeddings are detected simultaneously.

If two components are related, they have the same father or one of them is the grandfather of the other. So, the set of elements sharing a father is represented by a sub-graph structure, describing the directional proximity as well as the partial surrounding or embedding.

The contours of the previously detected photographic elements are included in this structure building, with a specific label, because they are likely to influence topological relationships.

A segmentation structure is illustrated in Fig. 6.

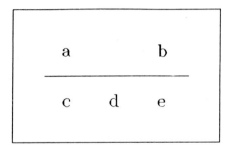

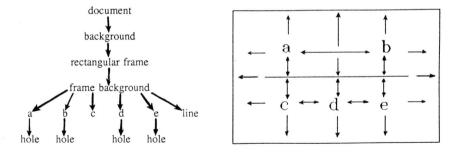

Above : Original image
Left : Hierarchical structure   Right : Proximity relationships
Fig. 6 : SEGMENTATION STRUCTURE EXAMPLE

5.2. Structure analysis

What is aimed at in this analysis is twofold: first, a content type must be assigned to connected components; second, elementary elements must be merged into sets, thus building a layout structure.

Both the available information types, i.e. the internal information and the topological relationships, are used in both these steps. As far as possible, the internal information used is limited to the set of measurements performed for each component. It prevents from scanning the contour coding, only used in the following specific recognition steps.

The component structure is updated merging, splitting and assigning original or previously created objects to a content type. This processing uses internal information as well as topological relationships and the decided assignment of a type to an element does not depend only on its internal information. At this point, it may be decided that a component has the same type as its father, whatever this type.

Rules based on the internal information have been defined in such a way that they require no arbitrary decision to be made on the element size, such as the maximum size of a character. This explains that criteria based only on internal information are limited. Examples of such criteria are based on the eccentricity.

The applied topological rules can be divided into two types. Some of them use only the existence of relationships and allow the assignment to a content type. Others complete the content type identification and create component subsets, searching a sense to a set of relationships. Some of these rules use internal information as secondary criteria.

First, black background areas are detected starting from the hierarchy root. The background areas could be characterized by their relative size, their number of included components, and their surface of information / surface of included inversely colored elements ratio.

Topological assignment criteria are for instance the number of descendant levels and the partial surrounding of other objects determined from the proximity sub-graph. Here are some examples of topological assignment rules:

- A very small component without many brothers is generally of the same type as its father.

- Elements with more than 2 descendant levels or a great number of sons or surrounding other objects are necessarily of the graphical type.

- Elements neighboring a great number of components in one direction are graphical.

At each hierarchical level, each set of components sharing a father is divided into subsets according to the proximity relationships.

Here are some examples of rules:

- Symbols lines are determined by the merging of a great number of elements, with no more than one descendant level, whose features are similar and which create a regular chain in the proximity graph. Such lines may then be split into words, which implies that the elements are characters.

- Symbols lines are likely to be merged into paragraphs, that may include underlining lines, whose detection is easy using the proximity graph.

- A symbols line which cannot be split into words is considered as a graphical element if its components have quite similar features (for instance, it could be a CGM dashed line).

• A component is linked to some of its neighbors of the same type, if it surrounds them partially or if their distance is lower than a fixed value. This rule allows for instance to recognize some objects detected as photographic (multilevel or bilevel) as belonging to the same photograph.

When searching for symbols lines, the horizontal and vertical directions are first analysed. If unsuccessful, the oblique directions are taken into account.

Those graphical elements or areas whose structure is too complex to be completely and efficiently recognized (e.g. handwriting, signature ...) are detected and considered as bilevel raster graphics. The CCITT T6 coding will be applied to these objects. Complexity criteria use mainly internal information.

Finally, isolated elements whose content type has not been decided and which do not belong to any component set, are classified according to criteria deduced, for instance, from the average size of the characters in the document.

Fig. 7 illustrates the results of the bilevel segmentation.

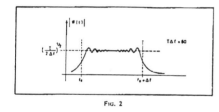

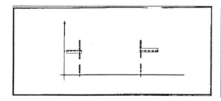

Upper left :   Original image   Upper right :   Characters structure
Lower left :   Processable graphics   Lower right :   Raster graphics

Fig. 7 : BILEVEL SEGMENTATION RESULTS

The last segmentation step aims at generating the ODA layout structure from the structured sets of components. This structure consists of a set of overlapping blocks, each of which is associated with one components subset.

The characters may then be submitted to an OCR. Each block associated with a content identified as graphic is submitted to the specific recognition module.

6. GRAPHICS RECOGNITION

6.1. Principles

The graphics recognition aims at extracting the graphical primitives, recognizing some simple graphical objects and coding them according to CGM. The information yielded by the segmentation on the layout structure remains of course very useful for this recognition and coding module.

Much work has been done on graphics coding, especially for the purpose of automatically inputting technical drawings. However, most systems work directly on the binary image combining techniques such as skeletonizing and polygonal approximation (see for instance [9], [10], [11]). We also explored this direction, with particular thought for the hardware implementation of the algorithms. We thus found it possible to use fast and local algorithms, easy to implement in dedicated circuitry, so as to extract linear structures from the binary image. This work is described in [12].

However, there is a fundamental disadvantage with such an approach in our case: because of the complexity and diversity of an office document, a very precise and complete module for the segmentation between text and graphics is required. We have shown that this segmentation yields a lot of useful information on the layout structure and the topography of the connected components. But, if we return to the binary image, we lose most of this information, or at least its retrieval becomes harder.

We therefore work on the contours of the connected components, which are chain-coded as previously described. On the one hand, the information yielded by the segmentation may thus be kept; on the other hand, we must retrieve linear structures from the contours of the connected components and not from a skeleton and for this we must solve new problems which do not exist with a skeleton-based method.

There are less publications on the work performed in this direction; however, Cugini [13] introduces an original method for inputting engineering drawings where the work is performed on the contours and not the line skeleton.

6.2. Linear segments extraction

Starting with the hierarchical structure of connected components, where the contours are chain-coded, the first step consists in extracting linear segments which are good approximations of the contour. This results in a new internal coding of each connected component and does not affect the structure.

Several methods are available for such approximations. Many of them are based on the recursive division splining, whose principle is to divide recursively the curve as long as a straight linear segment is not a good approximation of it. Other methods are based on the sequential curve following and progressive construction of the linear segments. Wall [14] introduces one algorithm with very low complexity computations. The general idea is to compute the algebraic area of the surface between the curve and its linear approximation.

The problem with such a sequential method is that the angular points may be displaced. Because of this, an angle detection must be added. However, this method remains much faster than the recursive division splining.

Once a polygonal approximation of the contours has been extracted, the actual lines should be retrieved. Graphics can be divided into the two main following parts :

- lines

- large black areas

When the approximation is over, the contours of the lines look like this:

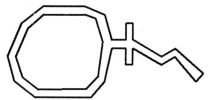

and those of black areas like that:

Intuitively, we see that there is a line if segments can be paired. Two segments can be paired if:

- their distance is not above a fixed value (considered as the greatest possible width of a line),

- they have the same direction

- they delimit a black area.

The lines are therefore extracted searching for each segment whether it can be paired with another one. In this case, the double path is followed as long as possible, evaluating the middle line and the thickness. If the segment cannot be paired, it belongs to an area and the current path is followed as long as no pairing is possible.

When following the lines, the extraction can be stopped because either:

- the end of a line in the original figure has been reached,

- or the followed line has led into a black area,

- or a point where several lines intersect has been reached

In those cases, a decision is made to possibly join segments across an intersection and determine the real intersection. For instance, segments are joined across an intersection if they have the same direction.

Fig. 8 shows a typical result of this method on the polygonal approximation of the contours.

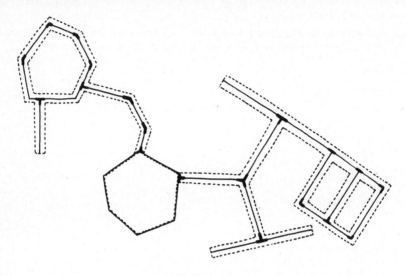

Dotted : Original contours
Black : Pairings and middle lines
Bold-faced : Junction points

Fig. 8 : POLYGONAL APPROXIMATION RESULTS

6.3. Higher level recognition

Now, the set of segments can be considered as curves, which may be open or closed. The module is designed to code this graphical information according to a standard such as CGM. We therefore have to recognize graphical primitives, such as lines, polygons, circles or rectangles. Such primitives can be found following the chained segments and analysing the global set curvature, the angular points and the angle measurements, as well as the number and type of junction points.

However, because the hierarchical layout structure has been kept, we can also aim at recognizing higher level objects. For instance, if a closed line encloses several parallel equidistant lines, this can be recognized and coded as a hatched area. Several small linear segments with the same direction may constitute a dotted line. Many intersecting horizontal and vertical lines can be regarded as a grid. Sets of curves that are close to each other may represent one single object. At this point, topological relationships, such as inclusion and proximity, are then quite useful.

7. USER INTERACTION

This system has two main funtionalities. First, the paper documents can be archived in a standardized and compact form and partly or completely retrieved later using any tools handling ODA documents. Second, printed contents can be inserted into a document being edited.

The ADE is one tool in a system for handling office paper documents in compliance with the ODA. Apart from the ADE, this system includes a structure editor, handling both the logical and layout structures and their conformance with the ODA classes definitions, different dedicated editors for characters, geometrics and raster graphics and a common user interface. Using some of these different tools in an ADE session yields new functionalities based on user-supplied information. Some possible interaction schemes are introduced in the next paragraphs.

The possible user help covers two main aspects. The user may supply a-priori information at the beginning of a session and correct some segmentation and recognition results.

When selecting the ADE, the user is asked via the common user interface for some information such as the name of the document and its quality, the sizes of the pages to be scanned, the bilevel rendition method to be applied to photographic objects (for instance, the screening type). He may also provide information likely to help the segmentation and recognition steps. For instance, the multilevel-bilevel segmentation may be avoided knowing that there is no photograph in the scanned document. The user may also specify areas in the document that are not to be analysed, for instance because their quality is too poor for the segmentation and recognition: the CCITT T6 is used for their coding.

Another level of a-priori information is being studied and relates to the class of the analysed document. A document class definition describes a model that specifies how to construct the logical and layout structures of documents that are members of that class. For instance, some rules indicate relationships between layout and logical objects. Others associate a common content with some objects or define how composite objects are built from subordinate objects. Such information may be used first for checking the consistency of the segmentation results with the class requirements. Morever, some layout objects may be associated with class-defined logical objects. For instance, an address or a logo are likely to be automatically extracted. Obviously, the corresponding class definition has to be known by the structure editor.

Suppose that, after each page has been processed, the user is requested to confirm the results. There may have been some errors in assigning content types to objects and after selecting the latter the user indicates the correct type. He states so the way he wants the information to be coded. For instance, the distinction between graphical objects, coded as graphical primitives, and too complex objects coded as bilevel raster graphics, is relatively arbitrary and the user may change the automatically taken decision. Graphical primitive coding may corrupt the original information or yield a less efficient data compression in very specific cases. Changing the coding implies either that the geometric recognition module has to be applied or on the contrary that the information has to be coded as bilevel raster graphics without approximation.

The last interaction level consists in correcting the recognition results. Because only the graphical objects are submitted to a recognition module, possible errors can be corrected editing the erroneous contents via the Geometric Editor.

8. CONCLUSION

In this paper, a system for changing a paper document to a standardized electronic form has been introduced.

Many researches are being carried out throughout the world on the automatic document analysis (see for instance [15], [16], [17]) but only sub-systems are marketed. Among them are the Optical Character Readers which recognize different fonts and possibly discard graphical parts as well as graphic analysers which recognize some basic graphical objects. The latter are often restricted to specific documents such as electronic diagrams.

Our system is being developed. A first stand-alone version offering the main functionalities has been implemented. The segmentation and recognition steps are still studied: some segmentation rules are likely to be refined, the level of recognized graphical objects may be improved. However, major improvements relate to the available a-priori information and involve more specific modules than enhancements of the present system. For instance, semantic information on the document content (e.g specifying if this is an electronic diagram or an architect map) improves the possible understanding level.

In a longer-term step, recognizing the logical structure of a document whose class is known could be attempted. More ambitious objectives are to recognize the class of the scanned document among a set of pre-defined classes or even to derive a class definition from a set of scanned documents.

REFERENCES

[1] ECMA 101 Standard. June 1985; ISO DP / 8613

[2] CGM Computer Graphics Metafile ISO / DIS 8632

[3] **OHTA Y.I., KANADE T., SAKAI T.** "Color information for region segmentation" in *Computer Graphics and Image Processing*, vol. 13, no.3, pp. 222-241, 1980.

[4] **POSTL W.** "Halftone Recognition by an Experimental Text and Facsimile Workstation" in *Proceedings of the 6th Conference on Pattern Recognition*, Munich, Germany, Oct. 1982, pp. 489-491.

[5] **KITTLER J.** and **ILLINGWORTH J.** "Minimum error thresholding", in *Pattern Recognition*, vol. 19, no. 1, pp. 41-47, 1986.

[6] **WHITE J.M.** and **RHORER G.D.** "Image thresholding for optical character recognition and other applications requiring character image extraction" in *IBM Journal of Research and Development*, vol. 27, no. 4, July 1983, pp. 400-411.

[7] **NADLER M.** "Survey of Document Segmentation and Coding Techniques" in *Computer Vision, Graphics, and Image Processing*, vol. 28, pp. 240-262, 1984.

[8] **CEDERBERG R.L.T.** "Chain-link code and segmentation for raster scan devices" in *Computer Graphics and Image Processing*, vol. 10, pp. 224-234, 1979.

[9] **HARRIS J.F., KITTLER J., LLWELLYN B., PRESTON G.** "A modular system for interpreting binary pixel representations of line-structured data" in *Pattern Recognition Theory and Applications*, edited by J. Kittler, K.S. Fu and L.F. Pau, D. Reidel Publishing Company, pp. 311-351, 1982.

[10] **GROEN F.C.A., van MUNSTER R.J.** "Topology-based analysis of schematic diagrams" in *Proceedings of 7th International Joint Conference on Pattern Recognition*, Montreal, vol. 2, pp. 1310-1312, 1984.

[11] **LANDY M.S., COHEN Y.** "Vector graph coding; efficient coding of line drawings" in *Computer Vision, Graphics and Image Processing*, vol. 30, pp. 331-344, 1985.

[12] **TOMBRE K.** "Segmentation and line extraction for recognition and coding of graphical parts in a document" in *Proceedings of International Seminar on Symbol Recognition*, Oslo, Norway, 1985.

[13] **CUGINI U., FERRI G., MUSSIO P., PROTTI P.** "Pattern-directed restoration and vectorization of digitized engineering drawings" in *Computers and Graphics*, vol. 8, N. 4, pp. 337-350, 1984.

[14] **WALL K., DANIELSSON P.** "A fast sequential method for polygonal approximation of digitized curves" in *Computer Vision, Graphics and Image Processing*, vol. 28, pp. 220-227, 1984.

[15] **DOSTER W.** "Different states of a document's content on its way from the Gutenbergian world to the electronic world" in *Proceedings of 7th International Joint Conference on Pattern Recognition*, Montreal, pp. 872-874, 1984.

[16] **MAKINO H.** "Representation and segmentation of document images" in *Proceedings of the Computer Vision and Pattern Recognition Conference*, Washington D.C., pp. 291-295, 1983.

[17] **WAHL F.M., WONG K.Y., CASEY R.G.** "Block segmentation and text extraction in mixed text/image documents" in *Computer Graphics and Image Processing*, vol. 20, pp. 375-390, 1982.

OFFICE SYSTEMS: Methods and Tools
G. Bracchi, D. Tsichritzis (Editors)
Elsevier Science Publishers B.V. (North-Holland)
© IFIP, 1987

AN INTERACTIVELY FORMATTING DOCUMENT EDITOR BASED ON THE STANDARDISED OFFICE DOCUMENT ARCHITECTURE

W. Horak, G. Krönert

SIEMENS AG, Munich
Private Communication Systems and Networks Division

ECMA ratified its standard ECMA 101 "Office document architecture" in June 1985. Based on this standard the paper presents system concepts and intermediate results of an ongoing prototype implementation performed by SIEMENS in cooperation with other European partners in an ESPRIT project funded by the CEC, since autumn 1983. Part of the project is an interactively and incrementally formatting document editor, which is controlled by document classes.

1. INTRODUCTION

International standards committees are currently making great efforts to draw up standards that will enable to interchange between open systems processable documents containing character text, data in tables, geometric graphic images and raster graphic images. Specifically the ISO (International Organization for Standardization), the CCITT (International Telegraph and Telephone Consultative Comittee) and the ECMA (European Computer Manufacturers Association) are working on a frame work with a series of parts that describe an office document architecture (ODA), content architectures for several content types, an office document processing model, a document profile, an office document interchange format (ODIF) and conformance combinations.

In September 1985 ECMA issued its standard ECMA 101 "Office Document Architecture" /1/ which covers above parts including two content architectures, one for character text and one for photographic (i.e. raster graphic) content. Corresponding parts are going to be issued as ISO DIS 8613 in April 1986 /2/. Additions regarding data, tables and geometric graphics are under development.

Since 1982 the authors have been working in the ODA standardization /3, 4, 5, 6/ and since autumn 1983 they have been leading the ESPRIT project 121 "handling of mixed text/image/voice documents based on a standardized office document architecture" /7/. ESPRIT is the acronym for the "European Strategic Programme of Research and Development in Information Technology" initiated and sponsored by the Commission of the European Communities. The main goal of project 121 is to design and prototype, till October 1987, cooperative tools for a userfriendly handling of ODA conforming documents at office workstations. The project is evaluating the ODA standard and will contribute to the further development of the document and content architectures in ECMA, ISO and CCITT. The partners in this project are SIEMENS (Munich) as prime contractor, TITN (Traitement de l'Information Techniques Nouvelles, Paris) as second contractor and QMC (Queen Mary College) Industrial Research Ltd. (London) besides CRIN (Centre de Recherche Informatique de Nancy) as subcontractors.

In spring 1986 an additional ESPRIT project is going to complement the tasks of project 121. In this project, called "Piloting of ODA "(PODA), SIEMENS, Bull, ICL, Olivetti and TITN will be the partners in order to promote and evaluate ODA.

2. COMPONENTS OF THE PROJECT

The project comprises the four main components shown in Figure 1:

The *Common User Interface* provides uniform access to all other components. It uses a bit mapped high resolution screen with multiple display windows, menues, icons and a mouse as pointing device. It is mainly tool-based, i.e. the user picks up an icon of a tool, e.g. an eraser, and applies it to an object. But for some operations the menu-based approach seems to be more suitable. The semantics of the tools is application-independent, which makes for consistency and predictivity (see section 6).

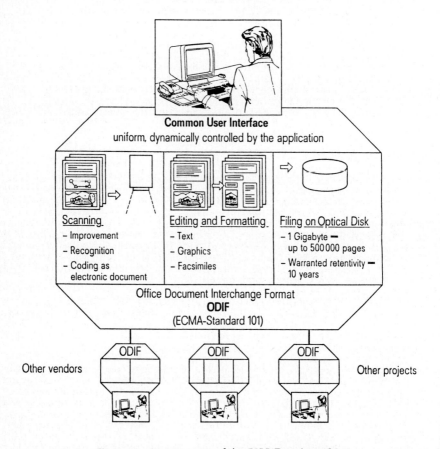

Figure 1: Components of the ESPRIT project 121

The *ODA-Document Editor* is for the interactive editing and automatic layout of electronic documents whose content contains a mixture of characters, geometric graphics and raster graphics. It is controlled by ODA Document Class Descriptions. Depending on the document class loaded, it transforms into a specialized report editor, order form editor, business letter editor, etc. Routine tasks, such as layout generation, chapter numbering or insertion of standard paragraphs and logos, are performed automatically. The architecture of the editor is derived from ODA. It is described in section 5.

The *Document Archiver* is for the long-term filing of mixed electronic documents on a digital optical disk as replacement of conventional filing cabinets. The GIGADISC of THOMSON-ALCATEL is used. It has a capacity of 2 Gigabyte with a warranted retentivity of 10 years.

The *Automated Document Entry* (ADE) /8/ closes the gap between paper documents and electronic documents. It has to convert printed information into an electronic format which can be displayed, edited, archived and printed again. The ADE can either be used in close cooperation with the editor in order to capture the content of single figures or paragraphs during document preparation (see section 6) or to capture the entire structure and content of sequences of printed pages.

All components are implemented on SUN II workstations of SUN Microsystems with UNIX 4.2 bsd, C and Objective-C (see section 5.3).

By the following the document editor is described in more detail preceded by a short description of ODA and of its processing model .

3. DOCUMENT ARCHITECTURE MODEL

3.1 Document structures, objects and content portions

Any given document is characterized by its *content* and its internal organization. The content consists of *graphic elements* such as graphic characters, control characters geometric elements and photographic elements ODA distinguishes between a document's *logical structure* and its *layout structure* The logical structure associates the content of the document with a hierarchy of *logical objects*, whereas the layout structure associates the same content with a hierarchy of *layout objects*. Examples of logical objects are summaries, titles, sections, paragraphs, figures, tables, etc. Examples of layout objects are pages, columns and areas with contents of different categories. Both structures are tree structures.

Objects have attributes which specify *properties* such as the dimensions of layout objects, or they may also express *relationships* among objects There are, for example, attributes of logical objects, which control the mapping from the logical structure to the layout structure (layout process). About 40 attribute types are standardised in ODA.

The architectural model distinguishes between composite objects and basic objects. *Composite objects* consist of components that may be other composite objects and/or basic objects. *Basic objects* are at the lowest hierarchical levels, and it is only through them that *content portions* are directly associated. In other words, the content of a document is structured from two sides, the logical structure and the layout structure.

Depending on the category of their graphic elements, each content portion is structured and presented according to a certain *content architecture*. A content architecture defines presentation attributes of basic objects as well as the set of graphic elements and control functions with their coded representation. ECMA 101 currently defines a *character content architecture* and a *photographic content architecture.*

Each object in the interchanged data stream is represented at least by the attributes "object identifier" and "object type" The *object type* assigns additional attributes that may be applied to objects of that type ODA distinguishes the logical object types "document logical root", "composite logical object", and "basic logical object".The layout object types are "document layout root", "page set", " page", "frame", and "block".

An object of the "page set" type may consist of a title page and continuation pages, either having different layout areas. Frames define boundaries within a page for the layout of the content. For example, frames can represent header, column, and footer areas.

Blocks are created by the layout process within lowest level frames . All frames and blocks are positioned relative to the coordinate system of their immediately superior object and are entirely contained within the area of that object.Within a page, frames and blocks may be positioned in such a way that they intersect partially or fully.

3.2 Object classes and document classes

Objects of the same type with additional common characteristics can be subgrouped into *object classes*. Logical object classes with objects of the "basic logical object" type are, e.g., the classes "paragraph", "footnote" and "figure title". Layout object classes of the "frame" type are, e.g., the classes "header frame", "column frame" and "footer frame"

Object classes can be defined by the application by means of *object class descriptions*. Object class descriptions can be perceived as a set of rules (grammar), or as templates according to which document structures can be produced. Object class descriptions contain attribute evaluation rules, which specify, in the form of constant or variable expressions, property rules, relation rules, content rules and construction rules.

Content rules specify *generic content portions*, which have either predefined content portions or define by means of content generators how content can be derived. Predefined content portions are the content portions of logos .Content generators are expressions to produce page numbers or section numbers.

Construction rules are expressed by the attribute "generator for suborddinates" and they occur only in composite object definitions. They define for the objects of the class concerned, (1) the object classes to which their constituents may belong, and (2) possible sequences in which these constituents may occur in the document structure. Construction rules are represented by expressions that allow distinct sequences, arbitrary sequences , options, and repetitions to be specified

Relation rules are expressed by the attribute "layout object class", which specifies the object class of the instance into which the content is to be layed out, and the attribute pair "layout category" and "permitted layout category", which have as value a name and express that matching names establish the mapping relation.

Similar documents can be grouped into a *document class*. Document classes are classes such as "business letter", "report", "memo","order form". Like object classes, document classes are not standardized. They can be defined by the application by means of *document class descriptions*. A document class description has to contain the object class descriptions for all objects which are allowed to occur in a document of that class.

Attributes which control the automatic generation of the layout structure are gathered in *layout styles*. Attributes which control the presentation of objects are gathered in *presentation styles*. These document styles can be regarded as composite attributes and can be referred from object class descriptions as one unit.

Figure 2 shows the overall document architecture model. The *document profile* contains information for handling the document as a whole. It consists of a set of attributes, that specifies the author, the issue date, which kind of content, structures and definitions are present in the document etc.

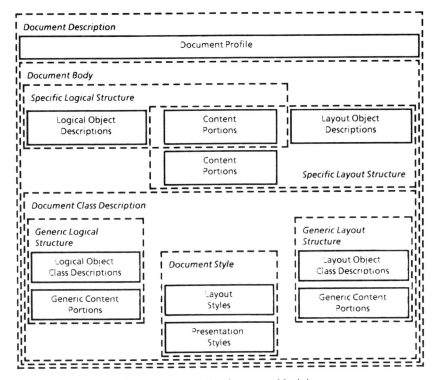

Fig 2: Document Architecture Model

4. DOCUMENT PROCESSING MODEL

Figure 3 illustrates how the different parts of ODA can be involved in document processing. Three main processes are distinguished:

The *editing process* comprises "content editing" and "logical structure editing". Structure editing includes creating or deleting an object, changing its position in the structure, and modifying values of property and relational attributes controlled by the generic logical structure. Content editing comprises adding or deleting graphic elements and control functions. The results of editing steps are the input for the automatic layout process.

The *layout process* comprises "layout structure generation" and "content layout". Both processes cooperate like co-routines. The basic principle of the "layout structure generation" is that the logical tree structure is traversed in pre-order and simultaneously is built up in pre-order a layout tree structure, which is correct in the sense of the generic layout structure. This generation process is driven by the attributes in the layout styles. The "content layout" fills the content into the empty blocks, which are generated as leaves of the layout tree structure. This may lead to the situation that the "content layout" requires again empty blocks from the "layout structure generation".

The *imaging process* maps the layout structure onto a physical presentation medium (paper, screen) and creates an image of the blocks's content elements controlled by

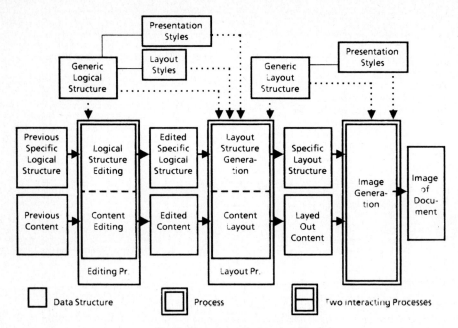

Fig. 3: Document Processing Model

the presentation attributes of the blocks and the control functions embedded in the content.

Manual intervention is taken into account by the model only for editing the content and the logical structure, even though editing of the layout structure and the definitions is possible.

Figure 4 details the layout process by an example:

The order of the layout process in which content portions are poured into frames building up blocks is determined by the pre-order of the logical objects in the logical structure tree.

Starting with the top level logical object the layout attribute "layout object class " is applied which references the "report page set" definition. A layout object of the class "report page set" is created and the first element in the sequence construction of the "generator for subordinate objects" in the "page set" definition is evaluated. This creates via the "title page" definition a layout object of the corresponding class. The generation process is continued till the first lowest level frame is generated into which the content of the first basic logical object has to be poured. It is a "header frame" which has an attribute "layout categories" specifying the layout category "1". Only those content portions of basic logical objects can be poured into this frame, which are subordinate to logical objects with an attruibute "required layout category" specifying the same layout category.

Walking down the logical tree from the root at the first possible path and searching for a matching layout category delivers the "heading" whose subordinates can now be laid out within the "header frame". Reentering the logical tree walk leads to a stop at "section 1" with the layout category "2". A new frame is needed and therefore the generation process at the layout side moves on one step. It produces a specific logical structure   generic layout structure

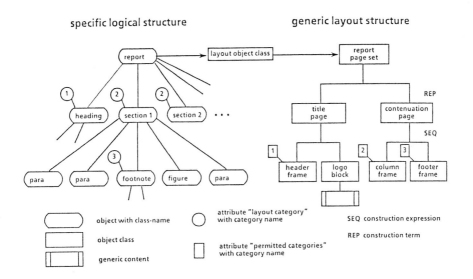

Figure 4: Layout Process Example

"logo block", which has already a predefined content, and moves on to evaluate the second element in the sequence construction of the "page set" definition. This produces the first "continuation page" and finally the next lowest level frame which has a layout category specified matching to that at the logical side. Now the sub-tree rooted at "section 1" can be laid out within the "column frame"

5.THE ODA DOCUMENT EDITOR

5.1 Requirements

Requirements to an ODA document editor can be derived from both, the ODA model and a WYSIWYG (what you see is what you get) design. These requirements shape the editor's architecture.

ODA determines the functional power and thus the steps involved in processing a document. But it is to design whether the editor is of the interactively formatting type or has a post-connected batch formatter.

Since to both, the logical objects and the layout objects, attributes can be attached, the document structures can be regarded as attributed trees. Editing involves generation or modification of the logical structure This requires an *editor for the logical structure*. The layout structure is generated or modified during the automatic layout process and can - to a certain extent - be manipulated by the user in a layout revision process. This requires an *editor for the layout structure*.

Depending on the content type characters, geometric graphics, or photographics, the basic objects have their own internal structure defined by the content architecture. A corresponding *content editor* must therefore exist for every content architecture accepted by the document editor. These editors manipulate the content elements of basic logical objects and position them within blocks, whose dimensions are also

294 W. Horak and G. Krönert

calculated by the content editors. This requires them to cooperate with the structure editors.

ODA regards each document as a member of a document class. From this follows that an ODA editor must be *adaptable to document classes*. This resembles syntax-controlled editors for programming languages. However, these editors have to process only one hierarchical structure, whereas the ODA editor has to process the two coupled structures. This is a unique feature. By reading in the document class description the ODA editor is transformed into a tailored tool which relieves the user of many class specific routine jobs. The editor thus becomes, for instance, a report editor, a business letter editor, an order form editor, etc. An ODA document class description consists of the definition of logical object classes and of layout object classes. Such an object class description consists of a set of rules which determine how the structure trees have to be built up and attributed correctly.

The *WYSIWYG principle* ideally requires that the layout of an edited document part and of its displayed environment, e.g. the page, is updated after each editing step.Normally, a lot of effort is necessary to achieve this. Therefore, existing document editors are either logically oriented with a post-connected batch processing process, or they are layout oriented and show after editing steps only the new layout of the page, which may get an arbitrary length. Pagination is only done on a special user command, because it is a time-consuming operation. In order to effect real WYSIWYG characteristics in an acceptable period of time, a refined document layout strategy is necessary:

The layout effort can be reduced considerably by the concept of incremental layout. It involves layout updates only of those parts which really require it. I.e pages may only be given new numbers or entire blocks may only be shifted. Since the layout structure is held in the ODA editor as an attributed tree, incremental layout essentially means that a correct attributing for the layout structure tree is calculated Standard procedures /9,10/ are available for this.

After completing an incremental layout process, the entire document is laid out in a valid way. However, usually the user can see only a part of the document on his screen, so that during editing it would be sufficient if only this part were validly laid out. This consideration leads to *delayed incremental layout*. After an editing step only the displayed environment is laid out consistently and the rest of the layout objects remain possibly invalidly attributed. An editing step is now immediately permissible again, and is followed by the same action. In pauses between not immediately following editing steps incremental formatting is carried out step-by-step for the rest of the layout objects until either the entire document is validly laid out or the user again initiates an editing operation. Thus the layout process fully utilizes the computing time not occupied by the editing process and hinders the user's editing speed as little as possible. Only at the end of the editing session the document needs to be laid out completely to allow printing.

5.2 Editor architecture

Above requirements defined already the outline of the editor's architecture as shown in Figure 5 /11/. The interchange format (ODIF) of a document consists mainly of three parts, the profile, the definition part and the object part. The definition part is used for the automatic adaption of the document editor. This is done in the following way:

From the definition part, two attributed grammars are derived, one for the control of the logical structure editor and one for the control of the layout structure editor. Roughly speaking, these attributed grammars are generated by filling in attributes of the definition part into templates for attributed productions. These templates are derived once from the ODA processing model and can be used then for every transformation of the ODIF definition part into the pair of attributed grammars.

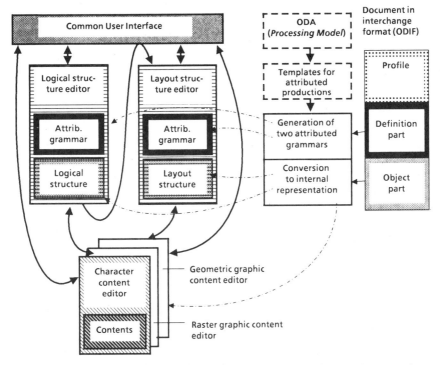

Figure 5: Architecture of an ODA document editor and internalization of interchanged documents

After each change in the logical structure, e.g. insertion or deletion of a figure, the logical structure editor executes semantic functions of the attributed grammar which result in instructions to the editor for the layout structure.

After the layout structure editor has generated or modified the corresponding layout object or objects, the layout structure tree is, in general, inconsistently attributed. The calculation for consistent attributing is now activated in line with the strategy of delayed layout. The layout structure editor and the content editors have to cooperate in this process and exchange attribute values, similarly to scanners and parsers in compilers. If the layout of a basic logical object has to be recalculated, the layout structure editor passes the maximum dimensions for a block to the content editor as an inherited attribute. The content editor then fills the logical object's content elements into this available area and thereby generates the actual block dimensions which are returned as a synthesized attribute to the layout structure editor. An analogous interaction occurs during content editing.

In this project three content editors exist for character text, geometric graphics and raster graphics. In another ESPRIT project 1024, called PODA (Piloting of ODA), components complementary to this project will be implemented, such as a data content editor (also for spreadsheets), a voice content editor or another independent tool, a document class definition editor for the production of document class definitions.

5.3 Status of the prototype implementation

The framework of the editor prototype is implemented in the Smalltalk-like programming language Objective-C. I.e. all interfaces between the components are programmed in Objective-C. Inside of the components, conventional programming languages, like C or Fortran, or again Objective-C can be used. The two structure editors and the editor for character content are programmed completely in Objective-C. The editor for graphics is partly implemented in C, since the Graphical Kernel System (GKS) on which this editor is based is written in C. The combination of C programs and Objective-C programs is easy, because a pre-compiler translates Objective-C to C.

Since Objective-C is an object-oriented programming language, programming in Objective-C means specification of classes. A class defintion consists of class variables, class methods and the declaration of instance variables and instance methods. During run time instances of these classes are generated. Each instance possesses its own set of instance variables, as they are declared in the corresponding class definition, and each instance accepts and performs each of the instance methods, which are specified in the corresponding class defintion. Class variables exist only once in the class and class methods can only be sent to the class and not to its instances. An example of a class method may be "new object", and when it is sent to the class, then the class generates an new instance of this class. Classes can be defined in a hierarchy, i.e. a class may have a "super class" or "subclasses".

In this hierarchy a class inherits all variables and methods of its superclass, however it is possible to overwrite such inherited methods.

Figure 6 shows the structure of a document represented by instances of different classes. Each instance may refer to other instances, which enables to express the document structures. The implementation of the Document Handler is the programming of the corresponding classes. Because of clearness, classes are collected to class groups in this figure.

For each document exists an instance of a class representing document descriptors. Such an instance has references to the top of the logical structure, to the top of the layout structure, to a set of instances of classes, which are used for the representation of ODA object definitions, and a set of instances for the representation of fonts. The instances for the ODA object definitions are generated during adaption time and contain the attributed productions, which are derived from the ODIF definition part, i.e. each such instance corresponds to an ODA object class definition.

The class groups for logical and layout objects contain for each ODA object type a corresponding Objective-C class. The instance variables of such a class express all attributes which can be attached to an ODA object of that type. The attribute evaluation is performed by a cooperation of these instances and the instances representing ODA object definitions, i.e. by performing methods and interchanging messages.

One of the attributes attached to basic objects is a reference to a descriptor of its content portion(s). The content can be accessed by two ways, namely from a logical point of view and from a layout point of view. The instances representing these descriptors can be regarded as the interfaces between the structure editors and the content editors.

6. USER BENEFITS - A SCENARIO

This chapter gives an impression, how the user can work with the document editor. The basic concept of the common user interface is that objects, like an archive, a document, a chapter, etc., are displayed on the screen together with icons representing tools, such as an eraser, a keyboard, a brush etc. The user may now pick

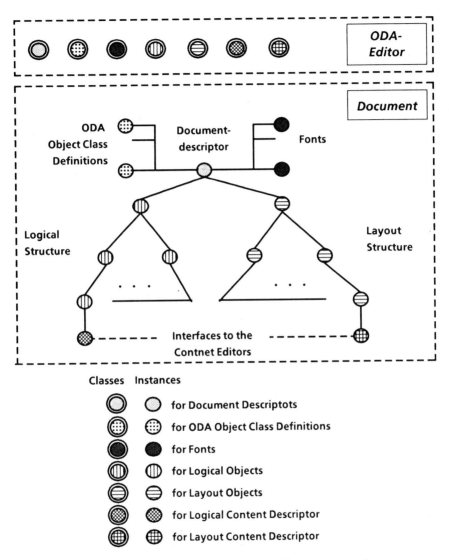

Classes   Instances

○ for Document Descriptots
⊕ for ODA Object Class Definitions
● for Fonts
⊕ for Logical Objects
⊖ for Layout Objects
⊛ for Logical Content Descriptor
⊕ for Layout Content Descriptor

Fig. 6: Objective-C implementation of the document editor

up a tool by pointing at it and selecting it via a mouse and apply it to an object, to a range explanation of an object or to a sequence of objects, just as he is used to do it on his desk. For some operations, however, as selecting an alternative, a menu-oriented approach will be prefered.

Let us assume, the user starts his work by opening the document archive and putting a document from there onto his desk in order to prepare it. Assume that the document is a not yet finished report. The document is shown to the user in two display windows (Figure 7): The "partial view" window shows a part of the document with its content

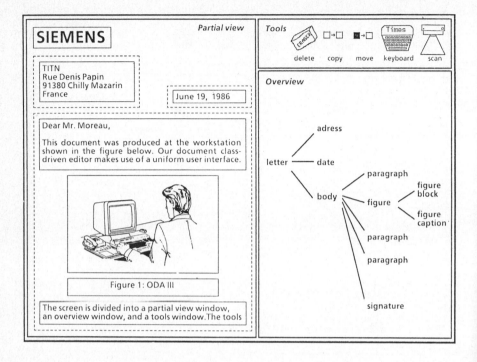

Figure 7:   User Interface: Examples of tools and document representation

laid out according to WYSIWYG as for printing. The "overview window" provides a representation of the logical structure of the document, either in a tree form or as a structured "contents list"..

Assume the user wants to move the already existing second chapter, which consists of 12 pages, behind the fourth chapter. In a conventional WYSIWYG editor, the user has to mark in the content stream the beginning of the chapter, then to scroll through the 12 pages and to mark the end of the chapter. After this selection, the user may move this content range, which corresponds to the second chapter, behind the content of the fourth chapter. Now the chapters are in the desired order, but the chapter numbers and subchapter numbers have to be renumbered manually. With the described ODA document editor it is much easier: By means of the "mouse" the user selects in the overview window the second chapter, which is represented there either as a node of a hierarchical tree or as an entry in a table of contents, and moves it behind the node or entry of the fourth chapter in the overview window. He has not to worry about renumbering, which is done automatically. Immediately after the editing step, the user may check the new layout caused by his editing step in the partial view window.

Now the user wants to append a paragraph at the end of the third chapter. For this reason he selects the last paragraph of the third chapter and calls for a new logical object by applying the "new-object-tool". Now the document editor provides a menue with a list of all logical objects which may be inserted at this location. This list depends on the construction rules of the current document class and the selected object. In our case the document belongs to the class "report". This class, for example, may be defined, such that the list consists of 'paragraph', 'figure' and 'chapter head'. The user now selects the 'paragraph', because he don't want to insert a chapter, neither a figure. The "new-object-tool" guides the user and assures that the document structure created is consistent with the document class.

Assume that the user wants now to insert a photo from a journal between two existing paragraphs of his report. He selects the preceding paragraph and applies the "new-object- tool", which now shows only two alternatives, namely 'paragraph' and figure'. The user selects 'figure'. This causes an iconographic display of two tool sets, one for the creation of geometric graphic objects and one for the creation of rastergraphic objects. The user selects the rastergraphic tool set, which causes the single tools of the set to be displayed to him. It is a "brush tool" for manual cration of rastergraphics and a "scan tool". The user selects the "scan tool" and after a request on the screen he puts the journals page on the flat bed scanner: The page is scanned and displayed in the overview window. In this overview facsimile the user selects the rectangular area containing the photo. Depending on the nature of the selected area's content, which is analysed by the entry system and may be of type bilevel, halftone or multilevel, the content is appropriately encoded and forwarded to the raster graphic content editor. It is then automatically zoomed into the column between the two paragraphs by the raster graphic content editor's layout process. If, because of a close column or page boundary, there is not enough space for the photo, after the preceding paragraph, the photo may be placed on top of the next column or page and the remaining space on the preceding column or page may be filled with content of the succeeding paragraph.If now the user applies the "new-object-tool", a figure caption object is instantiated and the user may type its content after having selected the keyboard tool.

Internally, operation is characterized by the fact that the user interface is separate and independent of the application.

Because the user interface is independent of the application programs, all objects which are to display the user interface on the screen must be sent to the user interface by the application as so-called display objects. The user interface incorporates received logical objects or layout objects into the corresponding display object tree These display object trees correspond to the part of the ODA layout structure or logical structure that is currently visible, and they are administered by the user interface. Modifications to a structure result in the application for modified objects sending corresponding display objects to the user interface so that this can bring the display object tree up to date. Display objects themselves have methods by which they can represent themselves on the screen. These methods use what are termed display primitives which are provided by the user interface.

If the user wants to apply an operation on a display object, the user interface asks the object "behind" it in the application if this operation is allowed, or which operations can be used. If the user has selected an allowed operation, the user interface sends the relevant message to the application object which performs the operation itself. Following the operation, display objects are again sent to the user interface informing it of the resultant modifications.

REFERENCES

/1/ ECMA: Standard ECMA-101, Office Document Architecture, September 1985

/2/ ISO/TC 97/SC 18/WG 3: ISO/DP 8613
     Information processing - Text and office systems - Document structures
     Part 1:General Introduction
     Part 2:Office Document Architecture
     Part 3:Document Layout and Imaging Process
     Part 4:Document Profile
     Part 5:Office Document Interchange Format
     Part 6:Character Content Architectures

/3/ Horak, W.: "Interchanging mixed text image documents in the office environment", Comput. & Graphics Vol, 7, No. 1, pp. 13-29, 1983

/4/ Horak, W.; Krönert, G.: "An object oriented office document architecture model for document interchange between open systems", Proceedings of GLOBECOM '83, San Diego, November 1983, pp. 1245-1249

/5/ Horak, W.: "Concepts of the document interchange protocol for the Telematic Services-CCITT Draft Recommondation S.a", Computer Networks 8 (1984), pp. 175-185

/6/ Horak, W.: "Office Document Architecture and Office Document Interchange Formats: Current Status of International Standardization", Computer, October 1985, pp 50-60

/7/ Horak, W.; Tartanson, F.; Coulouris, G.: "Handling of mixed text/image/voice documents based on a standardized office document architecture", ESPRIT 1984 Conference, Brussels, North-Holland, pp. 395-410

/8/ Meynieux, E.; Postl, W.; Seisen, S.; Tombre, K.: Office Paper Document Analysis, in this proceedings

/9/ Kennedy, K.; Warren, S.K.: "Automatic Generation of Efficient Evaluators for Attributed Grammars," Conf. Record of 3rd ACM Symp. on Principles of Programming Languages, pp. 32-49, 1976.

/10/ Möncke, U.; Weisgerber, B.; Wilhelm, R.: "How to Implement a System for Manipulation of Attributed Trees," 8th Professional Congress "Programmiersprachen und Programmentwicklung", Informatik Fachberichte, Vol.77, pp. 112-117, Springer, 1984

/11/ Krönert, G.; Friedrich, J.; Schneider, U.; Lauber, G.: "Requirements on a Formatting Document Editor based on the ECMA Standard 101", ESPRIT Technical Week '85, Brussels, North Holland

OFFICE SYSTEMS: Methods and Tools
G. Bracchi, D. Tsichritzis (Editors)
Elsevier Science Publishers B.V. (North-Holland)
© IFIP, 1987

INDIVIDUAL NEGOTIATION SUPPORT IN GROUP DSS

Rajan SRIKANTH and Matthias JARKE

Graduate School of Business Administration, New York University
90 Trinity Place, New York, NY 10006, USA

Fachbereich Informatik, Johann Wolfgang Goethe - Universitaet
Dantestr. 9, 6000 Frankfurt 11, West Germany

Abstract. Multiperson decision support systems can be viewed as the decision-level component of office information systems. Negotiation support is an important task of such systems. Besides mechanisms for representing and evolving group joint problem representations, such DSS should also provide an environment in which decision makers are supported in developing, analyzing and reinforcing their individual negotiation position. Recognizing the diversity of research approaches to negotiation modelling in the literature, this paper synthesizes an integrated model from which a knowledge-based individual negotiation support environment using tools from different areas can be designed. Role and architecture of such a component are described in the context of MEDIATOR, a database-centered negotiation support system under development at NYU.

1. INTRODUCTION

In an increasingly complex and turbulent business environment, decision makers will have to rely more and more on advances in information/communication technology for support [Huber and McDaniel, 1986]. While traditional single-user decision support systems (DSS) help explicate individual decision makers' problem views, thus improving managerial communication, modern office communication technology [Tsichritzis, 1985] can serve as a vehicle to support multiperson decisions more directly.

A number of researchers have begun to study the design and potential impact of so-called Group DSS [Gray, 1981; Huber, 1982; Turoff and Hiltz, 1982; Bui and Jarke, 1984; DeSanctis and Gallupe, 1985; Goncalves, 1985]. Knowledge sharing and negotiation support in different time/space organizational settings have emerged as critical goals of such systems [Jarke, 1986]. While knowledge sharing refers to the cooperative aspects of GDSS, negotiation support is needed where there is a conflict of interests.

The MEDIATOR project at New York University attempts to integrate both of these aspects into a comprehensive DSS architecture for multiperson decision making that is

302   R. Srikanth and M. Jarke

not necessarily cooperative. A common static framework for knowledge sharing and negotiation protocols is achieved by a specialized database architecture [Jarke et al., 1986]. Process aspects of multiperson decision making are embedded into a framework of evolutionary systems design [Shakun, 1981]. MEDIATOR offers two kinds of negotiation support components: group negotiation support for integrating individual positions into a group decision, and individual negotiation support for each party to defend its position. The former has the main purpose of achieving a common representation of the problem and then evolving this representation through consensus-seeking (via problem redefinition) and compromise (via concession making) towards a jointly acceptable agreement. Since communication is the main goal, a relatively simple mutually understandable language must be used for the joint problem representation.

In contrast, an individual negotiation support component has to provide a rich set of tools for analyzing the decision makers' perceptions of their own as well as their opponents' bargaining position. This requires an understanding of the mechanics and dynamics of the cognitive aspects of the negotiation process. Each of the many research areas that have contributed to our understanding of negotiations has modeled this problem in its own idiosyncratic way. Unfortunately, none of the approaches represent the full richness of negotiation processes and outcomes. This paper is an attempt to integrate major contributions of several disciplines into a unified model of negotiations that in turn serves as the basis for the design of a knowledge-based individual negotiation support environment within the MEDIATOR architecture. While we cannot claim to have developed a comprehensive *theory* of negotiations, we at least expect to provide a model for a uniform *systems environment* in which tools from different areas can be applied. Future work will have to show to what degree general theories can be developed from the integrated model.

This paper is organized as follows. Section 2 reviews the contributions of six reference disciplines with respect to their potential usefulness in individual negotiation support. Section 3 presents the integrated model along with two examples, and provides some justification by mapping the approaches taken by each area into it. Section 4 provides a brief overview of the MEDIATOR architecture and describes a knowledge-based design for its individual negotiation support component based on the integrated model. In section 5, relationships to other GDSS, potential application areas, limitations and future plans are discussed.

2. APPROACHES TO UNDERSTANDING NEGOTIATIONS

Negotiations are a part of everyday life. Whenever there is disagreement or conflict of interest between two or more parties, they negotiate. However, negotiations vary substantially in their fundamental characteristics like the underlying motivation, the nature of the relationship between and within the parties, the specific features of the issue under negotiation, and the negotiation process itself (see [Raiffa, 1982] for a detailed analysis).

Theories to explain the negotiation process have been proposed by researchers from different disciplines, including Game Theory (bargaining), Economics (decision making under uncertainty), Process Analysis (joint decision-making process), Sociology, Industrial Relations (collective bargaining), Politics (international negotiations, terrorism, etc.) and, Psychology (behavioral styles and negotiation strategies, etc.). It is the purpose of this section to summarize major contributions of these areas as far as they appear to be related to the goal of designing a negotiation support system. In doing so, we shall compare the approaches on their: *focus* of attention - what parts of the negotiation process they seek to describe, *level of analysis* or detail, *realism* or extent of simplifying and limiting assumptions, and *determinancy* or prescriptive power.

2.1. Game Theory - Bargaining

Game theory attempts to model negotiation behavior as a rational-choice, self-interested behavior toward a given array of values. It is primarily geared toward analyzing the decision "to negotiate or not to".

Elementary game theory assumes two parties, or organized collectivities, making choices from among a set of alternatives to reach an agreement. The set of all alternative courses of action open to both "bargainers", the relation between each possible pair of actions chosen and the bargaining outcomes, and the utilities assigned to these outcomes, are assumed to be known to both bargainers. The pattern of demands and concessions was shown to lead to an agreement which maximizes the product of the utilities of the two bargainers [Nash, 1950, 1953; Zeuthen, 1930].

Harsanyi [1956] suggested the concept of "maximum risk of no agreement" to explain the process by which the Nash outcomes were reached. This introduced considerations of uncertainties and probability into the bargaining process. Harsanyi [1962], extended this method to cases where the two parties "do not know (and know that they do not know) each other's utility function (preferences and attitudes towards risk)". This, he suggested, leads to "compounded expectations" which converge by two mechanisms: the usage of "stereotype utility functions" and the process of mutual "adjustment" of expectations as bargaining proceeds.

The implications of no agreement or "stalemate" on the bargaining process were studied by Schelling [1963] and later on by a host of others. Schelling pointed out that the time required to reach an agreement was costly to (both) bargainers and that this cost was an important factor in determining the final outcome. Bishop [1964] introduced "discount rates" to model concession making behavior and suggested that the bargainer with the lower discount rate has the bargaining advantage. Cross [1969] developed a detailed theory for the implications of this "time cost" on bargaining. He suggested that each bargainer chooses the demand that maximizes present value, discounted according to the time it would take to get it. An important contribution of this work was the concept of disproportional effects of the bargaining process on the two bargainers because of subjective estimates and asymmetric information.

After Harsanyi [1962], Cross was the first to revitalize the concept of "learning" in the game by suggesting that the bargainers perceptions of their own time costs --and expectations about their opponent's-- evolve in response to bargaining behavior and its consequences. Bargaining can be visualized as the process of reducing and eliminating the gap between the final outcomes estimated by the two participants on the basis of their perceptions of their relative bargaining strengths. Harsanyi [1967-68] tackles the problem of uncertainty about the pay-offs for the opponent by proposing that each bargainer actually imagines that he is faced by a probability distribution of different types of bargainers --each with characteristic pay-offs-- and bases his strategy on the expected value. He also uses estimates of his opponent's expectations about him. In [Harsanyi, 1972, 1976; Harsanyi and Selten, 1972], a two-person bargaining game with incomplete information is reinterpreted as an n-person Bayesian game. Selten [1975] notes: "the dynamics of the bargaining process appear to be a vehicle for credible exchange of information". Limiting assumptions that each of these theories makes are discussed in [Crawford, 1985].

Research on non-cooperative games and dynamic game theory takes a slightly different approach. Rao and Shakun [1974] model concession-making as a sequential decision problem and develop a dynamic programming model to solve it. Going one step further, Shakun [1981] models conflict as a problem with initially no feasible solution. Redefinition of the problem is required for a feasible solution to emerge. Shakun develops a "goals/values referral process" as a possible model to describe how the system is redefined in search of a solution.

Game theory views negotiations as strategic exercises and is perhaps the only area that has attempted to address all aspects of a negotiation. It is, however, handicapped in its attempts to model the negotiation process because it deals with a scenario where the values or preferences are fixed and so outcomes are inherent in the very structure of the game. The process of change in the values is something that game theory does not capture.

2.2. Economics - Decision Making Under Uncertainty

Uncertainty in a negotiation process can arise from two sources: (1) uncertainty about the outcomes/states of nature also called "risk", and (2) uncertainty about the opponent's preferences.

Analysis of decision-making under "risk" has been dominated by the expected utility theory. It is widely accepted as a near normative model of rational choice and a particularly good determinant of economic behavior [Keeney and Raiffa, 1976; Savage, 1954]. The assessment of alternatives under the expected utility theory is based on: the expected utility of the outcomes/consequences of the alternative, "asset integration" which refers to whether or not the utility resulting from the choice increases the total "wealth" of the decision maker and, "risk aversion" or the preference for certain returns compared to uncertain ones. The utilities of outcomes are weighted in the ratio of their probabilities. If two outcomes have the same utility, then the one with greater probability was always preferred.

The expected utility model is basically a "constant utility" model; it assumes that each outcome has a time-invariant utility value. In the "random utility" model, the utilities are described as random variables and this assumption is often used to explain the "intransitivity of alternatives" and changing utilities for outcomes. Coombs, et. al. [1970] have sought to explain the cognitive processes behind such a phenomenon. They conclude that different decision rules are used under different situations by the same decision maker and propose a contingency approach to choice theory, using cognitive factors, particularly information processing variables, to determine the "how much" and "how" of information storage and retrieval, how a decision problem is formulated and consequently, how it is solved.

Simon's [1947] theory of bounded rationality shows that human beings use "decision heuristics" in their decision making to reduce the information processing overhead. These decision heuristics are entirely subjective and as a result tend to be biased. Kahneman and Tversky [1979] have shown experimentally that expected utility theory is systematically violated. They identify a "certainty effect" -- people prefer certainty, a "reflection effect" -- people are risk averse in choices involving sure gains but risk seeking in choices involving sure losses (this phenomenon is often referred to as the problem of "framing"), and an "isolation effect" -- people disregard components that alternatives share, and focus on components that distinguish them. The isolation effect explains inconsistent preferences and intransitive preferences. In their Prospect Theory, Kahneman and Tversky propose that people do not evaluate the desirability of an alternative the new total state that results from the choice but by the net gains or losses in choosing that alternative. This value function, is concave for gains and convex for losses with a steeper slope. Yet another decision heuristic that is often used is the "availability" of relevant information. This refers to the vividness with which the information is stored. Vivid information is more readily "available" and so tends to bias decision making [Nisbett and Ross, 1980]. Clear unambiguous feedback from the negotiation aids in the formulation of more such heuristics. There are many of these heuristics that contradict the expected utility maximization theory and its basic tenets.

Notwithstanding the effects of cognitive limitations, decision and judgmental biases, expected utility theory remains the major normative theory of decision making. However, the use of the "utility maximizing" concept is tempered by combining it with the "satisficing" concept proposed first by March and Simon [1958] (see also [Raiffa, 1982] and [Tietz, 1983]). Another major theory that needs to be mentioned is the "equity" theory which emphasizes people's desire to achieve fair outcomes as a result of their easier acceptability [Schelling, 1963], and the ability to maintain goodwill in recurrent relationships. This theory has since been extended to incorporate a "mixed-motive" flavor into it - to maximize own gain as well as divide outcomes equitably.

In summary, this approach has focused on the *decision-making* process in a negotiation. Its normative models form the backbone of most present-day scientific business decision-making. The disadvantages of such an approach are that though it is high in its determinacy, the sources of such determinacy are artificial constructs like indifference curves, pareto-optimality etc. Some of the concepts are in reality unoperationalizable or tend to have poor construct validity. Moreover, the rationality assumptions ignore as irrational many interesting aspects of negotiations like preference intransitivity, power, persuasion and coercion, etc.

2.3. Process Analysis - Joint Decision Making

Based on earlier economic theory, Siegel and Fouraker [1960] view the process of negotiation as a joint decision making problem involving a combination of concessions and convergence. Two negotiators start from distinct initial positions that represent the initial aspirations or the positions they want the opponent to believe they desire. They then inch incrementally toward each other by making concessions until they converge to a common point. Cross [1969] and Bartos [1974] view negotiation as a *learning process* in which the parties react to each other's concession behavior. But this theory assumes symmetry of information. Findings of the concession/convergence approach are available to both parties. So there is no advice on how to bargain best that is not equally accessible to the other side. This obviously results in a stalemate. Another problem of this approach is that it has not overcome the problems of determinacy. Concession rates cannot be calculated easily and change over time. This approach does not allow for considerations such as use of power, tactics and negotiation skills which might affect the concession rate at any point in time.

A remedy that has been suggested for this is that the negotiation could be considered a "teaching process" instead of a learning process, but this further reduces the already low determinacy of the theory. A more fundamental question is whether it reflects the nature of real-world negotiations. Often the approach is applicable only when the variables under discussion are quantifiable and discretizable. Only then can distinct initial positions be identified and incremental concessions made. Since only the concession rates are considered to the exclusion of other variables, an incoherent mosaic of piece-by-piece concessions may emerge. Another important aspect of negotiations ignored in this approach is that frequently the list of items under negotiation is in itself a matter of negotiation.

As an answer to the drawbacks of the concession/convergence approach, Zartman [1977] presents a formula/detail approach: negotiations proceed by finding the proper "formula" before implementing "detail". According to Zartman, "negotiators begin by groping around for a jointly agreeable formula that will serve as a referent, provide a notion of justice, and define a common perception on which implementation details can be based. Power makes the values fit together in the package and timing is important to making the formula stick". His emphasis is on the process of negotiation as a process of *searching* - first for a single formula (similar to Shakun's [1981] goals/value referral process) and then for the implementation of this formula through the specification of details. He claims that while the concession/convergence approach is by nature reactive and passive, the formula/detail approach is associated with an "active search for a solution" and thus enhances the probability of creative solutions. It also leads to greater satisfaction than concession-making approaches since concessions tend to be viewed as losses.

This approach allows for the inclusion of power as added value in the process of selecting and modifying values. The concession/convergence approach can be thought of as the process of negotiation of detail after a formula has been found. Unfortunately, the approach suffers from a total lack of determinacy.

In the "progressive construction" approach, the issues under discussion are decided upon only one issue at a time. This can be conceptualized as a group decision making situation on a complex topic that is spread out over time, like disarmament.

The analysis of negotiations as joint decision making processes focuses on a macro-level observation of the process and its dynamics - the "how" of negotiations. As is to be expected in such an analysis, the underlying mechanics of individual values, preferences and motivations - the "why" - is ignored. The advantage of such an approach is that it gives us a way to look at negotiations as a dynamic search process -

incremental and goal oriented. Theoretically, this opens up the possibility of applying search techniques developed by areas such as artificial intelligence to analyze and possibly support a negotiation.

2.4. Sociology

In a sociological scenario, negotiations are seen as involving dual, conflicting motivations: the individual's (competitive) desire to maximize his own utility and the collectivistic (cooperative) desire to reach a "fair" solution. Literature in anthropology emphasizes the significance of "reciprocity". Reciprocal exchanges create bonds of friendship that hold society together. Homans' rule of distributive justice says that men view as fair, rewards that are proportional to the receipent's contribution to society. This norm of fairness can be seen as a state of equilibrium. Any deviation generates forces that attempt to restore it - that is why it became a norm in the first place. In addition, society institutionalizes and imposes sanctions on deviants.

In agreeing to reach a "fair" solution through the equal distribution (not division) of the maximum pay-off that each side can rationally expect, this approach does not allow for strategic misrepresentations or "bluffing". It is in the interests of each negotiator to make his opening bid as close to giving zero pay-off to his opponent as possible. This way, each negotiator can through the initial tentative acceptance form an idea as to his opponents position and what he can rationally expect from the negotiation.

Once the initial tentative offers have been accepted very reluctantly, the size of the opening concession gains importance. This is invariably a function of some factors extraneous to the negotiation process itself - psychological or social. A rational bargainer in this approach will expect a reciprocation of his offer. The rule of thumb that can be used to judge whether a particular concession has been reciprocated equally is seen as the state such that the negotiators have no need to revise their original expectations about the ultimate agreement. This implies that the fairness in question is only "perceived fairness". Failure to match concessions is not seen as "unfair" if the negotiator perceives that his opponents preferences have changed. Response to unfairness comes either as withdrawal or in the form of behavior that maintains the negotiators expectation about the outcome. Unexpectedly large concessions lead to revision of opponents expectations and unexpectedly small ones bring sanctions or stop further opponent concessions. Negotiators must be skillful enough to spot fair concessions and discriminate unfair ones.

The notion of the desire to achieve fairness as being the driving force in a negotiation has some limitations. It is based on a decision heuristic that is very vague and ill-defined -- the concept of "fairness". By its very nature, such an approach lacks determinancy and is open to a multitude of interpretations. However, this approach reveals the importance of societal norms, group norms, and ethics as factors of interest in studying negotiations.

2.5. Industrial Relations - Collective Bargaining

Labor negotiations can be described as "the deliberate interaction of two or more complex social units which are attempting to redefine the terms of their interdependence" [Walton and McKersie, 1975].

Three major propositions underly the explanation of conflict in this approach: (1) differences in goals, interests or values of the two parties [March and Simon, 1958; Axelrod, 1970, Pondy, 1969; Deutsch, 1971; Cormick, 1971], (2) interdependence among the parties [Walton and McKersie, 1965; Walton et al., 1969], and (3) perceived opportunity for interference [Goldman, 1962; Pondy, 1967].

Perrow [1961] describes operative goals in an organization as being "those that are embedded in the major operating policies and daily decisions of the personnel". They could refer to both means and ends. In general, greater incompatibility in goals leads to greater conflict. Dispersion or distribution of power among the bargaining parties was also important in determining the extent of conflict [Cormick, 1971; Dubin, 1960; Darkenwald, 1971]. In general, the more evenly distributed the power, the greater the conflict. Control structure as one determinant of official power also influences the occurence of conflict. Ambiguity about jurisdiction, i.e., differences in perception of authority relationships also affects conflict formation [Walton et al., 1969]. Deutsch [1973], in a socio-psychological approach to understanding negotiations, identifies six major sets of variables that affect negotiation behavior: characteristics of the conflicting parties, prior relationships between/among conflicting parties (the first time a concept of "history" has been introduced), nature of issue giving rise to conflict, social environment within which conflict occurs, strategies and tactics employed by the conflicting parties and, the consequences of conflict to each of the participants.

Kochan et al. [1975] suggest that the most effective strategy for resolving conflict lies in recognizing the underlying goals that the parties are seeking in the process and accepting the legitimacy of their efforts to pursue their goals.

The Industrial Relations approach recognizes the fact that conflict is dynamic as manifest in the constantly changing nature of the goals but does not attempt to understand the actual mechanisms of this process. It does not discuss the effects of individual differences in risk-taking propensity, motivation, perception etc., and their dynamics. It does however, provide an approach where the existence of power-dependency relationships is formally acknowledged as an important determinant of negotiation outcomes.

2.6. Psychology

People, as participants in a negotiation, communicate positions, send signals by making demands and concessions, respond to signals from the opponent, and through a sequence of such exchanges arrive at a solution to the problem under negotiation. Negotiation, in this approach, can be defined as a process of value and behavior modification through exchange of communications.

Spector [1977] identifies four primary factors that affect the negotiation process from the "microlevel perspective" of negotiator psychology: (1) the individual personality needs of the negotiator; (2) the personality compatibility among negotiators; (3) negotiator perceptions of his opponents strengths, weaknesses, positions, values, preferences, alternatives and intentions and his expectations of the opponents strategies and actions; and (4) persuasive mechanisms actually employed to modify the bargaining positions and values of the opponent to achieve a more favorable (from his point of view) convergence of interests.

Several researchers have studied links between single psychological factors and negotiation behavior [Rubin and Brown, 1975; Spector, 1975]. The results have been mixed. The failure to find intuitively obvious relationships has been explained as being the result of poor operationalization of the psychological constructs. However, a significant amount of research and case studies have shown that negotiator "personality" as manifested in predispositions towards the opponent and his motives for actions are important determinants of negotiation behavior. Similarly, perceptions of the opponents' strengths, weaknesses, intentions, commitments and goals affect the negotiator's response, the tone of interpersonal communication, and the learning process. Mutual power and influence relationships, employed effectively and credibly, provoke changes in negotiator values/perceptions and can lead to eventual concessions and convergence to an agreement [Zartman, 1974]. Finally, the interaction between the personalities of the two bargainers (soft against hard, etc.), and the interaction between the bargaining context and personality factors (certain characteristics are triggered by certain situations) decide the bargaining style of the negotiator, according to this approach.

Trying to understand the psychological aspects of negotiation gives a feel for its micro-level elements: the underlying factors and motivations that drive a negotiation. If we can look beyond manifested negotiation behavior to its origins and identify the *driving* factors distinctly, the negotiation's objective of *value change* is half achieved. The problems with the psychology approach are its obvious lack of determinancy and the almost too intricate and involved inter-relationships among the innumerable variables. Its strength is itself its weakness in some ways - it focuses on the negotiating parties, and their ability to modify the values of the issues at stake. It does not deal extensively with the negotiation process itself. Moreover, as yet, there is no single unified theory which combines all the single-trait research into a meaningful overall psychological theory of negotiations.

3. A UNIFIED MODEL

We have seen how the negotiation process has been studied and explained by researchers in different fields. They vary in perspective and in focus, in the level of analysis, the level of detail, in their assumptions and in their objectives. In short, the approaches present different "windows" to understanding negotiations, even though a few of these approaches address a number of aspects of negotiation (e.g., game theory or the model by Deutsch [1973]).

In contrast, a negotiation support system needs a more holistic approach that integrates the different perspectives into a uniform model that enables us to design a DSS to support the negotiation process. While this may not be feasible in the short run, the model to be constructed in this section should at least be sufficient to serve as the foundation of a negotiation support environment in which a decision maker can embed existing and forthcoming tools from any of the different areas. Inasmuch as these approaches seek to describe the same phenomenon, it appears possible and indeed desirable to integrate them, relaxing their assumptions and enhancing their descriptive power, in a joint framework that captures all major dimensions of the negotiation process.

3.1. The Model

As a starting point, we propose the two-person model of negotiations shown in Figure 1. (Extension to other cases will be briefly discussed at the end of this section.) The model claims that for describing or prescribing a negotiation we need information about: the environment, negotiator needs and values, perceptions and expectations, available experience, the decision-making process(es) that are used, the manifested bargaining behavior and the evolving state-of-the-problem as the negotiation progresses. These components influence and change each other dynamically, as indicated by the arrows in the figure. It is our claim that they can be used as a backbone structure for a negotiation support environment. As there is no coherent theory of the interaction between the components, the decision maker must apply judgement and intuition when using the tools provided in the system.

- **Environment:** This refers to the state of the world, i.e. the aggregation of technological, economic, political and social factors of the environment in which the negotiation is set.

- **Experience:** This refers to the accumulated store (in the negotiators memory- primary storage, or in the memory of those who are accessible to the negotiator for consultation- secondary storage) of information about former experiences- both general and specific. This can mean the history of former experiences, the inferences drawn from them (stereotypes), the patterns of strategies used under various environmental circumstances, their results, generalizations (decision heuristics), etc.

- **Negotiator Needs and Values:** These stem from three sources:

  1. The *systemic needs/values* refer to the specific manifestations of characteristic motivations and preferences imposed on the negotiator by the "system" in which he exists. For instance, the legal system enjoins in its members a need for fairness and a respect for authority- the law.

  2. The *group needs/values* refer to the needs and values that a negotiator inherits by virtue of his being a member of certain groups. These groups might be the actual constituents he is representing in the negotiation or they might be the subconscious affiliations of the negotiator. In the former case, the needs/values are consciously imposed upon the negotiator in the context of the negotiation. In the latter case, they act as subconscious referents for the negotiator. Which of these actually surfaces or dominates is a function of the negotiation context at any particular point in time. For example, a

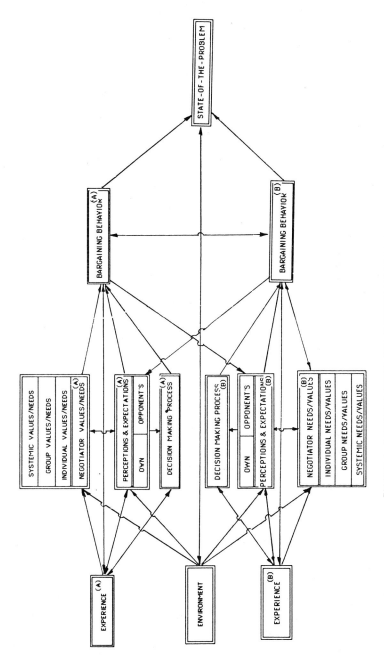

FIGURE 1. A UNIFIED MODEL FOR UNDERSTANDING NEGOTIATIONS

union representative has a conscious affiliation and allegiance to the
needs/values of the labor he represents, but also show subconscious
affiliation to groups like sex, countrymen etc., and demonstrates
needs/values that are representative of them.

3. The *individual personality* refers to the individuals own needs,
motivations, and preferences, such as need for social approval, need for
cooperation and friendship, need for achievement, needs for play,
seduction, exhibitionism and so on as well as his preferences among
these needs and the values he attaches to them.

Which of these three catagories of needs/values dominates or which
combination manifests itself is also influenced by the environment (both
physical and psychological), and by the negotiation and previous experience.
Note that both of these change over time as the negotiation progresses.

- **Perceptions and Expectations:** This represents the negotiator's "problem
  representation". It constitutes the "psychological" aspect of the environment
  for each individual negotiator where he visualizes positions or "states-of-the-
  world", the objectives/goals, the issues under consideration, the alternatives
  available, attitudes towards those alternatives, constraints towards making
  choices among alternatives, commitments, intended actions, and the possible
  strategy to be used. He does this evaluation for himself and also makes a
  subjective estimate for his opponents.   The problem representation
  undergoes constant modification and change. It can be modified by changes
  in the physical environment, changes in the state-of-the-problem as the
  negotiation progresses, changes in needs and values occasioned due to
  various factors, changes in experience through the availability of new
  information on past precedents, and very importantly, feedback from the
  actions or bargaining behavior of the opponents. The perceptions and
  expectations of one's own position are influenced by and in turn influence
  those of the opponent's position.

- **Decision-Making Process:** This represents the inferencing part of the
  model where alternative actions are evaluated by the use of decision models
  or judgemental and decision heuristics/biases. Examples of these include the
  estimation of expected utility, aspiration levels, axioms of equity and
  fairness, mixed-motive optimizations etc. The outcome of this process is a set
  of choices among the alternative actions for a given state of the physical
  environment, a given set of experience histories of decision processes and
  inferences, and a given subjective evaluation by the negotiator of his own
  and his opponent's problem representation as moderated by his needs and
  values at that point in time. It is a dynamic process that changes nature
  continuously as a function of these other components of the negotiation
  process.

- **Bargaining Behavior:** This represents the actual bargaining behavior of
  the negotiator; it includes the making of demands, offers, concessions,
  threats, promises, strategic posturing through suppression, distortion or
  misrepresentation of information, deception and bluffing, the use of power
  and influence strategies etc. This process is influenced by the manifest needs

and values of the negotiator, his perceptions of his and the opponents problem representation, the outcome of the decision making process and, very importantly, the pattern of bargaining behavior of the opponent. At any point in time, the actual bargaining behavior is a complex function of these variables and any one of them may be overridden by the other, particularly the lower order variables (that do not show a hierarchical influence relationship over this process in Figure 1).

- **Outcome - State-of-the-problem:** This represents the offers and concessions of the bargaining entities and shows the state of the problem resolution effort at any point in time. When agreement has been reached between the offers of the bargaining entities, it represents the culmination of the negotiation process. In the stages prior to agreement, it serves as a referrent state for the revision of expectations and perceptions by each bargainer, and as a vehicle of change for the environment at each stage of the negotiation process.

Figure 2 gives two illustrations of the model. The first example uses the model to describe negotiations among management and labor in a manufacturing firm that is trying to cut personnel costs due to severe financial problems. The second example describes negotiations among the marketing and engineering departments of a car manufacturer working with different goals on the design of a new car for the 1990's. This example is based on a real application studied in the MEDIATOR project but, as the first one, is highly simplified for purposes of exposition.

Our model has sought to integrate the complexities of the negotiation process into a simple framework of interacting components in what we hope, is an intuitively sound manner. The model derives its strength from two factors: first, its ability to accomodate a global perspective of the negotiation process without sacrificing the insight that a narrower focus on one or a few of the components can provide. and second, its emphasis on the dynamic nature of such a process. The major drawback to this model is that we do not yet have empirical evidence to support the choice of components and interactions directly. However, some validity is given to the model by studying its relationship to the reference displines -- see the following subsection. Inasmuch as our goal is not to develop new negotiation techniques, but to support existing and forthcoming ones by computer/communication technology, this degree of validity may be sufficient. In order to provide realistic negotiation support, the two-person model is easily adapted to other typical decision settings:

- *Full cooperation*: There is no necessity for individual perception and expectation components because a joint problem representation can be used instead. The bargaining behavior is limited to an exchange of offers; no strategic bargaining occurs.

- *More than two parties*: Each player's individual negotiation support system provides the same components as in the two-person case. The only extensions needed are in the perceptions and expectations component where each individual has a seperate representation for his perceptions and expectations of each of the other parties as well as his own. While in principle this may lead to complex information structures, these are simplified as it is often assumed that n-person bargaining situations can be considered as a two-

	Example 1. The Union-Management negotiation		Example 2. Interdepartmental Negotiation	
	Union Representative	Management Rep.	Engineering Department	Marketing Department
Environment	* General recession - rising unemployment/costs	* Severe financial loss	* advances in fuel-efficient engines. * projected shortage in steel supply 5 years from now.	* Competitors have announced the "car of the century" projected growth in the market for luxury sedans
Experience	* Past experience of union/management in negotiating with each other. * Settlements reached by other unions in same circs	* Strategies used by other companies	* Exp. with mktg. in last proj. - they want the impossible!! * That Mktg.Mgr cares only about his image.	* Engg -"they are unimaginative and lazy" * Last time had to invoke the director's authority..
Negotiator needs and values	* Minimize retrenchment & losses to constituents * Constituents must recognize my efforts - must keep face.	* Cut costs to an acc. level and save company * Use the opportunity to reinforce position of strength.	* Must keep down: workload on body shop, minimize retooling, and redeployment/retraining. * Must show that Mktg.Mgr that he cannot shove me around.	* Must beat competitors product * Inc. market share by -30% * I have got to look good - I must make it to the VP's post
Perceptions and Expectations	* There may be other choices. The union will come up with something reasonable.	* Possible alternatives- take pay cut,agree to phased lay-off, or bargain for min retrenchment. Mgmt will be tough but reasonable. Will reciprocate. Must ensure min retrenchment.	* Design should have very good fuel economy. Other things are not too important. Marketing will propose total change - too costly.	* Design should have lots of new/extra features. Styling must be improved. Engg. will possibly resist any change on grounds of cost. * We must show that we can earn more thro' better pricing.
Decision-making process	* Maximizing approach - must minimize losses to constituents, yet be "fair".	* A target reduction in costs. Will accept any proposal that satisfies	* Minimize tooling expenses, R&D investment reqd., and steel consumption.	* Maximize saleable features May accept compromise on some
Bargaining behavior	* Begins stridently opposing -concede mild pay cut,limited lay-off, and so on.	* Proposes drastic retr-enchment, marginal concessions. Threatens shut-down when union "unreasonable". New proposals..	* Start - propose just a new engine - make alt. proposals/ concessions - at times refuses to take responsibility for the project.	* Start with "dream car" - often complain that Engg is unreasonable - threaten to again go to the director - make concessions
Outcome "state-of-the-problem"	* Position of union/mgmt totally at odds. Concessions bring them closer. New proposals change focus. Finally reach agreement.		* Start with seeming total disagreement. Concessions/new proposals bring them closer to an agreement. Changes in environment force constant revisions till the product is finally on the road..	

FIGURE 2. TWO REAL-LIFE EXAMPLES IN TERMS OF OUR MODEL

party situations because of coalition formation.

- *Third party intervention* in the form of a mediator or arbitrator: The mediator/arbitrator can be considered a third player in the game but with no personal interest or motivation except to help both parties reach an agreement.

3.2. Relationship to the other Models

In an attempt to justify the proposed model, this subsection interprets the approaches described in section 2 as special cases of the unified model which emphasize the study of particular components and make simplifying assumptions about the others.

- **Game Theory**: This subset of the model focuses on some aspects of the Bargaining Behavior and some aspects of the Perceptions and Expectations component (particularly in games with unknown opponent utility functions). It assumes away the Decision-Making Process as being rational utility maximizing and assumes that the needs/values of the negotiator do not change. There is little consideration of the effect of former experience (through stereotypes) or the dynamics of the environment (except time costs). Dynamic game theory does consider the feedback from the changing state-of-the-problem.

- **Decision Making Under Uncertainty**: Here, the main focus is on Decision-Making Process, and Perceptions and Expectations. The effect of a dynamic Environment in altering the perceptions and expectations as well as the appropriateness of the decision-making process or decision heuristic are also considered. Certain standard Needs/Values (risk aversion, fairness or equity, mixed-motives) are included while others are ignored. The main subject of this kind of model is the interplay between perception as affected by cognitive limitations, bounded rationality etc., and decision heuristics/biases.

- **Joint Decision Making**: This approach concentrates on the components of State-of-the-problem and the interaction between Bargaining Behaviors. It takes cognizance of the important changes in Perception that occur during the course of bargaining, as well as the effect of cognitive limitations but other Perceptions as being constant. The Decision-Making Process,, for instance, is perceived as useful only to determine the intial position from which bargaining may commence. The theories look at negotiations as a process of search through the problems space to find a solution.

- **Sociological Approach**: This theory assumes that the Decision-Making Process is one of own utility maximization subject to a need for fairness. The Perception of fairness/unfairness of the opponents' bargaining behavior shows concern for the feedback process that changes Perceptions and Expectations and so determines Bargaining Behavior. Little consideration is given to effects of Experience or the Environment (except social norms which can be thought of as group needs/values).

- **Industrial Relations**: Here the focus is almost exclusively on the Perceptions and Expectations component as the main driving force behind conflict. Group needs/values are thought to dominate the negotiator values and shape Expectations and Perceptions of the Environment - the interdependence and the chance of interference as well as beliefs about power distribution, control etc. The dynamic nature of Perceptions and Expectations is viewed as a function of feedback from the state-of-the-problem, bargaining behavior of opponent and changes in the environment and consequent changes in group needs/values. The role of the individual needs/values of the bargainer and of the decision-making process are largely ignored.

- **Psychology**: This approach analyses the interplay between the different subcomponents of the negotiator's needs/values and their effect on the Bargaining Behavior. To a limited extent, psychology also studies the Perceptions and Expectations component as it can be affected by Bargaining Behavior. It does consider the effect of the Environment in triggering certain needs and fixing certain values.

We have attempted to show how the different approaches can be visualized as subsets of our model. In doing this we have concentrated on the main thrust of assumptions and research approach in each field. Some of the more intricate and involved pieces of research in some fields had to be omitted.

4. DESIGN OF AN INDIVIDUAL NEGOTIATION SUPPORT ENVIRONMENT

Our primary objective in studying the different approaches to understanding negotiations and developing a unified model was to develop a framework that would be capable of facilitating the assessment of negotiation situations from the viewpoint of individual decision makers in a multiperson decision support system setting. Before doing so, we summarize the global multiperson DSS architecture (MEDIATOR) in which the individual negotiation support environment is to be embedded.

4.1. MEDIATOR Overview

Based on experience with a GDSS for cooperative multiple criteria group decision making called Co-oP [Bui and Jarke 1984; Bui, 1985], the MEDIATOR project at New York University attempts to develop a comprehensive multiperson decision support system which also addresses issues of non-cooperation. Work on MEDIATOR thus far has focused on aspects of decision maker interaction and system structure rather than individual negotiation support [Jarke et al., 1986], and on case studies in interdepartmental negotiation support [Giordano et al., 1985].

From a *system perspective*, MEDIATOR can be understood as a specialized multiuser micro-mainframe database management system as depicted in Figure 3. Decision makers or players employ private data and tools on individual workstations -- and data from shared corporate or external databases -- to come up with an individual problem representation they are willing to share with a human group leader or mediator (though possibly not with other negotiating parties). A section of the group database contains a group joint problem representation synthesized by the mediator from individual

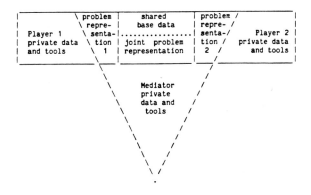

FIGURE 3: MEDIATOR Design -- Communication through Data Sharing

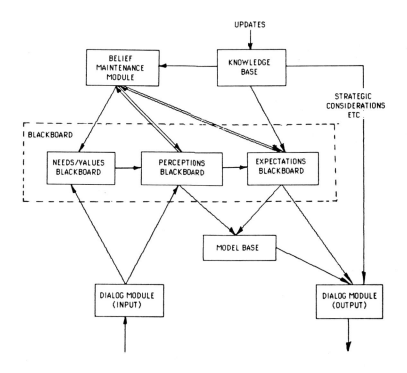

FIGURE 4. ARCHITECTURE FOR AN INDIVIDUAL

NEGOTIATION SUPPORT SYSTEM

problem representations using specialized private data and tools. The group joint problem representation is visible to all members of the group but not outside the group. Database transaction concepts similar to those used in CAD/CAM databases are being developed to enforce these rules.

The use of database concepts carries over partially to the *problem representation perspective*. Relational decision matrix structures generated by interactive multiple criteria decision methods [Jacquet-Lagreze and Shakun, 1984] are employed for the individual and group joint problem representations. Extended view definition facilities coupling model bases and databases are used for the creation of individual problem representations, and view integration techniques from database design are employed for synthesizing group joint problem representations [Jarke et al., 1986].

Finally, there is a *process perspective*. Expanding on an idea by Shakun [1981], negotiation is viewed as a process of cooperative evolutionary system design where the "system" is the group joint problem representation and the design goal is to reach a representation in which at least one decision alternative is acceptable to all players. In contrast to traditional system design, the problem is represented as a time-varying mapping from control space (the decision alternatives) to criteria space (the criteria used by any of the decision makers) to utility space (the preference structure of each decision maker). After the initial view generation and integration steps which are intended to achieve an initial common terminology and background knowledge, the main tools for evolving the group joint problem representation are those for *consensus-seeking* through problem redefinition in any of the three spaces (e.g., expansion of the set of alternatives or criteria considered), and for *compromise* through concession-making or application of axiomatic game-theoretic solution methods.

4.2. Individual Negotiation Support Environment

In the context of MEDIATOR, the individual negotiation support environment comprises a major part of the "private data and tools" offered to each player in his or her local workstation. It should enable a negotiator to consciously analyze his own and his opponents' behavior, and to articulate and examine the underlying motivations, assumptions, attitudes and strategies. Such an analysis, though perhaps infeasible in the midst of a heated negotiation, would serve a very useful purpose as a preparatory exercise before a negotiation, as a tool for analysis during protracted negotiations, for post-negotiation review, and possibly for training and refining negotiation techniques.

However, the internal mechanics of the components of the unified model and their interactions are too complex, dynamic and numerous for a human to keep track of. To overcome this limitation, knowledge-based systems could be envisioned as "cognitive aids" to the process. That, in a nutshell, is what the individual negotiation support system attempts to be. The cognitive process in the context of a negotiation can be structured in terms of the unified model, and instantiated with insights and specific methods that the different approaches supply. The structure of a system built around the unified model is proposed in Figure 4. The main components of this system, as well as their relationship to each other and to the unified model can be described as follows.

- The **knowledge base** manages relatively stable information in three areas. *Psychological models* take the form of psychological profiles and rules about the possible characteristic needs/values, attitudes, patterns of possible behavior, etc. *History of experiences with specific opponents* contains a selective record of previous behavior toward and by opponents and all that is known about them. The *general experience bank* accumulates knowledge of possible negotiation scenarios, typical strategies in such scenarios etc.

- The **model base** manages a variety of decision-making models and heuristics that might be used by decision makers based upon personal predisposition, perceptions and expectations, or perceived state-of-the-problem (see [Bui, 1985] for a description of a "content-oriented model bank" in GDSS which contains a subset of the models needed for this component).

- In contrast to the knowledge base which provides general and temporally relatively stable memory aids, the **blackboard** captures information about the evolving state of a particular negotiation problem. The *needs/values blackboard* contains the verbalized own needs/values and perceived needs/values of the opponent as moderated by the knowledge base. The *perceptions blackboard* stores the verbalized perceptions of own and opponent's "problem representation" -- the goals/objectives, issues under discussion, alternatives available, preferences, constraints, commitments, etc. as moderated by the perceived needs and the knowledge present in the knowlege base about the opponent and that relevant to his perceived psychological profile. Finally, the *expectations blackboard* contains the expectations about the opponent's possible actions and intentions as moderated by the perceptions blackboard content and the information available in the knowledge base about the opponent's past behavior and that of others in similar situations. Each of these subcomponent blackboards consists of two (and more if there are more than one opponent) parts that have to communicate and cross-check each other for internal consistency. They are all constantly under revision by the users perceptions of the bargaining behavior of the opponent and by changes in the environment in addition to the moderation mentioned above. This concept is similar to actor formalisms as proposed by Hewitt [1976].

- The **belief maintenance module** is responsible for the maintenance of internal consistency in the decision maker's belief system (cf. [Doyle, 1979]). It keeps track of the changing perceptions (which can be thought of as assumptions), state-of-the-world, environmental factors and available knowledge (psychological models, past experiences with opponent, general experiences). In accordance with these, it revises the perceived needs/values, the perceptions of own and opponent's problem representation, and the expectations.

- Finally, the **dialog module** of the individual DSS has to be enhanced to guide the user throughout the negotiation process. This involves eliciting information concerning his perceptions of opponents' and own needs, problem repesentations and expectations. It also includes blackboard manipulation, holistic problem understanding, and attention focusing. The dialog module lets the user access data and model management facilities to select decision-making models, to generate possible actions, and to present reports of expectations, choice of action, and summaries of historical records of strategies used in similar situations.

Space restrictions prevent a deeper discussion of this architecture and many details are yet to be worked out. Nevertheless, it seems a feasible though ambitious approach which implements the unified model and relies on components operational in existing AI systems. Moreover, a comparison of Figures 1 and 3 demonstrates a good fit between the global MEDIATOR architecture and its subjective mirror image in each individual negotiation support environment. This correspondence was further highlighted in a recent experiment that employed MEDIATOR for simulating a real hostage negotiation case, in order to study the usefulness of the multiperson model for individual negotiation support (in this case: support for the negotiator who attempts to get the hostages released).

A number of negotiation support tools reported in the literature could be embedded into such an environment. Many of these tools come from the domains of game theory and multiple criteria decision making, possibly combined with considerations of uncertainty (e.g., [Bui, 1985; Kersten, 1985; Shakun, 1985]). A commercially available system [Nierenberg, 1984] claims to assist in the training of negotiators by helping them articulate and therefore clearly understand their perceptions of the problem from their own and their opponent's viewpoints. While this is just a surfacing tool with no prescriptive suppport, another commercial package (Negotiation Edge by Human Edge, Inc.) asks Its user a structured set of questions from which advice on a negotiation strategy is inferred. Unfortunately, no support is given for adapting this strategy to the course of the negotiation process, and the large number of questions to be answered prevents frequent repetition of system usage during the negotiation. Undoubtedly, more tools will appear in the future.

5. CONCLUSION

The discussion in this paper should have demonstrated one negative and one positive result. On the one hand, the multitude of representations proposed by the different areas appears to make it presently impossible to come up with a comprehensive *group* negotiation support system that "objectively" covers all aspects of a negotiation situation in a fashion acceptable to all group members. Machine communication among group members will therefore have to be limited to relatively simple, mutually understandable representations.

On the other hand, the unified model should make it possible for *individual* decision makers to articulate and enhance their personal understanding of the negotiation position, by structuring their thinking in a much richer framework, using tools from the various areas. Coherence among these tools is then provided partially by the unified model which describes the interactions among different descriptive and prescriptive techniques in terms of the model components and relationships concerned, and partially by the decision maker himself, using the blackboard and knowledge base components of the proposed system as cognitive aids.

This argument carries over to a human mediator or group leader, perceived as a particular case of an individual decision maker. It leads us to believe that the

MEDIATOR architecture -- which does include such a human mediator -- should be able to provide more powerful group decision support than a fully automatic GDSS approach, especially when geographical dispersion limits direct communication among decision makers outside the system.

Besides raising a host of interesting design and evaluation questions, the proposed individual negotiation support environment and its integration into the MEDIATOR framework leads to another important observation. Since the individual model (even the part of it that is represented in the system) is so much richer than the "group joint problem representation", the "individual problem representation" component in MEDIATOR (Figure 3) --whose role is to compress the "private problem representation"-- will almost unavoidably lead to loss and distortion of information, even in a cooperative setting. Research in the treatment of incomplete or distorted information will therefore play a crucial role for the success of multiperson DSS.

REFERENCES

Axelrod, R., 1970. *Conflict of interests*, Markham, Chicago, IL.

Bartos, O.J., 1974. *Process and Outcome of Negotiations*, Columbia University Press, N.Y.

Bishop, R.I., 1964. A Zeuthen-Hicks theory of bargaining, *Econometrica 32*, pp. 410-417

Bui, X.T., 1985. Co-oP: a DSS for Cooperative Multiple Criteria Group Decision Making, Ph.D Dissertation, Graduate School of Business Administration, New York University, New York, NY.

Bui, X.T. and Jarke, M., 1984. A DSS for cooperative multiple criteria group decision making, *Proceedings 5th International Conference on Information Systems*, Tucson, AZ, pp. 101-113.

Coombs, C.H., Davis, R.M. and Tversky, A., 1970. *Mathematical Psychology*, Prentice-Hall, Englewood Cliffs, NJ.

Cormick, G.W., 1971. Power, Strategy, and the Process of Community Conflict: A Theoretical Framework, Ph.D. dissertation, University of Michigan, Ann Arbor, MI.

Crawford, V.P., 1985. Dynamic games and dynamic contract theory, *Journal of Conflict Resolution 29*(2), pp. 195-224.

Cross, J.G., 1969. *The Economics of Bargaining*, Basic Books, New York, N.Y.

Darkenwald, G.G., 1971. Organizational conflict in colleges and universities, *Administrative Science Quarterly 16*, pp. 407-412.

DeSanctis, G. and Gallupe, B., 1985. Group decision support systems: a new frontier, *Data Base 16*(1), pp 3-10.

Deutsch, M., 1971. Toward an understanding of conflict, *International Journal of Group Tensions 1*, pp. 42-54.

Deutsch, M., 1973. *The Resolution of Conflict*, Yale University Press, New Haven, CT.

Doyle, J., 1979. A Truth Maintenance System, A.I. Memo 521, Artificial Intelligence Laboratory, Massachussets Institute of Technology, Boston, MA.

Dubin, R., 1960. A theory of power and conflict in union-management relations, *Industrial and Labor Relations Review 13*, pp.501-518.

Giordano, J.L., Jacquet-Lagreze, E., and Shakun, M.F., 1985. Un SIAD pour la conception de produits nouveaux, aspects multicriteres et multi-acteurs, Note de Recherche, Universite de Paris-Dauphine, Paris.

Goldman, R.M., 1962. Conflict, cooperation and choice: an exploration of conceptual relationships, in N.F. Washburne (ed.), *Decision Values and Groups*, Macmillan, New York, N.Y., pp. 410-439.

Goncalves, A.S., 1985. Group decision methodology and group decision support systems, *DSS-85 Transactions*, San Francisco, CA, pp. 135-142.

Gray, P., 1981. The SMU Decision Room Project, *Transactions of the First International Conference on Decision Support Systems*, Atlanta, GA, pp. 122-129.

Harsanyi, J.C., 1956. Approaches to the bargaining problem before and after the theory of games: A critical discussion of Zeuthen's, Hick's, and Nash's theories, *Econometrica 24*, pp.144-157.

Harsanyi, J.C., 1962. Bargaining in ignorance of the opponent's utility function, *Journal of Conflict Resolution 6*(1), pp. 29-38.

Harsanyi, J.C., 1967-68. Games with incomplete information played by Bayesian players, *Management Science 14*, pp. 159-182, pp. 320-334, pp. 486-502.

Harsanyi, J.C., 1976. Time, information and incentives in noncooperative games, Working paper CP-381, Center for Research in Management Science, University of California, Berkley, CA.

Harsanyi, J.C. and Selten, R., 1972. A generalized Nash solution for two person bargaining games with incomplete information, *Management Science 18*(5), pp. 80-106.

Hewitt, C., 1976. Viewing control structures as patterns of passing messages, *Artificial Intelligence 8*, pp. 323-364.

Huber, G.P., 1982. Group decision support systems as aids in the use of structured group techniques, *DSS-82 Transactions*, pp. 96-108.

Huber, G.P. and McDaniel, R.R., 1986. Using information technology to design more effective organizations, in Jarke, M. (ed.), *Managers, Micros, and Mainframes: Integrating Systems for End Users*, John Wiley and Sons, Chichester, UK.

Jacquet-Lagreze, E., and Shakun, M.F., 1984. Decision support systems for semi-structured buying decisions, *European Journal of Operations Research 16*(1), pp. 48-58.

Jarke, M., 1986. Knowledge sharing and negotiation support in multiperson decision support systems, *Decision Support Systems* 2(1), pp. 93-102.

Jarke, M., Jelassi, M.T. and Shakun, M.F., 1986. MEDIATOR: towards a negotiation support system, *European Journal of Operations Research 18.*

Kahneman, D. and Tversky, A., 1979. Prospect theory: an analysis of decisions under risk, *Econometrica 47*, pp. 263-291.

Keeney, R.L. and Raiffa, H., 1976. *Decisions with Multiple Objectives: Preferences and Value Tradeoffs*, John Wiley and Sons, New York, N.Y.

Kersten, G.E., 1985. NEGO group decision support system, *Information & Management 8*, pp. 237-246.

Kochan, T.A., Huber, G.P. and Cummings, L.L., 1975. Determinants of intra-organizational conflict in collective bargaining in the public sector, *Administrative Science Quarterly 20*(1), pp. 10-23.

March, J.G. and Simon, H.A., 1958. *Organizations*, John Wiley and Sons, New York, N.Y.

Nash, J., 1950. The bargaining problem, *Econometrica 18*(1), pp. 155-162.

Nash, J., 1953. Two person cooperative games, *Econometrica 21*, pp. 128-140.

Nierenberg, R., 1984. The Art of Negotiating computer program (product review), *The Arbitration Journal 40*(3), p. 70.

Nisbett, R. and Ross, L., 1980. *Human Inference: Strategies and shortcomings of Social Judgement*, Prentice-Hall, Englewood Cliffs, N.J.

Perrow, C., 1961. Goals in complex organizations, *American Sociological Review 32*, pp. 854-865.

Pondy, L.R., 1967. Organizational conflict: concepts and models, *Administrative Science Quarterly 12*, pp. 296-320.

Pondy, L.R., 1969. Varieties of organizational conflict, *Administrative Science Quarterly 14*, pp. 499-505.

Raiffa, H., 1982. *The Art and Science of Negotiation*, Harvard University Press, Cambridge, MA.

Rao, A.G. and Shakun, M.F., 1974. A normative model for negotiations, *Management Science 20*(10), pp. 1364-1375.

Rubin, J.Z. and Brown, B., 1975. *The Social Psychology of Bargaining and Negotiation*, Academic Press, New York, NY.

Savage, L.J., 1954. *The Foundations of Statistics*, John Wiley and Sons, New York, N.Y.

Schelling, T.C., 1963. *The Strategy of Conflict*, Oxford University Press.

Selten, R. , 1975. Bargaining under incomplete information: a numerical example, in O. Becker and R. Richter (eds.), *Dynamische Wirtschaftsanalyse*, J.C.B. Mohr, Tubingen, Germany.

Shakun, M.F., 1981. Formalizing conflict resolution in policy making, *International Journal of General Systems* 7(3), pp. 207-215.

Shakun, M.F., 1985. Decision support systems for negotiations, *Proceedings of the 1985 IEEE International Conference on Systems, Man and Cybernetics*, Tucson, AZ.

Siegel, S. and Fouraker, L.E., 1960. *Bargaining and Group Decision Making*, McGraw-Hill, New York, N.Y.

Simon, H.A., 1947. *Administrative Behavior*, Macmillan, New York, N.Y.

Spector, B.I., 1977. Negotiation as a psychological process, in I.W. Zartman (ed.), *The Negotiation process*, Sage Publications, Beverly Hills, CA.

Tietz, R. (ed.), 1983. *Aspiration Levels in Bargaining and Economic Decision Making*, Springer-Verlag, Berlin.

Tsichritzis, D. (ed.), 1985. *Office Automation*, Springer-Verlag, New York, N.Y.

Turoff, M. and Hiltz, S.R., 1982. Computer support for group versus individual decisions, *IEEE Transactions on Communications COM-30*, 1, pp. 82-90.

Walton, R.E. and McKersie, R.B., 1965. *A Behavioral Theory of Labor Negotiations*, McGraw-Hill, New York, NY.

Walton, R.E., Dutton, J.M. and Cafferty, T.C., 1969. Organzational context and interdepartmental conflict, *Administrative Science Quarterly 14*, pp. 522-542.

Zartman, I.W., 1977. *The Negotiation Process*, Sage Publications, Beverly Hills, CA.

Zeuthen, F., 1930. *Problems of Monopoly and Economic Warfare*, George Routledge and Sons, London.

OFFICE SYSTEMS: Methods and Tools
G. Bracchi, D. Tsichritzis (Editors)
Elsevier Science Publishers B.V. (North-Holland)
© IFIP, 1987

EXTENDED MODELLING CONCEPTS FOR END-USER ORIENTED INFORMATION SYSTEMS

Roger M. TAGG

Independent Consultant, 6 Beechwood Avenue, Little Chalfont,
Buckinghamshire HP6 6PH, U.K.

New generations of computer systems, now being planned for user organisations, involve offering to individual end-users access to a range
of computing facilities (personal, organizational or external) from a
single workstation. In these systems, the user will have to find his
way through a potentially complex combination of application and
service functions, together with their associated collections of information. The user will require support in this process, and this
support needs to be based on a uniform set of models which describe
the objects of interest and their inter-relationships. This paper
looks at a set of 12 possible types of model which would be useful
in this way, and suggests some areas for more systematic research
and experimentation.

1.   INTRODUCTION

1.1   Changes in Orientation in Planning and Design of Information Systems

The identity of the "prevailing theme" in Information Systems (IS) planning and
design has been subject to considerable change in the last 10 years of Informatics History. The theme has moved beyond that of simply delivering single-
application functionality. It has probably now also changed from the classic
database theme of multiple access to shared data - which clearly addressed a
problem, but one which is now generally regarded as not being the whole problem.
Linking of cooperating systems has also been a recent theme, viz the work on
Open Systems Interconnection (OSI), but again this can be regarded as only one -
albeit important - element in future IS planning.

With the increasing number and range of computing facilities that are now
becoming available to end-users in organisations through terminals, workstations
and linked personal computers, a significant change in orientation seems called
for. According to such a change the new prevailing theme could be expressed as
"arranging to make available at each user's workstation all the information
handling facilities he requires, in a flexible and integrated manner". It is
this theme that characterises the phrase used in the title of this paper "End-
User-Oriented Information Systems".

1.2   Finding the Right Title for the Concept

The length of this title reveals a difficulty in deciding exactly where this
new theme belongs. It is clearly wider in scope than "Database" or "Office
Automation". "Office Information Systems" is a preferable title, but still
contains a possible connotation of being limited to traditional administrative
environments - which may not be appropriate for such environments as research
or production. "Management Information Systems" would be quite an accurate
term, but again suffers from connotations (as the failed concept of the late
1960's!). Perhaps a really suitable title has yet to be found.

1.3   State of the Art

Developments in this area are currently led into two directions. One is the
opportunistic appearance of commercial products aimed at capturing markets in
End-User IS software. Such products are often more notable for the novelty of
their interface than for their underlying architecture. Examples are Xerox
Star [1], Cullinet Goldengate [2] and IBM Office-by-Example [3].

The other direction is research into fundamental architectures, of which the
work of Tsichritzis and his collaborators [4], and of Neuhold [5] are interesting examples.

The position of the author of this paper is somewhere between these two main
lines of advance. As a consultant advising organizations planning for End-User
IS, one needs solutions based on the software that is likely to be available.
There appears to be a need to bridge the gap between the ideas of the researchers and the developers of successful commercial software. By surveying the
possible use of some of the models that have emerged from the research in
practical use of an End-User IS, it is hoped that both sides may derive some
benefit.

2.   THE END-USER'S NEEDS

2.1   End User Interfaces

Much of the literature on end-user needs seems to concentrate on "simple interfaces for simple end-users". The typical tools involved are such things as
question-and-answer dialogues, hierarchical menus, relational-based query
languages and spread-sheets. These tools do not always conform well with the
natural concepts of the users: the limitation of relational querying to flat
views of relatively well-formatted data being a much-quoted example. Exactly
what are the natural concepts that need supporting is rather more difficult to
answer.

Studies have been carried out to investigate the efficiency and "naturalness"
of certain types of view, eg Shneiderman [6], and research into the cognitive
factors involved is taking place currently. However there is no single stereotype for end-user behaviour. End-users can be categorized in many ways (see
Codasyl EUFC Report [7]) and can be at many different levels of skill in using
computer facilities (see Hall [8]). Needs for different views stem from differences in background in pre-computer information practices as well as from the
nature of the dominant tasks performed by the different end-users.

2.2   Forms - a Possible Unifying View

The concept of "forms" has been the most significant recent proposal for provision of a unifying end-user view concept. Forms offer a view of data that
almost everyone with a little appreciation of administrative procedure can
understand. They can also support most of the structures of data that need to
be treated as a unit in the user's operations with the data. However the
concept needs extensions, eg to allow nesting of forms within other forms, and
the assembly of forms into collections and documents which may include many
types of form including free text, graphics etc. There are also cases where
forms are not the most efficient concept for the user: an example arises with
statisticians and others who may prefer to use matrices (possibly N-dimensional)
or transposed (vector) views. The ubiquitous spreadsheet, while of form-like
appearance, contains arithmetic rules and hence involves extensions to the
intuitive concept of a form.

2.3   The Need for a More General Architecture

In recognition of these factors therefore, for a truly general end-user-orient-
ed facility, a rather more flexible architecture is required. This architecture will clearly include forms and the sorts of extensions mentioned above.
But it should also support a fuller range of potential end-user "natural"
concepts, both in terms of data views and procedure views.

Such an architecture might seem in danger of asking too much of the end-user.
But the test is whether it can blend the needs of simple users (who can stick
to well-defined paths), expert users (who can create the constructs which
enable them to work most efficiently) and those on the learning curve from more
simple to more complex use. Information will be complex as long as organisations and businesses are complex. It should be an aim of an IS that it
should not be unnecessarily more complex than the real world it describes. If
IS are to support more of the work done in organisations, then at least some
end-users will have to go along with the resultant complexity.

This argues against the idea of a universal simple solution to the requirement.
"Mouse-icon-window" technology, for example, is a useful MMI innovation, but it
does not itself address the full range of concepts involved. The same is true
of a free-form natural language approach. With more formal languages, relational
languages as they currently appear are not fully comprehensive - and those languages which are potentially more general in application, eg PROLOG, tend to
deal with information at too low a level. SMALLTALK is a possible exception,
and it will be discussed later in the context of the Object-Oriented approach.

Possibly the most significant comment from the end-user point of view is that
requirements are always evolving. End-users rarely see IS in terms of the
Design-Implementation-Operation life-cycle that the DP profession has forced on
them. With the likely faster rates of change in business practices, users will
want to be adding not only new procedures, but also new sources of data, types
of data, communications facilities, algorithms etc. If new MMI or software
aids become available they will want to use those too, if it helps their
effectiveness. As they acquire new tools, they will want self-explanatory
features, help and - if they are going to use the tools frequently - training
in how to use them faster. When they get used to the tools they may want to
tailor them and create their own short-cuts - possibly in the form of higher-
level concepts - to make their use still more effective.

2.4   Directory Enquiries - a Key End-User Requirement

This pattern of continual incremental enhancement of the end-user's facilities
suggests that a key requirement will be some sort of "Directory Enquiry"
service. This would help his understanding of the IS objects and tools that
are available to him - not only for the purposes of using the IS but also in
his own efforts to make further enhancements to the IS. This Directory service
will clearly be built on top of an extended Data Dictionary (alias Information
Resource Directory or System Encyclopaedia). The best way of offering a
suitable Directory service to the end-user is a subject which is itself a
current research topic, eg Sutcliffe [9]. But however the service is offered,
a more fundamental issue is that of the models of IS objects and tools on
which the underlying directory will be built. Without a consistent approach to
such models it will be difficult for end-users to see their way through the
complexity of a collection of heterogeneous but interlinking facilities. The
search for suitable models will be the subject of the remainder of this paper.

3.   THE SEARCH FOR SUITABLE MODELS

3.1   The Influence of Database

The database field is a very fertile source for possible models of the End-
User's information "world". Many variations on Bachman Diagrams, Entity-
Relationship Models, Relational Models and Semantic Models have been proposed.
These are often towards a canonical view of shared data rather than views of
data visible to end-users.

Database-oriented models also tend to be concerned with views of data without
the complementary views of procedure. While some aspects of procedure can be
masked by procedures or new definitions internal to a data model, in general the
data model has to be supplemented by a procedure model - Data Flow Diagrams are
one popular convention in this area.

3.2   Extensions of Database Models for End-User IS

The relational models had already started to introduce modelling into the end-
user area, but further developments were suggested in the early 1980's.
"Perceived Records" - potentially hierarchical structured objects seen by the
user of a Query Language - were proposed by the British Computer Society Query
Language Group [10], while Codasyl EUFC [7] proposed more general structures
for user-perceived forms which could include structures as complex as Bill-of-
Materials. These latter proposals also included a basic language for manipulating forms in a general dataprocessing/office automation environment. Forms
with associated procedures were also proposed by Tsichritzis [11], and messages
with associated rules by Hogg [12]. Multi-media messages have also been
subjected to modelling approaches, for example by Christodoulakis [13].

3.3   Apparent Models Underlying Commercial Products

Recently, efforts in developing models and architectures for end-user facilities
appear to have been overtaken by a number of commercial product announcements.
The Xerox Star and Lisa facilities bring with them a whole set of implied models.
Yet the applications at present are relatively self-contained, and it is unclear
whether the models will be suitable for more open, heterogeneous systems. However the object-oriented basis is promising (see below). There is also a whole
"pack" of "integrated" products for micros, of which the leader appears to be
Lotus. These are based on spreadsheet models, very simple flat databases and
word-processing formats - but as far as connecting to external sources of data
and procedures, they are very much geared to import/export using primitive
physical file transfer protocols. Cullinet's Goldengate product aims to ease
the transition by having a link to IDB, another product which gives relatively
transparent access to mainframe databases (not necessarily only in Cullinet's
IDMS). This transparency can also be provided for DEC, Data General and Wang
integrated office products. A significant feature of Goldengate is that it
offers a Directory facility. This is based on a quite flexible model which
allows all the main object types required and a nestable "folder" concept to
provide an aggregation/container facility. The directory can also include the
objects available to the Goldengate user through IDB - see reference [2].

3.4   Models Proposed Specifically for End-User IS

Modelling approaches specifically oriented to end-user facilities have only
begun to appear more recently, as a by-product of research into "office" IS.
A notable example is that of Gibbs [14] which developed out of research at the
University of Toronto. This approach builds on both the theoretical developments referred to in the previous paragraph and the object-oriented approaches

inherent in Xerox's Star and other recent office software. Another noteworthy
approach is that of Neuhold [5] of the Technical University of Vienna, which
concentrates on a number of separate models each of which supports one aspect
of the end-user's potential directory needs.

3.5   The Object-Oriented Approach as a Basis for Models

Since both of these last two approaches mentioned contain a significant "object-
oriented" element, it is worth looking slightly closer at the basic suitability
of such an approach for the purposes in question in this paper.

For a view on what constitutes orthodoxy in the object-oriented approach,
reference is made to papers on Smalltalk and its related manifestations, eg [15],
[16]. Any system is regarded as a collection of objects that communicate by
sending and receiving messages. All objects are instances of some object class,
and the classes in a system conform to some categorisation and/or aggregation
structures. Part of the class definition includes the storage required, the
types of messages understood and the methods (procedures) involved in respond-
ing to the messages. The system is thus viewable as a network of myriads of
small cooperating virtual processors, each holding the data and procedures for
a particular object instance. An alternative view is of "intelligent" data
objects, each containing the rules of how to process themselves under different
circumstances. In any case such an approach makes a serious change from the
traditional "procedure on data" view prevailing in previous approaches. Instead
of having sequences of procedural statements, one has a small set of basic
functions whose results depend on the object classes involved. Chains of
messages and "method" executions are then set off by various events or triggers.

However there is a question over how far a pure object-oriented view is entirely
appropriate for end-user oriented IS. Certainly there is a gain in having
higher-level representation of information for repeated tasks - "procedure-on-
data" may be relatively slow compared with manipulation of intelligent objects.
But are all elements of IS amenable to "objectisation"? Is it significant that
in Xerox Star one can have Function Icons and Data Icons?

A key practical problem that the object-oriented products have is how to incorporate facilities which the end-user would like to add but which are currently
in "procedure-on-data" rather than object-oriented form. This could be a
temporary problem, but a more permanent one might be that end-users do have
some tasks where the "procedure-on-data" approach is what they would like to
continue with. Possibly Xerox Star has recognized this by allowing object
classification to include such separation.

A further problem would appear to be that, in most current commercial implementations, Smalltalk and other object-oriented programming languages
(OOPLs) do not seem to be suitable as general end-user tools. They seem more
appropriate for specialists or intermediaries who will contract to build the
extensions the end-users require. Such contracting is likely to continue to be
required for some time, because of the complexity of the underlying information
handling needs - and of course to avoid wasting excessive end-user time and
effort re-inventing wheels. But there will probably be a class of users who
can build their own extensions, given a language rather easier than Smalltalk
but more powerful than the simple icon or menu interfaces.

However on the positive side, the object-oriented modelling approaches both in
products like Xerox Star and Lisa, and in theoretical models like those of Gibbs
and Neuhold, do seem to get closer to providing the support for the views which
end-users will need - at least compared with previous approaches. The next
section will look at some such possible end-user needs and see what underlying
models could be used to support them.

4.   END-USER VIEWS POTENTIALLY SUPPORTABLE BY MODELS

This section proposes 12 areas where a view which could be useful to an end-user could be supported by a model. In some cases, several views could make use of the same type of model - but the analysis here is by the type of end-user view. Each view is discussed under three headings:

- User need (describing what it is that the user needs to find out within his "Directory Enquiry")
- Underlying model (discussing what the nature of any underlying model should be)
- Examples (some references to known research work where suitable models have been proposed, with examples of diagrams where available. Comments on the suitability of example models are included in some cases).

4.1   Overall Structure of User-visible Concepts

User need: understanding of the meaning and inter-relationships of the main
           concepts offered to him in the IS (mainly for training purposes).
Underlying model: a conceptual data model at the "meta-meta" level rather than
           the "meta" level: ie the "Data Dictionary Schema" of the ANSI DAFTG
           [17].
Examples: Tagg [18] has shown examples describing the architectures of
           a) the British Computer Society End User Systems Group [19] (Fig 1)
           b) Gibbs of University of Toronto [14] (Fig 2).

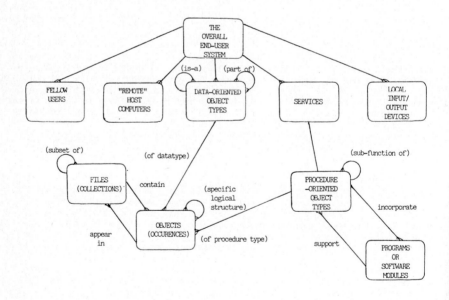

Figure 1 - Data Model of Major Concepts (BCS EUSG, from [18])

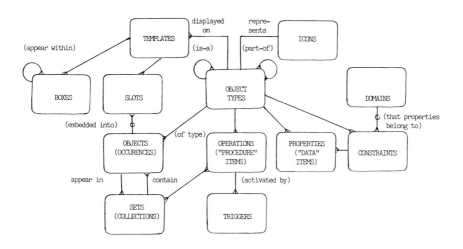

Figure 2 - Data Model of Major Concepts (deduced from [14])

These two Bachman diagrams - being the only examples investigated of this type
of model - show some interesting differences. The BCS model makes a clear data/
procedure distinction, while the Gibbs model is truer to the object oriented
approach. The Gibbs concepts are also perhaps more appropriate to the designer
of the IS than to the end-user.

4.2   Conceptual Data Structure

User need: reference information when doing ad-hoc querying, or when adding
          new, related, predefined functions to the IS.
Underlying model: some view of the conceptual data model, whether "external"
          or "local conceptual", at the normal "meta" (ie Data Dictionary
          Instances) level.
Examples: many from research, fewer in commercial products. Query-by-Example
          [20], when offered with multiple windows, is a potential exception:
          Cullinet's Goldengate works along these lines, but generally the
          model is simply a set of lists of relation contents. A more
          graphical model was that offered with Senko's FORAL-LP [21]: this
          represented the binary model by a connected graph with which the
          user interacted by light pen. End-user access to displayed Bachman
          diagrams has also been proposed, and Neuhold [5] proposes an "Object"
          Structure and Relationship Schema" in the Entity-Relationship format -
          including sub-types (Fig 3).

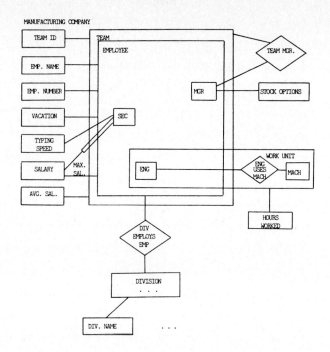

Figure 3 - Object Structure and Relationship Schema (from Neuhold [5])

This diagram is an interesting attempt to combine Entity-Relationship modelling and object-oriented approaches. But it is not clear from the example whether the concept of rectangular boxes within other boxes always has the same meaning. SEC, MGR and ENG are clearly sub-types of EMPLOYEE, but TEAM is a <u>collection</u> of EMPLOYEES rather than a super-type. Also, presumably, WORK UNIT is neither a super-type or a collection, but a join.

4.3   Object Type Classification Structure

User need: a picture of which object types are sub-types or specialisations of
           other types, and which hence inherit their characteristics:
           a) standard "system" object types, for tutorial purposes
           b) environment-specific, ie installation or user defined
           c) sub-collections of object occurrences within a type, ie with no
              additional characteristics (user "files" or "subsets").
              In all these cases the user's need is for reference both when re-
              trieving and when creating new object types as sub-types of exis-
              ting ones.
Underlying model: essentially a "is-a" hierarchy - in the sense of Tsichritzis
           and Lochovsky [22], or an entity sub-type structure. However there
           are potentially problems of "multiple inheritance" which could de-
           stroy a strict hierarchy (see Figure 5) and practical cases where
           new object types are formed by the union or intersection of two
           "subset" object types.
Examples: Smalltalk and Clascal (the language underlying the Apple Lisa) are
           both built on this model. But it is not clear what they offer in
           terms of a user-understandable view, eg diagrams or structured lists.
           Neuhold proposes an "Object Classification Schema" (Fig 4),the

example of which is purely hierarchical, and which is supported by an "expert system" to control which subsets of the hierarchy are displayed to the user. Gibbs proposes an "is-a" hierarchy (Fig 5), but the example here is plainly not strictly hierarchical. From the evidence of these two proposals it would seem that both the model and the presentation of the classification structure are in need of further research and experimentation.

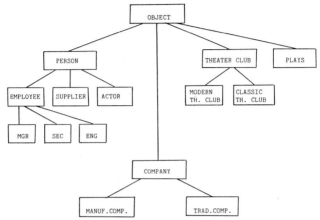

Figure 4 - An Object Classification Schema (partial) (from Neuhold [5])

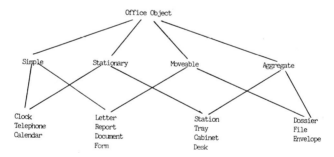

Figure 5 - An "is-a" Hierarchy (from Gibbs [14])

Figure 4 represents the sub-type or "is-a" relationship structure removed from Figure 3 - which overlaps with that meaning of "boxes within boxes" on Figure 3. Figure 5 shows both "multiple inheritance" of object properties (it is not a strict hierarchy) and also "orthogonal classification" (Simple / Aggregate is an alternative sub-classification to Stationary/Moveable).

4.4   Object Type Composition Structure

User need: details of which object types are composed of aggregates of objects of other types, in order to understand how operations on subsidiary objects affect the more complex, compound objects which include them:
a) make-up of complex object types, eg forms, messages, documents, mixed media objects, user-defined aggregates.

b) constituents of an object type in terms of more basic object
   types, eg numbers, integers, text, words, digits, pixels, bits
   (ie an "abstract data type" hierarchy)

c) "container" hierarchies, eg folder, in-tray, desk, station (Fig12).

Underlying model: the structure required here is analogous to a component assembly structure, such as may be found in manufacturing applications.
   The structure clearly represents a different type of concept than in
   4.3 above, but again hierarchies of variable depth - and nodes with
   more than one parent - can occur. However, there may be further
   differences between the examples a) b) and c) above which could
   justify further subdivision. For instance in c), the container
   object does not consist of its lower-level objects as in a) and b) -
   it contains them. The set of objects so contained is not the same
   as the container!

Examples: many of the examples given in research literature fall into this
   group. Christodoulakis [13] shows a generalised structure for multimedia messages (Figs 6 and 7). However these examples do not show
   all the possible directory data (eg repeating of included objects,
   either/or situations). Also the Vector/Raster split is not in the
   same "dimension" as the Image Text/Statistical Part distinction.

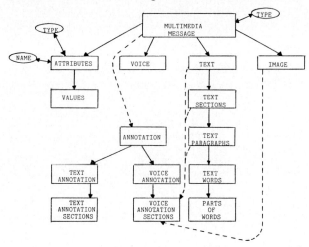

Figure 6 - Multimedia Message Structure (from Christodoulakis [13])

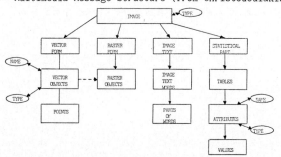

Figure 7 - Multimedia Message Structure (Image Part)
            (from Christodoulakis[13])

The proposed ISO standard Office Document Architecture (ODA) [23] includes example of both "generic" (eg for the class of objects called "reports") and "specific" (ie for a particular report)logical structure (Figs 8 and 9). The dotted relationships in Fig 8 appear to represent relationships other than "is composed of", with the circular ones denoting potential repetition.

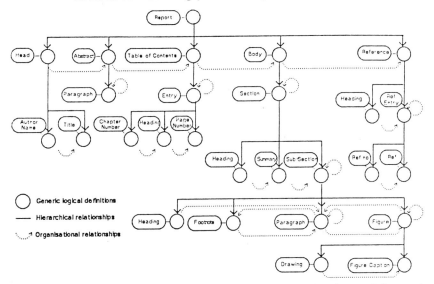

Figure 8 - Example of a Generic Logical Definition of a Class of Document Named "Report" (from ISO ODA [23])

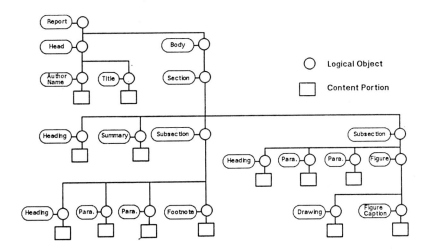

Figure 9 - Example of a Specific Logical Structure of a "Report" (from [23])

Rabitti [24], separates "conceptual" (ie a specific data aggregation structure) and "logical" (ie a generic abstract data type
structure) (Figs 10 and 11). These represent a view of modelling
fairly close to, but not identical with, the ODA structures.

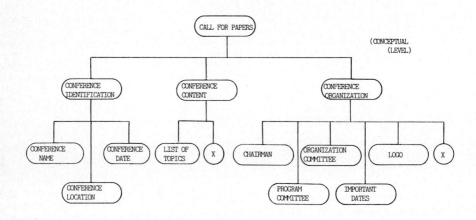

Figure 10 - Conceptual Document Composition Structure (from [24])

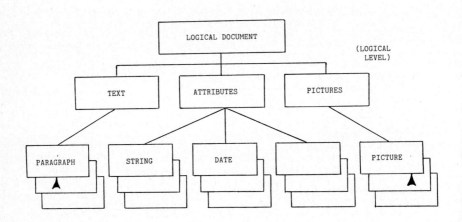

Figure 11 - Logical Document Composition Structure (from [24])

Gibbs [14] proposes a "part-of" hierarchy (Figure 12), which shows
a "container" hierarchy with occurrences of "contained" objects at
the lowest level. It is presumably possible for some to appear
(eg as copies) in many different containers, so a strict hierarchy
may not be appropriate.

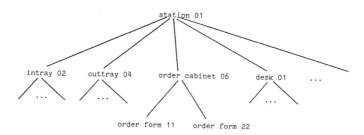

Figure 12 - "part-of" Hierarchy (from [14])

This area of object composition structure is clearly one of the less
well-understood ones. What is happening is that certain relationships are being segregated from the main conceptual data structure
and expressed as separate hierarchies. However whereas the sub-
classification relationship ("is-a") in 4.3 is fairly well understood,
composition is less so. Some examples appear to mix two different
relationships in the same hierarchy.

No examples have yet been seen of a model showing how "views" of
objects are derived from other views and ultimately from the objects
themselves, but both views involving joins and those only involving
projection are perhaps just special cases of the aggregation structure. There are many threads in this area of modelling - again there
seems much opportunity for research and experimentation.

4.5   Layout Structure

User need: understanding of how a displayable object (eg form, message, document)
is to be laid out, to help the user in assembling data when generating such objects.
Underlying model: very similar to the composition structure in 4.4 above, but
showing the inter-relation of "layout objects" (eg containers such
as windows, templates, boxes and slots - or fixed value objects such
as logos, standard text or fixed value numbers) and the data objects
which are to be embedded.
Examples: The ISO ODA proposals, which approximate fairly closely to the IBM
DCA/DIA, may well form a de facto as well as de jure standard here
(Figs 13 and 14). The examples again show the generic/specific
split. Rabitti [24] also addresses this aspect of modelling, but
defers to ODA for the details. The position of ODA in Layout modelling may also have an influence on Composition Structure modelling
(4.4 above). This is also suggested by Rabitti, but there must be a
question as to whether a "document" view is sufficiently general for
all object types.

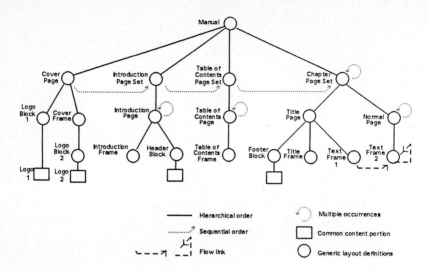

Figure 13 - Example of a Generic Layout Definition of a Class of Document Named "Manual" (from ISO ODA [23])

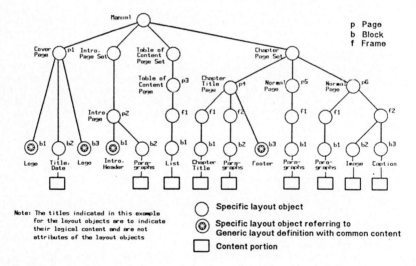

Figure 14 - Example of a Specific Layout Structure of a "Manual" (from [23])

4.6   Value Glossary/Thesaurus

User need: the user often needs to know about the structure of the possible
          different values of particular domains or attributes. The most
          common case is the "Thesaurus", used in many bibliographic IR
          (Information Retrieval) where certain values (words) may imply that
          other words also apply (eg "Fission" and "Fusion" both imply
          "Nuclear Reaction"). But the same need could arise in non-IR

applications; for example a geographical code signifying
"Buckinghamshire" could imply also another code signifying "Home
Counties" or "South East" which in turn imply "UK".
Underlying model: basically the same as in 4.3, ie a sub-classification
        hierarchy.
Examples: most IR software has this model and many packages offer some graph-
        ical representation. However this area has not yet pervaded the
        thinking of many researchers or software developers <u>outside</u> the IR
        field.

4.7 Messaging Point Structures

User need: identity of possible destinations/sources of mailed messages, and
        relationships to roles and individuals.
Underlying model: this could possibly involve 3 separate sub-models:
        a) role hierarchy
        b) role/person relationships (m-n list)
        c) point-to-point links allowed (connection network)
Examples: Tsichritzis and Gibbs [25] propose two structures, "canplay" and
        "haspath" which correspond to a) and c) above. Fig 15 shows an
        example of a "canplay" structure: like the previous example this is
        again a version of a subclassification ("is-a") structure.

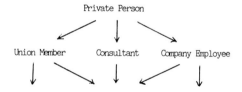

Figure 15 - A "canplay" Relationship (from [25])

A commercial product example can be seen in the ICL product
"Executive Action" [26].

4.8 User Access Permission Structure

User need: a) structure of user groups for access control purposes which the
        user knows about or is a member of
        b) hierarchy of access permissions granted by the user or by other
        users to whom he has, directly or indirectly given granting
        authority.
Underlying model: may be a single, or several, composition hierarchies as in
        4.4. Persons may be members of more than one group, and may be
        granted permissions from more than one source. The amount of any
        structure that should be displayed to any particular user would
        itself depend on access permissions.
Examples: no suitable diagrammatic examples have been found, but many im-
        plementations of permission-granting hierarchies are available in
        commercial products, especially database systems. In research papers
        a more common approach is to use constraints - eg Woo et al [27].

4.9   Procedure Structure

User need: given that users may still sometimes need to take the "procedure-on-
           data" view, they may need to call for information on menu structures,
           calling patterns, or inventories of sub-tasks. This will also be
           relevant if users are trying to append new procedures into the
           structure of an existing procedure base.
Underlying model: effectively analogous to the composition structure models in
           4.4, though the "part-of" relationship may mean rather more than
           simple containment; there may be repeats, sequence or possible
           parallelism.
Examples: many models and presentations have been proposed, both in design
           methodologies and application generators. Graphical aids are now
           appearing with many products. In the area of integrated end-user
           facilities, Neuhold has proposed an "Operation Classification and
           Structure Schema" (see Fig 16).

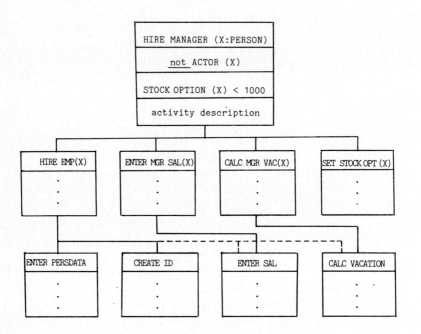

Figure 16 - Operation Classification and Structure Schema (from [5])

Sutcliffe [9] has proposed a "map" interface (Fig 17), which
provides scope for graphical interaction by the user.

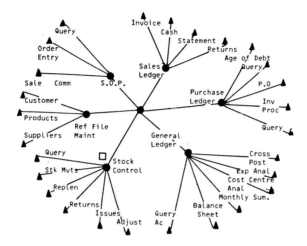

Figure 17 - Example of "Map" Interface (from Sutcliffe [9])

4.10 Procedure/Data Interaction Structure

User need: a) tutorial on which procedures do which actions on which object
              types, for understanding of packaged/predefined services
           b) a view of office "form" flow, or more generally of "chains" of
              object behaviour triggered by external events or by results of
              previous procedures.
Underlying model: essentially some sort of procedure dependency model. This
           can either be regarded as pure procedure dependency with associated
           data flows (and possibly also data stores as in Data Flow diagrams);
           or as a graph of messages passing between objects and causing method
           execution within the objects. Triggers, both external (ie caused by
           outside events such as the passage of time) and internal (ie set by
           the results of method execution within the chain) may be additional
           useful object types within this model.
Examples: Data Flow diagrams are widespread, and graphical support is now
           appearing in automated design tools - but this is aimed primarily
           at the specialist designer. Office-by-Example [3] includes a
           trigger mechanism, but there does not seem to be a graphical user
           directory aid. This is also true of Gibbs' model. Neuhold, however,
           has proposed a "Behaviour Schema" (see Fig 18). The example includes
           an external trigger. It is similar to a Data Flow diagram, though
           exactly what the parallel in data object terms of the "data flows" is,
           is unclear. It is also unclear as to how such a model can present
           the "which function works on what" in an appropriate form.

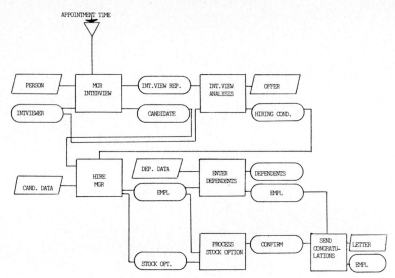

Figure 18 - Behaviour Schema (from Neuhold [5])

Another interesting example is the Toronto TLA research product [28], which proposes the concept of "sketches" which are either form look-alikes or "pseudo-sketches" which describe form flow. "Sketch graphs" are also proposed, but it is not clear how these will appear to the user.

4.11 Software Module Mapping Structure

User need: assuming the end-user has facilities for either acquiring (either as packages or as organisation-developed software) or personally programming (in a "language" or through an Application Generator) additional software modules, he will have the problem of how to integrate them into the overall integrated facility. There may have to be an element of "objectisation". Once they are part of the system the user may like to know which modules are supporting which procedures – or which object-dependent methods.

Underlying model: again a variation on 4.4, ie the object type composition structure. The modules can themselves be regarded as objects. The number of levels of assembly may be limited, since the procedure hierarchy will already be covered by 4.9. However it will certainly be possible for the same module to be used for more than one procedure.

Examples: none known apart from the conjectural one in [18] (see Fig 19 below).

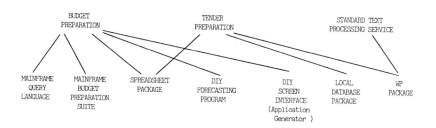

Figure 19 - Example of Service Assembly Structure (from [18])

4.12   Network and Host Processor Structure

User need: the assumption that access to facilities in a distributed network
             will be transparent will not always be justified. Transparency may
             not stretch to certain heterogeneous host systems or dialled-up
             access. Even if it does, the user's task may be dependent on
             specific reference to objects such as host processors.
Underlying model: would simply be an annotated map of the network and process-
             ors to which access within the integrated facility can be arranged
             and where access by explicit naming may be required.
Examples: none known.

4.13   Other User-Relevant Information

These are just a small number of additional user "directory" needs,
which are not appropriate to coverage by models as such. In some
cases they are concerned with occurrences of objects rather than a
meta-level view.
a) user commands, actions or responses permissible at any stage.
   This could be just a simple list, although the procedure structure
   (5.9) might have some relevance.
b) occurrence statistics, eg on values or value ranges of an attribute. These are often kept in practice at the meta-level in DBMS
   and query systems, for optimisation purposes. The user might
   also like a handle on this data.
c) occurrence details such as which object instances are currently
   "in" which container object or other aggregate (eg document).
   These are officially answered by queries against the actual
   object occurrences, but there may be a case for building in some
   of these as standard once "part-of" relationships are defined
   between object types.

5.   REQUIREMENTS FOR STANDARDS FOR END-USER SUPPORT IN A UNIFIED SYSTEM

When planning end-user oriented IS which involve integration between heterogeneous services over a potentially distributed environment, it is clear that
a system based on a set of integrated standard models will have much greater
usability and a longer life. Given the difficulties in enforcing standardisation of models of any sort, however, the best approach to building a system
may be to define a level of interface such as that variations in the MMI of how
directory facilities are offered can be linked to a standard view at that interface.

As far as model structure below that level is concerned, there are some possibilities of de facto standards for certain of the models. Examples are the
ODA models, IR-type Thesauri and Data Flow diagrams. However despite the best
efforts of researchers, notably Tsichritzis and his collaborators [4], there is
still a lot to do in other model areas and in integration between them.

In the related area of MMI for the directory facilities, there are also oppor-
tunities for standardisation efforts - though the lack of experience of use of
most of the methods may make this a longer-term goal. In any case a range of
different standard interfaces will be needed, depending on the technical features of each kind of workstation (eg colour, graphics, windows, interaction
techniques etc).

Another area for possible standardisation effort is that of standard "languages"
for the user to interact with any of the facilities in the system. Some of the
points about variability of workstations also apply here, but there are some
candidates appearing in current commercial products from which one or more
future standards might be drawn. Examples include:

        -Natural language (eg INTELLECT)   -Query-by-Example (QBE)
        -SQL   -Query-by-Forms
        -Euronet Common Command Language
                            (CCL) [29]   -Lotus spreadsheets
        -Pick "ENGLISH"   -Smalltalk

A final area for possible standardisation - and one which is key in any attempts
to build open (ie distributed) systems is that of data interchange. The ISO
ODA proposals address this to some extent, as do DCA/DIA within IBM. But levels
of the OSI 7 layer architecture also need to be considered. Protocols at a high
level will also be needed for non-document interchange, eg tables or spread-
sheets. Multiple media, eg vector graphics, image and voice will also require
consideration.

6   CONCLUSIONS

As discussed at the beginning of this paper, there is a need to accommodate a
shift in the prevailing theme of Informatics. The new theme involves looking
at things from the point of view of the end-user at his workstation who has
access to a whole variety of local and remote facilities. Research and
Development effort needs to be reoriented to this new pattern of IS which is
likely to form a more realistic "fifth generation" than that mooted so far.
The needed research involves merging several disciplines - there is no place
for jealous demarcation disputes between Database, Office Automation, Communications and MMI specialists. To risk committing heresy in some peoples' eyes,
it might be appropriate to conclude that the time has come to relegate "Database" to the engine room where it belongs and to tie one's flag to the mast of
more general Informatics.

7   REFERENCES

[1]   Smith, D.C.S., Irby, C., Kimball,R., Verplank,B. and Harlem, E.,
       Designing the Star User Interface", Byte 7(4) April 1982, pp 242-282
[2]   Cullinet Software Inc., Goldengate Summary Description, Product
       Documentation 1984
[3]   Zloof, M.M., A Language for Office and Business Automation, Proc.
       AFIPS Office Automation Conference, Atlanta, Ga, USA, March 1980
[4]   Tsichritzis, D. (Ed), Office Automation, Springer Verlag 1985
[5]   Neuhold, E.J., Objects and Abstract Data Types in Information Systems,
       Submitted Paper, Technische Universitaet Wien, Austria 1985
[6]   Shneiderman, B., Improving the Human Factors Aspect of Database
       Interactions, ACM Trans. on Database Systems 3(4) 1978, pp 417-439
[7]   Codasyl End User Facilities Committee, Journal of Development 1983,
       Canadian Government EDP Standards Committee, 1983
[8]   Hall, P.A.V., Man-Computer Dialogues for Many Levels of Competence,
       Proc. ECI Conference on Information Systems Methodology, Venice 1978
[9]   Sutcliffe, A.G., Use of Conceptual Maps as Human-Computer Interfaces, in
       People and Computers: Designing the Interface, Johnson and Cook (Eds),
       British Computer Society/Cambridge Univ. Press 1985, pp 117-127
[10]   British Computer Society, Query Language Group, Query Languages - a
       Unified Approach, Heyden Press, UK 1981
[11]   Tsichritzis, D., Form Management, Communications of the ACM 25(7)
       July 1982, pp 453-478
[12]   Hogg, J., Intelligent Message Systems, in [4], pp 113-133
[13]   Christodoulakis, S., Vanderbroek, J., Li, J., Li, T., Wan, S., Wang, Y.,
       Papa, M., and Bertino, E., Development of a Multimedia Information System
       for an Office Environment, Proc. VLDB Conference 1984, pp 261-271
[14]   Gibbs, S.J., An Object-Oriented Office Data Model, Technical Report
       CSRG-154, University of Toronto, January 1984
[15]   Borning, A., The Programming Language Aspects of Thinglab, a Constraint-
       Oriented Simulations Laboratory, ACM TOPLAS 3(4) October 1981, pp 353-387
[16]   Kay, A., New Directions for Novice Programming in the 1980's, in
       Programming Technology, Pergamon Infotech State-of-the-Art Report 1982,
       pp 209-248
[17]   ANSI/X3/SPARC Database System Study Group, Database Architecture
       Framework Task Group, Reference Model for DBMS Standardisation, National
       Bureau of Standards, USA May 1985
[18]   Tagg, R.M., Object Modelling in a Generalised End-User System, Unpublished
       Paper, BCS End User Systems Group, UK 1985
[19]   Tagg, R.M. and Sandford, M.R., Where to Now the Mouse has Arrived?,
       Computer Bulletin II/42 December 1984, UK, pp 2-8
[20]   Zloof, M.M., Query-by-Example: a Data Base Language, IBM Systems Journal
       1977 (4), pp 324-343
[21]   Senko, M.E., The DDL in the Context of a Multilevel Structured Description:
       DIAM II with FORAL, in Database Description, Douque and Nijssen (Eds),
       North Holland 1975
[22]   Tsichritzis, D. and Lochovsky, F.H., Data Models, Prentice Hall 1982
[23]   Campbell-Grant, I.R., Office Document Architecture, Fifth Working Draft,
       ISO/TC97/SC18/WG3 Working Paper, February 1984
[24]   Barbic, F., and Rabitti, F., The Type Concept in Office Document Retrieval,
       Proc.VLDB Conference 1985, pp 34-48
[25]   Tsichritzis, D. and Gibbs, S.J., Ettiquette Specification in Message
       Systems, in [4], pp 93-111
[26]   International Computers Limited, Executive Action: Introduction, ICL
       Technical Publication No R00490, 1986
[27]   Woo, C.C., Lochovsky, F.H., and Lee, A., Document Management Systems, in
       [4], pp 21-40

[28] Hogg, J., Nierstrasz, O.M. and Tsichritzis, D., Office Procedures, in
      [4], pp 137-165
[29] Negus, E.A., EURONET Guideline: Standard Commands for Retrieval Systems,
      Commission of the European Communities, December 1977

AUTHOR INDEX

A
AHLSEN, M., 33

B
BERARD, C., 45
BERTHIER, F., 59
BITTON, D., 115
BRITTS, S., 33
BUTSCHER, B., 97

C
CARINO, Jr., F., 159
CENCIONI, R., 79
COUTAZ, J., 59

D
DELGADO, J., 97
DEMURJIAN, S.A., 173

F
FALOUTSOS, C., 137

H
HAMMAINEN, H., 45
HOLLAND, S., 79
HORAK, W., 287
HSIAO, D.K., 173

J
JARKE, M., 301

K
KARSENTY, S., 67
KODECK, F., 79
KREIFELTS, Th., 197
KROMMES, R., 79
KRONERT, G., 287

L
LAUSEN, G., 247
LOCHOVSKY, F.H., 17

M
MAIOCCHI, R., 223
MARSHALL, R.G., 173
MEDINA, M., 97
MEYNIEUX, E., 267

O
OBERWEIS, A., 247

P
PADGHAM, L., 1
PERNICI, B., 223
POSTL, W., 267

S
SEISEN, S., 267
SRIKANTH, R., 301
SULONEN, R., 45

T
TAGG, R.M., 325
TOMBRE, K., 267
TSCHICHHOLZ, M., 97
TURBYFILL, C., 115

V
VAN NYPELSEER, P., 209

W
WOETZEL, G., 197
WOO, C.C., 17